DRAGON DAYS

The story of Miss Bardahl and the 1960s kids who loved hydros

Jon Osterberg

© Eileen Crimmin photo 1965

All text © Jon Osterberg 2012

Published by Peoh Point Publishing

Edited by Judith A. Sylte

All photo copyrights strictly enforced.
Full effort was made to identify photographers and/or photo-collection owners.
Unidentified photos were purchased from vendors. Please contact the author if you can identify unknown photographers or collections.

All rights reserved.
No portion of the contents of this book may be reproduced by any means without written permission of the publisher.

Library of Congress Control Number 2012911217

ISBN 978-0-615-65841-4

Produced by Lookbook Press
lookbookpress.com
Seattle, Washington, USA

Front and back-cover design:
Sean Osterberg

Cover photo:
© Jan Kaulins
Fine Art Photography
P.O. Box 237
Manitou Beach, MI 49253
jankaulins.com

Cover concept, back-cover photo:
© Jon Osterberg 2007

To order *Dragon Days*, go to dragondaysbook.com

Table of Contents

	Foreword	5
	Introduction	7
	Hydrospeak: a primer for laypersons	9
Chapter 1	Beginnings	13
Chapter 2	The core crew: *Bardahl*'s family tree	24
Chapter 3	Building a better *Bardahl*	33
Chapter 4	Racing and the new-boat blues	41
Chapter 5	*Miss Bardahl* redo	59
Chapter 6	Routine, rigor, and Thousand Island	63
Chapter 7	Musson strikes gold	66
Chapter 8	If you can't win, be spectacular	73
Chapter 9	*Thriftway* passes the torch (or *Bardahl* steals it)	85
Chapter 10	Dollars and sense	103
Chapter 11	It's about corners, not chutes	107
Chapter 12	Breaking, learning, innovating, and The Checklist	111
Chapter 13	She has a great personality	116
Chapter 14	Ron Musson, the person	118
Chapter 15	New boats, new players	128
Chapter 16	By the slimmest of margins	136
Chapter 17	"Never been so embarrassed"	152
Chapter 18	Back on top	157
Chapter 19	Harnessing nitrous	163
Chapter 20	New and improved: the cabover cometh	169
Chapter 21	Tricks and innovations	174
Chapter 22	Recommissioning the Dragon	182
Chapter 23	Three Gold Cups	194
Chapter 24	Green roostertails	209
Chapter 25	*Tahoe Miss* regains her stride	212
Chapter 26	Exiting in a blaze of glory	223
Chapter 27	Reflecting on excellence	228
Chapter 28	Finishing the cabover	234
Chapter 29	Black Sunday	243
Chapter 30	The Checkerboard Comet	257
Chapter 31	Lost: *Miss Bardahl* hydroplane	271
Chapter 32	First a facelift, then a rebirth	288
Chapter 33	The Dragon roars again	305
Chapter 34	Completing the puzzle, extending the legacy	311
	Acknowledgments	319
	Bibliography	321
	About the author	325

For Leo and E.K.

Foreword

Skip Schott and I sat under a white tent canopy alongside the Columbia River in Kennewick, Wash., shaded from a scorching sun. It was July 25, 2009, and we were munching sandwiches inside Lampson Pits, seated on canvas folding chairs next to the restored 1962-65 *Miss Bardahl* hydroplane.

Skip is one of the 1965 *Bardahl* crew members who now reprises his role on the restored boat, I'm the team historian and general go-fer guy, and it was the weekend of the annual Columbia Cup race. *Bardahl*, nicknamed the Green Dragon, was there to run exhibition laps against other vintage hydros.

A group of people on a pit tour had just left, and we were amused to see its tour guide was a boy in his early teens who read a semi-accurate account of our boat's history from note cards. I commented that when I was his age, I was befriended one day by *Notre Dame* driver Jack Regas, who shielded me and two friends from Seafair security guards after we'd hopped the fence and snuck into Seattle's restricted "hot pits."

Skip knew I had started a book chronicling the history of *Miss Bardahl* and asked how it was progressing. I winced and confided I was struggling with how to tell the story without using the first-person narrative style, which could come across as self-absorbed and egotistical with undue emphasis on me. First-person voice also might simply be bad journalistic form.

On the other hand, *Miss Bardahl* had been the object of my ardent affection as a youth, and as an adult I actually had played a key role in preserving the hydro for future generations. To make a long story short, the boat was "lost" for many years before I hunted it down and found it decaying outdoors in New Hampshire.

The dilemma was, how do I write about that without sounding like it's a story about me, instead of the boat and *Bardahl* team?

"But it *is* your story," Skip said. "Just tell it as you saw it. Don't worry about using first-person – you experienced all of this, and now you're wearing the goddam green shirt! Now *you'll* be the one who sees some kid at the fence and invites him over to the other side."

Skip was referring to the green monogrammed *Miss Bardahl* crew shirts that owner Dixon Smith had given each of us on the team, and which we proudly wore that day in Kennewick. (Mine had a fresh mustard stain on the front. Oops.)

Eventually I decided Skip's advice made sense, and sharing it here in writing serves as my disclaimer of sorts. I even took his advice a step further and peppered this book with anecdotes from my youth, because many of these personal tales might be experiences shared by the reader. I include them *not* to spotlight me, the individual – rather, they celebrate a *commonality* among many baby boomers in the Northwest and throughout Hydro Nation.

Non-native Washingtonians, and even young locals, are baffled by hydroplane racing's revered place in Northwest history. But the puzzle comes together a bit and you gain some perspective when you vicariously experience what it was like growing up near Seattle in its pre-professional sports era.

What began as an arcane, comprehensive history book of the 1962-65 *Miss Bardahl* (with a market of maybe 20 people worldwide – what was I thinking?!) has broadened into a narrative of *Bardahl*'s glory days, set against the backdrop of 1950s and '60s Puget Sound life as seen through the eyes of a skinny Lake Hills kid.

At the core I suppose I'm hopelessly sentimental and nostalgic. My wish is that you'll spot your own similar experiences in some of these stories, reminisce, and smile.

Jon Osterberg
Redmond, Washington
May 2012

Introduction

Seattle has generated its share of polarizing sports figures over the years. Names like Alex Rodriguez, Shaun Alexander, Billy Joe Hobert, Sean Kemp, Jim Owens, and Bill Muncey trigger contrasting perceptions among fans who either loved 'em or loathed 'em.

Hydroplane racing, once revered by a generation of Jet City baby boomers, now polarizes the Emerald City. Many who grew up near Seattle feel unbridled excitement when the growling speedboats kick roostertails skyward, and certainly some newer-generation fans share the buzz.

But for many around high-tech, uber-green Seattle, hydroplanes elicit a casual apathy at best, or worse, derisive cynicism. A yawn or a sneer.

Seattleites embraced their two big-time sports, Husky football and unlimited hydroplane racing, before the SuperSonics arrived in 1967. In those days Seafair crowd estimates of well over 100,000 were not merely hyperbole, and each of the three network TV affiliates – KING, KIRO, and KOMO – televised Seafair live all day Sunday, with plenty of weekday qualifying to boot. The daily newspapers – the morning *Seattle Post-Intelligencer* (dubbed the *P-I*) and the afternoon *Seattle Times* – devoted barrels of ink year-round to hydro racing.

It began when Seattle Chrysler dealer Stan Sayres' revolutionary hydro, *Slo-mo-shun IV*, set a world straightaway speed record and then whipped the field at the 1950 Gold Cup in Detroit. Sayres won more than just a trophy. He snatched the power base of hydro racing from the factory-laden Midwest and firmly replanted it in soggy Seattle. Washingtonians took great pride in this.

Sayres' boats, *Slo-mo IV* and *Slo-mo V*, reigned over the sport until 1956, then gave way to a succession of other dominant Seattle craft: *Miss Thriftway*, *Hawaii Kai III*, and *Miss Bardahl*.

Ole Bardahl's third *Miss Bardahl*, which raced from 1962 through 1965, marked the pinnacle of the round-bow conventional hydros. *Bardahl* won three consecutive Gold Cups and National Championships in 1963-64-65. Its driver, Ron Musson, was arguably the best of his era, and perhaps any era. The record book tells us that.

Less is known about how *Bardahl*'s implausibly young crew, led by the older Hall of Fame crew chief Leo Vanden Berg, infused the sport with innovative technical advances and fussy quality control that gave *Bardahl* its winning edge.

This boat and team spanned the waning years of minor-league Seattle. It was a less haughty age, a time when the citizenry still loved hydros while yearning for big-league sports – an NBA franchise, American League baseball, an NFL team, and years later a top-flight MSL soccer club.

It was a time when Northwest youths spent their summer days outdoors building forts in the fir and alder woods, playing fly-up at the schoolyard, listening to transistor radios at the beach, and towing wooden hydros behind their bikes. Curfew was signaled by the streetlights turning on at dusk, and parents sometimes didn't lock their doors at night. There were no cable channels, no remotes, no computers, no smart phones. Social media existed in science fiction, if at all. Kids either played together in person or talked on a land-line telephone (which for thrifty families was on a shared party line).

When Ron Musson and his radical new cabover *Miss Bardahl* met their horrific demise in an explosive crash at Washington, D.C., in 1966, it not only robbed hydro racing of its innocence, it marked the end of a Seattle sports era.

Renowned driver Chip Hanauer aptly describes hydroplane racing as "part of Seattle's cultural fabric." The weaving began with Sayres in 1950, and that hydro fabric arguably was strongest during the summer of 1965.

Hydrospeak: a primer for laypersons

This glossary appears at the front of this book rather than the rear. Unlimited hydroplane racing, like any avocation, is drenched in lingo and technical jargon that baffles the layperson. Happily for those reading this book, the author is the among the least-gifted mechanical minds of our time, which means that hydro jargon deciphered here should be within *anyone's* grasp.

The following terms appear throughout these pages, and knowing them now will boost your understanding and pleasure as you read ahead.

Unlimited versus **limited hydroplanes.** "Unlimited" is the largest, fastest class of hydroplanes, and they run with the fewest restrictions. In *Miss Bardahl*'s day they were mandated to be between 25 and 40 feet in length, propeller-driven, could not use jet power, and had to weigh at least 5,000 pounds without fuel. Otherwise they were unlimited – hence the name – though in later years the unlimiteds gained more restrictions. "Limited" comprises many classes of smaller hydros restricted by, among other things, engine size and horsepower. In *Bardahl*'s day, the largest limiteds – with a minimum length of 19 feet – were the 7-litres (427 cubic-inch engines).

Roostertail. The long, voluminous plume of spray behind a hydro kicked up by its propeller.

APBA. The American Power Boat Association, based near Detroit, has been the governing body of hydroplane racing for most of its existence. More directly, unlimited hydros in *Bardahl*'s day were governed by the APBA's **Unlimited Racing Commission**.

ADI (anti-detonation injection). Water, or a mix of water and alcohol, can be injected into motors to increase power and reliability.

Allison. An American piston aircraft engine made by Allison, a division of General Motors, and used in World War II fighters like the P-38 Lightning, P-39 Airacobra, and P-40 Warhawk. The Allison V-1710 was a 12-cylinder motor with 1,710 cubic inches; the 111 and 113 models weighed 1,385 pounds and were rated at 1,500 sea-level takeoff horsepower. The later G6 model, not available to hydros until after the Korean War, weighed 1,595 pounds and was rated for aircraft at 2,200 sea-level takeoff horsepower ("war emergency power" with ADI).

Rolls-Merlin. Rolls-Royce of Great Britain built the Merlin (named after a falcon) piston engine for World War II fighters including the Spitfire and Hurricane, and the Lancaster bomber. To boost wartime production, Rolls licensed Packard Motor Co. of Detroit in 1940 to build Merlins, starting in 1941; the Packard V-1650 Merlin became the workhorse that powered P-51 Mustangs. It was a 12-cylinder motor with 1,650 cubic inches, and of the 168,040 Merlins built during the war, Packard built 55,523. The dash 7 and dash 9 models later used in hydroplanes weighed 1,715 and 1,725 pounds respectively. The dash 7 was rated for aircraft at 1,315 sea-level takeoff horsepower (and 1,720 at war emergency power); the dash 9 was rated for aircraft at 1,380 sea-level takeoff horsepower (and 2,280 at war emergency power with ADI).

The Allison 111/113 and the Merlin dash 7 were approximately equivalent in power, and the Allison G6 and the Merlin dash 9 were approximately equivalent. Hydroplane teams "hot-rodded" these engines significantly to boost power, which also marred reliability.

When adapted for use in hydroplanes, Allisons and Rolls-Merlins were installed right-side up but backwards, relative to an airplane. Rather than spin an airplane propeller at the front, the crankshaft now turned a boat propeller at the stern using a gearbox tailored for hydroplanes. Merlin-hydro teams also rotated their carburetors to the top of the motor. (In aircraft, Merlin carburetors were mounted at the bottom, behind the propeller, while Allison carburetors were mounted on top, downdraft style.)

Manifold pressure. Think of an engine as a big vacuum. When a piston strokes downward, it sucks a mixture of fuel and air into the cylinder. Manifold pressure is a measure of how much mixture is being *sucked* into the cylinders. Higher inches of manifold pressure means more power, until you go too high and blow an engine.

Boost. Often used synonymously with manifold pressure, boost usually refers to air that's *forced* into the cylinders with a supercharger or turbocharger, which acts as a pump.

Manifold pressure and boost actually tell a pilot the same thing, just in different ways. When a supercharger is present, manifold pressure also can be used to measure how much air-fuel mixture is being forced into the cylinders.

Supercharger. Also called a blower, it compresses and rams the air-fuel mixture into the engine to increase power, which is measured by manifold pressure. The supercharger is gear-driven off the crankshaft. Allison 111 and 113 models had single-stage, single-speed superchargers, while the Allison G6 had a two-stage supercharger with a primary stage and a more-powerful auxiliary stage. Late-model Merlins used by hydros had compact two-stage, two-speed superchargers; race teams typically used low speed, and *Miss Bardahl*'s was locked in low speed.

So, why use low speed when high speed spins the supercharger faster, creating more boost? Because high speed is needed by aircraft at high altitude, generally above 20,000 feet, where the air thins. But at sea level and at all hydro venues (even Lake Tahoe at 6,225 feet), high speed doesn't help because it uses way more horsepower to run the blower than low speed, which delivers plenty of pressure at low altitude.

Turbocharger. Technically a "turbosupercharger," a turbocharger produces roughly the same result as a supercharger – increased power – but via different means. Turbochargers harness exhaust gasses to spin a turbine, which drives a compressor, which rams the air-fuel mixture into the engine. In *Miss Bardahl*'s day, only *Tahoe Miss* raced with a turbocharger, in 1965.

Sponson. The pontoon-like riding surface on the front half of a hydroplane. Conventional hulls have two, one on each side. When racing at full speed, only about one square foot of each sponson touches the water, hence the term "hydroplane." The bottom center section of the hull between each sponson is called the **tunnel**; it traps the cushion of air on which hydros ride.

Afterplane. The entire rear section of a hydroplane, beginning at the back of the sponsons.

Angle of attack. The designed angle, front to back, between a sponson's planing surface and the water surface. When that angle is measured laterally from the inside to the outside of a sponson's planning surface, it's called **dihedral**.

Battens. Horizontal wood strips under the deck, or on the hull's bottom, to which exterior plywood is fastened.

Cowling, or **fairing**. A structure on the exterior of an aircraft or boat, for reducing drag. In *Bardahl*'s day, hydros typically had fiberglass rear cowlings surrounding the tail and cockpit, and some hydros had removable engine cowlings.

Nontrip. Located on the side of a sponson and the afterplane, it's where the surface is angled to prevent catching or "tripping" on the water during a turn.

Gearbox. Custom built for hydroplane use, the gearbox transfers power from the engine's cylinders to the propeller shaft and propeller. Hydroplane gearboxes run just one speed. *Miss Bardahl*'s has a step-up gearbox ratio of about* 3.04:1, so that an engine turning 4,000 rpms turns its propeller at more than 12,000 rpms. (*Gearbox ratio can be changed depending on the size and layout of the racecourse and prop combinations.)

Ballard. Community in northwest Seattle, annexed into the city in 1906, home to a large Scandinavian population throughout the 1900s. Home of Bardahl's worldwide headquarters. Ballard once was defined as a place where aging Scandinavians drive slowly for countless blocks with their blinkers on, and never turn.

Lake Washington. A 22-mile-long, glacier-carved freshwater lake bordered by Seattle on its western shore and on its eastern shore by (south to north) Renton, Kennydale, Bellevue, Kirkland, and Kenmore. Key hydroplane landmarks on Lake Washington included (counter-clockwise) the U.S. 10 (now I-90) floating bridge; Stan Sayres Memorial Pits and the hydroplane racecourse; Seward Park; Jett's Marina, near Rainier Beach; Kennydale; the East Channel, site of world-straightaway-record runs; Hunt's Point, Stan Sayres' home and *Slo-mo-shun* base; and Sand Point, former site of a naval air station, also the site of world-straightaway-record runs. Lake Washington surrounds Mercer Island, which lies directly east of Stan Sayres Pits.

Spokane. Washington's second-largest city, 280 miles east of Seattle via Interstate 90. Non-Northwesterners often mispronounce it Spo-CANE; it's Spo-KAN.

Coeur d'Alene. Pronounced Core-duh-LANE, the north Idaho city and lake were named for the local Native American tribe, which French fur trappers called "heart of an awl" because of the natives' clever trading skills. Coeur d'Alene hosted the Diamond Cup hydro races from 1958-68. Coeur d'Alene lies about 30 miles east of Spokane via Interstate 90.

"Eastern races," "back East." Inaccurate terms often used by ignorant Washingtonians to describe *Midwest* race sites like Detroit and Madison.

"The Coast." Often used by ignorant Eastern Washingtonians and Idahoans to describe Seattle's locale. In reality, Seattle borders Puget Sound; the Pacific Ocean coastline lies 90 air miles to the west.

Seafair. Seattle's annual summer civic celebration, first held in August 1950 to celebrate Seattle's status as "boating capital of the world." Also the name of the organization (formerly Greater Seattle Inc.) that stages Seafair events. When hydro fans say a driver "won Seafair," that actually could mean the Gold Cup, World's Championship, or a host of subsequent corporate-sponsored regattas as well as the Seafair Trophy Race.

Hawaii Kai III. When Henry and Edgar Kaiser's hydroplane debuted in 1956, the name on the side of the boat was *Hawaii Kai III*, to promote Henry's planned community on Oahu. Crew member Pete Bertellotti told the *Unlimited NewsJournal* that an "Okina" (apostrophe) was added to the boat's name midway through 1957 – *Hawaii Ka'i III* – because Edgar Kaiser told the crew, "Without it, Kai isn't a nice word." Indeed, missing the Okina can greatly change a Hawaiian word's basic meaning, and the way it sounds. However, most Hawaiian references say "Kai" merely means ocean, or sea. With all due respect to the Kaisers, this book uses *Kai*, without the Okina.

Names of core team members. In common journalism style, the writer introduces a person by noting his or her full name, then uses only the last name on subsequent mentions. That would cause problems in this book, as four people from the same Smith family play a prominent role in *Miss Bardahl*'s history: Burns Smith, sons Dixon ("Dax") and David Smith, and Dixon's son, Ryan Smith. To avoid confusion, this book makes a style exception for those four people and generally cites their first names.

Chapter 1

Beginnings

The diminutive driver flashed a crafty smile. San Diego's late afternoon sun lit up his tanned face as he regaled teammates with details of their latest victory. It was Oct. 3, 1965, and Ron Musson had just toyed with and sped away from his biggest adversary, *Miss Exide*, in the final heat of the San Diego Cup on Mission Bay.

"Blew his doors off," said one crewmember, summing up the heat and race. "*That* was a dominating performance! We made hydro history today!"

In the final race of the 1965 season, Musson capped *Miss Bardahl's* brilliant career with blazing speed and a perfect score of 1,200 points. In the process, he earned *Bardahl* a third consecutive National High Points crown and shattered every major competition record with marks that remained unbroken for years: fastest 3-mile competition lap, 117.870; fastest 15-mile heat, 116.079; and fastest 45-mile race, 115.064.

Bardahl won each heat with ease and finished the 1965 season with four race victories. She won 12 out of 29 races altogether over four years, finished a record 57 heats in a row without an engine failure, and never raced again. A rarity among hydros, she ran her entire career under one name – *Miss Bardahl* – while earning a spot among hydroplane racing's all-time greats.

Few people could have envisioned such a sizzling finish after watching the Green Dragon slog through much of her maiden 1962 season.

This is the legacy of the third *Miss Bardahl:* Rich in promise but an underachiever early on, the 30-foot unlimited-class hydro flourished following a minor makeover to become a sweet-riding, ultra-reliable, record-setting speedster. And after three years of hard racing had weakened her tired hull, *Miss Bardahl* achieved even greater feats by harnessing new advances pioneered by a smart, savvy, young crew.

* * * *

In 1922, a 20-year-old immigrant named Ole Bardahl arrived in the Pacific Northwest from Norway. He possessed little money and knew no English, but he found work in a local sawmill and soon began picking up the language.

Years earlier a teenage girl had caught his eye in Trondheim, Norway. One year after Ole arrived, Inga Benjaminsen followed, traveling alone by boat and train.

"She was 18 when she came over," said Evelyn Bardahl McNeil, the older of Ole and Inga's two daughters, in a March 2011 interview. "They were kids, just 18 and 20. I can't imagine doing it. First he came by himself. There was nobody here that he knew, he had $32 in his pocket, and that was it. He ended up in

Everett because a friend of the family lived there and said that the streets are paved with gold, like they told all the young immigrants. Everett, of all places!

"The thing that was most interesting is my father was a boxer, he was a skier, and he was tough as nails," Evelyn continued, "but my mother at 18 went all by herself on the boat, 10 days, to Halifax I think. And then all the way across Canada on the train. She didn't speak a word of English and didn't know anybody. I don't know how she did it. She landed in Vancouver and then went down to Everett. They had zero, nothing."

The couple began building a life together, teaching themselves English. Inga lived and worked as a maid in a mansion on Seattle's Capitol Hill – "in those days they didn't live together if they weren't married; they were well brought-up children," Evelyn commented – and a year after arriving they were married in Seattle. Ole soon started a successful business constructing houses for Boeing workers.

"I have a housing project named after me," Evelyn said. "He built the first housing project for war workers, and I have 100 houses named after me in the south end, 'Evansvale.' He went to the banks and said I've gotta have money, and he got funding. He always could get money."

"He was one of Seattle's first 'tract housing' carpenters, building eight, ten houses at a time," said Jerry Zuvich, who worked for Bardahl decades later, including nine years on the *Miss Bardahl* crew. "He enjoyed picking out wood. He could identify every piece we'd put in that boat – spruce, white oak, mahogany, whatever. He knew the grain and would say, 'That's not a good piece to use there.' And that was okay, because he knew."

Ole Bardahl later started a company with a chemist he met in a college mining class. The chemist had ideas for manufacturing oil additives and soap, and after buying him out, Ole founded Bardahl Manufacturing Corporation in Ballard in September 1939. Bardahl's signature product was an additive that helped oil cling to metal, reducing engine friction and wear on moving parts.

Bardahl later constructed a large factory near the heart of Ballard at 1400 N.W. 52nd Street, topped by a prominent neon sign that still illuminates the community at night with "ADD BARDAHL … ADD IT TO YOUR GAS … ADD IT TO YOUR OIL." It was a time when Seattle's skyline to the south was dominated by the 42-story Smith Tower, for decades the tallest building west of the Mississippi.

Bardahl recognized the practical and publicity value of using racing as a test laboratory for his products. Over the years Indy cars (starting in 1950), hydroplanes, and aircraft raced under his Bardahl banner and touted its benefits.

"We used all of our racing activities as a high-test laboratory for our auto products," Ole Bardahl told the *Unlimited NewsJournal* in 1980. "In a car, the parts just don't get the strain that they do in racing."

Bardahl sales boomed when its 1950s TV commercials parodied the then-popular "Dragnet" program with cartoon characters Sticky Valves, Gummy Rings, and Blacky Carbon, who were vanquished by a detective who soaked them with "world famous Bardahl" oil.

As hydromania further enthralled Seattle in 1957, Ole Bardahl sponsored Norm Christiansen's basement-built mahogany-decked hydroplane, a short (27' 4") craft that debuted the year before as the U-4 *Tempest*. Powered by a World War II-era V-12 Allison engine *(see Hydrospeak)*, the renamed *Miss Bardahl* showed surprising speed at times but lacked durability.

Scrappy driver Norm Evans, from scenic, orchard-lined Lake Chelan in north-central Washington, throttled the Allison-powered *Bardahl* to fourth overall in the 1957 Mapes Trophy Regatta on Lake Tahoe, and he later snared fourth at the Sahara Cup on Lake Mead, where *Bardahl* won a heat for the first time.

Now hooked on hydro racing, Ole Bardahl jumped fully into the sport as an owner, not merely a sponsor, and organized Bardahl Chemical Corporation for the sole purpose of owning and operating *Miss Bardahl*. For $6,000, Ole ordered a new hull for 1958 from Ted Jones, the sport's top designer, and the new *Miss Bardahl* was built by Jones' 26-year-old son Ron, who in the 1970s would become a renowned unlimited-class hydro designer and builder.

Ted Jones rented a building in the South Park district of Seattle, at 7th Ave. South and South Kenyon Street, that was slated to become a Caterpillar bulldozer shop. Ron constructed *Miss Bardahl* there. Initially two brothers helped, but when Ted stopped by one day he was dismayed by their slow progress and fired them on the spot. Ron finished the boat, which was painted in Bardahl's corporate colors of metallic green, yellow, and black, and delivered it just in time for the 1958 Apple Cup Regatta on Lake Chelan.

Ted Jones drove *Miss Bardahl* on its maiden run on Lake Washington at dusk on Monday, May 5, 1958, before turning it over to regular driver Norm Evans. The crew then bundled up the hull and towed it east via U.S. Highway 2 and Stevens Pass.

Miss Bardahl roared to victory May 11 in Evans' hometown race, a rarity for a new boat. Now numbered U-40 (the "U" stands for "unlimited" and "40" is its registration number), Ole's 30-foot long, 12-foot wide, Allison-powered hydro – nicknamed the Green Dragon by the media – averaged 101.618 mph in the final heat to outrun *Miss U.S.1* of Detroit for the Apple Cup. It was a popular victory, with friendly and approachable Evans being a fan favorite.

But Evans apparently did something to draw Ole's ire and was terminated June 13, 1958, "for the good of the operation." Ole quickly replaced Evans with Mira Slovak, the "Flying Czech" refugee pilot revered by America for commandeering a passenger plane across the Iron Curtain to freedom, from Prague to Frankfurt, in 1953. Slovak was without a ride in 1958 because his *Miss Wahoo* had been beached by owner Bill Boeing Jr.

"Something happened between Mr. Bardahl and Norm Evans, and they fired him on the spot," said Slovak, who was hired June 17, 1958. "Mr. Boeing took one year off and said we're gonna come back in 1959. So he gave me the *Wee Wahoo*, a little boat, and I was driving *Wee Wahoo* to keep my hands in it."

Slovak and *Bardahl* were beaten a few times along the way in 1958 but took first place at the Buffalo Launch Club Regatta (a.k.a. National Sweepstakes) in Buffalo, N.Y., and the American Speedboat Championship (a.k.a. Rogers Memorial Trophy) in Washington, D.C., to accrue the most points for the season and earn the overall National Championship. *Bardahl* was quick at times and certainly reliable, finishing 25 out of 27 heats started under the care of crew chief Del Gould and lead engine mechanic Rudy Boppel.

"That was an unsteady boat. It was a rough boat, a pretty bumpy boat," Slovak recalled. "The championship really belongs to Norm Evans as well as me because he won the first race, and then I finished it. But that was an uncomfortable boat, I didn't like the boat at all. *Exide* was even worse," he said, referring to his 1963 ride.

Mira Slovak, on bow, teamed with Norm Evans to earn *Bardahl* the 1958 National Championship.
– photographer unknown, from Nostalgic Thunderboats Unlimited

Bardahl sponsored but did not own the first *Miss Bardahl*, in 1957.
– used with permission of Kirk Pagel

Crew chief and "relief driver" George McKernan in a 1960 test run.
© Bob Carver photo 1960

Musson won the 1960 Silver Cup driving the stock-Allison powered *Nitrogen Too* (later *Miss Madison*).
– used with permission of Sandy Ross

Ron Musson won national titles from 1954–58 in three classes of limited hydros.
– photographer unknown

Musson and *Bardahl* joined forces in 1961, wining seven of 12 heats.
© Bob Carver photo 1961

At Buffalo, Slovak encountered a champion limited-class hydro driver named Ron Musson, who was there racing the smaller hydros, and whom Slovak would later face in unlimited-class events.

* * * *

Hydromania had first captivated my entire family soon after relocating from Los Angeles to Seattle's Magnolia neighborhood in 1950. Dad in particular was quickly allured by the spectacle of speed and roostertails as well as the David-and-Goliath drama of Seattle versus Detroit. My brother Dave (eight years older than me) and sister Judy (ten years older) attended the first Seattle race with Dad in 1951, where they excitedly watched the new *Slo-mo V* win but were horrified to see *Quicksilver* disintegrate, killing its driver and riding mechanic.

My parents divorced in 1956 and my father moved to an apartment in Ballard, just three blocks east of Bardahl's headquarters on N.W. 52nd. My earliest memories include taking walks with Dad to see if *Miss Bardahl* was being prepared by her crew. My heart would race when we found the manufacturing plant's big, roll-up metal door open, revealing inside the sleek U-40 with its metallic green paint, black bow scallops, and yellow sides – the original Green Dragon.

This was the 1958 hull that raced through the 1961 season. I loved its streamlined, swept-back green tail fin. After I inherited my older brother's balsa wood *Thriftway Too* hydro model and repainted it as *Miss Bardahl* – using Testor's No. 54 metallic green model paint – the tail soon became problematic. It was tough for a young boy to play gently with such an exciting model, one with a delicate tail, which I broke countless times. Countless times I pleaded with Dad to fashion a new one. He patiently complied.

My earliest memory of attending a hydro race dates to 1958, when I was 4. I remember Dad and Dave hacking away blackberry vines to clear a spot on a hillside in the 3900 block of Lake Washington Boulevard. The pavement ran below, and across the street grew deciduous trees between which I caught spotty glimpses of the racecourse.

I recall glistening wood hulls with lime-green trim roaring by not far from the beach, undoubtedly *Gale V or VI* racing in an outer lane. The second *Miss Bardahl* debuted that year, but my memory of that race doesn't include a metallic green boat.

* * * *

The next two racing seasons were not as kind to the *Bardahl* team. 1959 began with promise as new crew chief George McKernan replaced *Bardahl*'s Allisons with more-powerful Rolls-Royce Merlins *(see Hydrospeak)*, and bold ex-*Hawaii Kai III* hydro jockey Jack Regas took over the helm. Jensen Motor Boat Company's slomoshun.com website states that Jensen worked on the Green Dragon between December 1958 and May 1959, doing significant modifications.

Bardahl won fast heats at the Apple Cup and Detroit Memorial but won neither event. Regas had the Green Dragon screaming across Lake Coeur d'Alene in the Diamond Cup, but *Bardahl* hit a wake and dug a sponson. A blast of water tore through the bottom and slammed the cockpit cowling into Regas, fracturing his skull and putting him in a coma for days.

An anguished Ole Bardahl announced his retirement from hydro racing, and the 1959 Gold Cup took place in Seattle three weekends later without the U-40. Ole later reconsidered, hired Burien milkman Bill Brow to drive, and following repairs by Jensen's team *Miss Bardahl* returned to action at the Silver Cup in Detroit, but the boat never finished higher than third overall the rest of the year. Still, with crew chief McKernan behind the wheel as "relief driver" at the final race on Lake Mead after Brow dislocated his shoulder in a fall, *Bardahl* captured second overall in the 1959 national point standings behind *Maverick*.

Unlike in 2012, "Maverick" also described America's infatuation with television Westerns in 1959. The show of that name ranked No. 6 in the national ratings behind No. 1 "Gunsmoke," "Wagon Train," "Have Gun Will Travel," "The Rifleman," and a non-Western, "The Danny Thomas Show."

In 1960 the Green Dragon really lost her roar. Ole hired a rookie driver, Jim McGuire of British Columbia, Canada, who took fourth at Chelan, then slid too wide on the Detroit River in the Detroit Memorial Regatta, smashing a dock and *Bardahl*'s sponson. *Bardahl* returned to Seattle for repairs, missing the Buffalo race. McGuire was dismissed after a poor Diamond Cup showing, and Brow returned for the rest of the year with tepid results: Seattle, did not finish; Detroit (again) Silver Cup, missed for more repairs; Washington, D.C., fourth. Brow scraped together a third and a second at Madison and Reno, placing *Bardahl* fourth overall in the season standings.

For Ole Bardahl's daughter Evelyn, that year's Reno Regatta on Pyramid Lake was particularly momentous, as she related in the summer 1992 edition of *Hydro Legends*.

> *It was in 1960 in Reno. I was eating breakfast with Bill Muncey and Bill Stead. I was looking for a ride out to the course – I didn't want to rent a car – and I asked Bill Muncey for a ride. He said he had to go to an interview and Stead wasn't going until later. But he got me a ride with another driver, Rex Manchester. It was a 30-mile drive and the beginning of a wonderful romance. We had a date set up before we even got there."*

Evelyn Bardahl Nicolaysen married Rex Manchester on May 5, 1961.

* * * *

As a 6-year-old, I coveted and treasured those balsa wood models my brother Dave had built of *Miss Thriftway* and *Thriftway Too*. One day Dave's neighborhood friend Ernie came to our house, and Ernie thought it would be amusing to re-enact the 1957 crash that had destroyed *Miss Thriftway* and injured driver Bill Muncey. Whether amused himself or vexed by peer pressure, Dave looked on as Ernie laid our balsa wood *Thriftway* on the floor in a jamb, slammed the door, and shattered the model. Ernie laughed. I cried.

In the 1950s and early '60s the Pacific Northwest was gripped by hydro fever. Fans flocked to outboard and limited-class races at Seattle-area venues like Green Lake, where racing had started in 1929; Lake Washington, which held races at several sites; Lake Sammamish, at Alexander's Resort and Vasa Park; Cottage Lake; and a crazy, winding, 40-mile round-trip sprint each April on the Sammamish Slough, which was dredged, straightened, and shortened in 1964.

Eastern Washington towns like Moses Lake, Electric City, and Wenatchee staged races. Even remote sites like Lake Osoyoos near Oroville and Lake Cle Elum north of Roslyn hosted inboard or outboard races. In 1960-61, Lake Cle Elum hosted six classes of outboard hydros at Driftwood Acres Beach, but the Aug. 27, 1961, event was delayed by stiff winds and eventually canceled, ending future races there.

* * * *

On Dec. 2, 1960, *Miss Bardahl* team manager Larry Weir had told *The Seattle Times*' Bud Livesley that "the boat is finished, as of now." Crew chief McKernan confirmed, "Boat operations have been suspended and the crew released," citing a formal letter he and Weir had received from Ole Bardahl, who at the time was in Montreal on business.

It was the second time Ole had quit since Jack Regas' serious injury in 1959. However, Bardahl's advertising manager said, "1961 plans will be developed after the first of the year." On May 19, the *Times* quoted Ole as saying, "I'm definitely out of racing."

Fans figured Ole Bardahl truly had quit or had at least grown apathetic about hydro racing when he skipped entirely the first two races of 1961, in Detroit and Coeur d'Alene. At the latter a paltry six unlimiteds showed up to compete July 23. Newspapers had reported *Bardahl* would race for the Diamond Cup with Mira Slovak at the wheel, but the Green Dragon never appeared. The *Times* reported in July that former crew chief McKernan had taken a job as a port engineer for a fish-packing plant in Alaska.

That week hydros shared headlines with Gus Grissom, who followed pioneer Alan Shepard and became the second American astronaut to fly into space, and who narrowly swam to safety when his *Liberty Bell 7* Mercury space capsule sank after splashing down north of the Bahamas in the Atlantic.

Miss Thriftway sported its familiar livery for the Diamond Cup but a new name, *Miss Century 21*, to promote Seattle's upcoming World's Fair, the Century 21 Exposition. Muncey and *Century 21* beat *Miss Spokane, Cutie Radio* (driven by 18-year-old rookie Billy Schumacher), *Miss Burien,* defending Diamond Cup champ *Seattle Too,* and *Fascination* in an event marred by 3,000 youths partying obnoxiously in downtown Coeur d'Alene the day before.

The 1961 Diamond Cup had come and gone without a glimpse of the Green Dragon. But the *Bardahl* team wasn't dead. In fact, it had been hard at work for weeks rebuilding the hydro's sponsons under the direction of new crew chief Tom Thorning, George McKernan's brother-in-law.

* * * *

That summer of 1961, kids on the other side of our block started a ground-level straw fort in the crotch of an old multi-trunk maple tree next to Lake Hills Community Church. Word spread and soon a dozen kids were at work, gathering tall grass baked tinder-dry by the July sun. We wove the grass around sticks and branches to form the walls of our fort.

That was a variation of our annual spring pastime, where we'd burrow deep into the blooming Scotch broom that grew thick on a nearby hillside, then hollow out a cavity the size of a tiny room that couldn't be seen from the outside. One of the older kids stole a *Playboy* magazine from his dad and stashed it there, and we'd gawk at its pictures inside our hideaway.

Most of the kids in my Lake Hills neighborhood east of Bellevue cheered for the Seattle boats, but one family two doors down disagreed. The three boys – Peewee, Gary, and Mike, roughly my peers but a few years older – and their parents cheered for Detroit's *Gale*s. No wonder. Their dad knew Pat Solomie, crew chief of the *Gale V* (and later, *Miss Smirnoff*), and the week before Seafair in 1960 or '61, Pat drove down our Lake Hills street towing the big mahogany and lime *Gale V* and parked it right in front of the boys' house. That drew a horde of kids and made the three brothers instant celebrities.

Solomie and the *Gale* crew stayed each year at the Hill Top Inn, a hotel on the north side of U.S. 10 ("The Sunset Highway") in Eastgate that was demolished years later for I-90 construction. My dad saw renowned *Gale* driver Wild Bill Cantrell there once in the hotel restaurant, introduced himself, and they chatted over coffee. "Nice guy, and quite a character," Dad said of Bill.

* * * *

Six weeks before the Seafair race, on June 25, 1961, Roger Maris smashed four home runs as the Yankees won a double-header over the White Sox, giving Maris a league-leading 40 homers over teammate Mickey Mantle's 38. The press dubbed them the "M&M boys."

On July 28, the *Seattle Post-Intelligencer* and *The Seattle Times* announced the return of a hydro jockey who along with Muncey would compose half of what reporters soon called hydro racing's own M&M boys. Ron Musson, a native of Akron, Ohio, would drive the recently rebuilt *Miss Bardahl*.

Musson was a rising star in the unlimited ranks, a 32-year-old crackerjack driver who had first raced outboards at age 15 and dominated his limited-class-hydro foes during the 1950s aboard boats like *Chromium* and *Chro-mate*. Overall, Musson won national titles (earned by compiling the most points in a full season of racing) five years in a row from 1954-58: 135 cubic-inch class, 1954-56; 225 class, 1957; and 266 class, 1954-58. In 1958 he beat Bellevue, Wash., driver Chuck Hickling to win the 266 national title on Lake Washington.

Musson also had won seven individual national championship races in the limited ranks – the top regatta each year – dating to 1952. One of them was the 1956 championship for 7-litre hydros, at that time the next-largest class to the unlimiteds. Musson seemed destined to be a giant in unlimited hydro racing despite his modest frame. Dark haired, tan, and somewhat stocky at 5 feet 7 inches and 155 pounds, the man was experienced, crafty, fearless, and blessed with great driving instincts. He also flew Cessna airplanes for fun.

In 1959, Musson was an unlimited-class rookie when he drove *Hawaii Kai III* to victory at Madison, Ind., and in 1960 he won the Reno Regatta on Pyramid Lake with the *Kai* despite shedding most of its left sponson on lap three of the final heat, in which he still averaged 107.752 mph. Musson also led for the first nine laps of Gold Cup heat 1A on Lake Mead before running out of fuel. Earlier that year he had won the 1960 Silver Cup in Detroit aboard Samuel DuPont's new *Nitrogen Too*, an underpowered boat that Musson drove past Bill Muncey and *Miss Thriftway* in two out of three heats. Musson benefited that day from the wrench-twisting of Graham Heath, an Allison expert and close buddy who worked on Ron's boats and later became a much-revered crew chief.

Muncey campaigned to get Musson the *Bardahl* seat. "I wanted Ron in the boat because he's a good driver, it's as simple as that," he told the *P-I*'s John Owen. "Sure, he gives me trouble, but he knows what he's doing out there. I want to race against the best, and he's one of the best."

Returning in 1961 for his second year with the *Bardahl* team was a 44-year-old U.S. Army automotive equipment inspector named Leo Vanden Berg from Seattle. Vanden Berg had been a crew member for the 1959 Gold Cup winner and national champion *Maverick*. When *Bardahl*'s new crew chief Tom Thorning assembled his 1961 team, Vanden Berg stayed, among the dozen who agreed to be per-diem volunteers.

Bardahl fans witnessed the Green Dragon's swift and dramatic resurgence when Musson took the helm for the 1961 World's Championship Seafair Race, held Aug. 6 on Seattle's Lake Washington. Boats were slotted into three tiers based on qualifying times, with the seven fastest grouped into the World's Championship event. Slower boats competed for the Seattle and Queen's trophies.

Musson's first ride in *Miss Bardahl* actually came on Sunday, July 30, one week before the Seattle race. On Thursday he qualified *Miss Bardahl* at a three-lap average of 109.535, good for sixth on the ladder. The crew spent Friday tailoring the cockpit for its new pint-sized driver.

Apparently it was a good fit. Musson soundly beat the fleetest of the fleet in his first two heats, including Muncey and *Miss Century 21*, and averaged 106.027 for all three heats to win the race. His two early heat wins gave Musson the margin he needed to survive hull and mechanical woes in the final, where he hobbled home fourth yet still captured the $10,000 top prize on overall points.

Distinguished *P-I* sports editor Royal Brougham wrote the next morning, "If you want the plain facts, the *Bardahl* out-performed the former *Thriftway* and Musson out-drove Muncey."

Or to quote its TV ads: Bardahl did it again.

* * * *

Mom worked part time at the Frederick & Nelson department store in Bellevue Square, where Kit Muncey – wife of renowned driver Bill Muncey – was a customer. One day Mom brought home Bill's autograph on a slip of paper. Mom liked the hydros, but unlike me her fondness had its limits.

KING-TV had first televised Seafair in 1952, with Bill O'Mara announcing, and KOMO-TV jumped onboard in 1954 with Keith Jackson. Both stations later televised Chelan's Apple Cup and Coeur d'Alene's Diamond Cup, as well. Nearly each year from 1961 through 1975, all three of Seattle's network-affiliate TV stations – KING, KOMO, and KIRO – covered the hydros' every Seafair move.

In the early '60s Seafair qualifying began on Tuesday preceding the Sunday race. Mom watched daytime soap operas on her days off, and in particular she liked a CBS show called "The Edge of Night." One August weekday as a dramatic "Edge of Night" plot neared its climax, the KIRO-TV announcer suddenly broke in: "We now take you live to the shores of Lake Washington…." and the screen cut to a black-and-white image of a low-budget hydro trying to scrounge up enough speed to qualify for the race. Mom fumed. I was delighted.

Dad took Judy, Dave, and me to Seafair each year, with one exception – 1961. I watched the race on KING-TV and KOMO-TV at home in Lake Hills, in our mint green (a hip late-1950s color) "rec room," seated in front of the Magnavox black and white console TV that Mom bought at Frederick & Nelson. KING's coverage was anchored by Rod Belcher, while KOMO's anchor was a soon-to-be nationally acclaimed sportscaster named Keith Jackson. Six radio stations covered the race live that year.

For luck, I hugged my *Miss Bardahl* balsa wood model during each heat Musson raced. My 7-year-old brain reasoned that the harder I squeezed, the more luck it should bring. And there at home in Lake Hills I watched Musson blaze past Bill Muncey and the other drivers to win the World's Championship Seafair Race.

* * * *

As the hydro race grabbed headlines, so did the mounting U.S. – Russia space race. "Miss Bardahl Beats Century 21" topped the front page of the Aug. 7 *Seattle P-I*, which ran a lower headline, "Russ Say Spaceman Landed Safely," followed by details of mankind's second orbital flight of the earth, by Soviet cosmonaut Gherman Titov.

Alan Shepard had become the first American to fly into space on May 5 when he rocketed 116 miles high aboard *Freedom 7* in a suborbital flight from Cape Canaveral; an American astronaut would not orbit the earth until John Glenn's flight in February 1962. Throughout the 1961 hydro season and for the next few years, the U.S. space program scrambled to catch up with the Soviets.

* * * *

Musson took third in the 1961 Gold Cup on Pyramid Lake, Nev., and was declared the winner of the abbreviated Sept. 10 Silver Cup in Detroit. *Bardahl* had posted that day's fastest speed, 108.089, while beating *Century 21* to win heat 1A, before driver Bob Hayward flipped his *Miss Supertest II* during a high-speed turn on the treacherous Detroit River in heat 2A and died. Officials canceled the rest of the race.

Bardahl broke a gearbox and did not finish her first heat of that year's President's Cup, but she came back to win the next two heats, including the final, to take third overall. She won the only heat she entered in the season's final race at Madison, Ind., giving her team great hope for the future: Despite skipping the circuit's first two races, *Bardahl* earned enough points to finish second overall to Muncey and *Miss Century 21* in the 1961 point standings. Musson's overall 1961 record: seven firsts, one third, and two fourths in 12 starts.

Ole Bardahl pondered what his team could accomplish with Musson piloting a new, improved *Miss Bardahl*. Asked by the *P-I*'s John Owen at the Gold Cup how he liked his new driver, Ole said, "Am I happy with Ron Musson? I just wish I'd had him two years ago."

For Ole, the thrill of racing was back. And Musson was the spark.

* * * *

Turbochargers, which harness waste exhaust for extra horsepower, were to become a key development in bolstering hydros' Allison engines. As this book goes to press the world's all-time fastest piston-powered hydroplane is the U-3 owned by Ed Cooper of Evansville, Ind. Cooper's thunderboat uses a 1,710 cubic-inch V-12 Allison engine equipped with a turbocharger. In 2004, U-3 driver Mitch Evans – winner of the 2003 Gold Cup, and son of 1958 *Bardahl* driver Norm – blistered the 2½-mile San Diego racecourse at a piston-record average lap speed of 162.602 mph.

Before turbine engines became common in hydro racing in the mid-1980s, many piston-powered hydros used turbochargers, including speedsters *Tahoe Miss* in 1965, *Miss U.S.* and *Lincoln Thrift* in the 1970s, and *Miss Madison* in the 1970s and '80s. A little-known fact: Which hydroplane was intended to be the first with a turbocharger? Answer: *Miss Bardahl*.

Sometime before 1961, the *Bardahl* team acquired a huge Switzer turbocharger. "It was there when I first went to work for Bardahl, a brand new one," said Leo Vanden Berg. Former Bardahl employee and crew member Jerry Zuvich concurs. "There was a turbocharger on the shelf, a great big one," he said. "This was a turbo you'd call 'sir.'"

Dixon Smith, also part of the 1960s *Bardahl* crew, said Ole contracted to have two of them specially designed and built for a Rolls-Royce Merlin, but they were never used. "They lay around in the corner, but we never did anything with them because nobody on our crew really understood turbocharging at the time. *Tahoe Miss* probably was the first hydro to use turbos, taken straight off of a P-47 D-10 Thunderbolt airplane," Dixon said.

Bardahl's turbochargers eventually were sold to Bernie Little, owner of *Miss Budweiser*. Their fate is uncertain. Vanden Berg said in 1989 he believed Little had sold them to an airplane racer.

Chapter 2

The core crew: Bardahl's *family tree*

A few weeks after the 1961 Seafair race, Dad drove Judy and me to Spokane, where we delivered her for freshman orientation at Whitworth College. For me, traveling through Eastern Washington was a huge adventure. This was pre-Interstate 90, and most of the route via U.S. Highway 10 beyond Easton had just two lanes.

Youths today can't relate to the terror of a baby-boomer kid riding helplessly, with no seat belt, as a Spokane-bound parent crossing a sagebrush wasteland mashes the gas, swings left across the center line to pass, and surges toward what looks like certain disaster with an oncoming car. Thank God for divided freeways.

Aside from sporadic terror on the blacktop, that 1961 trip seared exciting lifelong images into my 7-year-old mind: An enormous ancient log at a roadside display in Cle Elum. The Cascade Canal irrigation aquaduct, winding snake-like through the upper Yakima River canyon west of Ellensburg. The old two-lane Vantage Bridge. Roadside graffiti in Frenchman Coulee across the Columbia River from Vantage, where a smart-aleck had added "S&H Green Stamps" below the previously painted "Jesus saves." The pleasant smell of 25.9¢ Ethyl at full-service gas stations. Colossal high-voltage towers. Miles of barren, baked soil and sagebrush. Soaring Nabisco grain silos in Cheney.

We stayed one night at the Ridpath Hotel in Spokane, where it hit 100 degrees on Aug. 19. Archives show it surpassed 90 for five of the next six days: 100, 86, 94, 95, 96, and 92 degrees. I'd never felt such heat in Lake Hills. Despite it, I galloped around McMillan Hall on the Whitworth campus wearing a pillowcase for a cape, emulating George Reeves on television's "The Adventures of Superman." At dusk Dad and I said goodbye to Judy, and we motored westbound toward home via U.S. 2.

Somewhere west of the small farming town of Reardon we drove up a dirt road alongside a wheat field. We parked and crawled into sleeping bags in the back of Dad's white 1959 Chevy Impala station wagon on a night so black and clear we could see the Milky Way. Dad told me a story, the details of which are muddled and long forgotten, about how 1800s explorers sandbagged shallow Columbia River channels to create enough draft to float their grounded boats. We slept in the car and the next day drove north and toured Grand Coulee Dam, staggering in its immensity.

It was on that foray into Eastern Washington that I grew fond of Spokane, the Lilac City. And it was then that 19-year-old Skip Schott, one year removed from Spokane's West Valley High School, was already fully immersed in hydro racing as a crewmember of *Miss Spokane*, the Lilac Lady, Queen of the Inland Empire.

* * * *

Skip Schott had graduated from West Valley High in 1960 and worked in a cabinet shop for Kent Simonson, the representative owner of the community-owned *Miss Spokane*. Schott built cabinets by day, and at night he volunteered long hours as a crew member on the boat, but not for pay – "just for the glory," he said.

By 1961 Schott already had been around hydros for several years. At age 15 he had become friends with Dixon Smith through their common interest in running tethered gas-powered model hydros. In *Miss Spokane*'s early days, Schott's parents knew Norm Evans' father, and the Schotts would tow their 15-foot travel trailer from Spokane to Chelan and park it across the street from the Apple Cup hydro pits, in the alley behind the elder Evans' house.

"I really liked Norm," said Skip. "When I was a kid, he was really good to me and treated me not as a kid, but as an adult. That guy had balls made out of titanium. This is a man who crashed a crane down a ravine and was trapped for three days, and he crawled out and was fisticuffing with people within weeks."

At the August 1960 Seafair Trophy Race in Seattle, driver Rex Manchester had *Miss Spokane* out front in the final heat, mere moments from the checkered flag. Schott and the rest of the crew were ecstatic. "We jumped off the dock into the water to celebrate," he said years later. "We won the race! And then it got taken away from us."

Officials' red flares pierced the air and stopped the event just before Manchester could cross the finish line. *Miss U.S.1* had caught fire and driver Don Wilson dove overboard, halting the race.

When the final heat was rerun the next day, *Miss Spokane* got boxed in at the first turn as *Thriftway* surged to the front. *Spokane* charged hard and passed one boat but was unable to catch *Thriftway*. Manchester and *Spokane* finished second.

One year later, on Sunday, Aug. 27, 1961, Manchester had just won a heat of the Gold Cup on Pyramid Lake, Nev., and was leading the final lap of another heat when, rounding a corner, *Miss Spokane* fell into a deep trough and flipped.

"The wind had come up, and all we saw was the aluminum bottom of the boat," said Schott. "It went upside down, and Rex was trapped in the cockpit. He sucked a lot of water in before the divers got him out."

Manchester suffered a dislocated shoulder, severe cuts on his legs, and two sprained ankles. Knowing they could do nothing themselves to help Manchester, who though battered had escaped life-threatening injury, Schott and his friend Chuck Pierce jumped into a patrol boat to help retrieve *Miss Spokane*, which was floating upside down.

"It had a big air bubble in it, and we started towing it in," Schott said. "The divers jumped on its stern to catch a ride. When they did that the bow rose and belched a big air bubble. The bow kept rising, and obviously the boat was going down."

Schott spied a Clorox jug and a long strand of parachute cord in the patrol craft, and he quickly tied the cord to the jug and to the bow of the boat as it sank in 80 feet of water. Luckily the cord was 125 feet long, so the jug marked *Miss Spokane*'s location on the bottom of Pyramid Lake.

Manchester was rushed to Washoe Medical Center in Reno where he struggled to keep food down, eventually lost 20 pounds, and remained bedridden until Sept. 5, when he left the hospital in a wheelchair. But before that transpired, back at Pyramid on Aug. 28, the *Miss Spokane* team stood on the beach pondering its next steps.

"The boat's board of directors were broke at that point and owed money, so they said to leave the boat at the bottom of the lake," Schott explained. "And they all went home. Kent Simonson and his son Butch and I stayed there, and we recovered the boat."

The hull was raised and towed to shore just before sunset on Tuesday, Aug. 29.

Written accounts at the time cited "new financial backing" for the community-owned *Miss Spokane*. Years later Simonson and crew said that wasn't quite accurate: "The truth is, the crew supports the boat, and the wives support the crew," said Manchester.

* * * *

In May of 1958, 41-year-old civil service Army mechanic Leo Vanden Berg stood high on a railroad pier at Lake Chelan, looking down on the buzz of activity in the Apple Cup pits. He'd been interested in racing since 1938 when he worked at Pierce Automotive in Seattle and built engines for local car racers. Later, when Pierce raced his own cars, Vanden Berg was the driver at tracks like Silver Lake, Aurora Speed Bowl, and Civic Stadium. He loved hydros, too. He worked on outboards, owned one for awhile, and spent the night at Lake Washington to get a good spot for the family at Seattle's first Gold Cup race in 1951.

Born July 18, 1917, Leonardus C. Vanden Berg was a Seattle native who grew up in the city's South Park neighborhood at 1219 South Trenton Street, just a stone's throw below "Catholic Hill," where the original Our Lady of Lourdes Catholic Church (demolished in 1971) sat on the summit west of 14th Avenue South, between South Donovan and South Henderson streets. Leo was one of five kids, two boys and three girls.

"His oldest sister, Adriana, was a nun," said Mel Vanden Berg, Leo's son. "However, she met a gardener at the convent, and that ended that."

Leo was named after his father, Leonardus Quarrie Vanden Berg, a machinist at Seattle truck manufacturer H.R.L. Motor Company. Leo attended St. George School from kindergarten through eighth grade. During that time he and his brother, Francia, delivered newspapers, *The Seattle Times* and the *Seattle Star*.

Then tragedy struck.

"Our dad got hit on the head at work, and he was sick for two years before he died at age 41 from a brain tumor," said Ann Gustafson, Leo's younger sister. "My mom raised all five of us alone. She grew her own garden."

Leo described his mother, Margaretha, as a very small but powerful woman who was strict with her five kids. Though he was just 12 when his dad died, Leo soon found jobs in garages to help support the family. He later attended ninth grade at O'Dea High School in Seattle, then transferred to Cleveland High on Beacon Hill. He called Cleveland "just a three-mile walk" from home each day when he took a shortcut across the 14th Avenue S. Bridge and the Boeing Field runway.

Leo didn't finish high school and began earning money by purchasing wrecked or broken-down cars, dismantling them, and selling the parts to auto repair shops.

"He said he did that with many cars that are now valuable classics," said Mel. "He even had a Stuz but was unable to sell enough parts to recover what he paid for it."

Mylrea "Millie" Costain also grew up in South Park, the daughter of immigrants from the Isle of Mann. She too lost her father at a young age and endured a tough childhood. Leo (age 21) and Mylrea (20) got their marriage license in July 1938, were married and moved to Highland Park, where in June1939 they had a son, Len. Son Mel was born in May 1941, Leo served a stint in the U.S. Navy, and in 1943 the Vanden Bergs bought a house a few blocks east of their rental home.

"I remember my dad purchasing an army barracks that he had to dismantle, and from the lumber he recovered he built a two-car garage," said Mel. "I spent many hours helping him in the garage."

Sister Ann said Leo "was always working on cars" and seemed to have a knack for it, which led to a long career as an Army vehicle inspector at Seattle's Fort Lawton.

"He went to a GMC Hydromatic transmission class in Atlanta for the military when they first came out," said Mel, "and I understand he topped the class, which had engineers and other highly educated folks."

Despite his challenging teen years and associating with the sometimes-coarse car-racing crowd, Leo kept a level head and enjoyed simple pleasures.

"I never did see my father drink liquor," said Mel. "He loved ice cream, especially chocolate. We would drive all the way to an ice cream store in Rainier Beach to get ice cream cones."

Leo also harbored a soft side.

"He was given a live goose that he brought home to slaughter," Mel said. "He went to the back yard to cut its head off and was gone for a considerable length of time. My mother went to see why it was taking so much time and found him building a pen. He couldn't kill the goose. We had that goose for years, and my brother and I had to feed it. It got mean each time it laid eggs, so we knew she had eggs hidden somewhere."

Vanden Berg said in 1989 that his years as a Boy Scout leader helped him manage his *Miss Bardahl* crew members. They were older than scouts, of course, but the age gap between them and Leo spanned 20-plus years. Son Mel recalled Leo using his talents to "make for a unique experience" when their Boy Scout troop went inner-tubing in the Cascades. Leo wouldn't settle for simple tubes from cars, so he canvassed truck shops until he had enough giant tubes for the youths, then devised an efficient way to inflate them.

"He brought a gas-driven compressor along with the tubes," Mel said. "Our troop was the envy of others who brought only car tires, since we could do many more stunts and long chains."

Around that time Leo met Al Benson, another government worker who owned a C-class outboard hydro and helped get Leo interested and involved in boat racing. Benson later was drawn to unlimited hydros, and Leo got the bug too, leading him to that Chelan railroad pier during Apple Cup week in 1958.

Leo had been perched on the pier throughout time trials when a dark-haired man in *Maverick* coveralls approached him and asked what he was doing. "I've been watching you guys," said Vanden Berg. The man said, "Well, don't just watch us, come and help us."

So dark-haired Ricky Iglesias, *Maverick* team manager, walked down into the pits with Vanden Berg, who began working on the crew. "They blew the auxiliary stage off of their Allison the next day, and that's when I got acquainted with the aux stage," said Vanden Berg. "I helped their engine man Bill Newman build a new one. He was a factory-certified Allison mechanic. My job after that was to install the aux stage after switching engines, and align it."

In prior years Vanden Berg had attended Seattle test sessions at Jett's Marina as well as all of the Seafair races – "They weren't too particular about security in those days," he said – observing pit activity and lending a hand now and then by holding a rope, fueling a boat, or charging and installing batteries. Before Chelan he'd never met Iglesias, who randomly picked him out of a crowd.

"He always did that at every race, picked out some local guy to help for the weekend," Vanden Berg recalled. "He did that even after I was part of the crew. He was saving money – what for, I don't know, because *Maverick* was spending big money."

The team paid Vanden Berg's way to the races plus per diem and expenses. He sometimes put in 20 hours a day between his civil-service job at Fort Lawton and his *Maverick* duties. "I did that for years," he said, "working 40 hours a week and then helping *Maverick* for about 60 hours on evenings and weekends."

Mel helped his dad, doing odd jobs while the new *Maverick* was built at a Hallidie Machinery shop on First Avenue South in Seattle over the winter of 1958-59. After graduating from high school that spring, Mel worked for Ron Jones for a year and recalls "putting the fairline on *Miss Burien* and fixing *Thriftway Too*'s sponsons."

In 1959 Bill Stead won the Gold Cup plus four other races and the National Championship aboard the new *Maverick*, but owner W.T. Waggoner suffered health problems that July and retired from racing after the season. Leo Vanden Berg was out of hydro work – for awhile.

* * * *

Unlike many young men on hydroplane crews, Jerry Zuvich had never been to a boat race as a youth. He gained his mechanical experience in a realm quite foreign to unlimited racing: working as a commercial fisherman each summer. Zuvich's dad owned a purse seiner and drag boat.

"On a fishing boat, you have to learn how to get something running while you're working," Zuvich said. "I call it 'imagineering.' You have to imagineer a way of solving problems. You don't have the time or means to ask somebody who knows their way around it, you have to kind of think it out."

Zuvich grew up in the Queen Ann-Interbay-Magnolia area of Seattle, attending St. Margaret's elementary and then St. Martin's. He was unlike a lot of kids who played after school, riding bikes, watching TV, goofing off around the neighborhood.

"I was always working on the fishing boat," he said. "My dad never did get a driver's license, so as soon as I turned 16, I was his designated driver to go get groceries and pick up parts, because we always worked on the boat. In the spring as soon as I got out of school I had to go down to the boat and paint the bottom, paint parts, clean up. And then he and I had to change from bottom fishing – dragging – to seining. So there I was all the time, working on the boat."

Zuvich had two older sisters who also did quite a bit of work on the boat. Fishing was the Zuvich family livelihood.

"Back then, it was tough, just making a buck," he said.

In his late-teen years Zuvich and his dad fished southeastern Alaska between Ketchikan, Hoonah, and Juneau, which had pretty decent weather unless the wind was blowing under 20 knots. "Then the mosquitos would get you," he said. In later years Zuvich worked in Dutch Harbor and as a port engineer at Naknek, but it was after fishing southeast Alaska that summer of 1960 that Zuvich needed work and took a job with Bardahl Manufacturing Corporation on its canning line, in 1961. He was 20.

Although he'd never been to Seafair or towed a wooden boat behind his bike, Zuvich took an interest in the big green hydro housed inside the plant and offered to help *Miss Bardahl*'s all-volunteer crew, led by Tom Thorning. Among the volunteers was Leo Vanden Berg. After Zuvich became a shipping clerk he had access to a telephone and a delivery truck. The crew would leave shopping-list messages, and Zuvich would chase down parts.

Zuvich later witnessed turnover in the *Bardahl* crew and was the first and only full-time employee assigned to the 1962 hydroplane. He became friends with the people at nearby Sullivan's Auto Parts, who occasionally ground valves or knurled pistons for *Bardahl* when the race team was short on time. His friends also remember Zuvich hot-rodding a special car in 1965.

"I owned a 1959 Corvette, white with blue pockets on the fenders," said Zuvich. "I put a 421 Pontiac with tri-power in it because Billy Schumacher had a red 1963 fuel-injected Sting Ray, and I couldn't be outdone. I'm not sure exactly why we're still alive."

* * * *

Dixon "Dax" Smith and his younger brother David grew up around hydroplanes. Their father, Burns Smith, was an IBM engineer by day and skilled hydro mechanic and craftsman on evenings and weekends. Burns began as the crew chief for *Miss Seattle* and worked with several top hydros over the years including *Hawaii Kai III*, *Miss Seattle Too*, *Miss Bardahl*, *Notre Dame*, and *Miss Budweiser*.

Ron Musson knew Burns from their days racing *Hawaii Kai*, and after landing the *Bardahl* job, Musson asked Burns to go to work on the Green Dragon.

"I said, 'Yes, under one stipulation, and that is my kids are welcome around there,'" Burns told the *Unlimited NewsJournal* in 1977. Initially the *Bardahl* team said no, but later, "they very reluctantly said yes."

Dixon was born in August 1943. He became "Dax" in the same way many toddlers earn their nicknames.

"When he was very young, he couldn't pronounce his name," said David Smith. "Dixon was a big name for a little kid. But he could say something that sounded like 'Dax,' so my parents started calling him Dax, and he started calling himself Dax. He was 'Dax' well into adulthood."

As a youth Dax gained mechanical experience and knowledge working with his father, who had a shop in the basement of their home on Seattle's Beacon Hill. From an early age Dax was allowed to go downstairs and use power tools and help Burns fix car engines.

Dax later attended Cleveland High, a school of mixed ethnicity that could be rough around the edges. He was a bright student with great aptitude for math and physics, and in the timeless tradition of all smart kids, he sometimes drew the attention of the school's thugs.

"I got stuffed in a dumpster once or twice in high school," he said.

In high school and later as a University of Washington student, Dax drove himself and neighboring students around in the family car, a 1956 Chevy four door with a 265 V-8 and what he called a "slushbox 3-speed."

Burns Smith taught Dax about mechanics, but not so much about working on V-12 aircraft motors. It was an original *Slo-mo-shun* mechanic named Adam "Wes" Kiesling who influenced Dax considerably. Along with George McKernan, Kiesling was one of only two paid *Slo-mo* crew members, both being employees of Stan Sayres' Chrysler agency. Kiesling was crew chief of *Miss Seattle Too* in 1959-60, and he taught the teenage Smith how to assemble and take apart Rolls-Royce Merlin engines the summer between Dax's junior and senior years at Cleveland.

"Dixon's dad would drop him off, and he and Wes would build motors," said Schott. "You could throw a rock from PEMCO Insurance's headquarters and hit the old *Seattle Too* shop, a tiny white concrete or brick building in the South Lake Union neighborhood. It was so tight getting in, it had a garage door that a tilted boat would fit in with about an inch of clearance."

The address is 400 Minor Street N., across the street from Cascade Playground. In 2012, the former boat shop served as a PEMCO storage facility.

"Wes didn't teach me a lot about the *why*, which is so important, but which I wouldn't have understood until after learning physics and theory at the UW," said Dax. "He taught me about the *what*. He was a fussy mechanic who knew the entire Rolls manual and followed it precisely, which was important because the people who wrote it knew what they were doing and had things in there for a reason.

"Wes was a small thin guy, maybe five-foot-seven, maybe in his 60s," Dax recalled. "He could be grouchy at times, but he treated me well. I appreciated the opportunity because here I am, a high school kid being taught this stuff, as well as just running around for parts. It's an opportunity that most others my age didn't get."

Dax later earned a degree in both math and physics at the UW, with a minor in electrical engineering. In fact, many years later he was hired by Boeing as an engineer because of his education and practical engineering experience.

"Dixon could pass mechanical engineering or aeronautical engineering on a whim because he took those as electives," said David. "He's really good at that. I went into engineering because I didn't want to read and write and I thought I couldn't make it in arts and sciences. So every time I had a problem, Dixon would tutor me. He likes that situation, he very much likes to be the teacher."

* * * *

In the early days of Seafair, Burns Smith was drawn to hydroplanes.

"Dad would go down and camp out on Saturday night, find us a place, and then we would find him on the beach and we'd have our picnic and watch the races," said David. "We watched the *Such Crust* catch on fire, we were there when the *Quicksilver* went down. We were always at the races."

When he was in first grade, David Smith – two and a half years younger than brother Dixon – accompanied his uncle and cousins to the Sears, Roebuck and Co. store on South Lander Street in Seattle.

David had never been to the big store, and he'd never ridden an escalator until that day when his uncle coaxed him onto one.

"I hadn't tied my shoelaces real well, and they'd come unraveled," David said. "But I didn't know that."

David hopped on the escalator and his shoelaces dangled between the metal floor plates. When it came time to step off, David instead was jerked down as the plates and shoelaces slid under the floor.

"I smashed my face, and this thing is beating me up because my shoes are caught," David explained. "I'm screaming and yelling, absolutely terrified. My uncle and cousins laughed and said, 'Aw, just dust yourself off.' But that was a bad experience, and it took a long time for me to ever get on an escalator after that."

One Saturday a few years later, Burns Smith drove his daughter Rosann and sons Dax and David to Sand Point Naval Air Station on Lake Washington, where *Miss Seattle* shared a hangar with Bill Waggoner's *Rebel Suh*. While Burns and his IBM colleagues worked on *Miss Seattle*, the kids rode their bikes around the base and played on the boat. Then Burns trailered *Miss Seattle* to the dock, bolted a bench seat in the cockpit to accommodate two people, donned his green and white cotton lifejacket and an old helmet, and gave rides to volunteers as a thank you for their work on the boat.

After awhile Burns steered the hydro back to the dock, where he and the crew stood around chatting until Burns announced, "It's time. My kids are going for a ride." Unknown to them, he had arranged things beforehand. Burns instructed Rosann and her siblings, "You're going for a ride in the racebout, and you will *not* tell your mother."

Young David protested, "I don't want to go, Dad!" But Burns insisted, "No, you're gonna go, and this is going to be a great experience."

Rosann and David strapped on what he later described as "funky little lifejackets" and climbed into the cockpit, with David seated in the middle. In the mid-1950s, hydros had no sheet metal covering the driveshaft, and once Burns started the motor David looked down and saw the shaft directly below and between his feet, spinning rapidly.

"At this time in my life I'd gone 25, maybe 30 miles an hour in a boat, and soon we're doing a hundred-some miles an hour," David recalled. "And I am *petrified*. The boat's jumping around, and my father's grabbing me and gesturing, wanting us to look at the roostertail, because that's a big deal."

Rosann looked around and soaked in the spectacle, but David fixed his gaze downward the entire time. "I couldn't take my eyes off that shaft and coupling going round and round."

When they returned to the dock Burns was furious. "David, I can't believe the one time in your life you'll ever get to ride in a hydroplane, you wouldn't even look up." David started crying, and Burns said, "What is wrong with you?"

David sobbed, "I'm sorry, Daddy, but I was scared my shoelaces would get caught in the shaft," remembering his traumatic experience on the Sears escalator.

Later, David whetted his appetite for boat work by helping his dad on *Miss Seattle, Hawaii Kai,* and *Miss Seattle Too*.

"I would hold stuff for him, maybe put a fastener in or something like that," he said. "And as I got older, I did a little bit of work – hung around, didn't do much. But when Dad worked on *Hawaii Kai* when

Mascari owned it, there were a couple times they busted up the boat, and I got to work with my father on it. And in between all this we built three runabouts at home, just regular family ski boats," he said, explaining where he honed his woodworking skills.

With big brother Dax advocating for him, David would later work on *Miss Bardahl*.

"That was a very big time in my life to be able to do that," David said. "I didn't take enough time to enjoy it because I didn't really realize how good it was. Seattle didn't have the pro teams yet, we were heroes. And the other thing is, when I worked on the *Bardahl*, it was me – I wasn't with my dad, it was me, so I had to stand on my own.

"I was also the youngest person in the pits working on the boats, so my head was pretty big at the time, because I was pretty cool," he added with a smile.

Chapter 3

Building a better Bardahl

Following the 1961 season, Ole Bardahl once again – as he'd done in December 1960 – cleaned house. He released the entire crew except for Leo Vanden Berg, who had earned Ole's trust and was promoted to crew chief.

The subsequent crew thought the change might have stemmed from uncertainty over how parts and machine services were purchased.

"One thing's certain about Leo, he's as honest as the day is long," said Dixon. "That's one of the things Ole recognized. Ole had really implicit trust in Leo, and he knew Leo wasn't going to screw him."

Vanden Berg confirmed as much when asked about it in 1989.

"Yeah, I got along *real* good with Ole," he said. "Better than anybody. Because I understood what he wanted. Anybody who puts out dollars wants to know where his dollars are going, that they're not squandered. He said, 'You know, when other crew chiefs sell me the same cam rack three times, I've got to watch it.'

"When I first started as crew chief he'd give me, say, $500, and when that was gone I'd get $500 more," Vanden Berg explained. "And I always turned in all receipts; I checked right to the penny. Nobody ever did that before. And I'd turn receipts in right after every trip back East, for example. The other guys would wait half a year before they turned them in. So, towards the end there, I could get any amount I'd want."

Quality control also had been suspect before 1962.

"There was a lot of slip-shod work done earlier with the '58–'61 *Bardahl* team because of not overseeing things," Vanden Berg said in 1989. "Like, they'd put a heli-coil in crooked, and then the bolt would go crooked but they'd bolt it down anyway, which would put the wrong kind of stress through it."

In a 1980 interview Ole spoke highly of Vanden Berg. "Leo was a darn good employee and took a lot of pride in his work. I got nothing but praise for him."

Jerry Zuvich had gone to work for Bardahl Manufacturing Corporation in 1961, so he witnessed the team changes first-hand.

"In '61, at the end of the season, Mr. Bardahl and the crew kind of … uhh … broke up," Zuvich explained. "He came out one afternoon and asked me to straighten up the boat shop because he'd ordered a new boat. So I went over there and worked full time by myself for like a month or two. Leo Vanden Berg became the crew chief, and he was still on a volunteer basis. He worked at Fort Lawton during the day.

That was in early 1962, and that's when Mr. Bardahl ordered the boat from Ted Jones."

Ole hired Jones to construct a new *Miss Bardahl* for the 1962 season. Ron Musson had squeezed every bit of speed possible out of the 1958 hull, but he deemed that boat merely "pretty fair" and "a little jumpy." Ole was eager to give his new ace pilot a brand-new ride more to his liking.

Of the 1958 hull, Ole told the *Unlimited NewsJournal*, "I only kept the boat four years because I don't think a boat is safe after that, since bouncing in rough water can really shake a boat up."

In February 1962, Ted Jones "borrowed" a gifted carpenter named Bob Mackey from his son Ron, who lived and worked in Shelton at the time. Ted and Mackey began building the new *Miss Bardahl* – the third – in Jones' Kennydale shop alongside the East Channel of Lake Washington.

"Dad designed it but wanted someone else to do most of the construction," said Ron Jones. "Bob was working with me in Shelton at the time, and he took a leave of absence to help my dad. Bob stayed there for the length of time it took to build the *Bardahl*. And he did most of the hands-on work. He's excellent. My dad undoubtedly supervised and helped out. Dad wasn't, you know, unable. He could do his share too, but he was awfully busy."

Years earlier, Mackey had been one of three young Tacoma Vocational-Technical Institute woodworking graduates hired by Ron Jones to help with father Ted's boatbuilding business. Ted had hired Bill Muncey in 1955 to run the business end of the operation, and after awhile Muncey and Ron disagreed on Mackey's potential. Mackey was painfully quiet and introverted, not personable, and after a couple of months Muncey wanted to let him go. Ron protested, judging Mackey the best of the three young "wood butchers."

"I said, 'Give him a little time. He's got the ability,'" said Jones. "Muncey and I had quite an argument about him, but Mackey became the best boatbuilder in the country. Nobody could touch him.

"I would design a 225-class limited or something and we'd both build it," Jones explained. "We'd build the frames, put it in the jig together, but then I'd take one side of the boat and he'd take the other side. I would work my buns off, and at the end of the day he was always 15, 20 minutes ahead of me. He was so good. And he knew how far to go and not make a flower out of it. It wasn't made into a beautiful work of art, it was made into a race boat. And boy, Bob was the best."

Vanden Berg and other *Bardahl* team members concur that although Ted Jones oversaw construction of the new boat, Bob Mackey did most of the work. "Mackey, basically, was the main man," said Zuvich.

"Mackey was really good because he was fast and he was accurate," said David Smith. "Small, skinny, wiry guy. Huge amount of energy. He could work, work, work. He had more adrenaline than anybody I've ever met. Upside down all the time. Didn't complain."

Ted Jones told *Motor Trend* magazine that the 1962 *Bardahl* would incorporate major changes.

"No unlimited hydroplane has ever been built with the new *Bardahl*'s particular dimensions," he said. "She's the same length as most of the boats I've built, but she's wider … the width of the tunnel, and the inside are all different. The inside of the left-hand sponson is beveled. The main advantages are faster turning and more-rapid acceleration."

Those sponson angles later proved to be a problem, carving the water too deeply so that the hull reacted.

But *Bardahl* had other successful features that set it apart from other unlimiteds.

"Along with the '59 *Maverick*, it was the first low-deck design, the low profile," said Vanden Berg. "It had a lower crown than other boats. And the bottom was a little different, where it carried the center of gravity. Later, we were the first to use a cavitation plate. That was Ted Jones' idea to try and correct the ride that first season."

Most hydros at the time had a "rocker" bottom where, as with the runners of a rocking chair, the bottom's surface angle gradually curved at what's called the "break" – the point where the cushion of air packed underneath the boat spills out. *Bardahl* had a straight bottom, not curved – the forward surface was flat up to the break, a sharp angle behind which the rear surface of the bottom also was flat.

"Our break was farther back, too," said Zuvich. "Most boats were like 50/50 – on a 30-foot boat, the break was at 15 feet. Ours was more like a 60/40. The break was 10 percent farther back." In theory, it provided a larger cushion of air that enabled *Bardahl* to fly more, reducing water drag.

"And Leo's right about the lower profile," said Zuvich. "The core of that boat was very slight. And it's *really* small compared with the boat they ran in '61. I mean, that thing had a core that you wouldn't believe."

"The *Bardahl* was the lowest-profile unlimited built at the time," David Smith said. "The engine stuck up so much they couldn't even put a cowling on it. And Ron couldn't see over it, he couldn't see over the scoop or the aftercooler. So he looked out the side.

"Something else unique – the first time *Bardahl* ran, it had an outside skidfin," Smith added, referring to the aluminum blade attached to the bottom of the left sponson. The skidfin protrudes down, pierces the water and acts as a pivot to keep hydros from sliding out on turns. In *Bardahl*'s day, virtually all hydroplane skidfins were mounted on the *inside* of the sponson, which is where *Bardahl*'s was relocated soon after its christening.

Aside from that and a slew of mechanical innovations that came later, *Bardahl*'s construction was fairly conventional.

"It was pretty typical of all the boats in its day, except the shape of the hull," said Ron Jones. "It had laminated oak and aircraft birch frames and oak battens on the bottom. It had aluminum covering over the outside plywood skins on the bottom. It had aircraft spruce deck battens and five-ply quarter-inch mahogany decking."

"Later on we started putting more aluminum-clad angles in places on the frame to make it stronger, because with its lower profile it flexed more," said David Smith. "And unfortunately, those angles added some weight."

* * * *

In April 1962, while Bob Mackey and Ted Jones were building the new *Miss Bardahl* in Kennydale, my sister came home from college for spring break. Our family drove into Seattle to see the newly opened World's Fair, formally titled the Century 21 Exposition.

Seattle was a growing metropolis in 1962, not yet home to congested freeways and (aside from Boeing) business monoliths like Microsoft and Amazon.com. The 1960 census showed Washington with 2,853,214 residents (versus 6,724,540 in 2010), with 557,087 living in Seattle, the nation's 19th-largest city. Ninety-two percent of Seattle's population was white (which then included Hispanic/Latin), with less than 4.8 percent black and 3.1 percent Asian and Pacific Islander.

World's Fair admission for adults was $2. You could ride the Monorail into downtown Seattle and back for 75¢, and $1 bought you a ticket to the top of the Space Needle. Topped by a natural gas torch and aircraft beacon 605 feet above ground, the Space Needle was Century 21's centerpiece, painted "galaxy gold" (actually, orange) and "re-entry red" at the time, but other attractions appealed to me more.

For example, the Standard Oil exhibit gave away free samples of household oil in clear plastic tubes. The National Aeronautics and Space Administration (NASA) Pavilion featured exciting and timely exhibits, including John Glenn's *Friendship 7* Mercury space capsule from his February 1962 orbital flight. The Washington State Pavilion featured the futuristic Bubbleator elevator (and also a scary Cold War exhibit showing atomic bomb shelters), and at outdoor kiosks kids bought black felt hats embroidered with their names on the front.

But the biggest attraction for me was the stage where KING-TV Channel 5 broadcast its news shows, "Early Edition" at 6:45 on weeknights and "Weekend Edition" at 6:30 p.m. on Saturdays, for the duration of the fair. After anchors Charles Herring and Ted Bryant delivered their stories, and after Rod Belcher covered sports, on came "KING's cartooning weatherman" Bob Hale. He painted several large artboard placards for each show, on which he'd write forecast info like the expected high, low, wind speed, and chance of rain. Hale was a great cartoonist and his placards included recurring characters – seagulls, sunny Old Sol, Big Hi, and sometimes hydros.

After each "Early Edition" concluded and the stage lights dimmed, Hale autographed his placards and gave them away. During the six months the fair ran I procured four or five of those valuable, autographed works of celebrity art (as I perceived them). They sat in our garage at home, leaned up against the outer wall for a few years until they became so musty from the damp Northwest weather that I reluctantly let Mom throw them away.

* * * *

Spring break ended, and our family piled into Mom's newly purchased used 1962 Ford Falcon to drive Judy back to college in Spokane. We stopped for a picnic lunch at Gingko State Park in arid Vantage, where we spread a blanket on the ground near signs that read "Watch for snakes." We walked to the rim of a bluff overlooking homes far below and, further beyond, the Columbia River. A woman rode her horse alongside a road directly beneath us.

Someone commented that the entire vista would be inundated with water soon once the new Wanapum Dam was finished nearby (and indeed, that's what happened). We then left and drove east over the river on the old, steel cantilever, two-lane U.S. 10 Vantage Bridge for the last time. It was replaced by a new bridge two miles south, under construction since August 1960, that opened to limited traffic Oct. 4, 1962. Gov. Rosellini dedicated all four lanes on Nov. 9. Soon the old bridge was disassembled and stored nearby in Beverly, then moved 113 miles southeast to Lyons Ferry and reassembled in 1968 as the "new" SR 261 bridge across the Snake River.

* * * *

As the new *Miss Bardahl* took shape in Kennydale, crew chief Vanden Berg started assembling his new team. Bardahl shipping clerk Zuvich was a charter member, and because Vanden Berg worked until 4 p.m.

weekdays at Fort Lawton, Zuvich needed help moving the heavy crankshafts, heads and blocks that were too much for one man. Jim Schultz, a Boeing mechanic and taxi driver, was hired part-time.

"Zuvich was there five days a week, eight hours a day, plus working the evenings and weekends," said Dax. "He had, by far, the most amount of time working on the boat, and a lot of it was during the day by himself."

Construction on the *Bardahl* hull progressed, and when the bottom was finished the time came to roll the boat over, right-side up, to finish the deck. Zuvich drove east to Jones' Kennydale shop with Schultz; also on hand were renowned photographer Bob Carver and talented scribe Eileen Crimmin.

"I'd never rolled a boat over, so I called Leo at work for advice," said Zuvich. "There was me, Schultz, and Mackey. We had the boat half tipped over, and it was kind of dangling. Carver broke a stick behind my back, and I guess I lifted about a foot off the ground. He swore he'd never do that again."

As the boat neared completion, Vanden Berg filled out his crew with what he called "pretty good craftsmen."

"I always let my crew chief hire his men because if something went wrong, I couldn't blame him for the men I hired," said Ole. "My crew chief was in charge. I hired Leo as crew chief because he was a good conscientious fellow and used a lot of common sense. He was patient and didn't rush things. Generally, a boat conks out when small things go wrong."

Vanden Berg recruited Carl Comnick, a City of Seattle bridge foreman who custom-built the team's top-quality Rolls tools; Del French, a mechanic for Los Angeles – Seattle Motor Express (LASME); Hal Siegel, listed as the owner of Shoreline Taxi, whose parents owned Siegel Auto Wrecking; and Ray Welpley, a Transport Equipment superintendent who designed *Miss Bardahl*'s new trailer. All but Welpley appear in the 1962 *Bardahl* press kit.

"We often had to rebuild our own truck gearboxes," Zuvich said, recalling three LASME mechanics who worked with the crew over the years. "We had those Roadranger 13's or whatever those transmission are called, so you need to know what you're doing."

Also not listed in the press kit were Burns Smith and Ken Larson, a Northwest Orient Airlines flight engineer who later died in an Alaska plane crash. Both were ex-*Hawaii Kai* crew, and they worked on *Miss Bardahl* in 1962. Burns also recommended that Vanden Berg strongly consider hiring his son Dax, an 18-year-old freshman studying math and physics at the University of Washington.

"Leo hired my dad and Ken Larson as volunteers, and I came along as kind of a package with my dad," said Dax. "I had worked on the *Seattle Too* and done a little bit on *Hawaii Kai*."

The new *Miss Bardahl* hull was delivered to 1400 N.W. 52nd in Ballard in May 1962 – Jones' invoice: $9,400 – and the crew started work on its final configuration by installing the plumbing, wiring, cockpit, steering, gauges, tail fin and cowl. *Miss Bardahl*'s vital statistics: length, 30 feet 4 inches; width, 12 feet 5 inches; weight, 6,330 pounds, 7,100 pounds when loaded with fuel and 15 gallons of Bardahl oil. Her official owner was listed as Bardahl Chemical Corporation, and for 1962 she flew the burgee of Seattle Yacht Club rather than Queen City Yacht Club, her affiliation through 1961.

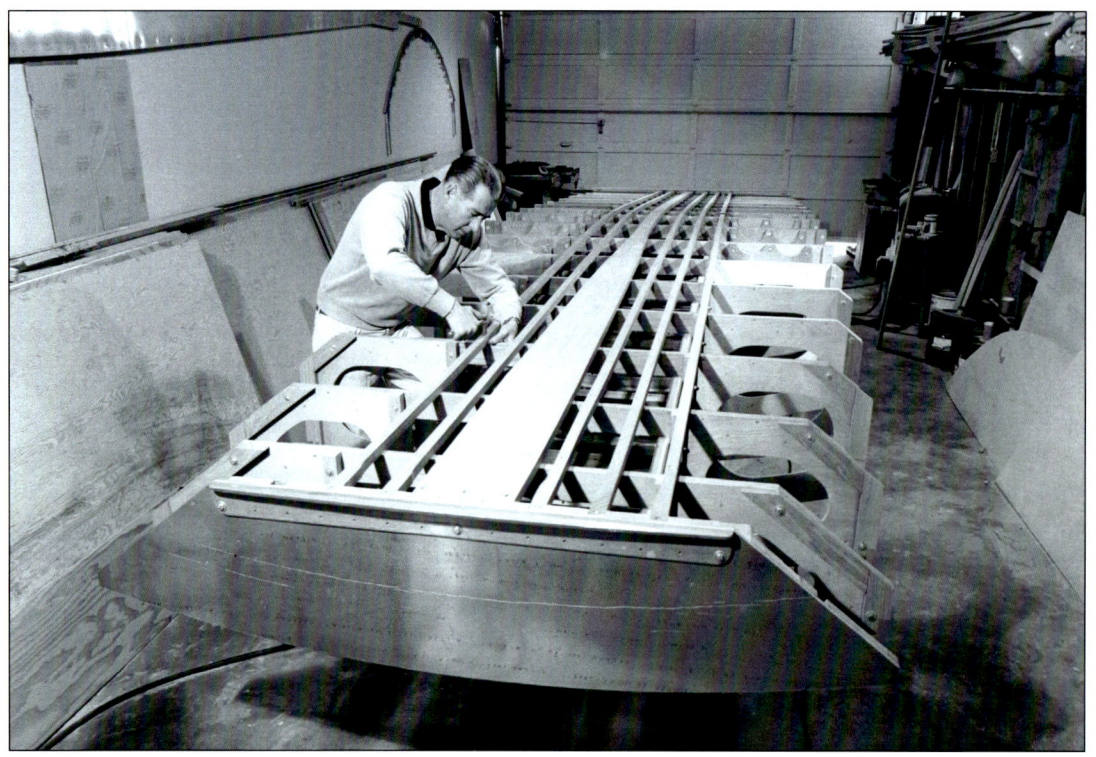

Ted Jones building the third *Miss Bardahl* in Kennydale, Wash., early 1962.
© Bob Carver photo 1962

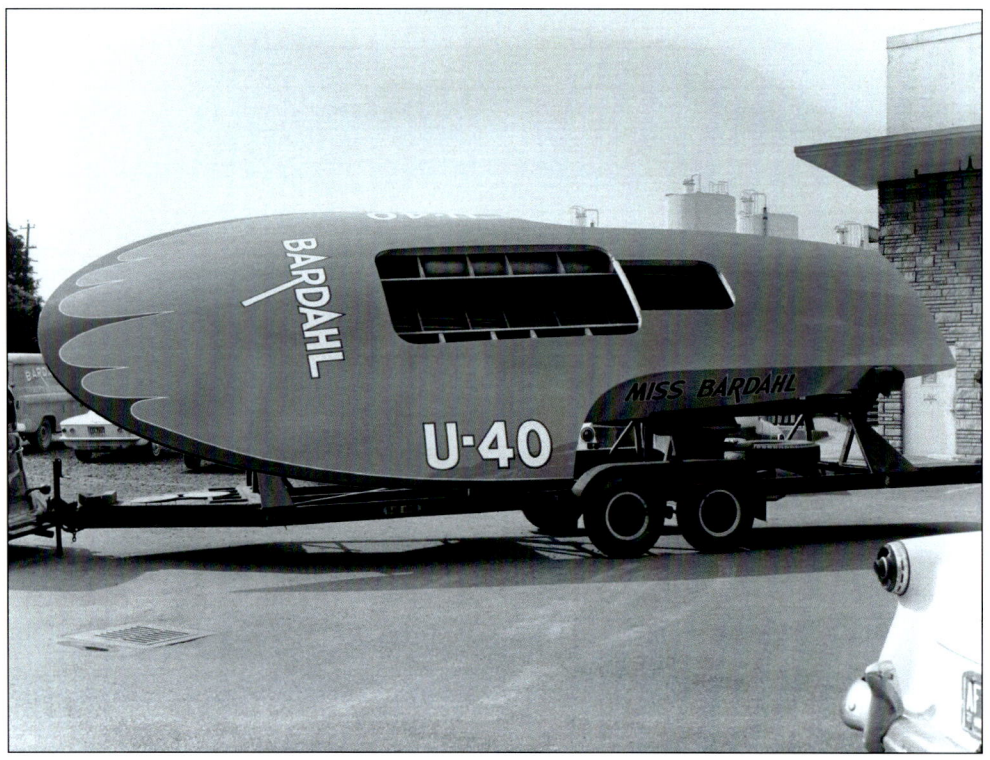

The new Dragon rolls out of the paint shop, spring 1962.
© Bob Carver photo 1962

All of the *Miss Bardahl*s resided in a spacious shop at the company's Ballard headquarters.
© Bob Carver photo 1962

Leo Vanden Berg, "Keeper of the Dragon" and Hall of Fame *Bardahl* crew chief from 1962–66.
© Eileen Crimmin photo 1964, used with permission of The Crimmin Collection

* * *

Telstar 1, the world's first communications satellite able to send and receive signals, was launched from Cape Canaveral July 10, 1962. That was a big deal, like the manned Mercury flights, and KJR Radio later began playing a new instrumental, "Telstar," by Tacoma band The Ventures.

My big sister Judy worked in the bakery of the P-X supermarket near our Lake Hills home each summer during college, and we enjoyed a nightly ritual that lasted three years: Just before closing time I'd walk three blocks to the store, where Judy let me choose one bakery item from among those destined to be discounted as day-old goods. Sometimes I'd get real lucky and find a jelly-filled donut among the pickings! Then we'd walk home together at dusk and recount our day.

The summer of 1962, several neighborhood kids built go-carts that we'd race downhill on S.E. 14th. We scabbed them together with scrap two-by-fours and plywood swiped from nearby building sites, plus axles and wheels scavenged from siblings' wagons, and nails and paint pilfered from dads' workbenches.

My cart was primitive – essentially a plywood sheet, plywood backrest, and two-by-fours with wheels and axles nailed on the ends. I nailed a rope into the front two-by-four at each end, near the wheels; I pulled the rope to pivot the front axle and turn. An older kid, Brad, built his cart with real hardware, including a steering wheel – but he accidentally rigged the steering cable so that when you wanted to turn right, you actually had to steer left.

Brad let me drive his cart down the hill one day. I got in, gained speed, and nearing the bottom sensed a car coming up behind me on my left. The logical part of my brain remembered, "Steer left to go right." But that felt so wrong, my gut simply would not allow me to actually turn the wheel left toward the car. So I turned the wheel right, which of course steered the cart left … and into the path of the approaching car, which blared its horn and braked. I was in no real danger since the car was going slowly. But the driver hollered at me, prompting raucous laughter from my peers.

Naturally, we built our own wood hydroplanes, too. Usually about 16 inches or 18 inches long, sawn from 5/8-inch or ¾-inch plywood. We'd nail on wood "engines," cowlings and tails, and some kids added sponsons, which was stupid because they made the boats more unstable on gravel. Someone discovered that if you pounded nails through the bottom of the boat and then hammered the points backward toward the stern, they made cool sparks on the street when you dragged your hydro after dark.

A few kids were meticulous with their boats, cutting them out with jigsaws and coping saws and carefully painting them to match the real hydros. That caused all kinds of angst when their hydros inevitably flipped on the pavement and scraped the fancy paint.

At age 8 I had no patience for precision or detail. I cut out awkward pointy-nose hydros – somewhat unavoidable when using a rusty old rip saw – and colored them with the only free paint around, Mom's dark brown house enamel. (That was before I could afford 10¢ bottles of Testors No. 54 metallic green and No. 12 yellow, which made *Miss Bardahl* paint schemes possible.)

Oh, and I cleaned mom's paintbrushes with gasoline, which added a crowning touch to my clumsy effort.

Chapter 4

Racing and the new-boat blues

The new *Miss Bardahl* was completed none too soon, just 10 days before the 1962 Diamond Cup Regatta. The boat marked the end of an era: *Bardahl* was the last unlimited built by Ted Jones. He designed three later unlimiteds – the 1963 *Tahoe Miss* and *Miss Exide,* and the 1964 *Mariner Too* – but the new U-40 was the last hydro Jones designed on which he worked with his own hands.

Bardahl's crew fought the clock on Tuesday, July 17, doing final preparations in the Ballard shop on the boat's systems, wiring, and Rolls-Merlin powerplant, while eight hydros sat lakeside 310 miles to the east in Coeur d'Alene, and two others were in transit.

Late on Wednesday afternoon, July 18, the Green Dragon finally took her maiden run on Lake Washington at Stan Sayres Memorial Pits. Musson throttled her up to 145 mph during a nine-minute session that he deemed a qualified success. Late that night the weary crew fired up its Ford C-750 truck and towed the shiny new metallic green and yellow hydro eastward via Aurora Avenue, Dearborn Street, and the Sunset Highway, U.S. 10.

Musson qualified *Miss Bardahl* on Lake Coeur d'Alene's 3-mile course at 108.434 mph, tied for third fastest behind *Miss Century 21* at 112.925 and *Miss Seattle Too* at 109.091. But *Bardahl* leaped out of the water and threw a rod in the first turn during heat 1B on Saturday and failed to finish. "Sure, we've got a few problems to work out," Musson said. "But this is gonna be a hell of a boat."

The next day *Bardahl* and *Seattle Too* swapped position several times battling for second on choppy water in heat 2B before *Bardahl* finished a close third at just 95.609 mph, earning 225 points – not enough to make the final heat. Driver and crew fretted over the hull's troubling tendency to porpoise at 135 mph, which made her tough to steer and taxed her engine every time the prop popped out of the water. In her first race, *Bardahl* finished a humble 10th overall.

Other boats making headlines that week included three new ones: the all-aluminum, twin-Allison-powered *Such Crust*; and nearly identical boats from designer-builder Les Staudacher of Kawkawlin, Mich., *$ Bill* and *Notre Dame*. They were the 35th and 36th unlimiteds built by Staudacher, who began his career as a church-pew builder.

Miss Seattle Too owners Milo and Glen Stoen hired former *Bardahl* crew chief George McKernan during the offseason to take over for departed crew chief Wes Kiesling, and an awkward mess developed when the *Too* co-drivers – Dallas Sartz and Bill Brow – couldn't resolve how to split time in the cockpit at Coeur d'Alene. Sartz bowed out for the Diamond Cup, saying, "I either drive it alone or not at all."

Former *Bardahl* driver Norm Evans was lucky just to be walking, let alone wrangling a raceboat. In July

1961 he had been driving a 20-ton crane northeast of Chelan when it overturned and tumbled into a dusty coulee. Evans, the father of two preschool boys named Mark and Mitch, lay mangled in the wreckage but somehow crawled 60 feet uphill to the road, where he attracted help before passing out. Evans spent two months recovering in a hospital and 10 more months convalescing, progressing from wheelchair to walker to crutches. On July 16, 1962, Evans had climbed into the cockpit of the Tacoma hydroplane *Coral Reef*, newly repowered with a Daimler-Benz Messerschmitt 109 fighter-plane engine, and roared around Lake Chelan. Evans said the boat performed beautifully. However, it broke down in Coeur d'Alene and failed to qualify for the Diamond Cup.

As for *Miss Bardahl*, her crew towed the flighty new filly home to Ballard for two weeks of frantic adjustments to give Musson a manageable ride for the Gold Cup.

Around that time, Schultz disappeared.

"He went out for a pack of cigarettes and never came back," recalled Zuvich. "His wife started calling after a couple days, I said I haven't seen him, and the next thing I knew she came out and picked his check up. I've never seen or heard from Schultz since."

* * * *

That same summer, a Columbia River camping trip marked a defining moment for a young boy from the Seattle suburbs who would become a key figure in hydroplane history. I learned about it from the boy's father.

Each summer brings reunions with hydro friends – people usually seen only at races or test sessions. My most enjoyable visits were those with Stan Hanauer. Stan lived a colorful life, and he was a great storyteller. A typical scenario: It's race week, the boats are testing, and a friend and I spot Stan. We exchange greetings, discuss what's new, and then the conversation shifts (at my prodding) to some fascinating anecdote of Stan's, usually unrelated to hydros – Stan using "dead reckoning" to navigate his sailboat across the Pacific in 50-foot seas, driving a transport truck in snow and ice over the original Blewett Pass hairpin roadway, hiking to the summit of Yakima Peak in winter just to ski down to Tipsoo Lake.

On a hot July 2002 day in Kennewick's Lampson Pits, Stan told me a story he didn't recall sharing with a writer before. It traces his son Chip's first interest in hydros and yields insight into the mindset that made Chip perhaps the finest driver to ever race them.

"Our family didn't attend hydro races regularly – that's not where Chip got interested," Stan said. "We were camping at Crescent Bar on the Columbia River when he was 8. Must have been around 1962. It was on Indian property – we paid 75 cents a night and got all the cord wood we wanted.

"Chip wandered off to the other side of the bar, where a Seattle outboard or inboard association was staging an event," Stan explained. "There were all kinds of little hydros. Chip disappeared for the longest time, and when we found him it turns out that's where he'd been, watching those boats run.

"On the way home, we're driving up the old Vantage hill on U.S. Highway 10 with Chip standing in the back seat, between his mother and me. He said, 'That's what I want to do.' Do what, we asked? 'Race those little hydros.' My response was, 'We'll talk about it when you have the money to buy one.'

"Well, Chip's mom was a real taskmaster, and if you said you were going to do something, she held you to it. You know, she dedicated her life to those two boys (Chip and brother Scott)."

Chip had a paper route, and he immediately started mowing lawns and painted a few fences around his Newport Hills neighborhood. He saved his money.

"Even then, Chip was very determined about something once he set his mind to it," Stan said. "So one day I got home from work and Chip met me in the front yard. 'I'm gonna buy a boat,' he said. We talked about it at the dinner table."

Chip had found a J-stock outboard with a motor, helmet, and life jacket for $175. And sure enough, he'd saved enough money. Father and son drove into Seattle and bought it all from a man who lived near Woodland Park, and Chip began racing.

"He often came in second, but he couldn't beat a girl named Janis Lee who always won. He'd tell me, downcast, 'I lost to a girl.' It was different in those days, losing to a girl. But she was so good, I'm absolutely convinced she'd be the best unlimited driver today if she'd continued. She came from a family of superb racers."

In an Aug. 3, 2010, *Seattle Times* online chat, Chip was asked about that. "Janis Lee was a girl I raced in outboards at places like Lake Sammamish when I was a young kid," he said. "She kicked my butt. Boy, am I glad she quit racing!"

Stan explained that Chip was always very good about doing chores and completing his homework, because he had to finish before he was allowed to race boats.

"So that's how Chip got interested in hydros," Stan said. "It wasn't what you'd expect, from the family attending Seafair or something like that. It started at Crescent Bar as an 8-year-old."

Chip's ability to focus, to concentrate so keenly on his driving task at hand, has been noted by many over the years. His determination to work and save $175 – in 1962 dollars, mind you – suggests that his mental discipline, which served him so well as an unlimited driver, already was robust at age 8.

Stan pondered a few moments, looking into the distance. He said, "You know, I think that was the same summer that Chip saw a classical guitarist at the World's Fair, and then announced he wanted to learn to play guitar. And he finally did, at age 42…."

But that's another Stan story.

* * * *

The *Bardahl* crew worked hard for two weeks to tame the new hydro's rocking-horse ride in time for the prestigious APBA Gold Cup on Seattle's Lake Washington. The Jet City sweltered, with the thermometer topping 80 degrees for a record-setting 11 straight days beginning July 20. Seven of those days ranged between 85 and 90 as Vanden Berg and crew toiled inside their N.W. 52nd boat shop in Ballard.

"We're trying to do in three weeks what takes three months to accomplish," Musson told *Seattle P-I* sports editor Royal Brougham. "But don't count us out."

Tuesday, July 31, dawned foggy and cool, but skies cleared at noon and gradually warmed to 75 degrees by the end of qualifying, or as it was called then, time trials. Spectators who used new bleachers on the east side of Stan Sayres Pits enjoyed a clearer view of the action as workers erected just one official barge, not two.

Trailer-firing outside the Ballard shop before the initial launch and christening.
– used with permission of the Museum of History and Industry

Lillian Bardahl Simpson swings the bottle to christen *Miss Bardahl* as Inga, Ole, Musson, Vanden Berg, and others look on.
– used with permission of the Museum of History and Industry

Vanden Berg, Musson, and crew prepare for the first test run July 18, 1962, at Seattle's Stan Sayres Memorial Pits.
– used with permission of the Museum of History and Industry

Musson prepares to start *Bardahl*'s Rolls-Royce Merlin engine. Note the lack of guy wires on the tail.
– used with permission of the Museum of History and Industry

Musson hit 140 mph on *Bardahl*'s maiden run July 18, 1962.
– used with permission of the Museum of History and Industry

At Lake Tahoe, site of the hull's first victory on Sept. 30, 1962. L to R: Jerry Zuvich, Leo Vanden Berg, unidentified (standing), Dax Smith, Ken Larson, Burns Smith; Ron Musson in foreground.
– Leo Vanden Berg collection, used with permission of Troy Cain

Fans who entered the pits with a $1 Seafair skipper pin found the hydro fleet parked on the northwest side, facing the lagoon. *$ Bill* sat near the white monorail flanked to the west by *Notre Dame, Miss Detroit, Miss U.S.1, Tempest, Bardahl, Gale VII, Gale V, Seattle Too, Miss B&I, Such Crust IV, Fascination, Tahoe Miss, Miss Madison,* and *Miss Century 21*. Arriving later was *Coral Reef*.

Musson was among Tuesday's would-be qualifiers. He pulled *Bardahl* away from the dock and roared around the 3-mile course for the fastest lap of the day, 114.650 mph, before breaking *Bardahl's* quill shaft – a thin spring drive that connects the supercharger to the crankshaft inside a Rolls-Merlin engine.

On Wednesday Musson tried again but returned to the pits after just one lap because the boat cavitated, like it had at the Diamond Cup. Cavitation is a loss of effective propeller thrust, the result of the blade popping out of the water instead of staying at least partially immersed. The propeller churns only air and speeds up, but the loss of "traction" not only slows the boat, it strains the engine, which first over-revs and then meets resistance when the prop drops back into the water.

The remedy required hull adjustments best done at the Bardahl shop, so the crew pulled the Green Dragon out of the pits and towed it to Ballard, where they worked through Thursday. Friday cooled to a high of just 63 degrees, and the crew set up camp again in the pits amid chilly showers. Musson charged onto the course, ran two warmup laps, and had the Dragon surging onto the front chute when suddenly it coasted to a stop.

"The engine was missing, so I shut it off," Musson said later. "We've had so many problems this week I wasn't going to take any chances."

Musson looked at the engine but found nothing obviously amiss … until he spotted the remains of a swallow, which had been sucked into *Bardahl's* carburetor air scoop.

The headline in the *Seattle Post-Intelligencer* the next morning read: Oops! The Dragon Swallows A Bird!

"The boat may have been running with the carburetor air scoop facing forward, for qualifying only," said Dixon in 2012. "That gives you a little more power as long as you're not running through roostertails."

Finally, on the last day of qualifying, Musson throttled *Miss Bardahl* around the lake in a steady rain Saturday afternoon at 109.459 mph to qualify for the Gold Cup, sixth fastest out of 12 boats. Bill Muncey and *Miss Century 21* topped the field at 116.212 followed by *Gale V*, 113.524; *Seattle Too*, 112.188; *Tempest*, 111.417; *Tahoe Miss* (the former *Miss Reno* and *Maverick*), 110.731; then *Bardahl* and six slower qualifiers.

Norm Evans and crew worked feverishly for two hours Saturday before the Chelan driver stormed onto the course in *Coral Reef* mere moments before the 4 p.m. deadline. He raised his arm to signal he was starting his qualifying run, but officials' red flares pierced the sky just seconds before he could cross the line. The referee would not stretch the deadline. For the Gold Cup, at least, it marked the end of Evans' comeback from his near-fatal 1961 crane crash.

* * * *

Gold Cup week had many subplots and sidenotes. *Gale VII* of Detroit was an interesting one. Never a competitive craft – and second in weight only to the twin-engine, 11,616-pound behemoth *Such Crust* – the 8,866-pound, Packard V-16-powered, 36-foot-long *VII* managed to lumber through three laps at an average speed of 100.309 mph. By comparison, the *P-I* listed *Bardahl* at 6,995 pounds and speedy *Century 21* at 6,647.

As a sidenote, Skip Schott later questioned *Such Crust*'s publicly reported weight. "I saw 13,000 pounds on the scale with my own eyes," he said, having watched it suspended from a crane and weighed.

When Chuck Hickling qualified *Tempest* on Thursday at 111.417 mph and sprinted around at 113.208 mph on the third lap, it likely marked the hull's fastest speeds ever.

A Friday announcement said former *Gale* head wrench Bud Meldrum had taken over as *Notre Dame* crew chief, replacing Marty Handshaw. That same day *The Seattle Times*' Matt Sayre wrote, "Ron Musson is so hot on the *Bardahl*'s throttle they had to devise a way to heat the oil before he stepped into the boat. A lap around the pond at cruising speed is accepted procedure. But watch Musson. His 'cruising lap' measures about 300 yards. After that, he flies."

The thinly equipped *Miss Madison* team included Musson's good friend, Graham Heath, who had built winning *Nitrogen Too* motors for Musson in 1960. Heath was responsible for *Miss Madison* making it through the entire 1961 season on a single Allison engine and an all-volunteer crew. He later would be named Crew Chief of the Year for 1965 by the Unlimited Racing Commission and earned accolades for his Allison engine wizardry with teams like *My Gypsy, Miss Owensboro, Kentuckiana Paving*, and as an adviser to Ed Cooper's U-3 camp.

Former *Bardahl* and *Wahoo* driver Mira Slovak was enticed to offer his observations in 1962 for ghost-written *Seattle Post-Intelligencer* articles. "When I drove for Bardahl, if you asked for a new prop or a new gearbox, you got it," he noted. "A businessman wants to have a good product representing him."

Slovak added, "Ron Musson is a pretty rough driver, a real charger. If the engine can hold up under his feet, *Miss Bardahl* could be up there."

Gale V driver Bill Cantrell offered an opinion that contrasted with the bombastic anti-Seattle rants of his boss, Lee Schoenith. Surveying the Gold Cup venue, Cantrell said, "No place in the world can touch Seattle as a place to hold this race."

Signifying the popularity of hydro racing in 1962, six radio stations covered the Gold Cup live: KAYO, KFKF, KING, KIRO, KOL, and KVI.

During Gold Cup week and throughout the April – October World's Fair, the front page of *The Seattle Times* featured a daily tally below the masthead. On Aug. 1 it read, "Fair Attendance: Yesterday, 55,383; Total, 5,054,691." Elsewhere an article announced, "Fair To Offer TV Coverage Of Gold Cup. TV sets in six locations to accommodate fair visitors who have an interest in the thundering hydros."

* * * *

Sunday morning, Aug. 5, 1962, brought gloomy gray skies, but hardy hydro fans still turned out in droves, including those aboard 1,130 boats on the log boom. Winds stirred Lake Washington and delayed racing for an hour while Bill Cantrell and Musson drove out to test the conditions. "It's rough, but it won't get any better," Musson said.

Six boats including *Bardahl* pounded toward the first turn at the start of heat 1A, roostertails flying, with Dallas Sartz and *Miss Seattle Too* on the outside. The *Too* hopped, nose-dived, and disintegrated in a towering geyser of spray and debris, leaving Sartz with a badly broken thigh and lacerations. He was plucked from the water, conscious, and transported to the hospital.

The rerun saw Cantrell surge to the front in *Gale V* and build a 20-second lead over *Bardahl* after five laps, the halfway point of the 10-lap, 30-mile heat. But in the south turn of lap eight *Gale V* blew its supercharger with a loud bang and expired, yielding the lead to *Bardahl*. Soon after, a patrol boat's red flare pierced the sky and stopped the heat when Bob Gilliam tried to restart his stalled *Fascination*, which belched a harmless stack fire. *Bardahl* was declared the winner at an average speed of 100.773 mph.

Bardahl and *Century 21* met in heat 2A. Muncey led out of the first turn and ran the first three laps at 108 mph to build a comfortable cushion over Musson, who ultimately finished second at 97 mph to Muncey's 101. That left Muncey and *Century 21* with 800 points, needing only to finish ahead of *Bardahl* and *U.S.1* in the final to win the Gold Cup.

Under drizzly gray skies at 7:40 p.m., *Such Crust IV* took the inside lane at the start of the final heat with *Miss Madison* leading the six-boat field across the line. But again it was Muncey and *C-21* on top exiting the south turn as *Bardahl* and *Notre Dame* dueled for second. Musson, unable to keep up with Muncey's 109-mph first lap, sagged to third and the 225 points he knew would be enough to secure an overall 925 for second place in the final standings. After a long day of accidents and delays, Muncey took the checkered flag just after 8 p.m. to win his fourth Gold Cup. He had won all three of his heats to score a perfect 1,200 points while averaging 100.074 for the 30-lap, 90-mile event. *Bardahl* and Musson, who ran just 81 miles because heat 1-A was stopped during lap eight, averaged 96.799. Both boats took a victory lap before the applauding hometown crowd.

It was the last Gold Cup of its kind. The following year, hydroplane racing's top prize became a 60-mile race comprising four five-lap, 15-mile heats, instead of three 10-lap, 30-mile heats.

"We're real happy with our finish here," Musson said. "This is a new boat and we're taking one step at a time. Considering the lack of time we had to get ready, I think the boat performed very well."

The Gold Cup dominated Monday's local front-page headlines, appearing above somber news from Brentwood, Calif., about an American film star: "Marilyn Monroe Is Found Dead At Home." The afternoon *Seattle Times* also ran a photo of John Glenn's Mercury space capsule being unveiled that morning in the NASA Pavilion at the World's Fair, visited that day by U.S. Attorney General Robert Kennedy.

Dax Smith had impressed Vanden Berg with his Gold Cup work on *Miss Bardahl*, and the crew chief offered him an official spot on the team.

"I was hired after the Seattle race in 1962," Dax said. "I was 18, about to turn 19, going to college, and I worked on the boat evenings and weekends. We were paid a monthly salary. We did not get paid overtime. We did get a percentage of the prize money, and we did get per diem. That's basically how I put myself through college, and I graduated not owing anybody anything, with a little bit of extra money. But I also devoted my whole summer to it. I didn't have any time off all summer. Jerry was the same way."

Miss Seattle Too was salvaged from the bottom of Lake Washington by Marine Power & Equipment and on Tuesday, Aug. 7, was towed to Lake Union. After a crane hoisted the battered remains onto a trailer the *Too* was taken to its nearby shop at 400 Minor Street N. — the shop where Wes Kiesling had taught Dax about Rolls-Merlins two summers earlier. Owner Milo Stoen said the only thing that appeared salvageable was *Seattle Too*'s motor.

On Wednesday the hometown boats *Miss Century 21* and *Miss Bardahl* were proudly parked for a two-day display at the World's Fair west entrance, near the Washington State Coliseum. Meanwhile, 130 miles to the southwest off Washington's coastline, Bobby Kennedy and family enjoyed a successful day catching salmon near Westport.

* * * *

When Paul Lowney's "This Is Hydroplaning" was published three years earlier, in 1959, the softbound color book became sacred text for hydro fans. My friends and I never tired of reading it. We persuaded my 15-year-old sister, who was admired for her artistry, to draw pictures of our favorite boats that she rendered from the book's many photos. I can see Judy in my mind's eye sitting at our formica dinette table at home, surrounded by a handful of kindergartners, bringing *Miss Pay'n Save* to life with Crayons and rich watercolors.

Pay'n Save, winner of the 1959 Apple Cup, later became the *Miss Seattle Too* that disintegrated in the 1962 Gold Cup.

Judy was a hydro nut in her own right. One brisk late-November day in 1957, Dad took her to Lake Washington near Sand Point to watch driver Jack Regas break the world mile-straightaway speed record aboard Judy's favorite hydro, *Hawaii Kai III*, the "Pink Lady" owned by industrialist Edgar Kaiser. As Regas throttled the *Kai* across the water at 187.627 mph, the spectacle of the roaring craft excited Judy so much that she jumped up and down on the dock – quickly drawing the ire of renowned hydro photographer Bob Carver, whose photos were blurred by Judy's gleeful bouncing.

Judy's love of hydros had started at age 7, in 1951, when most Seattleites got their first taste of the thunderboats.

I started out with no interest in hydros whatsoever. That very first race, the word "hydroplane" meant nothing to me. I had no idea what we were going to see, but Dad said, "This is going to be really great!" So we went down there among all the crowds, and everybody was rooting for Slo-mo IV. *The boats were kind of milling around before the start of the race, and I remember everybody saying, "Where's* Slo-mo?" *People thought it had a mechanical breakdown or something. And all of a sudden, at what seemed like the very last moment, it came flying under the floating bridge, and there was an air of exultation from the entire crowd! Everyone was screaming and jumping and saying, oh, here it is after all!*

Slo-mo IV *wasn't a particularly impressive-looking boat compared to some of the others. It seemed like it was smaller and didn't have a fancy streamlined look like some of the boats did back then. So in my mind ever since it's been kind of like "the little engine that could," the modest boat that turned out to be a hero for Seattle. But I'll never forget how everybody was so worried, "Where* is Slo-mo?" *Before I could see it, you could hear far off in the crowd this rising excitement, and then suddenly it appeared. And of course, the best part of all the hydros was the sound, the roar that made every hair on your head and arms stand up and salute, and also the thrilling sight of the flying roostertails.*

The Detroit boats had sort of an "art moderne" look, an architectural style from the '30s and early '40s, that sort of modernistic streamlined look. Slo-mo *wasn't flashy-looking to my eyes. I picked* Quicksilver *as my favorite entirely on the basis of its impressive, fast-sounding name. Dad, on the other hand, had already read up on hydros so was rooting for* Slo-mo, *which I thought was a pitiful name for a boat, one that obviously didn't have a chance of winning.*

We always staked out a spot on the beach with a blanket and we took a thermos, cooler, and probably sandwiches. But we didn't stay strictly on the blanket, we walked around and got as close as we could to the pits. This is the old Mount Baker pits. I watched them lifting the boats in and out of the water, and I was fascinated with all of that. It became an annual event, Dad, Dave, and me.

We were totally Slo-mo *fans while they were running, and after that I really liked* Hawaii Kai, Wahoo, *and* Miss Exide. *I certainly remember the various* Thriftways, *and for a long time we had immense prejudice against* Thriftway. *My recollection is that once the* Slo-mos *were history, everybody in Seattle was now supposed to love the* Thriftways, *there was very much this local embrace of the* Thriftways. *And in my opinion, they were just interlopers. I couldn't develop the affection that we'd had for the* Slo-mos, *but I can't tell you exactly why, although it's true that I didn't like Bill Muncey. I liked* Hawaii Kai *because I thought the name was very musical, and the color to me was so cool compared to all the other boats. I thought it was creative and futuristic, not necessarily that it was a "pretty" or "girly" color.*

I remember Wild Bill Cantrell, when the hydro ended up in someone's yard. He was kind of a character. And of course, everyone in Seattle despised the Gales *and all the Detroit boats. It was like our civic duty as Seattleites to feel that way. My perception was that we Seattleites felt like we understood the soul of hydroplaning in a way that people from Detroit simply couldn't, that they were all about the engines and the mechanics, and that we were all about the Zen of it. Those were good years.*

What stands out in my mind about the later races is that every year the crowd got drunker and wilder. Back in the early days, I suppose there may have been drunks, but I was either oblivious to them or they kept it under wraps. In later years it seemed like people were puking on the ground and peeing in front of everybody.

* * * *

At some point during the 1962 season, likely after the Gold Cup, crew chief Vanden Berg stumbled upon a possible source of *Miss Bardahl*'s vexing supercharger failures. It stemmed from Ole Bardahl's insistence that his boat not have guy wires supporting the tail. Ole rarely gave direction on boat setup and race strategy, leaving that to his talented team. But he had witnessed an accident in which a driver was pitched out of his boat and got caught on a guy wire. The driver wasn't badly hurt, but the potential for severe injury was there.

"That's one of the few times where Ole flat-out gave an order and said, 'This is my boat, and we will not have any guy wires,'" said Dixon. "Well, we had tremendous problems that year busting up the front of the engine. Every time we ran, we broke something badly."

Zuvich recalled how Vanden Berg would thump his fist on *Bardahl*'s tail fin while walking by, just to make sure it was securely fastened and hadn't shaken loose. One day when he did that his teammates working on the engine felt the entire boat shake.

"That was the big clue that said, 'Hey, here's the problem. Fix me.' The tail was really strong. It was mounted with a sturdy piece of aluminum T-stock that bolted to the transom, and it transmitted any tail vibrations. We were shaking pan nuts off the motor, breaking stuff in the blower," Zuvich said.

"The tail was buzzing," said Dixon, "and it transmitted through the boat and aggravated some weak parts in the front of the motor, just shattered some stuff. We'd come out with a hand full of gear teeth at times."

Despite Ole Bardahl's misgivings, Vanden Berg decided to put stainless steel guy wires on the tail, and to the crew's amazement, it cured a lot of engine trouble.

"I now understand why," said Dixon. "Back then, I didn't have the engineering background to understand, but there's something called 'torsional vibrations.' Every piece of metal is like a spring. It may be a very *stiff* spring, but still it's a spring. There are some natural frequencies involved and you can get the spring where, if you excite it at just the right frequencies, you can make it worse and worse until it tears stuff up. One of the ways you can excite it is, each time the propeller blade slaps the water, the gearbox keeps turning. The prop tends to stop momentarily, then it snaps ahead.

"Apparently, the tail was exciting some parts in the engine at just at the right frequency to shatter them. The problem was torsional vibrations. It's a real-world problem, and guy wires fixed it."

* * * *

Miss Bardahl underwent more modifications after the 1962 Gold Cup, and Musson liked what he found during weekend test runs on Lake Washington. "We've cut back the sponsons and the boat is riding as it should now," he said. "The cavitation is gone." However, his satisfaction proved to be short-lived.

After Vanden Berg and crew packed up their Dragon and rolling stock, Zuvich and Dax hopped in the Ford tractor truck with *Miss Bardahl* in tow and navigated Seattle's pre-freeway arterials to Dearborn Street, where they merged onto eastbound U.S. Highway 10, bound for Detroit and the Aug. 26 Spirit of Detroit Regatta. The renamed event replaced the annual Silver Cup in which driver Bob Hayward had died the previous year.

"The first couple years, I guess I did most of the driving, towing the boat around, until Leo became full time," said Zuvich.

"For the first year or two, Leo flew in and out of some of the races," Dixon said. "He had a full-time job at Fort Lawton, so he didn't do a lot of the traveling and truck driving. Jerry and I did the majority of hauling the equipment across the country.

"Both Jerry and I have seen the U.S.A. through the windshield of a cabover Ford truck about four times," he said, chuckling. "A truck *without* air conditioning."

Because they were energetic, confident, eager to compete, and perhaps simply because they were young – Jerry 21, Dax 19 just that month – the two teammates butted heads occasionally as alpha males will. Decades later, Dixon reflected on that 1962 season and admitted he harbored a little resentment at the time about Zuvich being in charge when they criss-crossed the country hauling *Miss Bardahl*.

"I didn't understand back then why Jerry was in control," Dixon said years later. "But the fact is, Jerry was a full-time Bardahl employee, and a little bit older."

Dixon described a typical summer day on the road in the life of a hydroplane crew member.

"You get up in the morning and eat breakfast together. You work hard all day, seven days a week, 10-12 hours a day. You have dinner together most of the time. By then you're so shot, you go to bed. And in 1962, we were typically sharing rooms. So you spend three and a half months straight essentially living together with these people. You spend more time working and living with the guys on the crew than you'd ever spend with your wife if you were married."

Aside from Zuvich and Dax, the other crew members were older, though Dave Smith – Dax's younger brother – did help at the shop occasionally. Vanden Berg had the not-so-easy task of herding his young protégées. Zuvich and Dax accepted responsibility, took their jobs seriously, and performed well, but they were youths, and occasionally they acted their age.

"I always told them on race night, 'Go to bed early; you've got to be sharp tomorrow.' Sharp up here," Vanden Berg said, pointing to his head.

Ultimately, in 1964-65, the entire crew would range from just 17 to 26 except for Vanden Berg.

"You know, later on when Jerry took over in 1967, they called them the teeny-bopper crew? Well, I had the *baby*-boppers," he said. "Dax was under age, and Dave surely was. I promised Dax's dad and mom that I'd take care and make sure he didn't drink, make sure he went to bed at night, all those things. They were both going to school; Dax was going to the University at that time and had just gotten his license, driving a '56 Chev."

"Leo had the youngest crew of the fleet," said Ron Jones, who tuned *Bardahl's* sponsons several times over the years and knew the team. "And they were also the sharpest. They were all very good.

"Leo told me his biggest job wasn't the boat, it was keeping the kids straight. He called them 'the kids,'" Jones said, laughing.

"The first year while the boat was getting straightened out, it was a mix of crew, old and young," Zuvich said. "The second year, it became younger, and I think maybe that's when some of the – I don't know, animosities or whatever – got stronger."

"Maybe Jerry felt like Dixon was trying to take his job, but I don't think Dixon actually meant it that way," said Roger Kruse, who maintained *Bardahl's* rolling stock beginning in 1964. "Dixon is a strong-willed, gung-ho, go-forward person, and Jerry's not quite as much. He's a good mechanic, he knew his boats and knew what to do, but he also liked to chase girls. Dixon was more like, stay there and get the job done. And Jerry was more like, get the job done so we can go chase girls."

"Jerry and I worked together very, very well at race sites, with excellent teamwork," said Dixon in 2009. "But we sometimes butted heads back at the shop, and it was usually over whose idea was better. Also, Jerry was a full-time Bardahl employee. He'd already put in eight hours when Leo and I would arrive in the evening all fired up with energy and enthusiasm, and at the time I couldn't understand why Jerry didn't have the same enthusiasm.

"A good way to describe it is, I'm a type 'A' personality and was even more so then," Dixon continued. "And what you learn on some teams is to be a good tolerater. And that's kind of how it was between some of the *Bardahl* guys. These are people you wouldn't necessarily choose as best friends to spend time with and eat dinner at each other's houses, but you can still be a very effective team."

Today Dixon has far more appreciation for Jerry's skill than he did when they were spirited young adults.

"What wasn't apparent to me then was that Jerry did in fact become a very good manager, and he demonstrated that as crew chief of the checkerboard *Bardahl* in the following years."

* * * *

August was Dad's favorite month to go boating in the San Juan Islands, and August 1962 was my first visit to Jones Island. We hopped into Dad's white '59 Chevy station wagon and trailered his 16-foot wooden blue and white Reinell to Sunset Beach in Anacortes. There we loaded supplies and camping equipment into the boat and motored northwest across the vast Rosario Strait and an often-choppy section that Dad called "hell's half acre." But on this trip there were no daunting waves or deep troughs from passing freighters, just placid salt water, singing seagulls, and blue skies.

Dad's boat was powered by a 35-hp Evinrude outboard that occasionally broke down in open water – he'd grumble about "that doggone impeller" and disassemble part of the motor to patch it together – and we'd explore the entire San Juan archipelago in this modest craft. Years later friends marveled, "You cruised the San Juans in that dinky boat?" We knew no different, and to our family a 16-foot Reinell seemed just fine.

Dad followed the Friday Harbor ferry route for the early leg of the trip, cruising between Blakely and Lopez islands, then through the scenic channel dividing Shaw, Orcas, and Crane islands and slightly beyond to Jones Island. We pulled into the south cove and set up camp on a rise to our left, with a sweeping view west across San Juan Channel to San Juan Island, the Wasp Islands to the south, and a parade of powerboats, sailboats, and ferries plying the waters.

We explored tide pools, watched deer, lit a driftwood campfire, and motored a short distance east to Deer Harbor for groceries. Dad always bought raspberries and variety packs of Kellogg's cold cereal: We slit the perforated face with our thumbnails and poured milk directly into the little foil-lined boxes. I can remember eating cereal in the warm sunshine while listening to Elvis Presley croon "I Can't Help Falling in Love With You" on Dad's bulky blue transistor radio.

* * * *

That August of 1962, Zuvich steered *Miss Bardahl*'s tractor truck down the highway, descending the eastern slope of the Rockies onto the plains. He twisted the knobs of the AM radio mounted on the dash, looking for a familiar station. Suddenly, through the static and undulating signals, the Everly Brothers boomed strong and clear.

"Wolfman Jack!" Zuvich recalled. "That was my station of choice. There's a radio station we could get for probably three of the five days it took to drive back East. When I first started in 1962, there were no freeways. People forget that. We did a lot of two-lane driving. Like when we went into Montana, it was always under construction to go to four lanes. But the Wolfman, once you got up on the flats, he was our guy. Old-time rock and roll."

Zuvich and Dax likely were tuned in to XERF-AM, a Mexican station in Ciudad Acuña, just across the border from San Antonio. Its 250,000-watt signal blasted across much of North America and the U.S., where even clear-channel AM stations were restricted to 50,000 watts. Wolfman Jack rocketed to rock and roll fame on XERF, just as depicted in the nostalgia film "American Graffiti," marketed with the tagline "Where were you in '62?"

Miss Bardahl and crew rolled down Jefferson Street in Detroit, turned right on Burns Drive and pulled into the pits alongside the river, near The Whittier hotel. Alas, the Green Dragon's appearance on race day, Aug. 26, was brief.

The *Bardahl* team assumed the race would be postponed because of steady rain, but it wasn't, which they learned 11 minutes before the start. Musson entered the bumpy Detroit River course too late for heat 1A and was disqualified for not being on plane at the one-minute gun; one account said it was after the race had actually started. *Bardahl* withdrew in protest and sat on its trailer the remainder of the day, along with Bob Gillam's two *Fascination*s. Aging veteran Danny Foster came out of a four-year retirement that week to drive *Gale VII* and lumbered to a second and a fourth in preliminary heats.

Wind, rain, and waves tormented the fleet until skies cleared for the final, in which *Century 21* and *Gale V* battled, with Cantrell forging ahead and pulling away for four laps. But after a 108+ mph lap, fastest of the day, *Gale V* blew its supercharger in lap five. Muncey inherited the lead and won, ending the day with 1,200 perfect points. *Notre Dame* took second, *Tahoe Miss* third. The Detroit race marked 50 consecutive heats run by Muncey's craft without an engine failure, dating clear back to Lake Mead in 1959.

The racing fleet trekked south to Madison, Ind., for the Governor's Cup Regatta over Labor Day weekend. There, surprised teams found Lee Schoenith quite cranky. He had retired his *Gale VII*, fired his crew, and withdrew *Gale V* from the race.

"We were beating Muncey in Detroit, and we broke down," Schoenith said. "We beat *Bardahl* in Seattle, and we broke down. I think I have the best boat in the country and the best driver in Bill Cantrell. But we couldn't run without breaking down."

On Saturday in the first heat of the two-day Madison race, Musson led briefly in lap one until Muncey forged ahead on the backstretch and pulled away to win at 104.819 mph. *Bardahl* finished second at 101.454.

On Sunday morning, debris dotted the Ohio River from two successive overnight rainstorms. *Bardahl* won heat 2A at 100.812 mph over *Tahoe Miss*. Then Musson took the inside in the final heat and hooked up with *C-21* in a screaming duel, holding a slim three-foot lead over Muncey at the end of lap four. Musson was pulling away ending lap five when officials flagged *Bardahl* and *Tahoe Miss* to run an extra lap for jumping the gun. *C-21* averaged 98.813 mph to win, Marion Cooper aboard *Miss Madison* took second, and *Bardahl* finished third but earned second overall for the Governor's Cup, including the day's fastest lap of 105.675 in the final.

The *Madison Courier* called the *Bardahl-Century 21* duel a "classic, chaotic, aquatic cutie."

By winning, *Century 21* wrapped up the national points title and notched 53 straight heats without a mechanical failure. *Yachting* scribe George Van wrote, "*Bardahl* grew flighty when she came close to top speed and couldn't stay with *Century 21*. When *Bardahl* wobbled, Musson wisely backed off."

Out in the Northwest, Elvis Presley caused a stir when he arrived in Seattle on Sept. 5 for 10 days to shoot the MGM film, "It Happened at the World's Fair." Jay Rockey, the Century 21 Exposition's public relations director, recalled Presley "was calm, well-spoken, nice looking, and clean." Visitors poured into the Seattle World's Fair to set a single-day attendance record on Sept. 15 of 106,860; total fair attendance since April now numbered 7,730,389.

Muncey and *Century 21* had arrived in Washington, D.C., as heavy favorites to win the Sept. 15-16 President's Cup on the Potomac River. *Tahoe Miss* changed drivers in D.C., a move that would kindle heated hydro battles for the next four years. Veteran charger Chuck Thompson, 48, replaced Col. Russ Schleeh, who soon after retired from the Air Force to join Douglas Aircraft.

C-21, *Bardahl*, and *Gale V* battled to finish in that order on Saturday in heat 1B of the President's Cup, with Muncey running a blistering 111.639 mph on the 3-mile course to break the Potomac heat record by more than 2 mph. *Bardahl* posted 107.933, *Gale V* 103.966.

On Sunday, Muncey won both of his heats to claim the President's Cup, his fifth straight race, and looked poised to make a clean sweep of the entire 1962 circuit. Muncey's heat 2B victory didn't come easily, however. *Bardahl* led into the first corner followed by *Notre Dame* and *Gale V,* with Muncey trailing in fourth. Musson led until turn one of lap two, where *Bardahl* threw a rod and coasted to a stop.

When Muncey won the final and set a record race average of 109.157 mph for the three 15-mile heats, posting 1,200 perfect points, he extended *Century 21*'s amazing record for consecutive heats finished without a mechanical breakdown to 55. Thompson earned two heat victories and finished second overall in his first ride aboard *Tahoe Miss*. Ever the charger, Thompson and *Tahoe* would prove to be tough competitors.

* * * *

In late September the hydros trekked cross-country to a new Lake Tahoe event organized by *Tahoe Miss*'s owner, casino magnate Bill Harrah. High winds whipped the mile-high Nevada lake and delayed qualifying for the first Harrah's Tahoe Regatta, held on a 3-mile course near Stateline, where hydros crossed into California near the end of the backstretch.

"Tahoe is probably my all-time favorite race site," said Zuvich. "Everybody had their own Sanikan painted in their colors; ours was green and black. The crews all had free hot dogs, and anything in the pits was free, because they felt you were part of the show. If you needed to go to town, Harrah had a cab waiting for you. If you needed to go to a machine shop, you'd jump in the cab with your part and go. You didn't have to ask somebody like an official – 'Gee, how do you get there? Where is it?' It was all covered, and it was done really nice.

"Every year, Tahoe was a joy," he continued. "And it's kind of funny that I tell people the biggest thing that stands out is that you had your own Sanikan. But that's how personal it got, they thought about what each crew needs. When you get down to having your own Sanikan, they're really looking to make you happy."

The *Century 21* team stood on the brink of going undefeated for an entire racing season. Muncey had dominated the fleet, yet his gruff Montana crew chief voiced caution.

"We've had engine problems every time we've raced here in the past," Jack Ramsey told *Seattle Times* columnist Bud Livesley. "Each race gets tougher. The pressure mounts each time out. The boat has to quit sometime. We only hope it does so because Bill turns off the key."

Calm water greeted the hydros on race day, Sunday, Sept. 30, when Bill Muncey's streak finally ended: *Miss Century 21* busted its crankshaft in heat 1B and was beached for the day. The persimmon and ivory champion's quest for an undefeated season slipped away.

Miss Bardahl finished second in her first heat, then surged to a commanding lead at the midpoint of the second heat before twisting a quill shaft that crippled her supercharger. *Bardahl* barely limped home in fourth. But there in the thin air on Tahoe's pristine waters, at the end of her freshman season, the Green Dragon won its first regatta by winning the championship heat wire-to-wire at 101.351 mph, with the day's fastest lap of 109.091.

Bardahl didn't appear dominant to Monday morning newspaper readers who noted her paltry 869 total race points. But the team had turned a corner, and the Tahoe victory later proved to mark the start of a new hydro era ruled by a metallic green and yellow charger.

Second place in the Tahoe regatta went to *$ Bill*, driven by Rex Manchester, while Morlan Visel – who ended a 10-year retirement to steer his *Hurricane VI* – took third. After posting a first and a second,

Thompson and *Tahoe Miss* were hosed down by a roostertail in the final. Of historical note, the revered *Miss Seattle* – formerly *Slo-mo-shun V* – earned third in heat 2B while averaging 85.066 mph.

Though pleased with the race victory, Musson and crew still felt hampered by *Bardahl's* porpoising ride that hurt its motors. All season long Musson had tried in vain to compel builder Ted Jones to correct his design.

"The whole '62 season, Musson tried getting a hold of my dad," said Ron Jones. "Every race, between every race, on the telephone. He even wrote him a letter. And he would never respond. He wouldn't talk to Ronnie. All year long, they couldn't get my dad to help them or answer them."

Vanden Berg recalled getting marginal help from Ted Jones, who suggested bolting a cavitation plate to *Bardahl's* transom, something untried in unlimiteds before then.

"That's the only solution he came up with all summer," said Vanden Berg. "We used that cavitation plate for the turns. It didn't do any good in the chutes."

Zuvich recalled the team's struggles to correct their new boat.

"The first year was the hardest," he said. "At every race, we worked at least one night straight through to change that boat. I have to hand it to Leo, boy. He projected the program, and every race we did something to try to make the boat understand that it's a race boat. It took until the last race at Tahoe before we won anything with it."

* * * *

Musson's victory at Lake Tahoe coincided with the latest milestone in America's space race with the Soviet Union. Three days after the Nevada regatta, astronaut Wally Schirra blasted into orbit aboard his *Sigma 7* Mercury spacecraft and circled the earth six times before splashing down in the Pacific. The flight was twice as long as the earlier orbital missions of John Glenn and Scott Carpenter, *Aurora 7* pilot.

Shirra witnessed a space-flight mystery that had baffled Glenn, Carpenter, and NASA officials on previous flights. "I, too, see fireflies," Shirra said at the end of his second orbit.

Glenn had reported seeing strange luminous particles suspended outside his capsule window while orbiting the globe, and when Carpenter also saw them, he solved the puzzle by pounding on the inner side of his capsule to create more "snowflakes." Scientists concluded they were particles of Florida frost that flaked off and reflected the sun's rays.

* * * *

Kids growing up in the 1950s and '60s had an omnipresent threat to distract them: nuclear bombs and the Cold War. Lake Hills Elementary School held occasional duck-and-cover drills, and our principal once told us in an assembly that if we ever saw a bright flash in the west toward Seattle, we should dive into a ditch and cover our eyes with our hands.

Mom took this threat seriously when the Cuban Missile Crisis escalated in October 1962. She bought canned food at the P-X supermarket and stored it in wood apple crates in the garage, instructing the family that if the Soviets attacked, we would carry the crates into the crawl space under our Lake Hills rambler, using it as a pseudo bomb shelter for the duration – however long that may be.

The Soviets backed down from the October confrontation after 10 tense days, but until then the threat of nuclear war, mushroom clouds, and radiation poisoning was very real in the minds of Lake Hills third-graders and American youth. It certainly negated much of the carefree delight that accompanied the World's Fair, which ended its six-month run Oct. 21.

One week earlier a very tangible disaster had struck the Northwest, though it paled beside the threat of nuclear war. A rare Pacific Ocean "extratropical cyclone" migrated north, and winds exceeding 100 mph blasted the region on Oct. 12, 1962, taking 46 lives and flattening forests, robbing the timber industry of more than 11 billion board feet of lumber. Steady winds hit 65 mph in Seattle with gusts of 80.

But for kids on my block, the storm was all just a really cool adventure that dazzled us with flying branches, soaring shingles, and exploding power-line transformers. Best of all, we got to use candles and flashlights for emergency lighting inside the house.

Power outages were not infrequent in my youth, and my "closet pyro" that dwells within all boys welcomed the chance to light candles and build a blaze in the fireplace. I always felt disappointed when the lights eventually flicked back on and the refrigerator resumed humming.

Chapter 5

Miss Bardahl *redo*

Ron Musson was not happy.

The scrappy little driver had expected his new boat would be a rocket in 1962, ready to conquer *Century 21* and all comers. Sure, new hydros need fine-tuning and a few races to work out the kinks. But *Bardahl*'s crew had thrashed hard all summer trying to tame the U-40's wild ride with little success.

Musson had expected to ride the new *Bardahl* to the top of his sport. He squeezed every bit of potential out of the hull, finishing third behind *Century 21* and *Tahoe Miss* in the 1962 national points standings. But he expected more.

"Ron Musson was one of the all-time greatest drivers that ever lived, and sometimes you don't need to have the fastest boat to win a boat race," said Ron Jones. "There were occasions when Musson won all by himself – he didn't have speed on anybody. He just won the boat race. Well, Ron Musson hated the way that '62 boat rode.

"I'll tell you, there are drivers who are really good, and if a better one comes along, the really good drivers are scared to death of them," Jones continued. "And a lot of those guys were scared to death of Ronnie Musson. He was *real* good. He knew when to move and when not to move. And if his boat wasn't behaving that day on that racecourse, he would attack it a little differently. He'd improvise and overcome the deficiency some other way.

"Though he wasn't technically oriented, Musson excelled at knowing how to make any boat perform its best. He had a feel for the boat that I don't think you learn. If you don't have it, just forget it, it ain't gonna come!" Jones said, laughing.

* * * *

On Sept. 7, 1962, Ron Musson was named to a full-time position at Bardahl International Corporation, the distributing company for Bardahl oil products. Musson's title: public relations director and coordinator of racing activities. His days as an electrical and plumbing contractor in Akron, Ohio, were winding down. He and wife Betty and the two kids moved to Seattle, where they settled into a Ballard apartment at 5210 Russell Ave. N.W., just a few blocks from the Bardahl plant.

In the spring of 1963, Ron Jones worked as a field coordinator and draftsman for the penitentiary in Shelton, Wash. While living there he rented a little shop in the woods where he and Bob Mackey built boats, including N-86 *Tiger Too*, a record-setting 225-class limited built in 1961 that Jones said was the first rear-engine, wide-transom, low-profile hydroplane. (Some claim the 48-class *Piranha* was the first wide-transom cabover, in 1962, driven by future unlimited star Mickey Remund.) Jones built the penitentiary weekdays and helped Mackey build boats at night and on weekends.

"I had worked for two or three days straight without a break, and boy, I was tired," Jones recalled. "I was home taking a shower. It was the middle of the day, and my wife beat on the shower door and said, 'You'd better come to the phone quickly, I think you'll want to talk to this guy.' It was Ronnie Musson.

"So I jumped out of the shower and took the phone, and Musson said, 'Ron, I'm going to tell you some serious things. You're not going to like a lot of it, but I'm going to tell you how it is. Your dad built us that new boat, and it's the worst piece of junk I've ever driven in my life. I'm gonna kill myself in it. I'm deathly afraid of it. It *will not turn*. It rides like a frog, and I don't want any more to do with it. And here's what Ole and I decided: If you'll come rebuild the boat, we will continue to run it. If you say 'No, I don't want to do that,' we are going to burn it. In a public place. On television. And we are going to say why.'

"That would have been ugly," Jones said. "I felt bad for Bardahl and agreed to try and fix it."

Jones begged his boss for a leave of absence and was granted just two weeks – a moot point, because that's all Musson would allow, anyway. The *Bardahl* team had little time to prepare for the '63 racing season, and Musson told Jones that whatever he did, he had to finish it in two weeks.

Miss Bardahl's poor riding characteristics stemmed from a Ted Jones innovation intended to boost performance. Hydros in the 1950s often hopped and leaped, and in the corners they oscillated like a rocking chair. Ted thought that came from the lateral running surfaces of the sponsons being too flat and reacting to the water. He thought if those surfaces were steep, it would soften the ride and cushion the blow.

"That was a misconception, and it was unfortunate because Dad really believed he was helping the cause," Ron Jones said. "But really, it hurt the cause badly."

Ted designed the 1962 *Bardahl* with the steepest sponson dihedral – angle of attack – of any hydroplane. Years earlier Naval architects had determined the optimum lift-to-drag angle of a running surface was 3 to 3.5 degrees, the point where you get the most lift with the least drag. Ted took note and built all of his boats that way, adding a slight twist to the sponson's angle of attack so that the outside of the running surface was at 4.5 to 5 degrees.

Miss Bardahl pioneered Ted's new idea for a much greater angle of attack.

"I think Dad had it up to like 7 or 8 degrees, and as it went forward it got up to 10 or 12 degrees," Ron Jones said. "It looked like a V-bottom boat on the bottom of the sponsons, they were so steep. They carved the water too much and reacted to it, making the boat hop and come over on its nose. When Ronnie drove the boat into a corner, the right sponson would bury because the boat leaned so far. The sponson was so steep it couldn't support the weight, and it would pierce the water. And sometimes in the turn, Ronnie saw water lapping onto the deck, and to a driver that says, 'We're going over.'

"That boat scared the tar out of him all year," he continued. "The first time it was launched it submarined when it pulled away from the shore. They ended up winning at Tahoe, but that was simply because they won the attrition battle. Dad had avoided those people all summer when they complained about the boat ride."

"The boat had a tendency to roll over on its nose, which breaks engines," said Zuvich. "It makes your manifold pressure jump up and down erratically. It's real hard on the blower gears. All that year of '62, we were changing dihedral and the angle of attack on those sponsons. We ran those things up, down, sideways, inside out, and it still would do the same thing. So the only thing left was to move the sponsons farther away from the propeller."

* * * *

Vanden Berg and crew turned *Bardahl* upside down and stripped it to provide access for Ron Jones and Bob Mackey, who rented a motel near the Bardahl shop and worked on the boat 12 to 14 hours every day. They ripped everything off the sponsons until only the frames remained, then started rebuilding. Jones shimmed the frames to flatten the angle of attack, and once he was satisfied with the dihedral – about 4 degrees on the main part and 3.5 on the small riding surfaces – they built new battens, chines, and planking.

Ted Jones had designed *Miss Bardahl* to be divided equally, fore and aft: The sponsons stopped about halfway back from the bow, at 15 feet, and the rear of the boat extended another 15 feet. Ron Jones believed the hull's center of gravity was too far forward, and one way to correct it was to shorten the sponsons. He and Mackey did that by sawing 11 inches off the rear of each sponson, up to the next frame, which moved *Bardahl*'s riding surfaces forward and lengthened their distance from the propeller.

"It was 11 inches because the rear two frames are 12 inches apart, and it just so happened we had a frame that distance," recalled Zuvich. "And that's where you need a frame for strength – at the back of the sponson. So the sponson got cut off, halfway for convenience, to that frame."

"I knew it was pointless to try fixing the boat without eliminating those sponsons," Jones said, "so I took 'em clear off and redesigned them totally, and moved the ends of the sponsons forward. I wanted to go another whole frame, but there was no way to make the deck match the sponsons in the amount of time we had, so I attached angled aluminum plates to cover the 11-inch gaps we'd created on each sponson. They're still there today."

The deck line never was altered to accommodate that change. Jones and Mackey finished the job in two weeks – barely. The result: shorter and wider sponsons.

Hydroplanes of *Bardahl*'s era had trouble keeping their propellers immersed, which strained shafts, gears, and motors. RPMs fluctuated as the props rose, dropped, rose, dropped, disrupting thrust and robbing momentum. Broken, jagged roostertails were common in the 1950s and '60s; long, low, smooth roostertails showing constant forward thrust were rare. Indeed, throughout the 1962 campaign the *Bardahl* camp often uttered the dreaded "C" word – cavitation.

Strut weight is another factor in proper hull attitude. The strut is the piece of steel bolted to the bottom of a hydro near the transom, and the propeller shaft runs through it. If you balance a hydro on two sturdy sawhorses, with the running surfaces of both sponsons resting on the sawhorses, and you rest the propeller on a scale, you'd gauge the strut weight. Ted Jones aimed for a strut weight of 300 to 400 pounds on his boats, and shortening *Bardahl*'s sponsons put more load on its propeller. Ron Jones estimates that after the sponson modifications were complete, *Bardahl*'s 1963 strut weight was around 800-900 pounds.

The result: *Bardahl*'s propeller would stay halfway immersed in the water as it should, constantly thrusting the boat forward, on straightaways and in corners. No more scrubbing off 25 mph every time the nose stuffs in the water. No more cavitating. The boat now would accelerate better because it lost less speed and torque in the corners. And with better balance, *Bardahl* could handle lumpy water nicely, staying parallel to the surface.

Vanden Berg then focused on moving the boat's center of gravity (CG) even farther back. Ron Jones said his father designed boats with their CG eight or nine inches behind the ends of the sponsons. *Bardahl*'s was originally farther back at 18 inches, according to Vanden Berg, yet the 1963 alterations shifted it aft even farther.

"We moved everything we could toward the rear to get the weight back, batteries and stuff," Vanden Berg recalled while examining the boat in July 1983. "When the boat was built, it had an 18-inch CG behind the sponsons. We changed it *way* back. By 1965 I think it was back about here," he said, gesturing toward the cockpit.

In 1989 Vanden Berg said the CG ended up at 52 inches behind the sponsons, perhaps a misstatement. Dixon Smith said 52 inches is way too far. Jones agreed.

"Leo may not have remembered exactly," Jones said. "I would say the CG was more like 32, and even that is a long ways. If it were something like 25 or 30, or 32, for an unlimited of its day, that was just unheard of. But it worked really well."

It was time to test the rebuilt Dragon on Lake Washington. *Bardahl*'s 1965 press packet described the 1963 scene:

> *Ron took her out, toured up and down the lake several times, slowly at first and then faster and faster. He tried turns at different speeds and accelerated hard to test for any cavitation. There was none. The boat rode level and steady as a rock. She slid through the turns without so much as a shudder, and when she came in Ron had that "cat that just ate the bird" look on his face, Leo had a kind of silly grin, and the rest of the crew looked as though they had just hit the jackpot at Harrah's.*

In 1963, *Miss Bardahl* was to be an entirely different raceboat. The new sponsons held the hull up through the turns, and she no longer went crazy, porpoising and banging from sponson to sponson down the chutes. For the rest of its career, compared with its rivals, the Green Dragon rode like it was mounted on rails. While others jumped and rocked and dove, *Bardahl* skimmed as smooth as silk.

"It turned very well after the changes. It was a whole new boat," Jones said. "Before, it wouldn't turn at all without getting up on its side. So every year after that I worked on it, because it was a wood boat and the water would soak the sponsons here and there, and they would get a little hook in them and I would straighten it out. Probably three times a year I planed on the sponsons and shimmed them and did whatever I had to do to get them straight again."

Chapter 6

Routine, rigor, and Thousand Island

Miss Bardahl's crew changed for the 1963 season, getting smaller and a little younger. Vanden Berg, 46, remained crew chief, logging long hours when he wasn't on the job as an Army vehicle inspector at Seattle's Fort Lawton. Zuvich, 22, continued to work full-time weekdays as the shipping clerk for Bardahl Manufacturing Corporation, working on the boat evenings and weekends. Dax Smith, 19, attending the University of Washington full time, did likewise.

Several 1962 crew members, including Comnick, French, Larson, Siegel, and Welpley, left the team. Burns Smith also moved on – "I decided I was too busy at home and I'd better bag it for awhile," he told the *Unlimited NewsJournal* – but his 17-year-old son David, who occasionally tagged along with Burns and Dax the previous year, helped out now and then at the *Bardahl* shop.

Joining the crew were two brothers with prior hydroplane experience: Scotty Freeman, a 44-year-old planner at Boeing, and his brother Gernie Freeman, 42, a receiving clerk for Seattle's Bon Marché department store. Bill Marshall, a gearbox expert and truck mechanic who worked for LASME, also came aboard.

"It worked out that we had more young blood than old blood, and we just went that way," said Zuvich. "So in '63, I don't think we had that many of the original group left as far as the older guys go."

Vanden Berg instilled in his team the importance of quality control, cross-training, and double-checking, about which he was rigid. The younger crew members bristled at times over what they perceived to be his inflexibility and militaristic style. Indeed, Vanden Berg was a known creature of habit who clung steadfastly to routines and ordered the same food from restaurant menus. But his quality control paid huge dividends, and four decades later the core crew – now sage and circumspect – would apply that same rigor with their rebuilt and restored *Miss Bardahl*.

"I had a team where everybody knew everybody's job, but they maybe excelled in one or two areas," Vanden Berg said. "Everybody got to do everybody else's job, so in case something happened to somebody, we could carry on. Like, Dax broke his shoulder riding a dirt bike. Well, that kind of tied him up a little bit. But we carried on just the same. He was there, working with one arm."

"The majority of the time we had an informal policy that if you did something major on an engine, before you closed it up, you got somebody else over to take a look inside," said Dixon. "Like, 'I did the crankshaft. Jerry, come over and look.' Or if Jerry did the cylinders, 'Leo, you come over and look.' If you're pressed for time, you didn't do it. But if you had the time, you did."

While Vanden Berg's penchant for routine and rigor paid dividends in racing, it also was a source of amusement for his young teammates.

"Absolutely, Leo was very much a creature of habit," said Skip Schott, who joined the team in late 1964. "We'd go into a restaurant and the waitress would come around and ask Leo what he wanted, and all of us would chime in together, 'Top sirloin well-done, Thousand Island, baked potato.'" Schott laughed. "That's what he ate every time. It was real difficult to talk him into trying something different. Art Louie had a Chinese restaurant up on 85th that we lobbied hard for, but we got to go there only once or twice."

When in town, Vanden Berg's restaurant of choice was The Golden Tides, west of Ballard on Shilshole Bay. "The Tides" became a *Bardahl* team staple for years, with dinner being part of the compensation for what was largely a volunteer crew.

* * * *

On May 1, 1963, Redmond, Wash., mountaineer Jim Whittaker became the first American to summit Mount Everest, stirring excitement around Seattle. About that time my peers and I established our own crazy little outdoor adventure: storm-sewer spelunking. One of the older kids on the block felt audacious one day and decided to crawl into the open end of a large storm pipe that emptied into a culvert near my elementary school. He came back with thrilling tales of exploring the unknown and, allegedly, ending up in a narrow vertical pipe covered by a grate that looked into someone's bathroom. "I saw a toilet, I swear!" he said.

My friends and I soon followed suit while Mom was busy at work. Our family's only flashlight had dead batteries, so instead I brought a home-made Christmas candle my sister had crafted by pouring melted wax remnants into a foil cupcake liner. We walked to the storm-sewer opening and sized up its 36-inch concrete pipe. With trepidation that I dared not reveal to the other boys, I crept into the darkness on my hands and knees. The slap-slap of my free hand – the one not holding the candle – echoed through the musty pipe.

We crawled for what seemed like a perilous distance but in reality was not quite a full neighborhood block. Then one of the older kids blew out my candle. He thought it was funny. Of course, *he* had a flashlight. I wanted out but found the pipe too narrow to turn around in, and feeling suddenly claustrophobic, I crawled backward as quickly as I could.

My friend's little prank spooked me, but apparently not enough. We crawled through that storm sewer several times over the next couple of years.

* * * *

In June 1963, the hydro fleet trekked to Guntersville, Ala., to kick off the racing season at a new event, the $10,000 Governor's Cup Regatta on Guntersville Lake. On April 17, 1962, Guntersville had been the site of Roy Duby's screaming run aboard *Miss U.S. 1*, where he set the world mile-straightaway record for propeller-driven craft at 200.419 mph.

As qualifying began June 21, halfway around the world 65-year-old Milan archbishop Giovanni Montini was elected the 262nd Pope of the Roman Catholic Church and chose the name Paul VI. Two days later, West Germans in Bonn cheered visiting President Kennedy who told them, "Your liberty is our liberty." On June 26 in Berlin he declared, *"Ich bin ein Berliner."*

Musson throttled his now-swift *Bardahl* to the top qualifying speed of 112.500 on Guntersville's choppy 2½-mile course and said, "We expect to win. We're running great." *Notre Dame* flipped on a swell but driver Col. Warner Gardner was unhurt, and his crew repaired the Shamrock Lady in time for Sunday's race. Chuck Thompson ran 109.796 mph in his spanking new *Tahoe Miss*, a Ted Jones-designed red and cream craft built by the *Tahoe* crew. It ran a two-stage Allison, weighed a hefty 8,500 pounds, and showed great chute speed but ran wild through the turns.

Other combatants included Don Wilson aboard Detroit's *Miss U.S.5*, the former *Hawaii Kai III*; Bill Cantrell in *Gale V*; Norm Evans and *$ Bill*; Jimmy Fyle with *St. Regis*, built in 1955 as *Tempo VII*; and band leader Guy Lombardo with his new four-seat *Tempo*. Missing were Muncey and his U-60, which had reverted to its pre-World's Fair name, *Miss Thriftway*. Owner Willard Rhodes, crew chief Ramsey and team had opted instead to prepare for the July 7 Gold Cup in Detroit. Bob Gilliam also withheld *Fascination*, which he said was geared for 3-miles courses and might strain its equipment on the shorter Guntersville oval.

Under overcast skies, Musson easily outran the field to win all three of his heats and capture the 45-mile regatta with 1,200 perfect points. *Bardahl* averaged 102.700 mph to beat *Gale V* and *Tahoe Miss* in heat 1A. In 2B he yielded lane one to Cantrell and battled *Gale* again, needing a 110-mph first lap to pull away and win a tight race at 106.000; *St. Regis* finished third. *U.S.5* and *Tempo* met mechanical misfortune in their heats, and Chuck Thompson was scalded when *Tahoe*'s exploding blower sliced a water line in 2A. In the final, *Bardahl* ran 100.446 to beat *$ Bill*, *Gale V*, and *Notre Dame*.

"I used to think *Hawaii Kai* was the last word, but it doesn't compare," Musson said afterward. "The *Bardahl* is the fastest boat I've ever handled, bar none. I don't want to change a thing."

Vanden Berg saw the race in Dixie as a turning point for Musson, where he finally learned he didn't need to drive pedal-to-the-metal all the time. "I told him he'd finally lost that little black cloud over his head, once he learned to conserve his equipment and drive just fast enough to win. That was in Guntersville, Alabama."

Chapter 7

Musson strikes gold

Miss Thriftway left Seattle June 25 for Detroit, as did a new boat with a somewhat *Bardahl*-like low profile, *Miss Exide*, to be driven by Czech freedom flier Mira Slovak. Sponsored by Exide Battery Company of Cleveland, Ohio, *Miss Exide* was designed by Ted Jones and built by Ed Karelsen, the veteran boatbuilder's first foray into the unlimited class. Jones reportedly questioned whether *Exide*'s construction was stout enough for an unlimited – rather than screw everything together, Karelsen used glue and a staple gun, as was his custom with smaller limited hydros.

"When Ted Jones saw how he was building the boat, Jones pulled out. He said I want nothing to do with it," Slovak said. "Staples. That's right, staples."

Karelsen built *Miss Exide* at the Stoen brothers' Minor Street shop in Seattle's Cascade neighborhood – the shop that previously had housed *Miss Seattle Too, Miss Pay'n Save,* and *Hawaii Kai III*. The boat shop occupied the first story, and upstairs were the Harrison Street offices of Pay'n Save Corporation and its president, M. Lamont "Monte" Bean.

"Monte Bean had made the stipulation with George McKernan, 'Don't ever, ever start up that boat here,'" said Bob Woolms, a *Seattle Too* and *Exide* team mechanic. "Well, one day we had to start it up. We backed it out of the shop, barely, and we hooked the water up and started it. Around the corner comes Monte. He said, 'Dammit George, my coffee cup was vibrating on my desk!' Boy, he was mad."

Karelsen and his crew set to work building *Miss Exide*, operating under time constraints.

"The problem with that boat is – and Mira will tell you this, too – we put it together too quickly," said Woolms. "It wasn't a very good job. That's why that thing blew up later, in Coeur d'Alene."

Once finished, the new red, blue and white hull with the checkered tail was trailered to Stan Sayres Pits at Lake Washington and christened June 7, 1963, as news media, rival crews, and fans looked on. Mira Slovak climbed into the cockpit and wiggled into the seat.

"When he started the boat up, there's a rock jetty that goes out, and Mira had to go out and around it," said Woolms. "But he veered toward it severely, and it kind of scared us because we didn't know what he was doing. So he went out on the lake, maintained about a 90 mile-an-hour speed and came back in. Mira used to call George McKernan 'Yoorge.' He said, 'Yoorge, I think we have a problem. I turned the boat to the left and it went right; I turned it to the right and it went left.' Yeah, we put the steering box in backwards. But he didn't tell the press, and nobody even knew it. He didn't want to embarrass George and the crew and the Exide Battery people."

For the first time, in 1963 the APBA Gold Cup would be hosted *not* by the race site affiliated with the previous year's winner, but by the organization that bid the most for the event. Detroit offered $36,250 to outbid Seattle, which offered a mere $25,500 on the assumption that Bill Harrah would bid $50,000 to hold the race at Lake Tahoe. However, Harrah abstained altogether.

Another change was the new Gold Cup format that comprised four 15-mile heats of five laps each, for a total of 60 miles, rather than three 30-mile, 10-lap heats for a total of 90 miles. Crews also would be allowed to make one complete engine change on race day, Sunday.

On June 29 and 30, Rex Manchester tested the newly rebuilt *Miss Eagle Electric*, formerly *Miss Spokane*, on sleepy Moses Lake in Eastern Washington. The Lilac Lady hadn't run since flipping on Pyramid Lake in 1961, but crew chief Kent Simonson pronounced her ready to race after Manchester hit 170 mph and made some brisk turns. The U-25 would skip the Gold Cup and stage her comeback at the July 27-28 Diamond Cup at Coeur d'Alene. On hand for the test was the boat's new sponsor, Dave Heerensperger, owner of Spokane's Eagle Electric and Plumbing stores.

Muncey and *Thriftway* topped the Gold Cup qualifying ladder on Monday, July 1, with a 113.207-mph average for three laps, including a Detroit course-record lap of 114.893. Having won the gold goblet in 1956, 1957, 1961, and 1962, Muncey was the heavy favorite, aiming to tie Gar Wood's record of five wins.

Wilson and *U.S.5* ran three laps at 109.169. The former *Hawaii Kai* had just undergone repairs to straighten its warped sponsons, the result of the hull being stored atop barrels.

Musson beat *Thriftway*'s mark on Tuesday by averaging 113.849 mph in *Bardahl*, with laps of 113.684, a record-tying 114.893, and 112.970. *Seattle P-I* sports writer John Owen described a playful aftermath.

Muncey: "Where did you get that?"

10-year-old son Wil Muncey, clutching a black jacket emblazoned with B-A-R-D-A-H-L: "They gave it to me. Can I keep it, Dad?"

Muncey, with a hint of a smile: "No, you may not."

Wil: "Please!"

Muncey: "Well, you can keep it, but I better not see you wearing it around here."

Wil: "Okay, thanks. Tomorrow they're going to give me a T-shirt."

Musson, witnessing the exchange: amused expression.

Elsewhere in the pits, the *Gale* camp was not so cheery. Its behemoth Packard-powered *Gale VII* tossed a prop, ripping a hole in its bottom, and its stern quickly sank to the bottom of the Detroit River. Driver Danny Foster stood knee-deep in water, perched on the bow, until a Gale workboat rescued him. *Gale VII* soon twisted in the current and slipped under, landing upside down on the river bottom.

That same night, gut-wrenching news came from Seattle. Undefeated track and field star Brian Sternberg, who had pole-vaulted higher than anyone in the world at 16 feet 8 inches, suffered a critical injury in a gymnastics trampoline accident at the University of Washington's Hec Edmundson Pavilion. The 20-year-old UW junior did a double-back somersault with a full twist, then landed on the back of his neck and dislocated his vertebrae, pinching his spinal cord and causing permanent paralysis from his neck down.

Musson's top speed lasted just one day. On Wednesday, crew chief Ramsey announced Sunday's Gold Cup would be the last for his Nifty Thrifty, which would retire after the 1963 campaign. Muncey then went out and roared around the pear-shaped 3-mile course at 116.463, including one lap of 116.756 that shattered his and Musson's course-record lap of 114.893. Other qualifiers included *Tahoe Miss* at 111.300, *Miss Exide* at 99.733, and *Tempo*, newly purchased from Lombardo by Florida business executive Bernie Little, at 99.388 mph. Former *Maverick* pilot Bill Stead qualified *Tempo* for regular driver Bob Schroeder.

Bob Gilliam announced in Seattle he had abandoned plans to race in Detroit, where late Wednesday *Gale VII* was raised from the riverbed, too damaged to be repaired by Sunday. No hydros ran Thursday on the Detroit River in honor of Independence Day.

* * * *

In the 1960s, firework stands popped up around Lake Hills long before July 4. A plywood Zebra Fireworks shack appeared in the west end of the P-X supermarket parking lot each year around June 10, shortly after school let out. We'd loiter around the shack hours on end, day after day, pining for the really tall 75¢ fountains and the fat $4.95 variety boxes of "safe 'n sane" pyrotechnic thrills.

Alas, I rarely had enough money to buy even a 35¢ Piccolo Pete, which when lit made a shrill whistling sound for about 10 seconds. My future brother-in-law Gordon was dumbfounded that anyone saw value in a Piccolo Pete, which he could mimic with his lips and tongue. He'd let out a shrill whistle for a good five seconds, then ask me for 35¢ and laugh heartily.

With just a nickel, a kid could buy a box of "snakes" – cylindrical black tablets that, when lit, magically sprouted serpentine ash for several seconds. Parents hated it when kids lit snakes on driveways or sidewalks, leaving dark burn marks. Mom insisted that I light my snakes on the underside of our metal garbage-can lid. Clever compromise.

Firework season was an adventure because we ritually scoured roadside ditches for glass pop bottles, which in those days could be redeemed for their deposit fee at any grocery store. Standard 12-ounce pop bottles fetched 3¢, while the large quart bottles yielded a whole nickel. We spent hours combing the shoulders of 140th Avenue and other nearby arterials looking for empties. Beer bottles were everywhere, but unfortunately they (as well as certain pop bottles) were "no deposit, no return."

Still, a kid could spend an hour combing the roadside, find eight or nine bottles, and get enough cash to buy himself a small fountain, or several 5¢ boxes of snakes.

Someone discovered that if you took a pair of pliers and squeezed a Piccolo Pete between the "o" and the "P," then lit it, the thing would explode like a firecracker.

1963 also was the year that Washington state outlawed firecrackers. Some kids still bought them on Indian reservations, but the King County Sheriff patrolled our neighborhood that July 4 and actually caught someone lighting off Black Cats inside a neighbor's mailbox.

* * * *

On Friday, July 5, veteran *Hurricane IV* and *VI* driver Morlan Visel charged around the Detroit River in *Miss Madison*. The former *Nitrogen* had been donated by its owner, Delaware industrialist Samuel DuPont, to the town of Madison, Ind., whose residents owned it and named it after their hotbed of hydroplaning. Visel had just completed a 109.2-mph qualifying lap when *Madison* apparently struck an 18-inch chunk of wood while entering the Belle Isle turn, lurched, and shredded off nearly its entire left side.

For Visel, filling in for unqualified rookie Buddy Byers and the departed Marion Cooper, it was just his second ride in the boat. Rescuers pulled him from the water with no pulse and in shock, but Visel was revived and hospitalized with a broken ankle, dislocated shoulder, and lacerations. Ironically, the Gold Cup was to have been Visel's and *Madison*'s last race anyway – the team had just reached agreement to buy DuPont's newer *Nitrogen Too*, an aluminum-core hydro.

George Simon un-retired his *Miss U.S.1*, which scampered around the course at 113.600 mph with Roy Duby at the wheel. Aboard Simon's other entry, Don Wilson boosted *U.S.5*'s speed to 113.326. Musson ran laps of 115 and 116 but decided not to shoot for Muncey's record. "I'm not as fat with equipment as he is. I'll wait until Sunday to race him," Musson said.

Slovak and *Exide* nearly lost their spot in the Gold Cup – only the 12 fastest qualifiers were allowed – until Slovak raised his speed late Saturday from 99.733 to 107.570. *Such Crust* and Leo Mucutza were bumped instead, being 13th on the qualifying ladder at 101.250. Also failing to crack the top 12 were Fred Alter in *Mariner Too* (the 1959 *Miss Buffalo*); Doc Terry aboard *Coe-Z Miss,* the former *Miss Lumberville*; and the damaged *Gale VII* (Foster) and *Madison* (Visel).

The final field was set. For the first time ever, no Gold Cup qualifier ran below 100 mph. Muncey and *Thriftway* ruled the roost at 116.463, followed by Musson and *Bardahl*, 113.849; Duby in *U.S.1*, 113.600; Wilson with *U.S.5*, 113.326; Thompson and *Tahoe*, 111.300; Cantrell in *Gale V*, 108.000; Slovak aboard *Exide*, 107.570; Gardner with *Notre Dame*, 106.592; Evans and *$ Bill*, 106.333; Walt Kade in *Miss Blue Chip* (the former *Breathless II*), 104.770; Bob Schroeder driving *Tempo*, 104.463; and rookie Jimmy Fyle in *Miss St. Regis*, 102.444.

* * * *

Qualifying week had taken place during calm water and sunny, 90-degree skies, yet clouds and early showers greeted the Gold Cup fleet on race day morning. *Thriftway* started the day as expected by winning heat 1A at 102.428 mph, followed by *Tahoe, Exide, $ Bill,* and *St. Regis. U.S.1* plowed through roostertails in the first turn, throwing Duby from the cockpit, knocking him unconscious against the cowl, and wrenching his back. *U.S.1* coasted to a stop and did not finish.

Bardahl dueled *U.S.5* in 1B past the starting line before the red boat sheared its left sponson, sending chunks sky-high. Wilson actually completed a lap before shutting down, and officials finally stopped the heat midway because of floating sponson debris. "We put two boats in the water and couldn't make it to the first turn," owner George Simon said in disgust.

Bardahl took an early lead in the 1B restart and won at 104.936 mph despite treacherous swells, with *Gale V* a close second at 102.622. *Notre Dame, Tempo,* and *Blue Chip* rounded out the finishers.

For the first time since *Bardahl*'s offseason overhaul, Muncey and Musson squared off, in heat 2A in which *U.S.1* did not start. Musson trailed Muncey on his outside hip up the backstretch during the pre-start milling period. Circling the Roostertail turn, Muncey drove a bit farther upriver, apparently wanting a long run to gain greater momentum and speed at the start. But Musson mashed the gas around the corner and got ahead of Muncey; when Thompson swung *Tahoe Miss* around the exit buoy on the inside position, he drifted out slightly toward lane two. Close to his right was *Bardahl*, with a slightly wider gap between *Bardahl* and *Notre Dame,* then *St. Regis.*

Muncey, aiming for an open slot between *Tahoe* and *Bardahl* that now had vanished, slowed and tried to squeeze in anyway but was hammered by roostertails. The other four hydros hit the line virtually abreast. *Thriftway*'s Rolls-Merlin gulped water, sputtered, and died; Muncey wallowed to a stop near the starting line in about lane two or three amid his competitors' wakes.

Musson poured on the power and screamed around the river, opening a modest lead over hard-charging Thompson and the rough-riding *Tahoe*. *Bardahl* ran lap one at a record 114.650 mph (which stood until 1976), extended its lead, and won the 15-mile heat at a109.489-mph average over *Tahoe, Notre Dame,* and *St. Regis*. *Thriftway* sprouted a giant stackfire and failed to restart until the leaders were on lap four, earning Muncey just 127 points and marring his chances for a fifth Gold Cup.

"I thought Bill was right on my tail all the way, until I finished my first lap," Musson said, presuming Muncey had squeezed into the gap between *Bardahl* and *Notre Dame* at the start and was stalking his stern. "When I finally saw him sitting there, I took it a little easier."

Years later, Wil Muncey recalled his father's reaction in the *Thriftway* team trailer after that heat. Bill Muncey cried while talking with Ramsey because he felt he'd let the team down and should have been smarter. "I'd never seen Dad cry before," said Wil.

* * * *

Randy Roe is a longtime unlimited crewmember who lives in the Detroit suburb of Taylor, Mich. The first hydro race he recalls attending was the 1963 Gold Cup on the Detroit River.

"People talk about where they were when they heard about JFK being shot, and have a mental picture of it," he said. "That's how I remember the 1963 Gold Cup – a group of mental 'photographs.' I was 6 and sat with Mom and Dad by the old pit area next to The Whittier, and it seems like it was a drizzly day. It was cloudy and dark for sure.

"The first 'photograph' would be when Muncey got washed down at the start of heat 2A. *Thriftway* just sort of disappeared when he tried to make a lane where there wasn't one. And then he was the only one there, dead in the water. Then came this enormously bright orange stackfire as he struggled to get restarted.

"As I watched *Bardahl* run down the backstretch, my mental photo was of something very purposeful, sharp, perfectly balanced like an arrowhead," Roe recalled. "The low profile combined with the hotrod all-black engine sticking up tended to accentuate the effect, I suppose. The other thing I remember is how well the *Bardahl* slid through the Roostertail turn, staying seemingly flat all the way."

* * * *

Heat 2B saw Wild Bill Cantrell steer *Gale V* to a 99.815-mph victory over *Tempo*, which Schroeder coaxed from last place, followed by Slovak and *Exide*. Kade and *Blue Chip* threw a rod in lap three and didn't finish, and Evans and *$ Bill* were disqualified for striking a buoy.

Bardahl's crew changed engines, and Musson enjoyed a cakewalk in heat 3A after Don Wilson, filling in for Duby, jumped the gun and then conked out in *U.S.1* before completing a lap. *Bardahl* averaged 105.469 and finished half a lap ahead of *Notre Dame* and *Tempo*, while *$ Bill* and *Blue Chip* did not start.

Muncey needed a win in heat 3B to have any shot at a high Gold Cup finish. But after installing a fresh engine, Muncey's chances were dashed by another dreary start that left him dead last in the first turn. Slovak throttled his new *Exide* into the lead but was passed on lap one by the wild-riding *Tahoe Miss*, which sped to the checkered flag at a heat average 104.814 mph. Thompson, who claimed he "opened her up and was going better than 190," benefited from an Allison with a two-stage blower set up by Bill Newman, who had been the mastermind behind *Maverick*'s two-stage Allison success. *Gale V* made up ground to take a close second at 103.250 with *Exide* third and *Thriftway* fourth. *St. Regis* conked on lap four and did not finish.

Musson and *Bardahl* entered the final heat with a perfect 1,200 points, while *Gale V* and *Tahoe* tied at 1,000. The Gold Cup would go to the boat scoring the most total points, and the most *Bardahl*'s challengers could earn was 1,400. Muncey tallied only 696 altogether, giving him the fifth slot in the final.

Onto the course roared *Gale V, Tahoe Miss, Exide, Notre Dame, Thriftway,* and *Bardahl*. Cantrell pushed *Gale V* hard to win at 105.551 mph, while Musson and *Bardahl* cruised to a comfortable second at 100.953 to earn 1,500 overall points and win the coveted Gold Cup. *Tahoe, Exide, Thriftway,* and *Notre Dame* followed in that order.

"I knew I just had to finish third to win," said Musson, now the winner of three straight races. "I only had two things on my mind: Keep from jumping the gun, and stay out of trouble."

Cantrell and *Gale V* earned second in the overall Gold Cup standings with 1,400 points. Third went to Thompson and *Tahoe Miss*, 1,225; Gardener and *Notre Dame* took fourth with 845; Slovak and *Exide* earned fifth with 844; and perennial winner Muncey finished a startling sixth in *Thriftway* with 823.

Bardahl averaged a record 105.212 mph in winning the 60-mile race. Following were *Gale V*, averaging 102.809 for 60 miles; *Tahoe*, 101.639; *Notre Dame*, 95.741; *Exide*, 94.351; and *Thriftway*, 90.888. Counting the laps completed before *U.S.5*'s accident halted heat 1B, *Bardahl* actually raced more than 67 miles.

George Simon retired his aging *U.S.1* – again – after the Gold Cup and returned the wrecked *U.S.5* to owner Joe Mascari, but Simon pledged to build a brand new boat for 1964.

The next day, Seattle news media reported the Gold Cup results and also showed President Kennedy welcoming Jim Whittaker and his American Everest team to the White House, where they received medals for conquering the 29,028-foot Himalayan peak.

* * * *

Sleeping outside on summer nights was a big deal as a kid. Usually we threw our Dacron bags right on the lawn and lay awake watching for satellites and shooting stars. On Gold Cup weekend in 1963 my next-door neighbor Paul suggested we set up his canvas pup tent in my backyard, which we did with his dad's help. We lay inside in our bags, eating buttered popcorn and listening to Alan Sherman sing *"Hello, Mudduh"* on the transistor radio. Inside the house, Mom watched her favorite evening TV shows. By 1963 America's most-watched programs had shifted from Westerns to "The Beverly Hillbillies," "Candid Camera," and "The Red Skelton Show."

Late that night, from inside our tent I heard the rumble of a V-8 with glass pack mufflers pull up to our curb. It was my brother Dave, who on July 5 had bought his first car, a 1955 Chevy Bel-Air convertible, two-tone blue, from Aurora Chevrolet for $700.

Later that month I witnessed a partial solar eclipse. Scientists warned observers about eye damage, so we built a viewing contraption out of a shoebox with pinholes we'd seen in the newspaper, but the thing didn't work and we missed the solar spectacle.

Chapter 8

If you can't win, be spectacular

In mid-July, colorful Indianapolis racecar driver Eddie Sachs was named the new chauffer of Detroit's 1year-old *Such Crust IV* hydroplane, replacing Leo Mucutza. Sachs had won the pole position at the 1960 and '61 Indy 500 and was currently enduring pseudo-celebrity status for being punched in the nose by 1963 Indy winner Parnelli Jones. Mucutza and Bill Cantrell tutored Sachs, who had gained notoriety for saying, "If you can't win, be spectacular."

Perhaps the Clown Prince of Indy sought even more notoriety by driving the conspicuous, spectacularly heavy *Crust*. On July 12 he took his first ride, steering the twin-Allison monster around the Detroit River while Mucutza worked the throttle. Afterward Sachs announced, "I'm serious, I'm going boat racing," and set his sights on the July 27 Diamond Cup.

"This is the toughest thing I've come up against," said Sachs, comparing *Such Crust* to Indy cars. "You turn the wheel and wait 10 seconds before it makes the pivot, and when it makes a pivot you have to work your hands to keep control."

Ultimately, *Such Crust* didn't travel to the Gem State after owner Jack Schafer couldn't find a sponsor to help offset the cost of transporting and campaigning his boat. But the *Thriftway* team attended, eager to atone for its Detroit performance. And Muncey wasn't about to relinquish his claim to being the top dog in hydrodom, despite steering into cascading roostertails – twice – at the Gold Cup.

"I think our boats are quite comparable in performance," Muncey said about *Bardahl*. "But I won't go along with him if Ron says he has a faster boat. He tried to beat our qualifying record at Detroit, but couldn't. His crew waved him in after two laps when they saw he couldn't beat us."

Musson likely was razzed by friends and foes for some sloppy driving of his own July 17, when he crunched his fender turning into the driveway of his Russell Park apartment in Ballard. *The Seattle Times* couldn't resist reporting the mishap by noting that aside from cars, Musson "drives *Miss Bardahl* with unerring accuracy."

While the newspaper took a playful angle, Leo Vanden Berg kept a wary eye on his diminutive jockey, who to him seemed to imbibe at inopportune times.

"I'd always go to Ron Musson's room every morning of qualifying to see what shape he was in," Vanden Berg said. "If he was in bad shape, the boat stayed apart all day. If he was in good shape, we had it running at 9 a.m."

Although Muncey avoided alcohol – Kit Muncey wrote in 1972 that "my husband was a moral, deepwater

Baptist" – he and Musson were on friendly terms, and Muncey was the only driver Vanden Berg ever saw Musson socialize with aside from Rex Manchester.

"At races, Ron was with a lot of the owners. He didn't fit in with the regular crew people. He and Muncey were kind of close, but Muncey was definitely not a drinker. Still, they worked together promoting races and stuff like that for a year or two, going to Canada and everywhere," Vanden Berg said.

Longtime hydro photographer Bill Osborne watched Muncey his entire career and knew him well in his later years.

"Bill didn't pal around with a lot of people," Osborne said. "Bill was not a pal-around guy. He had *utmost* respect for Ron, and he liked him, he liked what he did on the racecourse. He didn't necessarily approve of some of his off-course activities – Bill was an absolute teetotaler. But in later years we talked about people who Bill respected as drivers, and Ron was on his short list.

"Bill didn't have a lot of friends," Osborne continued. "He could do the public speaking thing, but he was hard in one-on-one situations in developing a relationship. I personally always felt that he didn't want to get hurt by disappointment. A lot of the media criticism stung him in the beginning. Later in life he got it figured out and said, 'Aww, it's just part of the deal. Bad coverage is better than no coverage.' Bill was a marketing guy. We talked about the Lee Schoenith feuds that he had, and I said, how can you drive for him? And Bill said, that was all staged."

Seattle Times columnist Hy Zimmerman wrote in 1963, "Bill is brash sometimes, sometimes he is argumentative. However, underneath the gruff and the bluff is thinly covered sensitivity. He is easily hurt, for he wants so much to be liked."

Vanden Berg said Muncey's crew chief Jack Ramsey "was a good egg toward me. He helped me a lot. Not in his secrets or anything so I'd be *more* competitive, but he wanted me to *be* competitive. I'd call him many times." Dax Smith recalled Musson and Muncey being friends, but said the *Bardahl* crew had a somewhat adversarial relationship with the *Thriftway* crew, their crew chiefs notwithstanding.

"We basically did not socialize with those guys," Dax said. "Except on rare occasions, we didn't talk to them a lot. We were not welcome around their race boat; they were not welcome around ours.

"There was a time when the *Thriftway* people were doing some development work on propellers, which they considered pretty classified," he explained. "For quite a while, they made a significant effort to wrap their propeller before they yanked their boat out of the water. They had good reason to do that; they had some pretty slick stuff going.

"So, being the inquisitive let's-piss-the-competition-off type that I am, I got a long lens for my camera, and I made great effort to do anything I could to take pictures of their propellers. I virtually carried that camera for about a month and a half anytime I was in the pits. I'd be in the cockpit working, and the camera would be there with me. I'd see the *Thriftway* lifted up and I'd pop up out of the cockpit, CLICK!, drop back down. It got to the point where I came up out of the cockpit, looked through my camera, and saw nothing: There's a *Thriftway* guy holding his hand up over my lens. 'We don't want you taking pictures of our boat. Not funny. You want your camera broken? Keep taking pictures. You're not welcome around our boat. Stay away.'

"Obviously, you have to retaliate for something like this," said Dax with a smile. "When they left in the evening, they taped a plastic bag around their prop, and they would very carefully take a marker pen and mark a couple of lines on the plastic and tape so you could tell if it had been unwrapped or not. Once they left, Zuvich and I would go over and spend 10 or 15 minutes very carefully marking the tape here, marking the plastic there – that kind of stuff. 'You want to play that game? We know how to play that kind of game.'

"All in all, we didn't have a really friendly relationship with the *Thriftway* guys," Dax said. "We got along, but I was invited out of their pits more than once, and we probably invited them out of ours. I was probably a little more aggressive about trying to find out what other people were doing than most. I guess I'm too snoopy sometimes. But that's part of racing, to find out what the other guys are doing."

* * * *

Musson took *Bardahl* out on Lake Washington July 19 for a pre-Diamond Cup shakedown, and Seafair queen Gail Reid got a 145-mph ride, one of the few given during that era. Six hours to the east, three hydros already occupied the Coeur d'Alene pits a week before the Diamond Cup – *$ Bill, Tempo,* and *Notre Dame.*

On the world stage, heavyweight boxing champion Sonny Liston knocked out previous titleholder Floyd Patterson at 2:10 of the first round on July 22 in Las Vegas, where contender Cassius Clay, the "Louisville Lip," drew attention by bolting into the ring after the fight to shake four fingers on each hand at Liston and shout, "You'll fall in eight, so don't be late!" Liston later said of their upcoming bout, "Clay? It'll take me one round to catch him, and half a round to knock him out."

The next day in Moscow the United States, Russia, and Britain ended talks sealing an agreement to end nuclear tests in space, in the atmosphere, and under water. It led to a comprehensive Nuclear Test Ban Treaty later signed by Dean Rusk, Andrei Gromyko, and Lord Home on Aug. 5. President Kennedy ratified it Oct. 7, and it took effect Oct. 10, 1963, raising hope where angst had prevailed during the previous October's Cuban Missile Crisis.

* * * *

Diamond Cup qualifying got underway Tuesday, July 23, 1963, on Lake Coeur d'Alene. Eight boats lounged in the pits under clear 90-degree skies when Rex Manchester and *Miss Eagle Electric* of Spokane qualified at 97.122 mph on the 3-mile course, easily beating the 90-mph minimum. But the next day gusty winds swept the lake into a froth, and the boats didn't budge from their trailers except for *Notre Dame* and *Tempo*, which made tentative test runs.

Tempo owner Bernie Little boarded three passengers – Bill Muncey, Norm Evans, and local race official Bob Maker – onto his "world's fastest runabout" and turned a 96.1 mph qualifying lap. Also on the scene was *Tempest*, carefully rebuilt by Chuck Hickling over the winter after being badly burned on Lake Washington in the 1962 Gold Cup.

On Thursday Musson sprinted around the lake at 113.208, the fastest lap of the week and day. Thompson and *Tahoe Miss* went 110.656 while Muncey and his Nifty Thrifty ran 109.312; Slovak coaxed *Exide* to an identical 109.312.

The next day Muncey woke up with a heavy foot and pounded *Miss Thriftway* around the Diamond Cup course at 116.129 mph for one lap. Musson immediately urged his crew to drop the Dragon onto the water, and he screamed across the waves at 118.421, a course record that never was broken. Musson also sizzled through a 117.391-mph lap; both speeds broke the previous Diamond Cup record of 115.632 set by Brien Wygle aboard *Hawaii Kai III* in 1959. Chuck Hickling put *Tempest* into the show at 105.469, but two also-rans failed to muster the necessary speed or stamina, *Fascination* and *U-Owe-2*.

Sportswriters made much of the duel between the M&M boys of hydro racing, Muncey and Musson, and the return to racing of colorful Czech freedom flyer Mira Slovak added to a spectacle that already included Wild Bill Cantrell, rough and tumble Chuck Thompson, local favorite Arlo Rexford (Rex) Manchester Jr., and other lively characters.

Coeur d'Alene race officials beamed with approval at the huge field, a reversal from 1961 when a paltry half-dozen hydros showed up. Thirteen now crowded the pits, and race committee commodore Carter Crimp said Ron Musson's help had been tremendous, working in his capacity as the Western representative for the Unlimited Racing Commission. Now, Crimp worried only about where he would park all the hulls that crowded the lakeshore below Tubbs Hill.

Fans enjoyed not only the hydros but the Blue Angels and Walla Walla Skydivers, both of which performed on Saturday and Sunday along with the thunderboats.

Northwest news media tended to overstate reports of "rioting" youth in downtown Coeur d'Alene during the Diamond Cup era, and articles in 1963 said police officials discussed their "battle plans" to present a show of force sufficient to deter any hooligan activity. In 1961 Idaho national guardsmen had in fact been called out to stem the mayhem, but 1962 had been more subdued.

* * * *

Coeur d'Alene is home to a passionate group of hydroplane enthusiasts called the Hydromaniacs. Indeed, the group endures years after the Diamond Cup ended its 10-year run, and the Hydromaniacs staged August 2010-11 exhibition events with restored vintage hydros. With such passion comes a natural bias, yet a thoughtful reflection on the Coeur d'Alene "riots" written by lifelong resident Dave Walker, drawing from *Coeur d'Alene Press* news stories, deserves serious attention.

Walker wrote that there are people who were smack in the middle of the disturbances who are amused at how the "hydro riot legend" has morphed over the years. The first Diamond Cup "riot" was in 1961, reputed to be the worst because it came unexpectedly. The *Coeur d'Alene Press* archives don't include the post-race Monday edition, but the *Press* mentioned no mayhem in later days.

Police were prepared in 1962 for the two-day (Saturday and Sunday) Diamond Cup. Saturday night crowds got fired up, as reported by the *Press* on Monday. A "disturbance" took place Saturday night around 11:00 p.m. and police had it under control in about two hours. Coeur d'Alene Police Chief Reine Schmidt said, "Last year's trouble was termed a riot. I don't believe this one was but it could have turned into a riot unless it had been contained." The story added an "estimated 500 youths, more than in 1961" gathered on Sherman Avenue, but police had prepared to "get tougher quicker" and did so. After being given 10 minutes to disperse, fire trucks sprayed water and police lobbed "tear gas bombs" on the remaining crowd. Several were injured and received hospital treatment.

Altogether fewer than 50 people were taken into custody, 14 charged with failure to disperse. Remaining violations were for minors possessing alcohol, open containers, disturbing the peace, public drunkenness, drunk and disorderly, and similar charges. Most of those charged were not from Coeur d'Alene. The

Desert Hotel (Diamond Cup headquarters) and Merritt's service station had broken windows, and some police cars were dented.

The 1963 Diamond Cup was another two-day affair at a time when Idaho's legal drinking age was 19, and Sherman Avenue had no shortage of bars. Monday's *Press* proclaimed "Crowd Unruly, 80 Arrested" and estimated 1,000 "young people" were involved. Police Chief Schmidt and Sheriff John Bender agreed that the 1963 ruckus never exceeded the "unruly crowd stage." Helmeted officers used tear gas, "wielded their nightsticks several times," and fire hoses were used. Damage reports showed only two broken windows, plus "trees, benches and garbage cans were broken up" as the crowd entered City Park; 41 were charged with failure to disperse, 14 minors were charged with possession, and "several" were charged with disturbing the peace, disorderly conduct, and drunkenness.

In subsequent years the *Press* reported, "Our small riot was under control almost immediately" (1964, when 60 were taken into custody for rowdiness, most from out of town); "At no time was there any indication of major trouble," and "Disturbances were practically non-existent" (1965, when 50 were arrested for rowdiness and traffic infractions). There was no mention at all of crowd trouble in 1966. For the final Diamond Cup in 1968, Sheriff John Bender said, "What few disturbances we had were normal for the size of the crowd."

That's how Walker summarizes The Great Diamond Cup Hydroplane Riots. But legend grows, especially when cultivated.

"In 1968, a 'ticket' to the Diamond Cup was a booster button that cost $1," Walker wrote on his blog. "A lousy buck. But people would walk 100 yards and around the fence rather than shell out a couple dollars. Even at the age of 13, I thought that was a pretty lowdown cheat. How could an event be funded when you can't even get people to buy a ticket? There was no money and there were no more Diamond Cup races. Thus, an era came to an end."

* * * *

Stephen Shepperd is another longtime North Idaho resident, a hydroplane enthusiast and historian, and a member of the Hydromanics. Shepperd had a memorable encounter with the *Bardahl* team in 1963, when he was 15. His anecdote starts by referencing a photo he'd received from an agency that created a Camel cigarettes ad featuring Ron Musson.

In the brown paper envelope was the picture and a letter from the William Esty Company advertising agency of New York City. They were the advertising firm that had created the ad for R.J. Reynolds.

The Esty agency indicated that R.J. Reynolds had forwarded a copy of the letter that I had sent them, and that they were pleased to send me a print of the picture used in the ad for my scrapbook. They instructed me to not use it for any purpose other than my personal use. They also thanked me for my interest in Camel cigarettes despite the fact that I was 15 years old and a non-smoker at the time. The letter was dated Jan. 15, 1963.

When the boats gathered for the 1963 Diamond Cup in late July, I was again working in the pit area. The day that the new Miss Bardahl arrived, I went home in the afternoon and brought back my prized picture of Musson.

I found Musson in the Bardahl team trailer and showed him the print, asking if he would mind autographing the photo for me. He smiled broadly, then laughed out loud and said that he would be more than happy to sign the picture. He then summoned Crew Chief Leo Vanden Berg from the trailer to show him the picture and to suggest that he also sign it. He marveled at the fact that a teenage kid (15) from Cd'A would have a copy of a picture of himself that he himself did not even have.

Both of them signed the picture, and we discussed how I had been able to secure the picture. We also talked about some common memories that we shared about prior Diamond Cup races. It was truly a highlight of my experiences as a pit worker and race fan.

From that day forward, he acknowledged me whenever we met, and we occasionally talked. He was a genuinely nice man, and he very well could have been the most successful driver in the history of the sport had he lived beyond the 1966 President's Cup disintegration of the cabover Miss Bardahl. I have to say that that day was one of the saddest days of my life and I remember where I was when I received the news that he had been killed. I felt a friend had been taken from me.

– Stephen Shepperd, 8/18/2010

* * * *

Exide and *Thriftway* dominated early 1963 Diamond Cup headlines, each winning preliminary Saturday heats. Slovak timed his start perfectly in heat 1A and ran away from *Tahoe Miss, Eagle Electric, Tempest,* and *Fascination,* which Bob Gilliam finally had qualified as the 14th entry. *Exide* averaged 99.191 mph. Sadly, Bob Miller's aging 1953 hydro, *U-Owe-2* (formerly *Gale IV*), lost its left sponson after barely qualifying at 90.103.

As was often his habit, Muncey lagged behind the field prior to the start of heat 1B, aiming for higher top-end speed at the line. Although this backfired on him badly at the Gold Cup, the tactic delivered in spades at Coeur d'Alene. Muncey found lane one open after Norm Evans slid out in *$ Bill,* and the M&M boys sped to the front. *Thriftway* and *Bardahl*'s screaming Merlins echoed off the pine-shrouded hills surrounding the lake, their roostertails soaring skyward as the sun-baked hydros rocked on their sponsons.

The ivory and green boats finished lap one with identical speeds, 110.429 mph, whipping the crowd into a frenzy. Musson gained a slight lead entering the first turn on lap two, but Muncey cornered "as if the *Thriftway* were lassoed to the buoys," wrote *The Seattle Times*' Bud Livesley. Muncey used the inside lane to good advantage, and *Thriftway* led *Bardahl* by a boat length exiting the turn.

Musson mashed the gas pedal on the backstretch of lap two and caught Muncey, passed him, and slowly stretched his lead around the south turn until he smacked a roller near the exit pin. *Bardahl*'s tail lurched out of the water and the prop spun freely, throwing an engine rod. The metallic green and yellow boat coasted to a halt. Muncey churned ahead aboard his ivory charger and won easily at a swift 109.267 over Evans in *$ Bill* and Bob Schroeder aboard *Tempo*.

Afterward Muncey said about his start, "Heck, just because I lost the Gold Cup doesn't mean I'm going to change the way I've been driving all these years. But there's no doubt about it, the *Bardahl* is a real fast hunk of machinery." Musson nodded and said, "Both boats are fast. In fact, they're just too darn close in speed.

"Being on the outside takes about 10 miles an hour more to overtake the inside boat," Musson said. "Of course, with a boat like the *Thriftway*, I simply didn't have the speed advantage."

Notre Dame beat *Fascination* in heat 1C while *Gale V* and *Mariner Too* did not finish. Cantrell had led for

Bardahl occasionally sported a nose cowl in 1963. L to R: Scotty Freeman, Leo Vanden Berg, Gernie Freeman, Jerry Zuvich, Dax Smith.
© photo by Stearns 1963, used with permission of Troy Cain

1962 Seafair Queen Gail Reid went for a July 1963 ride in *Miss Bardahl*.
© photo by Stearns 1963, used with permission of Troy Cain

Leaving Ballard for the first 1963 race in Guntersville, Ala., with *Bardahl* hooked to the Ford C-750 truck.
© photo by Stearns 1963, used with permission of Troy Cain

Musson and Reid leave the Stan Sayres Pits dock at Lake Washington. Note guy wires now added to tail.
© photo by Stearns 1963, used with permission of Troy Cain

1963 test session, Stan Sayres Pits.
– Marg Smith photo, used with permission of Dixon Smith

Musson relaxes during race week.
© Eileen Crimmin photo 1964, used with permission of The Crimmin Collection

1963 Diamond Cup, Lake Coeur d'Alene, Idaho. L to R: *Tempo*, *Bardahl*, *Thriftway*.
© Eileen Crimmin photo 1963, used with permission of The Crimmin Collection

Karelsen-built *Miss Exide*, salvaged following her 1963 Diamond Cup crash with Mira Slovak driving.
– photo by J. Richard "Dick" Olesberg, DDS, used with permission of Dale Olesberg

Bardahl exits south turn, Diamond Cup 3-mile racecourse, 1963.
– Rich Ormbrek photo, used with permission of The Crimmin Collection

two laps but blew *Gale*'s supercharger in lap three, and *Mariner* had fizzled earlier after lap one.

Heat 2A on Sunday saw *Exide* again win wire-to-wire as Slovak made another perfect start to average 94.537 mph in beating *Tempest, Tempo, $ Bill,* and *Fascination.* Rex Manchester shut down *Eagle Electric* after three laps when the aluminum sheathing on the bottom of the hull peeled off and wrapped around the prop shaft.

The M&M boys were rematched in heat 2B, but the expected battle never materialized. *Bardahl* stopped after crossing the starting line, thanks to a faulty fuel pump. *Gale V* lost its blower in turn one, and Muncey found himself chasing Thompson and *Tahoe Miss* for nearly two laps. But the casino craft broke its two-stage blower, leaving *Notre Dame* to battle *Thriftway* until Gardner's mount busted an oil seal and died. *Thriftway* was the lone finisher at 103.686; *Fascination* did not start.

Blaming *Bardahl*'s trouble on a bad fuel pump "was bogus," said Dixon in 2012. *Bardahl* had redundant systems and never would have failed to finish because of a bad fuel pump, he said. The 1963 Diamond Cup likely was the one time that Musson shut down, Dixon recalled in a 1987 interview.

"We were in a situation where we had run out of motors, just flat run out of motors. And there wasn't time to build new motors before the next race. We launched him, he went out and drove across the starting line, and he turned it off. That was probably one of the stupider things we ever decided to do, because it turned out he could have probably motored around and done quite well, if not won, without hurting the equipment much," Dixon said in 1987. "We never ever did that again."

The final heat matched two boats tied with 800 points, *Exide* and *Thriftway*. No one really expected the Stoen brothers' untested new steed to match strides with the reigning national champion, but it did. *Exide* snatched the inside, carved out a slight lead at the start and held it through turn one before Muncey crept ahead up the backstretch and through the south turn. Muncey and Slovak finished the first lap nearly tied. Then *Exide* bounced, dipped a sponson, and disintegrated amid a massive blast of wood and spray, pitching Slovak into the water with a broken jaw, severe facial cuts, and a broken ankle. *Exide*'s shattered remains quickly sank 126 feet to the bottom of cold, clear, Lake Coeur d'Alene, where it stuck its nose – or what was left of it – into five feet of mud.

"The *Exide* was right before me one moment; the next it was gone," Warner Gardner later said. He had been running "in the slot behind Mira and *Exide*." Gardner whipped around in *Notre Dame*, shut down, and dove into the water where he had seen the red hull gurgling below the surface. He needed to swim about 20 feet to reach Slovak. "I had a heck of a time locating him but, fortunately, the water is clear and I spotted his yellow life jacket. He was unconscious when I reached him. He was bleeding badly from a gash just under his lower lip. I just tried to keep his head out of the water until the patrol boat arrived."

Slovak, 33, was rushed to Lake City Hospital where he was reported in satisfactory condition. He broke his ankle, lost two teeth, and it took 27 stitches to close the lacerations on his face.

Exide's crash meant that all Muncey had to do was finish the race to pocket enough points to win his third consecutive Diamond Cup. "I knew from the way the other drivers were talking that they were going to go out and fight for it," he said. "I didn't want any part of it since I just had to finish to win. You can't win if you don't finish."

The final heat was a dandy. Amazingly, Bob Schroeder burst into the lead with the four-seat *Tempo* for three and a half laps before one of his gas tanks emptied, causing his fuel-starved motor to cough in the corners. *Tempo* slowed, and Evans in *$ Bill* and Hickling in *Tempest* surged past, battling deck to deck until the final turn, where *Tempest* nosed ahead and won by 45 feet at 99.889 mph to *$ Bill*'s 99.741. *Tempo* hung on for third followed by *Notre Dame* and the ambling *Thriftway*. *Fascination* did not finish.

The final Diamond Cup standings showed *Thriftway* on top, *Tempest* second, *Exide* third despite its demise, *$ Bill* fourth, *Tempo* fifth, and *Notre Dame* sixth. *Bardahl* finished even lower than her 10th-place debut the previous year by "earning" 12th place with zero points. Also earning Diamond Cup goose eggs were *Gale V* and *Mariner Too*.

Certainly, no one at the time could foresee what would follow, or that what would follow was even possible: *Miss Bardahl* would finish every heat the rest of her career. She never again broke down.

That night, Seattle television viewers watched *Exide* explode on KING-5's Diamond Cup highlights show hosted by Rod Belcher, and the same film was aired on KING's "Telescope" show at 8:00 Monday morning.

Salvage crews raised *Miss Exide*'s battered hulk on Monday afternoon as downcast owners Milo and Glen Stoen pronounced it unrepairable.

"There's nothing to rebuild," Milo said. "Everything forward of the cockpit, except part of the left sponson, is gone. Even the windshield is gone – I think Mira hit that when he flew out."

For the Stoens it was an ugly repeat of the 1962 Gold Cup, where 11 months earlier their *Miss Seattle Too* had exploded, sending driver Dallas Sartz to the hospital. *Miss Exide* had been built to replace *Seattle Too*. Slovak must have felt déjà vu as well, having suffered serious injuries when he barrel-rolled *Wahoo* in the 1960 Seafair Trophy Race.

In the August 1975 *Unlimited NewsJournal*, *Exide* builder Ed Karelsen offered his opinion about what caused his new boat to crash. "It was running downhill horribly. The shaft hole was drilled in the wrong place, none of the hardware fit, so we had to put the motor farther forward than it was supposed to be. It was out of balance and they didn't have time to change it," he said.

The week after the Diamond Cup, Bill Boeing Jr. offered his rebuilt *Wahoo* for sale, with proceeds to benefit a Seattle charitable organization for the arts. "I will make a gift of the boat and all the parts to PONCHO. It's for sale, through PONCHO, for $15,000." Not a bad deal for a proven hull that had first raced at Seafair in 1956.

The hydro fleet trekked across Washington via U.S. Highway 10 to Seattle, where half a dozen of them – *Gale V, Mariner Too, Notre Dame, Tahoe Miss, Tempo,* and *$ Bill* – camped at Sand Point Naval Air Station until Monday of Seafair week, when they caravanned along Lake Washington to the Stan Sayres Memorial Pits. That week, Army engineers from Fort Lewis built a 300-foot floating span from the east shore of the pits to the official barge. Meanwhile, Mira Slovak flew into Seattle's Boeing Field via chartered plane from Coeur d'Alene, his right foot and ankle encased in a cast, and went directly to Virginia Mason Hospital to recover from his crash. Before leaving Boeing Field, Slovak told the assembled reporters of his Diamond Cup ordeal, "I was spitting teeth like Popeye."

* * * *

My brother Dave still lived at home the summer of 1963, having just graduated from Sammamish High School. It was Dave's duty to mow our lawn. I was 9, and Mom didn't want me using the gas-power lawnmower until I was 10. She'd had a mowing accident years earlier, slicing her big toe, and to her age 10 seemed like the point I'd be mature enough to safely handle that chore.

But Dave was crafty. Now, in fairness, that's probably just my sour-grapes perception. Yet I recall one summer day in 1963, he saw me eyeing him as he circled our vast front lawn with the green and red Briggs & Stratton rotary mower. When he stopped to empty the bag of clippings he unfolded his diabolical scheme.

"You know what I like to do when I mow?" Dave said. "I like to pretend I'm a hydro driver."

The mower was his hydro; its motor was loud, and he said when he cornered around the lawn, he pretended he was turning on a racecourse.

That's all it took. I envied his role. *I wanted to mow.* "Show me how!" I said, and he promptly complied.

I remember how exhilarating it was to push that mower around the yard, turning left around imaginary buoys, that loud 4-horsepower motor approximating a Rolls-Merlin in my mind. And whether it was that day or sometime later, I remember mowing when Mom pulled into the driveway in her white Ford Falcon and hustled out, asking my brother something like, why on Earth is Jon mowing the lawn? Dave said, look, Jon's doing a good job, he's obviously big enough to mow, and he likes it.

I stupidly concurred and pled with Mom to let me mow. In the end she agreed.

I don't know this for a fact, but I think that was the last time Dave mowed our Lake Hills lawn. And after I had done it two or three times the novelty wore off. It wasn't so fun anymore. Soon it became passé, and later, a chore – one that I didn't enjoy again until, as an adult, I had my own house and yard.

But Dave was right. I *was* big enough, and he'd served his time mowing that big corner lot for eight years. Besides, soon he was off to the University of Washington and lived on his own. It was time for me to inherit the helm.

Today, I continue to envy my brother. He has a really cool riding lawnmower, something I've always wanted, while I still push my old power Toro around the yard.

Chapter 9

Thriftway *passes the torch* (*or* Bardahl *steals it*)

Associated Grocers shocked the hydro world on Friday, Aug. 2, by announcing that not only would *Miss Thriftway* be retired in 1963, the boat and team would retire very soon, after the Aug. 11 Seafair Trophy Race. Contrary to public assumption, no replacement hull would be built. There would be no more *Miss Thriftway*s.

Less certain were Bill Muncey's plans. For the interim he would operate his Thriftway grocery store on south Mercer Island, "pushing prunes" as he liked to say. (On Dec. 23, 1963, Muncey would open a second store, the Roostertail Market, in Mercer Island's Shorewood Apartments complex.)

"It would be difficult for me to join another racing team at this time," Muncey, 34, said. "The word 'retire' sounds so final. It sounds as if the only thing to do next is to die. And I have no plans along that line for some time." He added that without Rhodes and the *Thriftway* crew, headed by Jack Ramsey, it would be difficult to assemble a similarly successful racing team.

The announcement came at a time when the *Miss Thriftway* team was near its zenith, having been national champs three straight years, and Muncey was the reigning *Seattle Post-Intelligencer* Man of the Year in sports. *Thriftway* had won the Gold Cup in 1961-62, and although Muncey had been out-smarted and out-driven in 1963's premier regatta, he had rebounded nicely at Coeur d'Alene to snatch his third straight Diamond Cup. Now it appeared only one battle royale remained for the persimmon and ivory charger: a Lake Washington showdown with the ascendant, mercurial Green Dragon.

Representative owner Willard Rhodes released Associated Grocers' official statement, which thanked crew chief Jack Ramsey and Muncey for their tireless time and effort and spoke of pride in the organization's success. Of the team in general the statement said, "hydroplane racing is not a two or three month effort, but a year-round project that demands the devotion of the racing team for the full 12 months. These men have given of their time, have been away from their families, consumed their vacations, and so thoroughly dedicated themselves for nine years, we feel that we cannot ask them to extend themselves further."

The team planned to take stock of its equipment and resources over the next 60 days, and for the time being neither the boat nor any of its equipment would be for sale.

Following Associated Grocers' shocking news, the sport got a needed boost Aug. 3 when Milo and Glen Stoen announced they were buying the *Wahoo* from Bill Boeing Jr. and would race it at Seafair as *Miss Exide*. The Stoens said crew chief George McKernan and team would have the boat out of mothballs and on the water within days, and that the purchase included four Rolls-Merlin engines, two gearboxes, and various accessories. The quick little Jones-designed, Staudacher-built, 28-foot hull was about to get wet for the first time since 1960.

Glen Stoen told *The Seattle Times* no driver had been named, but "my choice is Don Wilson, if he is available." Wilson was unemployed after George Simon beached his *Miss U.S.* hydros. Driver speculation also centered on Russ Schleeh, who recently had tested the Tacoma hydro *Coral Reef*, and Billy Schumacher.

Swelling with confidence following his 118.421 lap in Coeur d'Alene, Musson told *Seattle P-I* scribe John Owen he was shooting for the Seattle course record of 120.267 mph set by *Maverick* in 1958. "We're going for 120. Can we do it? We'll come awfully darn close. I know we can do 119. I think we've got just about the fastest boat around."

Interspersed with hydro news, Seattle's daily newspapers touted the nightly Aqua Follies water spectaculars at Green Lake Aqua Theater, Nordstrom's purchase of Best's Apparel, a new Wigwam discount clothing store opening in Sunset Village shopping center at Eastgate, formal signing of the nuclear test ban treaty, and Craig Breedlove setting a new world land speed record of 407.45 mph in Utah. A *Times* photo headlined "Tiger on the loose" had a caption announcing, "California invader." Streaking across the page was Harry Schneider of Palo Alto, Calif., aboard his 225-cubic-inch limited hydro named *Tiger Too*, the futuristic cabover built by Ron Jones in Shelton in 1961. Schneider won the Seafair Green Lake Regatta in record-setting time.

* * * *

As Seafair qualifying opened on Tuesday, Aug. 6, news came that *Coral Reef*'s temperamental Messerschmitt powerplant would not be ready in time for the boat to appear in Seattle. Neither would the "new" *Miss Madison*, the former *Nitrogen Too*, for lack of a rudder. But *Exide* found its man to replace Slovak, 1956 Seafair winner Col. Russ Schleeh, 44.

Ron Musson steered *Bardahl* onto Lake Washington's 3-mile course that afternoon and achieved a feat that earned surprisingly little media attention: He became just the second hydro driver in history to turn a lap at 120 mph. But while blasting around the south turn in his third lap, *Bardahl* barked loudly as she jammed a rod through the side of her Rolls-Merlin. Musson the driver became Musson the spectator, forced to watch as rival Muncey whipped around the course for three laps at a speedy 117.052 mph. Musson had turned 120.000 and 117.904 on his two completed laps.

Musson later said, "We had nine gallons of oil when I started and only three inches were left when I got back. I think that's what caused me to throw a rod."

That was *Bardahl*'s last attempt at a qualifying record during the Musson era. Taking stock of their remaining equipment, Vanden Berg and team decided it was folly to set records and qualify fastest if it hampered their chances of winning on race day. "We're down to our last two engines and we can't take a chance," Vanden Berg said. That served as another turning point for Musson, who from that day forward became known as a gamer, much like later driving greats George Henley and Jim Kropfeld, notorious sandbaggers in qualifying who showed their true speed on Sundays.

The top teams clearly tried to psych each other out as Seafair time trials continued. *Thriftway* owner Rhodes said he had instructed Muncey to go just fast enough to beat *Tahoe Miss*, which had qualified at

115.139 mph. "Bill only had to do 116, but he calculated wrong," Rhodes said with a wink, noting their 117-mph speed. "We'll have tryouts for a new driver tomorrow." For his part, Thompson said he wasn't really trying for a fast run. "I wasn't even pushing the engine."

Bob Gilliam should have earned creative thinking awards for working the system to try and pocket some extra dough. He had his *Fascination* and *Fascination I* boats in Stan Sayres Pits on Tuesday, but yanked both when officials refused to pay him $400 out-of-state tow money for each hull. Gilliam had joined the Guntersville, Ala., Yacht Club, but officials noted his hydros' Seattle registry and offered him only $200 tow money per boat.

On Thursday the ex-*Wahoo* saw its first action in three years as Schleeh circled the buoys at test laps of 107, 104, and 108 mph. Musson fired up *Bardahl* for late-afternoon laps of 115.139, 115.139, and 114.650 on flat sticky water for an average of 114.975, third best on the time-trial ladder. And a celebrity pilot, visiting NASA astronaut Gordon Cooper, who had orbited the Earth aboard *Faith 7* on May 15-16, took *Tempo* out for a spin as lakeside thermometers hit 85 degrees.

Rex Manchester averaged 105.194 for three laps aboard *Miss Eagle Electric* for new sponsor Dave Heerensperger, 27, attending only the second hydro event of his life. "I became the sponsor just by chance," he said. "I read a story in the Spokane newspaper saying that anyone who had $5,000 could take over the boat. The crew rebuilt the boat this summer, spending $3,100 of their own money and 10 weeks' time."

The "new" *Exide* became the 10th Seafair qualifier Friday by averaging 112.111 mph for three laps with new driver Schleeh at the wheel. Watching was Mira Slovak, whose name remained painted on the side of *Exide*'s red tail cowling from its *Wahoo* days. The deck retained its mahogany finish and U-101.5 number, but white lightning bolts had been added, and a checkerboard pattern graced its tailfin.

Muncey blistered the course at better than 118 for three laps on Friday but officials waved off the effort, saying Muncey failed to signal the official barge that he was starting an official qualifying run. Thompson, too, ran afoul of officials when he brought *Tahoe Miss* back to the pits after laps of 118 and 116, thinking he had completed three circuits; officials never timed his first lap, not seeing a hand signal. Bill Cantrell ran speedy laps in *Gale V*, upping his qualifying average to 114.894, including one circuit at 116.379.

Fred Alter finally got *Mariner Too* into the show on Saturday after blowing equipment all week long, averaging just under 95 mph to become the 11th and final qualifier. Bob Gilliam relented and re-entered his *Fascination*s, but qualified neither boat after the U-88 blew its supercharger to pieces while trailer-firing. Ron Musson took Leo Vanden Berg out for a Saturday test spin so the crew chief could better gauge *Bardahl*'s performance.

"It bugs me, knowing how fast this boat will go," Musson said when asked by Bill Knight of the *P-I* how he felt about being the third-fastest qualifier. Musson credited Ron Jones' pre-season sponsor rebuild for his new-found speed. "Jones started over from scratch, and he deserves plenty of credit."

Farther uplake that afternoon, Spokane's Earl Wham won the 1963 Kirkland Kup limited-class hydro race on choppy water that sank two boats. Wham drove his 266-cubic-inch *Holy Smoke* past bigger 7-litre hydros. Other Kirkland racers that day included Bill Brow, Chuck Hickling, George Henley, and a Bremerton man driving a 225-class hydro named *Gotcha*. His name: Al Villwock, the uncle of Dave Villwock, unlimited racing's winningest driver.

* * * *

Race day dawned sunny and warm with no threat of rain. From the inside out, *Bardahl, Thriftway* and *Exide* pounded across the starting line in heat 1A. *Thriftway* zoomed ahead entering the south turn and *Exide* nudged past *Bardahl* coming out of the turn, and they stayed that way until the final lap when Musson surged up the backstretch, drove deeper than *Exide* into the north turn before decelerating, squeezed inside the former *Wahoo* and outraced her to the checkered flag by exactly half a boat length to claim second. *Thriftway* averaged a record 112.500 mph for the heat, while *Bardahl* ran 110.474 to *Exide*'s 110.429. *Notre Dame* and *Tempo* followed; *Gale V* never left the dock. Earlier that morning Bill Cantrell had suffered severe stomach pain and was taken to the hospital, after which both Fred Alter and Roy Duby agreed to fill in for Cantrell. But the mahogany and lime riverboat suffered mechanical woes and never raced all day.

$ Bill blew its supercharger in the first turn of heat 1B, and without a replacement, the California craft was beached for the day. *Tahoe Miss* pressed *Miss Eagle Electric* for the lead when red flares pierced the sky and interrupted the race. Coming out of the south turn, *Mariner Too*'s engine had belched a fireball that engulfed the cockpit, and driver Fred Alter "knew it was time to push out. I rolled into the water," which prompted flares. Alter suffered minor leg and arm burns and was plucked from the water by a U.S. Coast Guard helicopter.

In the rerun, Manchester pushed *Eagle* into the lead followed by *Tahoe* and *Tempest*, but Thompson closed the gap and trailed by only four lengths ending lap one. *Tahoe* passed *Eagle* before the south turn and ran an unofficial 115-mph lap to open a 12-second lead that stretched to more than 40 seconds by the finish, where *Tahoe* won at 112.126 mph followed by *Eagle Electric* at 101.541 and *Tempest*, which turned a 112-mph final lap to nearly catch Manchester. *$ Bill* and the ineligible *Mariner Too* did not start.

Soon after heat 1B ended the sky suddenly darkened, cool gusts blew, thunder boomed, and torrents of rain fell on unprepared Seafair spectators. The violent, unforeseen storm had moved briskly northward from southern Oregon, bringing lightning that a Weather Bureau meteorologist said was "as severe as I have seen since I left Wisconsin 30 years ago." Racing was delayed as fans bolted for cover, deserting the shoreline in droves.

Jack Butler, retired KING-TV broadcast engineer who pioneered live hydro telecasts, recalled the long 1963 delay. "We did an interview with Ole and his comment was, 'We came here to race, not to #@&! around.' That went on the air. I thought KING would lose its license."

* * * *

Dad took my sister and I to the races that day on Lake Washington. Judy was home from Whitworth College in Spokane for the summer and again worked in the bakery at the nearby Lake Hills P-X supermarket. That year she procured a day-old banana cake for us to enjoy during the race, and we sampled it not long after staking out our spot on the beach north of the hydro pits early Sunday morning.

Hydro fans always call Lake Washington's lakeside viewing area "the beach," but actually it's mostly a grassy hillside that gently slopes perhaps 50 feet or so from the shoreline up to Lake Washington Boulevard.

Most of Seattle's Seafair Sundays are sunny. Yet 1963 was the second straight year of stormy skies. Gray, threatening clouds had blown in for the 1962 Gold Cup as the day progressed, and it showered. We saw *Miss Seattle Too* disintegrate spectacularly and two other boats burned, delaying heats into the early evening.

The weather was even nastier in 1963 – at around 2 p.m. lightning flashed, thunder pealed, and dark clouds drenched us. We fled the beach, and Dad left the cardboard box containing Judy's half-eaten cake on the ground alongside a chain-link trash bin, not wanting to lug it around. Then we sought shelter under the madrona trees.

Eventually the storm passed, sunshine returned, the race resumed, and having earlier abandoned our lakeside spot we roamed the beach and the boulevard. Hours later we found ourselves near our morning site ... and there, still on the ground next to the trash bin, was the soggy P-X bakery box. Judy cautiously lifted the lid. When we saw her banana cake still inside was indeed untouched, we scavenged it, remarking between giggles how surprisingly fresh it tasted.

* * * *

Exide led across the line in heat 2A, but *Tahoe* roared past in the south turn and quickly stretched its lead as the combatants spread out. Thompson clocked 113, then slowed but still won by half a lap over *Exide*, *Tempest*, *Eagle Electric*, and *Notre Dame*. Thompson averaged a speedy 110.384 for the entire heat.

Bardahl and *Thriftway* squared off again in heat 2B, and Musson cut inside Muncey to steal lane one and dashed into the lead. Muncey trailed by just two boat lengths after one lap but Musson widened his gap around the south turn. The two Seattle hydros blasted up the backstretch with roostertails jabbing high until *Thriftway*'s supercharger came unraveled and she coasted to a stop exiting the north turn. Muncey's mechanical marvel, which just the summer before had chalked up 55 consecutive heats without a failure, deigned to finish its dazzling career at the end of a tow rope. *Bardahl* roared on and averaged 108.259 to beat *Tempo*, the only other finisher.

The final heat brought *Tahoe*, *Bardahl*, *Exide*, *Eagle Electric*, *Tempest,* and *Tempo* motoring out of what *Seattle Times* sports editor Georg Meyers dubbed Quill Shaft Lagoon. Musson trailed Thompson by 100 points and several seconds in elapsed time, so *Bardahl* had to win the final with a decent cushion to win the race. Likewise, Thompson had to win or finish a close second to Musson to ensure a *Tahoe* victory.

Hickling and *Tempest* held the pole position flanked by *Bardahl*, *Exide,* and *Eagle Electric* at the start, with *Tempo* far to the outside; *Tahoe* lagged almost a roostertail behind in lane two. Six blaring fighter engines shook the ground as *Bardahl* outran the field entering the south turn, but *Exide* pounded up the backstretch and briefly nosed ahead, while *Tahoe* closed the gap on both. Harrah's heavy steed smashed into a swell approaching the north turn, and the 5-foot-7-inch, 180-pound, 51-year-old Thompson later said he was bucked out the left side of the cockpit onto the deck but never relinquished his right-hand grip on the steering wheel. He pulled himself back in and tore after the field, passing *Eagle* and *Tempest* at the end of lap one, and then set his sights on *Miss Exide*'s checkered tailfin ahead.

Bardahl pulled away and stretched its lead through the south turn on lap two as *Tahoe* gained more ground on *Exide*, until Thompson passed Schleeh on lap three entering the south turn. *Bardahl* ran lap four at 110 mph to lead *Tahoe* by 11 seconds. *Tempest* died in the north turn and *Exide* did likewise on lap five before restarting, only to be passed by *Eagle Electric* 100 yards from the finish. By then Musson and *Bardahl* had already thundered past the official barge to win the heat at 108.303 mph, several seconds ahead of Thompson in *Tahoe* followed by *Tempo*, *Eagle,* and *Exide*.

Bardahl and *Tahoe Miss* finished tied with 1,100 points, but someone in the *Bardahl* camp had miscalculated the difference in total elapsed time for both boats entering the final. *Tahoe Miss* won the $25,000 1963 Seafair Trophy Race by 6.2 seconds.

"I thought we only had to make up 7 seconds," said Musson, who in reality had trailed *Tahoe* by 17 seconds entering the final. "If I had known it was more, maybe I could have gotten a little more out of the engine … I know I could have picked up six seconds."

Zuvich said in 1988 that Ole Bardahl generally left race strategy to his crew and seldom gave direction, except in some final heats. At Seafair 1963, Ole was frustrated that the team had been unclear about total elapsed time.

"That was one thing he questioned, as if Leo had time to stop and figure it out," said Zuvich. "Well, in the heat of the battle, it's pretty hard to put down your tools and put down your propeller and get your pencil out and start figuring each boat in minutes and seconds, you know? Today, a guy could probably throw it in a computer and have it. But back then, you long-handed it, and you're dealing with 60 instead of 100 when you're counting the numbers. It makes a difference, and it takes longer. So after that, he usually would get with Ronnie or somebody else and help out."

Miss Exide took third place overall followed by *Tempo, Miss Eagle Electric,* and *Tempest.* Thompson received a ceremonial dunking in the lake from his ecstatic crew, which included Harry Volpi, Bill Newman, Everett Adams, and George Goeschl. In winning the race, the red and cream casino craft set a new 45-mile race average of 109.459 mph on storm-tossed waters, breaking the old record held by an earlier Nevada hydro, *Maverick,* which like *Tahoe* had used powerful Bill Newman-built, two-stage Allison engines.

Thompson's racing persona was that of a burly, hard-nosed, unrelenting charger. A Detroit tough guy. But friends and hydro insiders thought differently.

"He was a tough driver, but otherwise he was a pussycat," said Zuvich. "He was a teetotaler. And his wife used to sit in the car and knit."

* * * *

Miss Bardahl was the hot new darling of Seattle fans in 1963. Standing alongside Lake Washington at Seafair that year, I remember *Bardahl* elicited near-universal cheers and thumbs up, while many boos and thumbs down greeted *Miss Thiftway* as she roared by. "Muncey wins too much," several people sneered.

The next year, I was dismayed to find the tables turned. Musson drew a few boos and thumbs down at Seattle in 1964. *Bardahl* had become the dominant boat, irritating some, although hydro journalists observed that all of the *Miss Bardahl*s remained generally popular throughout their years.

* * * *

1963 started an uninterrupted string of Seafair races for hydro chronicler Craig Fjarlie, longtime *Unlimited NewsJournal* editor and Associated Press hydro stringer.

"In 1955 I was 7 years old. I'm sitting on the front porch of my house in the Shoreline area, 148th and 5th Avenue, and qualifying was going on for the 1955 Gold Cup," Craig recalled. "I was sitting there with one of my friends who lived just down the block, and this is the days when channel 5 used to break into programming to show qualifying. My mom opened the door and said, 'Kids, *Slo-mo V* flipped!'

And we both dashed inside and watched the replays of the flip. I knew what *Slo-mo V* was, I knew about hydroplanes. I don't have much recollection before that, but I knew something about the sport, and it mattered to me.

"The first time I saw one run was the next year at Seafair," he continued. "We went down to that area, basically drove across the floating bridge to Mercer Island and back, and *Miss U.S. II* was out on the course. That was the first unlimited I saw run in person. Since then, I've been to every Seafair race from 1963 to present."

* * * *

As avid as I was about *Miss Bardahl* and Ron Musson, legions of Northwest kids also idolized Bill Muncey, and they lamented his departure from the hydro scene in 1963 and mourned him after his 1981 death. Years later I became friends with one of those lifelong Muncey devotees, Bill Osborne, and as aging baby boomers we continue to playfully needle each other over who was better, *Bardahl* and Musson or *Thriftway* and Muncey. Osborne explained how he became a hydro fan from somewhat afar.

I was raised on Vashon Island, and my father was a doctor, pretty successful. He liked snow-skiing, water-skiing, and he would watch the race on Seafair Sundays, but we were never allowed to go to the races. He just felt that was a waste of time. I saw my first boat in 1955 on television, and the first boat I saw in person was Slo-mo-shun V. I saw it on display, and a week later I saw Miss Thriftway *on display, and I thought those boats were really pretty neat. We could hear the boats run from Vashon as clear as day, the roar of the Merlins and Allisons. I'd run upstairs and turn on KING-TV, and my mother and I would watch time trials live and direct from Lake Washington, with Bill O'Mara.*

My favorite boat, in the beginning, was Slo-mo-shun V. *But in 1955 it flipped, and so* Miss Thriftway *became my backup boat. It wasn't my first choice, because I saw the* V *first and got to touch it, and it was several weeks later before I got to see the* Thriftway. *And I thought both of those boats were really cool. I never liked* Slo-mo IV, *I liked the* V. *It's a number thing, I guess. My favorite number is 5, not 4. The* IV *is a beautiful boat, wonderful history and all that. But when the* V *went away,* Thriftway *became my favorite boat.*

We lived on Quartermaster Harbor, a quarter of a mile west from the KIRO Radio towers. Technically, we were on Maury Island. My nearest good friend lived eight miles from me. My mother didn't have a car, so I spent a lot of time playing by myself down on the beach, inventing games, and I'd hear the boats run.

In 1955 I met Bill Muncey. My mother had the family car, we were in Seattle, and we saw the boat on display. I almost fell out of the car! We pulled over, looked at it, and Muncey was there. It was at a Thriftway store – not his Mercer Island store, somewhere else. I thought he was the coolest person I'd ever met in my life. He bent down, picked me up and put me up on the deck of the boat. I told Bill later, "You were so nice to me, that just made me want to know more about hydros and really get into it as a kid." It's amazing, the impact that professional athletes have on kids, and Bill wanted me to be as excited about his sport as he was. And here I was, just a 7-year-old kid. He had nothing to gain by that, he just did it because he had a passion.

The first time I actually went to the races, my dad went to a party at a doctor's house on Seafair Sunday, and the first race that I watched live was the 1958 Gold Cup. I was 11. I went down to the water, and I swear that in the test run Bill Muncey waved at me as he came by the shoreline. He was waving at everybody, but my story is, he was waving to me. By that time I had already written him letters, and he had answered them, and I got on his Bob Hale Christmas card list. When the boat had wrecked in 1957 I cried, I was just heartbroken.

I wrote him a letter and said, "I hope you're feeling better and wish I could come and see you, but I live on Vashon and can't." He wrote me back a hand-written note and thanked me for my interest and concern.

* * * *

The hydro fleet motored east for the next stop on the 1963 unlimited circuit, the Indiana Governor's Cup in Madison, Ind. During pre-race testing Aug. 27 on the Detroit River, *Mariner Too* driver Marv Henrich, 33, landed in the hospital when the *Too* disintegrated and sank.

"We were having a scrub race and going about 130 to 140 mph down the backstretch," said Walt Kade, who was directly behind in *Blue Chip*. "Marv's boat hit a swell, nosedived, and when she came down disintegrated completely."

The unlimiteds were already in Madison on Thursday, Aug. 29, when Seattleites celebrated the opening of the new Evergreen Point Floating Bridge, connecting Seattle's Montlake neighborhood with Bellevue, Kirkland, and the Eastside. Governor Al Rosellini, Seattle Mayor Gordon Clinton, and other dignitaries at the ribbon-cutting immediately began touting the need for a third Lake Washington span, a toll-free companion to parallel the original U.S. 10 floating bridge.

Later that day in Madison, Musson took national high-point leader *Miss Bardahl* out for a spin on the Ohio River. On his second lap he sprinted down the front stretch, charged into the downriver turn and hit a swell. *Bardahl* dug its right sponson, lobbed Musson into the water, and flipped upside down. Musson was fished out of the river by rescue boats and taken to King's Daughters' Hospital with five cracked ribs.

Bardahl fared better, breaking only its windshield, cracking its tail, and soaking its gauges. The crew turned the boat right-side up at the dock, loaded it onto the trailer, and towed it to an empty hangar at the Madison airport for round-the-clock overnight repairs.

"The flip broke off the windshield and Ron broke some ribs," said Zuvich. "The motor was drained and started, the oil tank was drained, and a new windshield was installed. Not much damage, basically."

"He was going pretty hot when he went into the turn," said crew chief Vanden Berg. "Ron just about spun out as he turned, then as he straightened out he hit this wake and over she went. It was lucky he wasn't going any faster."

"I can't remember much about the accident," Musson said in the hospital. "I didn't see the wake, I fell in it. Then I was face up in the water about 50 feet from the boat. I can't get my breath. My chest is still sore."

At home in Seattle, an anguished Betty Musson sought details, initially getting only second-hand reports of Ron's condition.

"I get a numb feeling inside every time Ron goes out in the boat," she later told *Seattle Times* reporter Bud Livesley. "I don't kid myself that what Ron is doing isn't dangerous. But this is the kind of man I married and this is what he wants to do."

As for *Miss Bardahl*, years later Vanden Berg said, "There was no real structural damage. That boat had a tendency to take water over the top of the sponsons every once in a while. It would lean that far. That nontrip was real short. If it would've been a little taller, even 2 inches, it would have helped."

Ole Bardahl and rescue patrolmen blamed the accident on a "big cruiser" plying the Kentucky side of the river and carving a large wake, but *Madison* team manager and race official Phil Cole said he never saw any such cruiser.

Elsewhere in the Madison pits, the *Exide* team was breaking in yet another new driver. Mira Slovak wanted to race again but instead chose to maintain his flying status as a first officer with Continental Airlines, which reportedly gave Slovak an ultimatum to choose between piloting jetliners and hydroplanes. Russ Schleeh also wanted to drive in Madison but had a business commitment that kept him in Los Angeles. So the Stoen brothers turned to former *Miss Burien* and *Miss Bardahl* driver Bill Brow, 38, the "world's fastest milkman" from Burien, Wash., to helm *Miss Exide*.

"Bill Brow was a personal friend of mine," said *Exide* crewman Bob Woolms. "He was a little bit hot-headed. You didn't pull anything over on Bill Brow, because he'd nail you.

"One time he was running the *Vitamilk* on Green Lake against Doc Johnston in *Annie's Dodge*," Woolms recalled. "He was a doctor, and he was a big guy, and he came too close to Brow and washed him down. When they came into the pits, he and Brow almost started fighting, because Brow was really upset. Other than that, Brow was a good guy. He took hydroplane racing to heart, boy. I mean, that was his life. I don't have anything bad to say about Bill Brow."

The Seattle Times reported that Bill Muncey and Rex Manchester volunteered to substitute for Musson in the Governor's Cup, but at Musson's suggestion Ole quickly recruited Florida redhead Don Wilson instead. Late on Friday afternoon, the day after the flip, Wilson steered the repaired *Bardahl* back onto the river for a half-dozen test laps. Brow also put *Exide*, now bearing "U-75" on its mahogany deck, through its paces.

"Ronnie was in the hospital, and we had gone up to see him," said Zuvich. "We asked him how hard he ran the boat, and he said, 'I only pull 100 inches of manifold pressure and go 3,800 rpms.' So that's what Wilson was instructed to do."

But Vanden Berg was baffled because *Bardahl* ran slowly, despite Wilson following the prescribed rpms and manifold pressure. Told not to exceed 3,800 rpms, Wilson turned laps of 105, 105, 105. Vanden Berg said to go up to 4,000 rpms and sent him back out, and Wilson ran laps of just 108, 108, 108.

"When Wilson was driving the boat, all of a sudden we were going significantly slower," Dax recalled. "He seemed to adhere to the guidelines we gave him on rpms and manifold pressures and stuff, and I can remember telling Leo to go ask Musson in the hospital, 'If you're running the thing harder, just *tell* us, so we can tell Wilson to do it. We're not mad at you.'

"Musson had a problem of not telling the crew how hard he ran the engine – either that or he just chose to ignore all the instruments in the cockpit," said Dax. "I think it was a combination of the two. We had been on his ass on a fairly regular basis about breaking motors, and he broke a fair amount of equipment. And of course, when you're building motors and he's breaking them faster than you can build them, you get a little upset. When you take two engines apart and one is obviously garbage inside and the other one is still pretty good, and the driver says he ran them both at the same rpm, you know that can't be. What I think we were trying to tell him was, 'OK, you broke it, fine; just tell us how hard you were running.'"

Zuvich recalled, "That night we went back to the hospital and told Ronnie what happened. I told him, 'We're not using oil and we're not using much fuel.' Ronnie says, 'Well, maybe it's 4,100 rpms, and maybe it's 110 inches (of pressure).' So we tried that the next morning, still went slow, and one thing leads to

Start of 1963 Seafair heat 1A, L to R: *Exide*, *Thriftway*, *Bardahl*. Muncey won at a heat-record 112.500 mph.
– Richard Hall photo, used with his permission

Col. Russ Schleeh driving the replacement *Exide*, formerly *Miss Wahoo*, Seafair 1963.
– Richard Hall photo, used with his permission

Ron Musson congratulates *Tahoe Miss* driver Chuck Thompson, right, on winning Seafair in 1963.
– used with permission of Sandy Ross

Musson broke several ribs, but *Bardahl* suffered only a lost windshield and cracked tail when it flipped qualifying for the 1963 Governor's Cup.
– photographer unknown, from the Leo Vanden Berg collection

Team *Bardahl* at Lake Tahoe, 1963, L to R: Ole Bardahl, Musson, Vanden Berg, Zuvich, Scotty Freeman, Gernie Freeman, Dax. Note the quick-change air trap below Dax.
– Marg Smith photo, used with permission of Dixon Smith

Vashon Unlimiteds' replica of the 1955 *Miss Thriftway*. The real one disintegrated in the 1957 Governor's Cup at Madison, Ind.
© Jon Osterberg photo 2007

another. 'Maybe I turn 4,200 rpms.' He kept going up like that."

Wild Bill Cantrell won heat 1A on Saturday in *Gale V* at an average of 104.874 mph over *Blue Chip*, the "new" *Miss Madison* (formerly *Nitrogen Too*) with rookie driver George "Buddy" Byers, and Indy 500 driver Eddie Sachs aboard *Such Crust; Tempo* did not finish. In heat 1B, Wilson drove *Bardahl* past a fading *Exide* on the last lap to win at 102.681 with *Miss Michigan* third; *Notre Dame* and *Tahoe Miss* did not finish.

"It handles differently and I'm still having a little trouble going through the corners," Wilson said of his new ride. "Ron is giving me lots of help."

"Bill Cantrell got really mad at us because Donny Wilson couldn't get the boat to turn like he wanted and damn near put Cantrell up on the Kentucky beach," Zuvich recalled.

Despite the heat win, Vanden Berg remained dissatisfied with *Bardahl*'s performance, and the team drove to King's Daughters' Hospital for yet another visit with Musson.

"Finally, Saturday afternoon Ronnie says, 'Well, maybe I run 4,400, 4,500, and pull 120 inches,'" Zuvich said. "And all of a sudden the boat was running within a mile an hour of what Ronnie ran. And that's where we left it. But Ronnie wouldn't admit to all of it at one time. We had to squeeze it out of him."

So the truth was out. Musson had fibbed about how hard he drove *Miss Bardahl* the entire time.

"I knew it; Donny Wilson proved it," Vanden Berg recalled. "That's where that '*Bardahl* bark' came from, that crackle that it got after a certain rpm. Musson ran it more than he said he did. We learned a lot about Ron Musson through Donny Wilson. We had a 'de-liar,' the camera and Donny Wilson.

"We had a photo recorder in the back," Vanden Berg explained. "But Musson never turned the switch on – 'Oh, I forgot.' One time we set it up and told him, 'Don't forget to turn on the photo recorder.' But we'd already turned it on when he left the pits; I'd reached back inside and flipped the switch. And we learned then."

Vanden Berg suspects Musson 'forgot,' fearing that the team would get angry at him for running the equipment so hard.

"You know, 4,000 used to be the magic number of maximum rpms at 100 inches," said Zuvich in 1988. "When you get above 4,000, you know it because the oil system tries to purge itself. The engine starts breathing so bad, and we used to have the old system – remember all the oil on the side of the boats when they ran years and years ago? That was because of blow-by; it happens above 4,000. But we weren't blowing oil this time. We used to come in and have to squeegee the boat off because it was just dripping with oil.

"So Wilson had to turn 4,500 rpms before he finally matched Musson's speeds. Ronnie was turning 4,400, and 120 inches. But he wouldn't let us know until the end," Zuvich said, laughing.

When racing resumed Sunday morning, *Notre Dame* pilot Warner Gardner stepped into a new life chapter: The previous day had been his last in the U.S. Air Force after 25 years. And Buddy Byers was eager to further explore his own brave new world, unlimited racing, although the term "rookie" hardly seemed appropriate for the 1961 7-litre national champion and mile straightaway record-holder in the largest limited-hydro class.

Gale V led wire-to-wire in heat 2A and averaged 108.346 mph to beat *Bardahl* and Wilson, who clocked 101.963. *Blue Chip, Notre Dame,* and *Such Crust* followed. In 2B, Brow got a bad start but stood on the pedal and scooted past *Tahoe Miss* in the downriver turn on lap four to win at 108.100. *Tahoe* took second at 106.487, then *Madison* and *Tempo*; *Miss Michigan* did not start.

Five boats earned a spot in the final heat and charged down the 3-mile course, under the Madison-Milton bridge. Brow and Cantrell hit the starting line first but Wilson powered *Bardahl* into the lead briefly in the first turn. *Exide* reclaimed the lead and won the heat, finishing 12 seconds ahead of *Bardahl* at a quick 110.974-mph average for the 15 miles. *Bardahl* averaged 108.281 followed by *Gale V* at 107.441 and *Blue Chip* at 99.282. *Miss Madison* blew its motor and did not finish.

Brow earned accolades for his first unlimited-class win, which set a new 45-mile Governor's Cup race record of 107.281 mph. *Gale V* claimed second overall with 1,025 points, and *Bardahl* took third with 1,000 but retained the national-points lead with two 1963 races remaining.

"The boat is yours, Bill. You did a real fine job," former *Exide* pilot Mira Slovak told Brow. Owners Glen and Milo Stoen removed "substitute" from Brow's driving title and announced he had earned the privilege to helm *Miss Exide* for the rest of the season. Brow praised his new ride, saying *Exide* handled similarly to his *Miss Vitamilk* 7-litre.

"*Exide* has more weight, of course," Brow said. "But otherwise, it handles virtually the same. The *Exide* is an ideal boat for a course such as this. The corners are a bit tight for these big boats, but they put a good boat in the water under me today."

For *Such Crust* driver Eddie Sachs, it was his first and last time competing in a hydroplane race. The following year he died in a fiery crash racing at the Indy 500.

The *Bardahl* team pondered its state of affairs. The crew liked Wilson's experience and professionalism, and he communicated well in reporting boat performance and instrument readings. Yet something seemed to be missing.

"I still, to this day, don't know whether we went slower because we didn't tell Don Wilson to push on the pedal hard enough, or whether Musson was just that much better of a driver," Dax said. "There was a lot of gnashing of teeth over that because, you know, we were still naive enough to think that a driver's a driver: You can swap those guys and it'll go just as fast. Musson probably made the difference in going faster, and Wilson probably wasn't pushing on the pedal quite as hard.

"We had engines that Musson essentially destroyed in one heat of racing," he said. "But we also won. So, I'm not saying that's *bad* if that's what it takes to get the job done. Just *tell us* so we know. We need to know what we're working with."

After Musson finally fessed up, the crew had a better sense of its situation.

* * * *

Midway through *Bardahl*'s 1963 breakout season, attention shifted to Seattle's other big-time sport, Husky football. Coach Jim Owens fielded a strong University of Washington team that went 6-4 and later played the Dick Butkus-led Illinois Fighting Illini in the 1964 Rose Bowl. KING-TV sports anchor and hydro broadcaster Rod Belcher called the radio play-by-play that year (altogether, he did so from 1960-65) on KING Radio 1090, and Husky fans grimaced during his Sept. 3 sportscast as he described star fullback

Junior Coffey's season-ending foot injury suffered in a preseason drill the previous day.

Coffey's injury had a silver lining, though. Seattle artists The Young Men recorded a fun parody of the Coasters' 1959 hit "Charlie Brown," titling their adaption "First Downing Charlie Browning." The lyrics praised backup UW fullback Charlie Browning and teammates like quarterback Bill Douglas and end Jake Kupp. The song got constant local airplay.

Washington jumped out to a quick 7-0 lead in Pasadena and looked to be in control until quarterback Douglas broke his leg. Illinois and its star linebacker Dick Butkus came back to win, 17-7, and the Huskies didn't play in another Rose Bowl for 14 years, when Warren Moon led them past Michigan in the 1978 classic.

I turned out for football in late summer 1970 at Sammamish High School, until a group of us foolishly quit the team rather than conform to coach John Stupey's rigid (and unfair, we whined) rule requiring short hair. Stupey had been the Huskies' center on the 1964 Rose Bowl team, and he sometimes joked that "Butkus kicked my butt."

* * * *

The President's Cup in Washington, D.C., was a two-day affair held two weeks after the Madison race. Ten boats showed up to vie for the honor of accepting the first-place trophy from President John F. Kennedy. Hydro jockeys circled a 3-mile course laid out directly below the takeoff runways for National Airport. Musson, unable to drive, was on hand to give substitute driver Wilson advice.

The Seattle Times' Washington Bureau writer Bill Prochnau wrote of the "proud but polluted Potomac River," and true to form, racers found the waterway littered with debris on Friday, preventing qualifying runs.

Washington state Senators Henry M. Jackson and Warren G. Magnuson attended a small luncheon for the *Bardahl* and *Exide* teams and had their picture taken with the hydros, which were tilted on display in front of the U.S. capitol building.

Cantrell steered *Gale V* to an easy win under cool, overcast skies in heat 1A at 104.610 mph to beat *Notre Dame, Tempo,* and *Madison. St. Regis*, the only Washington, D.C.-based hydro in the fleet, did not start. Heat 1B brought the hot dogs onto the river. *Tahoe Miss* led at the start but blew its gearbox in the first turn and died. *Exide* and *Bardahl* staged a close duel, with Brow winning by 200 yards over Wilson, 108.695 mph to 107.569. Judges later ruled that Wilson had cut inside the exit buoy just before the dash to the starting line, and *Bardahl* was disqualified. *Miss Michigan* took third but was awarded second following *Bardahl*'s disqualification. *Blue Chip* conked in lap three.

Initially, the judges had ruled Wilson's start legal. "I don't know if I made it," Wilson said of his infraction, "but I didn't endanger anybody and I didn't ruin anybody's start." In reversing their decision, the judges rescinded *Bardahl*'s 300 points earned for the heat.

Rain fell shortly before the start of Sunday's action and refused to let up. After four hours of deliberation, officials finally canceled the rest of the race and declared *Exide* – tied with *Gale V* at 400 points each – the winner based on elapsed time. *Notre Dame* took third based on elapsed time with *Miss Michigan* fourth, *Tempo* fifth, and *Madison* sixth.

By virtue of her Saturday disqualification, *Bardahl* earned zero points for the weekend and fell two points behind *Exide* in the national points race, 1,627 two 1,625. However, *Exide*'s total included points earned by Slovak in the previous hull, which rival camps contended should be counted separately. In the driver standings, Bill Cantrell moved into a first-place tie with inactive Ron Musson, both men totaling 5,100 points.

Soon the APBA's legal counsel, W. A. Smith of New York, ruled the points scored by both *Exide* hulls would be tallied separately. This returned *Bardahl* to the top of the national standings with 1,575 points to *Gale V*'s 1,450, *Tahoe*'s 1,218, and *Exide*'s 1,175. The season finale at Lake Tahoe would decide the National Championship.

First, *Miss Bardahl* faced a different challenge. The rough Potomac had pounded her into submission, leaving an ugly bulge above *Bardahl*'s right sponson where a broken frame had lifted the deck. The team towed the boat 145 miles to renowned boatbuilder Henry Lauterbach's shop in Portsmouth, Virginia, for repairs that were done rather crudely, but effectively.

"I remember we had to cut holes on both sides of the frame – this is after the race," Zuvich said. "The battens were all blown up. We went to Lauterbach's for a fix one day, put the boat underneath this shop building. We put a big jack at the top of the roof of the building, and we jacked the frame back down, put some angles and more bolts in it, never really pulling it apart because we didn't have time. And the boat didn't mind it at all; it went right back to running again. So that boat, to me, never had a down time.

"That's the only time I've been to Virginia Beach," he added. "They had a restaurant with great pies, and Leo was a pie eater, and I'm pretty sure that was with Leo. He liked his desserts."

* * * *

Musson was glum as the late-September Harrah's Tahoe Regatta approached.

"I'm going to have another checkup Monday, but right now it doesn't look like I'll be able to drive this weekend at Tahoe," the sore-ribbed driver said. "I can't use my right arm without a stabbing pain in my back. I'm going to be in that boat if I possibly can. But Don Wilson will be on hand in case I can't make it."

By Sept. 25, eight boats rested in the Lake Tahoe pits while mechanics struggled to adjust their Allisons and Rolls-Merlins to the 6,225-foot altitude. The *Bardahl* crew made savvy carburetor adjustments to maintain power, and they also brought their quick-change air traps that could be mounted to the afterplane, behind the sponsons, to provide more lift in the thin air.

"We could bolt them on and take them off in nothing flat," said Vanden Berg of the air traps. "We had all sizes. Quarter-inch aluminum plates, unpainted, polished a little bit. From race site to race site, with different water conditions, or wind, we'd change them."

On Thursday Chuck Thompson ran the fastest average speed of 107.641 mph for three laps around the 3-mile oval near Lake Tahoe's south shore. *Exide* averaged 104.516 with a fast lap of just under 110. *Eagle Electric* also qualified, at 105.7 mph. Sore-ribbed Musson took a few runs in the Green Dragon, but lingering chest pain bothered him too much in the corners, and he reluctantly conceded that *Bardahl*'s best chances resided with Wilson.

"Sure, I'm disappointed," Musson said. "The boat is running real good and Don will give it a good drive. But I'm not ready. It bothered me when I turned and the water was smooth. You're thrown against the side of the boat on the turns and my ribs are still tender. In the race I might dig into a big swell. I'm not sure I could handle the boat."

Brow upped his three-lap average to 112.578 mph on Friday with a fast circuit of 113.208; Wilson ran laps of 110, 110, and 111; and *$ Bill* and new driver Billy Schumacher turned 103. The 11-boat field was set.

Wild Bill Cantrell sewed up the 1963 driving title with a heat 1A victory at 103.607 mph, followed closely by *Eagle Electric* and Manchester at 103.250, *Madison* and Byers, *Tempo* and Schroeder, and *Fascination 1* with Bob Miller. *$ Bill* and Schumacher conked out on the first lap.

Wilson throttled *Bardahl* home first in heat 1B at 106.508 mph, with *Exide* and Brow a distant second at 101.656, then *Tahoe* and Thompson ahead of *Notre Dame* with Gardner. *Fascination* and Bob Gilliam did not finish.

Exide ran strong in taking heat 2A at 105.592 followed by *Tahoe Miss* and *Tempo*, while *Gale V*, though it finished second, was disqualified for hitting a buoy. Wilson and *Bardahl* bounced over the whitecaps and roared far to the front in heat 2B ahead of *Eagle, Madison,* and *Notre Dame* before officials stopped the race on lap three because of strong winds. The boats returned to the pits, where points from heat 2A stood to be voided if the B section could not be rerun and completed.

Officials waited more than two hours for winds to subside, but when gusts of 40 mph persisted, they called it a race. Because she had the fastest elapsed time of the truncated event, *Miss Bardahl* claimed her second straight Tahoe Regatta, won her third race of the year, and earned the National High Point championship for 1963. *Gale V* took second in the race and the national standings, and *Eagle Electric* clinched third for the race. Final national point standings showed *Bardahl* on top followed by *Gale V, Tahoe Miss, Miss Exide, Notre Dame, Tempo, Miss Thriftway, $ Bill, Miss Eagle Electric, Tempest, Miss Madison,* and nine others.

Ole Bardahl praised his relief driver. "That Wilson sure knows what he's doing, and he goes out to win," he said.

"When Musson got hurt and Wilson drove the *Bardahl* for a couple of races, I remember he was always talked about in very well-respected terms," said Skip Schott. "He got a lot out of the boat."

Hydro racing earned a key victory off the water in October when United States tax-court judge Howard A. Dawson ruled that hydroplane racing operation expense could be considered an advertising deduction. Dawson affirmed George Simon's assertion that he should be allowed tax deductions for $105,000 in costs to run *Miss U.S. 1* as an advertising vehicle for his United States Equipment Company. Washington Sen. Warren Magnuson applauded the ruling, which came after several previous tax claims had been disallowed for hydro owners Stan Sayres, Joe Schoenith, and Ole Bardahl.

In subsequent years, unlimited hydroplane racing would lose even more of its amateur-sportsman flavor and adopt a commercial mindset. The change wasn't immediately evident, but eventually colorful homespun monikers would give way to corporate titles. The "*Miss*" personal title nearly vanished. Names like *Quicksilver, Adios, Breathless, My Gypsy,* and *Maverick* gave way to floating billboards even more extreme than *Miss Thriftway, Miss Bardahl,* and *Miss Exide*: Harrah's *Tahoe Miss* became *Harrah's Club*, community-owned *Miss Madison* turned into *Rich Plan Food Service*, Bill Muncey drove boats called *Myr Sheet Metal* and *Atlas Van Lines*, and in 1973 owner Bob Fendler campaigned a boat named *Lincoln Thrift & Loan Association's 7¼% Special*.

* * * *

After the 1963 season Bill Muncey offered to help owner Shirley Mendelson McDonald improve her stock-Allison-powered *Notre Dame,* but only if she brought the boat from Detroit to Seattle. On Dec. 10, 1963, Muncey took *Notre Dame* out from Jett's Marina for a Lake Washington test run. But a fuel line worked loose, the bilge filled with gasoline, and the boat caught fire and burned to the waterline. Muncey escaped.

"I was accused of doing it on purpose to get Mrs. McDonald to buy *Thriftway*, so I could race her again," he said.

Rather than rebuild and convert the drop-sponson hull to Rolls power, McDonald bought a new, already-built hull from Les Staudacher on Dec. 19, and Muncey agreed to drive if the team were based in Seattle. So a new Shamrock Lady joined the Seattle hydro fleet.

* * * *

In my fourth-grade year my friend Mikey and I landed our first jobs. The local P-X supermarket was our hangout, and we often loitered in its two-man barber shop staffed by the adults who cut our hair, Dallas and Jonas. This was an old-school shop, not a hair salon – spinning barber pole, vinyl chairs, wall posters depicting your choice of hair styles, and the barbers wore white hip-length polyester smocks. Not a hair dryer or conditioner in sight, but plenty of Vitalis and Butch Wax.

One day Dallas must have decided that if Mikey and I insisted on hanging around, he should put us to work. So he offered us jobs: sweeping hair off the floor and shining customers' shoes. Sweeping was easy, but Dallas held a narrow view of how shoes should be shined. So he trained us.

Speed was important, because in those days of crew cuts and flattops and "Ivy League" trims (illustrated on the wall poster), buzzing hair with electric clippers didn't take long. Dallas taught us to tuck buffing rags into customers' shoes to protect their socks, then dip our bare fingers directly into the Kiwi shoe-polish tins. We'd smooth the polish around the shoes, wipe off our fingers, let the polish dry for a couple of minutes, then brush vigorously. Last, we'd buff with flannel towels to coax a fine shine.

I don't recall if customers tipped us for the shines or if they simply paid Dallas and Jonas. But I do remember we earned 50¢ an hour for our work.

Dallas and Jonas were a couple of hounds. They'd snicker with each other about the prominent attributes of ladies passing by, and they always kept a *Playboy* or *Saga* magazine stashed under the cash register. When they'd go on break to get coffee at the snack bar, Mikey and I peeked at their magazines. One time they caught us and got cross, making us feel like we'd done something dirty. But why wasn't it dirty for them?

That job lasted just two or three weeks because Mom hated the way the shoe polish stained my fingers and dried under my nails, so she made me quit. Perhaps she also sensed the barbers were hounds!

Eventually Dallas and Jonas gave way to two barbers named Wayne and Larry who cut my hair until ninth grade. At that time my good friend and neighbor Rick claimed he'd watched his sister, a hair dresser, cut hair enough that he could do it himself. So Mom would give me $3.50 for a haircut from Wayne or Larry, but instead, I'd trot up to see Rick, who truly was surprisingly adept with scissors and thinning shears, and he'd cut my hair for free. Then I'd take Mom's money to Valu-Mart and buy an LP record for $3.33.

Years later I confessed this to Mom, who deemed it more the behavior of a rascal than a delinquent. After all, I *did* come home with my hair cut. I suspect she even might have secretly admired my scheme a tiny bit on account of her own ultra-frugal nature.

Chapter 10

Dollars and sense

Because of its success, many people assumed the *Bardahl* team was lavishly funded, like Bernie Little's *Budweiser* teams of the late 1960s and beyond. That wasn't the case. Though the boat was operated with ample funds to make it a consistent winner, the *Bardahl* team budget likely didn't even rank in the top three at the time.

"We didn't ever spend money like *Tahoe Miss* on gee-whiz programs," said Dixon. "I'm reasonably certain Harrah's *Tahoe* people spent a lot more money. I'm sure the *Gale* people spent a lot more money. Look at the number of people they had working full time, the amount of stuff they built – of course, they were running two, three boats sometimes. But some of their experiments were not cheap."

"*Tahoe*'s budget was like *Budweiser* today," Vanden Berg said in 1989. "*Bardahl* might have been a little above average. But we didn't get to chrome everything. Ole was pretty good, but he still didn't want to *blow* money. Our annual budget was $55,000 for the whole year, except the year we ran the cabover it was $85,000. That was including the boat. I earned a salary of $800 per month the last two years."

Ole always made enough money available to get the job done, according to Dixon. That can be a real problem on some boats where the team doesn't get enough money, or it doesn't get enough money when it's needed – during the summer there's lots of money, but in the winter there's little.

"That's not the way to run a race boat," Dixon said. "I think if Leo would have gone to Ole and said, 'Look, we feel that we really need to spend this many dollars on getting forged pistons,' for instance, we probably would have got them. We weren't hurting for bucks."

Roger Kruse recalled there was always enough money to meet the needs and do a job correctly.

"Money wasn't a problem – if you needed to fix the truck, you fix the truck," he said. "They didn't say we can't afford to put brakes on it this week, we'll put them on next week. There was none of that. We got the trucks ready to roll, and we had very few breakdowns on the road."

David Smith, who joined the team in 1964 and remained through 1968 – the year the fifth *Bardahl* hull was dubbed the Checkerboard Comet – believes a few teams spent more money.

"We were good, not great," he recalled. "And great was *Tahoe*. I think sometimes *Gale* spent a little more than we did. Bernie and *Budweiser* didn't, because he was on a shoestring back then, running used equipment. He didn't have the big Anheuser-Busch kahunas yet. *Notre Dame* was in there; Shirley spent a lot of money with awful results. The year I worked with them in 1969, we spent more money than we ever did on the *Bardahl*, and I think we got second place almost every time. Around 1965, *Notre Dame* was buying brand new stuff, brand new engines. They just spent money in the wrong ways with the wrong people. Winning races is all about people.

"We actually got paid pretty well," David said of *Bardahl*. "When the *Exide* was running, they went through a lot of money, too, because they were doing experimental stuff and they had to pay their experienced guys."

The experienced guys David competed against in other camps enjoyed needling the young *Bardahl* crew members, particularly when the 1967-69 *Bardahl* was run by what the media dubbed the "Teeny-Bopper Crew." David recalled that most 1950s-'60s hydro mechanics were middle-age men who had worked on Allisons and Rolls-Royce Merlins during World War II.

"If you hadn't fought in the war, they thought you couldn't be a crew member, because you wouldn't know how to work on an engine from World War II. They'd ask, 'Were you in the war?' and we'd say, 'Of course not.' 'Well, then, you can't do this.' And so we loved rubbing it in whenever we won. 'We weren't in World War II, but we still beat you guys!'"

Skip Schott didn't join the *Bardahl* team until post-season 1964, but as a *Miss Spokane* mechanic he had been long familiar with his Ballard-based rivals.

"I know that *Bardahl* got a hell of a bang for their buck," said Schott, who was a Bardahl Chemical Corporation employee for a year. "Back then it was cheap to produce a real good race engine. You could buy, in a sealed crate, a brand new dash 9 Merlin for a thousand bucks, delivered. You could buy engines that had 300-500 hours on them for less than a dollar an hour. We bought five of them in Spokane for two thousand bucks, delivered.

"When I was with *Bardahl* we also did a lot of stuff in-house that other teams would send out," he said. "I think at that time, Shirley and *Notre Dame* were spending big bucks. And the *Gales* always spent a ton of money. Harrah's – those *Tahoe* guys got real payroll wages, medical benefits, retirement."

Tahoe Miss crew chief Everett Adams said in 1965, "We operate with five full-time crewmen."

Echoing his brother's assessment of *Notre Dame*, Dixon noted a missing correlation between big budgets and race wins with the mahogany and lime boats from Detroit.

"The *Gales* didn't run real well a lot of the time, so people didn't think they spent a lot of money," said Dixon. "They did. They spent a *bunch* of money, and they tried some incredible things. Some of the stuff should have done very, very well, and somewhere between the initial idea and the implementation, it got screwed up. They just could never get it all together. They had an electronic fuel injection in the boat before most people even knew that such a thing existed. And it *worked*. It worked very well."

Dixon believes that if Ole Bardahl had increased his 1964 budget by $50,000 to make the Green Dragon go faster, the team might not have known how to spend it anyway.

"We weren't smart enough at that point to do anything more than we did," he said. "Maybe we would have hired two more guys to make our jobs easier. That wouldn't have made the boat go faster, though."

By post-season 1963, *Bardahl*'s core crew was primarily three people – Vanden Berg, Zuvich, and Dixon, with Zuvich the only full-time employee – compared with *Tahoe* and *Gale*, which seemingly employed armies of workers. And *Bardahl*'s offseason work was volunteer, aside from meals at what the crew called "The Tides."

The *Bardahl* team's offseason routine was consistent for years: Tuesday night and Thursday nights, Vanden

Berg and the guys worked from 4 or 5 p.m. until 10 p.m.; on Saturdays they started at 9 a.m. and worked until 6 p.m. As racing season drew near they worked whatever hours were necessary – four or five evenings, Saturdays and Sundays.

"As best I can remember, we were not paid for winter work, the Tuesday night-Thursday night-Saturday work," said Dixon. "On Tuesday and Thursday nights, Bardahl bought us dinner, and on Saturday a lunch. We usually had dinner at the Golden Tides. It's a nice place, and that was part of the deal. Ole bought us dinner, and we worked for free on the raceboat. Saturdays, we'd get burgers or something, and Bardahl would pick it up. But we weren't specifically paid in the winter. Jerry was paid his normal monthly salary, but the Tuesday-Thursday-Saturday routine was free. He did that on his own.

"The thing that probably kept it all glued together was the stability of Leo, and everybody was interested in winning," Dixon added. "We weren't there to make money, we were there to win boat races. Had we been able to afford it and not starve to death, we all probably would have done it for free."

Dixon recalled being paid per diem while on the road in the summers, and the crew got 2½ percent of the prize money. "I made enough money in the summer to pay my way through the next year of college and save a few bucks."

* * * *

No person will make a great business who wants to do it all himself or get all the credit. — Andrew Carnegie

The best executive is the one who has sense enough to pick good men to do what he wants done, and self-restraint enough to keep from meddling with them while they do it.
— Theodore Roosevelt

Ole Bardahl struck a nice balance. He provided his team with the resources it needed to win while staying an arm's length away and trusting his guys to do their jobs without overbearing direction. Some hydro owners – successful or not – have been seen as hands-on pests by critics. The most successful owner in hydroplane history, Bernie Little, often accompanied his *Budweiser* drivers down the dock before heats and instructed them which lane to take, or ordered a crew chief to pull a motor that didn't "sound right" to his ear.

Dave Heerensperger, who racked up 25 career wins with his *Pay 'n Pak* and *Eagle Electric* hydros between 1968 and 1982, often was eager to lend a hand.

"When you're really thrashing, and you really had to get something done, who was there to help you? Heerensperger – one of the world's worst mechanics," said Dixon, chuckling. "But his intentions were good. Great guy. *Super* guy, and I'd work anywhere for him.

"I can remember at one point when my brother and I were working on the *Pay 'n Pak*, and we're just really thrashing. Heerensperger comes up to my brother and says, 'What can I do to help?' My brother says, 'Get out of here and let us do it!' Heerensperger says, 'Okay,' and off he goes."

Ole interacted with the team mostly through Vanden Berg. After Musson moved to Seattle from Akron on 1962 and added Bardahl Public Relations Director to his job description, Ole sometimes dealt directly with Musson on team affairs. But Ole understood about delegating authority and responsibility, and he trusted Vanden Berg, and Ole gave him a fairly free hand to run the race boat.

"I'm sure that Ole gave Musson some guidance at one point or another," Dixon said. "Ole was not a divorced-from-the-boat owner. He was not an absentee owner. But he was a good owner and didn't muck with the crew. He'd come out and chit-chat with you and ask you how things were going, but he didn't get into personalities and policies at our level. He stayed out of our hair."

Vanden Berg said Ole often visited the boat shop and asked if he needed anything, and if he really did, he got it. At race sites, Ole did not dictate strategy or tell Musson which lane to take in a given heat.

"He let us work out our own strategy," said Vanden Berg. "We'd work it out with the driver. The only question he always asked was, 'Vy didn't vee vin?' After we won, he didn't give a hoop. But why didn't we win – he always wanted to know. He always asked for an honest answer, and I always gave him the honest answer where maybe some of the earlier guys didn't. And it always satisfied him."

Zuvich's perspective of Ole was broadened by his dual role as full-time company employee and *Miss Bardahl* mechanic.

"Ole was involved, but never to the point to tell you how to run the boat," recalled Zuvich in 1988. "He was a good sounding board. You could talk to him. A lot of people are scared of Mr. Bardahl. He just calls a shot a shot, that's all. You don't pull the wool over his eyes. If you do, he'll tell you. And I've seen people do it, and I've seen them get mad because he said, 'You're a son of a gun.' Well, goddang it, you were! As far as I'm concerned, the man is as strong as a rock. If he couldn't afford something or didn't want to spend the money on it, he didn't hem or haw and pussyfoot around with you, he just said 'no.'"

* * * *

America endured a lingering nightmare that began Nov. 22, 1963, with President John F. Kennedy's assassination in Dallas, Texas. Seattle and the nation grieved as the ugly saga unfolded: the horrific mayhem at Dealey Plaza, Jackie Kennedy's blood-stained pink suit, JFK's death at Parkland Hospital, Lee Harvey Oswald murdering police officer J.D. Tippit, Jack Ruby gunning down Oswald two days later on network television, little John-John Kennedy saluting his dad's horse-drawn hearse during the funeral procession.

I was in Mrs. Bass' fourth-grade classroom at Lake Hills Elementary on Friday morning, Nov. 22, when the wood-cabinet intercom speaker above the black chalkboard crackled to life. The school office told us President Kennedy had been shot in a motorcade in Dallas. Mrs. Bass quickly turned the shocking news into a teaching moment and asked, "Can anyone explain what a motorcade is?" Someone answered, and the image my mind conjured up was actually that of a sedan chair, or what ancient Romans called a lectica. An absurd thought, even for a 9-year-old.

Not long after, the voice of our principal, Mr. Feaster, came over the intercom. His voiced broke with emotion before he aborted his announcement, and we heard him say off-mic, "I'm sorry, I can't…." School secretary Maybelle Weatherhead took over and impassively completed the message, forever seared into my memory: "To complete Mr. Feaster's announcement, President Kennedy has died from gunshot wounds he received today in Dallas."

On Sunday, Jack Ruby shot and killed Oswald at 9:21 a.m. Seattle time. We heard about it on the AM radio in Mom's Ford Falcon on the way to Bellevue Presbyterian Church. Mom was disturbed and voiced grave concern, not mere cliché, by lamenting, "What's this world coming to?"

Chapter 11

It's about corners, not chutes

The new year began with America still in mourning. A fresh, welcome distraction arrived Feb. 7, 1964, when an unlikely quartet of shaggy-banged Brits named John, Paul, George, and Ringo disembarked their Pan Am Boeing 707 onto the tarmac at New York's newly renamed JFK Airport. Two days later Beatlemania swept America when the young rockers performed on *The Ed Sullivan Show* before a record 73 million television viewers. The British Invasion was underway, and the Beatles led the assault.

Ron Musson spent the winter recovering from his cracked ribs. Happily, his race boat had blossomed magnificently in 1963, and the team needed only to strengthen its arsenal of equipment for 1964.

Unlike some teams that strived for high chute speed, the *Bardahl* team believed races were won in the corners and chose to excel at turning and accelerating. Because the Green Dragon typically ran at the front of the pack, observers assumed incorrectly it was very fast on the straightaways.

"No way," said Vanden Berg. "That boat wasn't fast in the straights. The best we ever made was 155, 160. It fooled you! That's a *corner* boat. I remember *Tahoe Miss* used to beat us on the straightaway all the time, and we'd pass him on the turns. *Tahoe* could go 180, but it couldn't turn.

"That's where we won all the races, in the turns," he said. "We ran nine-second turns where everybody else ran 11. Other boats rode differently. Ours wouldn't porpoise like they would in the turns, it would skim right through."

Vanden Berg and crew strategically chose gearbox and propeller combinations that gave them an advantage cornering and accelerating. *Bardahl* chose smaller props, as well, which kept rpms up through the turns and didn't lug the engine.

Vanden Berg suspected most teams banked their hopes on chute speed. It's a balancing act: You can set up a boat for speed on the straightaways, which Zuvich figured was *Tahoe*'s and *Gale*'s strategy, but doing so saps acceleration and cornering.

"I think I carried that through most of my racing career," said Zuvich. "You spend more time in the turns than you do down the straightaway, when you count both turns. The few seconds you spend at the end of the straightaway, you can't pass anybody because your boat is loose and flying. So if you make a boat turn or make a boat accelerate, you don't need the chute speed. Yeah, I think 160 in the chutes would have been a lot for our boat."

"Our boat wasn't a slouch in the straightaways," Dax said. "But there's a compromise there. You typically do not get beat from halfway down the straightaway to the entrance pin. Usually, you get beat through the corner and exiting the corner, from the exit pin to the first half. If you can make your boat accelerate and beat the guy halfway down the straightaway, you can stay on the inside and make him work. You need to be competitive, but you don't need that extra 10-15 mph on the straights, where the boats become unstable. And that's one of the things we worked on. Horsepower gives you acceleration more than top speed."

Even for a driver who doesn't hold the inside position, which often was the case for Musson running in lane two or three, superior cornering and acceleration trumps top end.

"Ron was good about getting the inside – he could hold the inside line no problem with that boat," said David. "Other people would flop around on the outside, cavitate, hippy-hop. That thing would just fly through the corner. And our boat was set up to be a drag racer, an accelerator, not a top-and boat. We could out-drag anybody. That's where we won.

"I remember Ron was really good in lane two or three, better than he was in lane one, because with a heavier boat you want to keep your momentum up. And if he could come out of the turn pretty much deck to deck with somebody and then nail it, he would take them. We didn't beat people with top end, we beat people by out-dragging them."

"Musson would always try to get the second lane, if I remember," said Gary Breakfield, who joined the team for the 1964 season. "That's where he ran, lane two."

Ron Jones is skeptical of any 1960s driver who said his boat hit 190 or faster in the chutes on race day. Such speeds were attributed to *Tahoe Miss*, *Hawaii Kai*, even to *Slo-mo IV*. Jones believes in Vanden Berg's assessment that *Bardahl* ran an honest 160, which was fast enough to win.

"After watching boats for a number of years, I fancied myself as being pretty good at estimating boat speed," Jones said. "I would always have said, on a good racecourse, they were running 165. But on an average racecourse, short courses, or rough water, 155-160 was probably pretty much true. You know, in those days, we used to hear about 200 mph and all that. That was somebody's pipe dream; 165 would have been real fast."

Unlike current hydroplanes, teams in the 1950s and '60s did not have sophisticated propeller programs that used computer-assisted equipment to machine precision props in their own shops. Jack Ramsey's *Thriftway* team generally is credited with pioneering "progressive pitch" in its blades, but otherwise the camps used what they could buy from manufacturers.

"We had Records, and we had some Carys, props that came out of Italy. That's where Record is, that's where Cary is," said David. "We probably had eight props. Sometimes we'd get props mid-season. I don't know how, they'd just mysteriously appear."

"That was the problem," Vanden Berg said. "If you could get blanks and cut them yourself ... but nobody worked on the propellers with self-interest; they always relied on somebody else."

"Most of the stuff was reworked by Howard Kruger," David said. "He didn't *build* the props, he'd rework them – change the pitch, the angle, the cup. He was the prop guru, and he was in Ballard. He was in the business a long, long time ago. I used to go out there with my father during the *Miss Seattle* days."

A May 1957 *Seattle Times* article quotes Kruger describing how, even at that early time, *Miss Bardahl* and *Miss Seattle* ran Kruger's three-blade props to eliminate cavitation.

Dixon hesitates to characterize *Bardahl*'s efforts as an experimental program.

"We got new props kind of on a continuing basis and figured out what works good," he said. "We did some playing around with things like going to smaller pitches, higher gearbox ratios … we did learn a few things, but I'm not so sure at that point we even understood what we learned. For instance, the boat behaved better with a smaller-pitch prop. If you put a smaller-pitch prop and a higher gearbox ratio in, the boat tended to behave a little better. But at least from my standpoint, we were kind of shooting in the dark on that one."

"No teams understood the technology like today," said David. "And we didn't have elephant-ear props, we just had cleavers, the ones that are straight across the back with sharp edges. They were forged props, they weren't cast, and they were hand-finished to get balanced. Howard had this magic he would put in them, and sometimes it worked and sometimes it didn't."

Vanden Berg made most of the decisions on which propellers and gearbox ratios to run, and it varied according to the size and shape of the racecourse. Seattle had a symmetrical 3-mile course, Madison's 3-miler had narrow 600-foot turns with longer chutes, and Detroit's unique layout was pear-shaped with a tight, tiny Roostertail turn and a wide, sweeping Belle Isle turn. In *Bardahl*'s later years, 2½-mile courses became more common. Water conditions also were a factor. Racers often battled rollers on the Detroit River and thick chop on Lake Coeur d'Alene, but found an ideal surface on Mission Bay.

"Usually for a race we'd have three engines laid out with gearboxes on them," David said. "Once we decided on the gearbox ratio, all three all got the same one."

Vanden Berg kept track of the props, recording how much running time each one had. Props broke infrequently, unlike during the turbine era when thin blades snap off occasionally and rip apart the transom. Teams in the 1960s used red dye to detect cracks, later evolving to zyglow phosphorescent paint with a fluorescent light, and when they found trouble they changed props.

"We'd try two or three props when we were testing and qualifying, and Ron would get his favorite," said David. "I'd lay them all out, the primary propeller, a backup that was his second choice, and sometimes a third choice. Sometimes he would say after a heat, 'I'm getting passed by the guy, I need some more top end,' and we'd choose another prop that would be 3 mph faster at a given rpm. But we didn't have the little short shafts like they use today, so we would have to take the nut off and take entire shaft out, the entire length."

"We tried different props constantly," said Gary Breakfield. "As soon as that boat came out of the water, we had a special cover made for the prop to hide it from all the other crews. It was a secret in their mind: 'What are they hiding? What did they have for a prop?' We never let anybody see it, we kept it hidden. We'd go down to the water and pull the cover off once it's in the water. Coming out of the water, Jerry would cover it up so no one could see it. That was really comical; we did that all the time. We kept people wondering what that hell we were doing."

Zuvich recalled Musson's preference for the two-blade props that Vanden Berg said were nicknamed a "kamikaze" style.

"They worked the best. We ran a couple of three-blade props that made it neater down the chute, but the boat wouldn't handle in the turn with it. I think we used it as a backup. It was a Cary three-blade," Zuvich said.

"Ron hated three-bladed props," David recalled in 2011. "Every time we put one on the Green Dragon – we tried one probably three times – Ron would say, 'Get that damn thing off.' It would jack up the ass end of the boat and plow the nose down, because three-blades by nature give you more lift. They're more efficient.

"We run with a three-blade now on the rebuilt boat," he continued. "If we'd had the prop that we run today on the boat back then, Ron would love the way that thing turns. It's a better prop for the hull, from a new era with better technology."

Despite how fast and hard *Miss Bardahl* ran for four seasons, she never had a significant propeller failure.

"As far as I know, that boat never threw a prop," David said. "Of course, the cabover did. That was the demise of the cabover. But the 1962 boat never threw a blade. And I don't think the bottom ever came out of that boat, not until we rebuilt it."

Chapter 12

Breaking, learning, innovating, and The Checklist

Miss Bardahl became the top boat of the unlimited fleet in 1963. Besides victories at Guntersville, Detroit, and Lake Tahoe, the Green Dragon led race-winner *Thriftway* at Coeur d'Alene before breaking down, and if not for miscalculating elapsed time entering the final heat at Seattle, *Bardahl* also might have won Seafair.

Much of *Bardahl*'s edge stemmed from Ron Musson's masterful driving, but equally important were the crew members, who tested new ideas and refined old ones. Engine failure still plagued them early in 1963, but unlike many teams that simply replaced broken motors with fresh ones and left it at that, *Bardahl*'s crew dissected each broken part and studied it.

"Every time you break an engine, you really ought to learn something," Dax said. "You broke it because something didn't happen like it should. We spent a lot of time analyzing broken stuff. And a lot of people don't. They break an engine and say, 'Aw, we just broke another one,' and they cart it off. You break an engine, and there's something to be learned there, no matter what. We looked at stuff and said, 'OK, it broke. Why? How can we make it better?' And we learned a lot, so things improved as we went along.

"I think one of the things you've got with a younger crew," he continued, "is you don't have the mindset, 'It's always been done this way.' There was nobody in the crew that had any serious objection to trying something new. A lot of crews, you'll hear, 'That worked great last year; don't mess with it.'"

Despite his age, military background, insistence on rigor and detail, and being pegged by family and friends as "a creature of habit," Vanden Berg was open-minded, flexible, and willing to experiment with new ideas, to adapt proven concepts into foreign settings.

"Leo in general was not an obstructionist who simply said, 'Well, I don't believe that, the Rolls guys didn't say to do that,'" said Dixon. "He allowed us to experiment. He was open to it, like the time we went to Jett's Marina and tested a Rolls that had three different flat-top pistons inside of it. We wanted to learn, and the fastest way to do it was to run all the pistons at once, rather than put them in separate motors. That thing went out and made a racket like you've never heard before!"

Perhaps Vanden Berg's open-mindedness was rooted in his own penchant for zany ideas. He once told his son Mel about a time in his youth, when he was buying and dismantling vehicles to sell the parts, that he modified one car so that it could be steered with the driver's seat reversed.

"He geared it so that it could go backwards as fast as it previously went forward," Mel said.

New knowledge bred new solutions: Vanden Berg and crew replaced their Rolls-Merlin engines' standard, recessed through-bolts with larger, stronger, tight-fitting straight ones. They reheat-treated the main-cap studs, which increased strength and hardness. They heli-coiled the main bearings and bolts, remachined oil passages near the main bearings to improve oil flow, and welded additional counterweights to the crankshaft. They took shot-peened rods and *re*shot-peened them, making them stronger.

"As far as I know, we were the first people to do some of that stuff," Dax said. "And reheat-treating some of the engine parts, making them harder, significantly improved our reliability. It probably did as much for our reliability as a lot of that stuff."

"We did those things to increase engine life," said Zuvich. "They didn't increase horsepower, but we bought ourselves an extra three minutes or so of hard running. The goal was engine longevity at the end of the day.

"At first, yeah, we were the first to try some of those things," he said. "But as crew members move and shift around, everybody gets it."

In fact, a few of *Bardahl*'s modifications came from the *Hawaii Kai III* team via Burns Smith, a crew member during the Pink Lady's latter days when the boat was owned by Joe Mascari. The *Kai* enlisted acclaimed California hot-rodder Ed Winfield to help sort out its engine failures, and together they pioneered some firsts in hydro racing: extra counterweights on the crankshaft, helicoiled cases, a new cam profile to slow valves at high rpm, and dash 9 end-to-end oiling, which hadn't been compatible with the hydros' aftermarket gearbox.

But *Hawaii Kai* aside, *Bardahl* pioneered many new ideas, such as reheat-treating the connecting rod bolts.

"My father brought rod bolts to a company near my Federal Way home to have them specially treated to prevent them from elongating," said Mel. "Then he'd stop by our home for a visit He did that so no one would find out this little secret for keeping the engines from cutting themselves in half."

Other firsts: Vanden Berg worked with Dick Gordon on a quick-change gearbox that could be swapped intact without disassembling it. And as might be expected, oil played a key role in *Bardahl*'s success as the Green Dragon was the first hydro to successfully run two oil pumps. *Hawaii Kai* had tried end-to-end oiling with limited success by placing a second pump on the generator mount, but *Bardahl* fitted all of its Merlins with a second oil pump on the hydraulic mount, an easy and highly effective improvement.

Vanden Berg also worked with Bardahl's chief chemist, Donald VanSteenvoort, to tailor racing oil for the boat.

"He made it to our specs," said Vanden Berg. "Then Ole sold it to other teams, or he was giving it away. We'd go back East with 300 gallons of oil and we'd run out in the middle of the season and have to ship some. He was giving away five here, 10 here, 20 there."

Fragile quill shafts drove racers nuts back then. Technically called a spring drive in the Rolls-Merlin, as opposed to a true quill shaft in Allisons, it was a weak link connecting the crankshaft to the supercharger, and the entire quill-shaft assembly comprised five pieces. The quill shaft often broke, particularly when strained as the propeller bounced in and out of the water. More than one team worked to strengthen them. *Bardahl*'s answer in 1964 was to combine the five parts into a two-piece quill initially machined in Akron, Ohio, later superseded by a solid, heavy duty, one-piece quill built by Mantel Gear Works in Seattle.

It's generally believed the Stoen brothers' team developed the first solid quill, on either *Miss Seattle Too* in 1962 or later on *Miss Exide*.

"We came out with a solid quill shaft, on *Miss Seattle Too*," said crew member Bob Woolms of his 1962 boat. "Who do you think wound up with a solid quill within three weeks? *Bardahl*. They copied it from us."

In truth, *Bardahl* didn't develop its solid quill until 1964. Regardless, *Bardahl*'s later versions eventually were perfected to last up to 10 hours.

"*Exide* was working on the same thing, only a different manufacturer," said Vanden Berg. "We first made a two-piece. That didn't work out too well, but it was better. Then we came out with the one-piece. We later found out the Gear Works in Seattle was making *Exide*'s, so we had them make ours, and we modified it *many* times. And then *Exide* got *our* modifications. We used to track time on them, and every one I had was numbered. We had about seven different types of materials, and we kept track of which kind would work the best.

"Another thing we did that others didn't do is knurl our pistons," Vanden Berg said. "They looked like a screwdriver with a knurled handle. We did it on the edges, where they rubbed. The knurling held oil and kept the pistons from scoring."

The *Bardahl* team ground its propellers to shape a "progressive pitch," something *Thriftway*'s team had done. Vanden Berg used gear ratios and smaller props suited for fast corner speeds. Though not the first to do so, *Bardahl* also experimented with three-blade props, one of which later propelled the cabover U-40 during its fateful, final race in 1966.

"I'm not saying that other teams weren't doing some of that, also," said Vanden Berg. "Like, I know others were putting different rod bolts in different mains, and all we were doing was reheat-treating them."

What really optimized all those improvements and innovations was Vanden Berg's strict quality control program. "We used to keep detailed time logs on all our engines and parts," he said. "And I made sure everybody was cross-trained, even though they excelled at certain jobs."

Zuvich continued Vanden Berg's cross-training practice with his own crews throughout his racing career.

"When you're testing and qualifying, you can go ahead and afford to have people switch around so they know what to do if someone gets hurt and can't show up," he said. "But there's no reason at a race why a person would walk into an unfamiliar area. You put your men in a familiar place."

* * * *

Vanden Berg also insisted that every task and all vital data be logged on a detailed checklist, which hung from *Bardahl*'s windshield on a clipboard. The team followed strict, well-defined processes that optimized their efficiency and speed.

"We all had specific responsibilities, and we knew what they were," David said. "Leo had a checklist, and we always filled out the same things. I never jumped into engine stuff, they never jumped into hull stuff. That's why we got in the water and always made the next heat, because we always did the same things. If Leo's checklist wasn't filled out, that boat never came off the trailer."

Skip Schott found the same diligence in place when he joined the team later. "We rebelled against the checklist just because Leo forced it down us, but we knew that it was the key, and we followed it," he said.

When interviewed by *The Seattle Times*' Dwight Perry in 2004, Dixon reflected on what in hindsight had become revered as The Checklist, on which much of *Bardahl*'s success hinged.

"Leo had a checklist on race day, and when you did something, you sign it off. At the time it was a real pain. Later on in my airline career, I learned how important stuff like that was. He was a great advocate of checking other people's work. That's what gave us the ability to win races. We didn't make as many mistakes as other people."

"I don't remember anybody else having a checklist," said David. "And we prided ourselves on changing an engine faster than anybody. We always made the next heat, no matter the crisis. We always got in the water. Part of that is because we worked really efficiently, but we also practiced. We practiced engine changes, we practiced getting the boat on the trailer."

"At races, each guy had specific areas of responsibility, well-defined," said Dax. "Barring something abnormal, we could go from one heat to the next and essentially not talk to each other, because we knew exactly what to do."

The checklist reflected the special roles Vanden Berg had assigned to each crew member. Zuvich was now an adept mechanic at building Rolls components and changing engines under race-day deadlines. Likewise for Dixon, who also tapped his physics and engineering knowledge to apply theory. Young David already was a skilled wood-worker after helping his father build three runabouts at home. And Vanden Berg, a mechanic by trade, delegated responsibilities to match his crew's strengths and then managed the operation.

"I did very little of the actual engine work, but I oversaw a lot of it," he said. "I watched things pretty close."

"Dax and I were mainly the engine guys," Zuvich said, explaining their race-day regimen. "He'd take one side, I'd take the other side, and Leo would take the coupler and line the engine up. Dax and I would hook up our hoses, and we each had a linkage for the throttle."

"Before the solid quill, we did quick quill-shaft changes between heats," Dax said. "Jerry and I did those right in the boat. There's a row of nuts around the blower that holds it on. We knew who was responsible to take *each nut* off. We *practiced* this stuff. We knew exactly what to do when a blower came off, we knew who was in the bilge doing what, who was handling parts, who was handling tools. We could go in and out of an engine probably as fast or faster than anybody else."

Working at the Bardahl shop, Zuvich typically rebuilt blowers and cylinders. Vanden Berg also did that along with hull work, which included rudders and props. Dax mostly did engine work, which in 1964 he estimates accounted for 70 or 80 percent of the crew's attention. Dax primarily rebuilt the bottom end – crankshafts, connecting rods, lower cases, and wheel cases. Once the individual engine components were prepared, everyone helped with assembly, though Zuvich and Dax tended to do most of it.

"We all kind of hung bearings and rods and assembled parts together," said Zuvich. "Leo, after the first year or so, spent most of his time with the hull, and spent a *lot* of time developing quill shafts. We had some real exotic quills. And Dax was really good with carburetion."

Dax also typically designed and installed the wiring on the boat. "I enjoyed it, and nobody else liked to do it," he said. "Electricity comes very hard to some people and very easy to others. For me, it's easy, so I did that kind of by default."

"At a race, I always worked the coupling end, the cockpit," said Vanden Berg. "And I always took care of the props. They all knew how to do it, but there were so many failures from previous years, that's why I took on that responsibility myself. And we all did hull work."

Later, David became the person primarily responsible for the stern, a role he carried through his 1970s *Pay 'n Pak* years.

"The whole time I worked on the *Bardahl*, which included the Green Dragon, the cabover, and also the checkerboard boat, I always had the back of the boat," he said. "I was usually the guy who threw the rope. Once the boat got onto the trailer I ran water through the engine to cool it off. Leo did the coupling and had the checklist. If we weren't changing the engine, Dixon and Jerry would handle the spark plugs and set valves. Then Reb would fuel the boat. We knew exactly what the drill was – before the boat ever came out of the water, the decision was made to change the engine or leave it alone. I would do a prop change occasionally after doing a dye check."

"Reb" was Gary Breakfield, who in 1964 charged batteries, handled the bow rope, put fuel and oil in the boat, and helped fill in wherever needed. Roger Kruse, who took care of *Bardahl*'s rolling stock, did likewise. The entire crew worked efficiently together, succeeding in part because it excelled at the simple tasks.

"We were one of the first ones up in the morning and in the pits," said Zuvich. "We concentrated on our own jobs and did all the little things some crews forget, like putting gas in the boat, putting rear plugs in, throwing a rope without letting go of both ends. Silly things like that cost some people races. It's not necessarily the fastest guy who wins the race – it's the guy whose team got the whole job done who wins the race."

Because of Vanden Berg's cross-training program, everyone was largely capable of filling almost any role, though they specialized for time and economy. But he recognized their strengths and assigned them accordingly. He kept personalities in balance. He was the glue that held things together.

"Leo was a good mechanic," Zuvich said. "But a crew chief's job is to organize, and to keep the crew, the boat, the engines, and the owner all level, and keep them apart from each other enough to get their jobs done. The crew chief's job, he's the juggler.

"And obviously, Leo was a good juggler."

Chapter 13

She has a great personality

Much of what made *Bardahl* the top boat of its day can be attributed to the 1963 preseason sponson rebuild, which gave the boat near-perfect balance and allowed Musson to unleash the Dragon's power and drive more aggressively. After that, the boat displayed many strong characteristics and very few weak points. "For its day, that boat was close to perfection," said Vanden Berg.

About the worst thing that could be said about *Miss Bardahl*, aside from its lingering tendency to lean too far on its right sponson in the turns, was that it leaked. Vanden Berg recalled it leaked where the sponsons fit onto the main hull. Toward the end of the boat's career it worsened, and the crew waited until three minutes before the one-minute gun to drop the boat in the water. David Smith doesn't recall leaky sponsons but suspects water shot in through the propshaft log underneath the hull.

Dixon learned more in 2001, during *Miss Bardahl*'s restoration.

"We found more hidden damage than I expected from when it was racing," he said in 2011. "Like under the fuel tank, there's an area we couldn't see, particularly the inboard of the left sponson, inboard of the skidfin. It was pretty busted up in there. There were many places it could have been leaking."

Leaks aside, from 1963 on the Green Dragon was a sweet machine. "The boat had a really good personality after 1962," said Zuvich. "It was a great little boat. Didn't seem to do anything wrong."

"The boat, after it had matured a year or so, was a darn good race boat for its era," said Dax. "The boat handled pretty well in general, probably as good as anything out there. It probably didn't push as easy as some boats, but it didn't push real hard. It took horsepower to make it go, but not a gigantic amount. I'm almost certain that we were making more horsepower than others during some of the time we were running, particularly towards the tail end, with that boat."

Bardahl's ideal balance gave it an edge in rough water. When a wave or roller launched the boat, it always remained level and came down flat. That enabled Musson to keep his foot on the throttle while wobbly competitors backed off.

"It was very, very good in sloppy water," David recalled. "If you look at all the times when that boat's out of the water, like that famous picture in Detroit, it didn't get out of attitude. It always landed correctly. It was balanced very, very well.

Beautifully balanced, *Miss Bardahl* rode level even when she left the water, like on the Detroit River in 1963.
© David Dixon 1963, from the Leo Vanden Berg collection

"Ron also was very good at handling that boat. He was a magician. Great driver. In those days, you couldn't just ram into the corner. You had to de-accelerate, or you got into the corner so fast that you slid out too far. When I rode with Ron, at the buoy before the entrance buoy, he would crank the wheel and start getting the boat to slide before it ever got to the corner, to stay with the buoys. And once he got in the corner he would reverse-steer the thing and work it on the propeller. At a certain point, probably three-quarters, he would start hammering the throttle and the boat would zing, just fly. The boat had so much torque and power it would not accelerate straight, it would torque to the left."

Ron Jones said that for what was expected of an unlimited during its era, *Miss Bardahl* had no weak points.

"I think it was probably the king of the mountain," he said. "I'm convinced that if Leo had wanted to run for the mile-straightaway record, the boat could have been set up to do that and probably could have gone 200 mph, with the right gears and the right propeller. It could have been altered. But Ronnie Musson's biggest thing was circle racing. It was set up to accelerate. And it did!"

Chapter 14

Ron Musson, the person

When you ask his contemporaries to describe Ron Musson the person, you get several perspectives. Ask about Musson the racer and virtually everyone describes a superb driver who combined skill, instinct, courage, and later, even prudence to top his craft.

"The girls just adored him, and so did the guys. He was everybody's bud. He was a really nice, nice man. He was our neighbor too, one of Rex's very best friends," said Evelyn Bardahl McNeil, Ole's daughter and widow of Rex Manchester.

"I didn't really care for him as a person. He acted either silly-crazy – you know, silly, not serious – or he'd be a loner. I went looking for him many times and found him alone in a bar, usually smashed," said Vanden Berg.

Can they really be describing the same man? Perception is reality, and perceptions are shaped by the personal values of the beholder, the lens and filter through which each person sees life a little differently.

As a youth I saw Musson as a heroic, do-no-wrong figure. I wanted to confirm that as an adult, and a profile emerged of a man who's certainly entertaining and charming, yet not always straight and pure. In other words, a real person, a guy with achievements but also flaws.

Ronald John Musson was born April 24, 1929, and grew up in Akron, Ohio, where his parents Glenn and Gayle owned Dauntless Plumbing and Electric. The family eventually lived in a house on the shore of Portage Lakes, so Ron grew up around boats and took an interest in racing. He started driving outboards at age 15, around the time he became a standout in football, basketball, and golf at Ohio Military Institute in Akron.

Glenn supported Ron's pursuit but was less of a racing enthusiast himself. Ron later graduated from Kent State College.

"My dad Ray Osborne, Ron, and an Akron jeweler named Jim McMullen were The Three Amigos," said Jim Osborne, who grew up in the north Akron suburb of Cuyahoga Falls. "All three of them bought Sid Craft-model hulls with 10-hp Hurricane Mercury motors and raced in the B-stock utility classes. Ron was really good-looking, young, brash. He must have had an olive complexion, because he was always tan. My recollection is he wasn't spoiled. He was a ladies' man, and definitely my best word to describe him is 'leadfoot' – in everything! He lived life to the limit."

"Ron was very macho, there's no doubt about it," said his stepdaughter, Josette Musson Hess. "And very competitive. Obviously, you don't get to the level he was and not be competitive. He drove limiteds before he went to the unlimiteds, and even as a kid they had motorboats, living on the lake in Ohio. So he was driving boats all his life."

Ron was very supportive of 10-year-old Jim Osborne and persuaded Glenn Musson to sponsor Jim in the Soap Box Derby. Ron also encouraged the elder Osborne to let young Jim race in the outboard JU class, the 5-hp beginner class for kids, and Jim recalls racing against Billy Schumacher once on the Choptank River at Chesapeake Bay. Jim also liked model airplanes and was impressed when he went to Ron's house one evening and saw the radio-controlled airplanes Ron kept in his basement.

"My dad had a '57 Pontiac Star Chief with tri-power, and at the same time Ron had a new Olds 98, a high-horsepower one," Jim said. "I remember they took a trip up to Toledo, dad riding with Ron, which normally would be an hour and a half trip via a turnpike almost all the way. They made it up there in like 45 minutes. My dad said he was so scared he wanted to get out of the car, and he made Ron promise that he would drive sane.

"Watching Ron race, his big thing was, whenever other people would back off, he would stay in it – *hard*. That's how he drove the inboards. That's how he got his reputation of being a winner. Everybody else would back off. He wouldn't," Jim said.

"He has no fear of speed – on or off the water," Betty Musson said of Ron years later.

"I always thought Ronnie Musson was sticking his neck out too far," said longtime unlimited driver and owner Bob Schroeder. "He was really stretching things, even in the limiteds."

"He was very friendly, very outgoing, very good with kids, always happy, always smiling," added Jim Osborne. "Even though I think he must have come from money, he by no means was aloof. He was approachable. Very articulate. I remember Ron always would make a big fuss over my little sister who was four or five at the time. He'd come over to our house, and he was really good with little kids."

Musson was in his mid-20s at this time, married to an attractive woman with coal-black hair named Florence. Ron and Florence May Zufall had married in July 1950, when he was 21 and she was 19. At that time Ron listed his address as 3404 Waterside Drive in Akron, a house on one of the Portage Lakes, mere blocks from Firestone Country Club. Florence, who had been a Coventry High School homecoming queen, lived just six blocks to the north in a lakeside home. They had a son, Glennie, likely named after Ron's father, whose first name actually was Glendal.

For a short while Ron and Ray Osborne co-owned *Chromium* and *Chro-mate*, the 135- and 266-class limited boats in which Ron gained fame when they were owned by Frank Hearn. Ron hauled the boats to races on a double-deck trailer designed to stack the hydros, one above the other, while Osborne stayed home running his machine shop.

"One day Ron came back from a race where he blew a motor because he'd been revving it up in the pits, out of the water," said Jim. "You blow up one or two Keith Black motors, and that's when my dad said goodbye, and they ended their partnership real quickly. It was shortly thereafter I think that Ron moved up into the unlimiteds."

Ron and Florence divorced in December 1954, and in 1956 Ron married Springfield, Ohio native Betty Lou Beichly, a former John Robert Powers – New York model whose father was Russ Beichly, the Akron University basketball coach from 1941-59. Betty was three years older than Ron and had two children,

Bobby and Josette, from her previous marriage to Bob Vallen that ended in 1954. Bud Livesley later described Betty as "blonde and pretty and warmly friendly. She is infectiously vivacious." Kit Muncey, wife of Bill, described Betty as "the ex-model with the volatile temperament."

Betty had grown up in Akron, attended West High and Akron University, and it was while working at her modeling school next door to Dauntless Plumbing and Electric in Akron that she got to know Ron, who worked there until they moved to Seattle in 1962. Many years later, Betty would run what her husband of 38 years, Wally Bostick, called a charm school in their Mercer Island home.

"Ron was my stepdad, but we grew up with him, my brother and I," said Josette. "My mother was divorced from my father when I was 2 years old."

Josette recalled Ron indeed was playful and, echoing what Osborne said, fun with kids.

"In Ohio, our whole neighborhood played. The fathers threw balls," Josette said. "In fact, Bill Muncey came to visit us, and that ended up in some kind of a game in the backyard, through the tomato patch with tomatoes all over everybody. Everybody made them out to be big rivals, but Ron and Bill liked each other very much."

Ron always loved his fast toys, whether it was outboards, go-carts, fast cars, model airplanes, or real planes.

"When we were growing up he bought my brother a go-cart, which of course my brother hardly ever got to drive because Ron was on it all the time," Josette said. "Then they always crashed it, he crashed into the trees with it.

"Ron always drove Oldsmobiles, and he always drove fast. Always. He also had a 1959 Corvette that was gorgeous. He always had really awesome cars. And then we had two different airplanes. The first plane we owned was a little two-seater, and then he moved up to a four-seater, and he flew all the time. He had his pilot's license. My grandparents lived in Florida, and the four of us would fly to Florida every year for Christmas in that plane.

"We moved to Seattle in 1962, and I remember being mad that we missed the World's Fair," Josette recalled. "I started school in September 1962. At first we lived in an apartment in Ballard while they were hunting for a house, and then our house was up above North Beach, on the edge of North Beach and Blue Ridge."

When asked what Musson's personality was like – how she would describe him if she met him at a party – Josette said that aside from being "very macho," he headed up a fairly normal household. He owned a dog named Baron, which true to Ron's nature was a macho breed – a black German Shepherd. When Ron lived in Ohio, he also had owned a boxer.

Ron liked Westerns and war movies, never missing TV shows like *Combat* or *Rawhide*.

"We always had to watch that kind of stuff. He was a manly man, what can I say," Josette said, laughing. "I would not call him a metrosexual, by a long shot!

"Now, you have to remember, I was a young girl," she continued. "I'm not looking at it from adult eyes, and I do think that makes a difference. Obviously, he was fun, everybody liked being around him. They had cocktail parties, you know. I think he was a big partier. He was no Bernie Little. Ron was not as gregarious as that, not boisterous at all. And when he was racing, the day he was driving, he didn't like to really talk to anybody. He kept completely alone, he didn't talk to fans until he was done. He kind of hid during the race."

When asked who Ron's friends were, Josette mentioned the Bardahl and Seattle Yacht Club social circles, and Gene Mittelstadt, who ran a local mortuary.

"I wouldn't say Rex Manchester was his best friend, but they were friendly," she said. "We had a big boat – 36 foot, 38 foot Owens. Ron would come home from work and he'd be tired, but he wanted to go out on that boat every night during the summer. He kept it down on Lake Union because it was wood, no salt water. It was the 60-something, all teak. He worked on that boat a lot, it took a lot of maintenance. So mom would pack stuff and bring dinner and we'd all go down, and he would back the boat out, then give it to me and say, 'Okay, you drive around.' And he'd go and sleep. He taught me how to put the boat back in. It was very relaxing for him to just be on the water.

"He was the type of person who just threw you into whatever. Like the year we learned how to scuba dive. We were out on the dock in Hood Canal, and I'd never had a tank on or anything. So he straps me up, and I'm pretty small, and he put these weight-belts on me and this tank and the whole thing, and just shoved me off the dock. I'm a really strong swimmer, but I just couldn't get back up!" Josette said, laughing. "So it was always learn by fire. You just did it and see what happens."

* * * *

Mira Slovak encountered Musson at the 1958 Buffalo Launch Club Regatta, which Slovak won aboard the original Green Dragon *Miss Bardahl*. Slovak recalls the wind always started blowing across the Niagara River after noon, and at the drivers meeting a short, dark-haired limited-hydro driver stood up and complained that the limiteds always had to run late in the day and got stuck with the rough water.

Slovak, seated in the back, knew what it was like to be jostled around in choppy water while driving his *Wee Wahoo* limited hydro. So he looked at the referee and said, "That's okay with us. Why don't you let the little guys drive ahead of us? Then they can avoid the rough water."

Something in Slovak's word choice struck a nerve with the short driver – 5-foot-7-inch Musson. He challenged Slovak saying, "What do you mean, little guys with the little boats?" Slovak replied, "Well, you're little, and you're driving a little boat."

"Musson glared at me, he got a little puffed up, really upset," said Slovak. "Later on I told him, 'You're really touchy, what for? I drive a little boat, and I'm a little guy, so what's the difference? A big boat can take the swells, and the little guys cannot take the swells.' It was like a joke, but obviously it backfired on me because he never liked me after that. I wanted to let it go, but he kind of remembered it."

Slovak lost contact with Musson and doesn't recall racing against him, and the few times their paths crossed, particularly at Tampa in 1966 as Musson and buddy Manchester rode past on a motorcycle, Slovak would say hello and Musson "kind of gave me an 'up yours.'"

Although in 2011 Slovak didn't specifically recall racing Musson, they did in fact compete. One time was the memorable heat 1B of the 1959 Sahara Cup on Lake Mead, a race that Slovak and *Wahoo* won. In that heat Slovak averaged a scorching 110.316 mph to win, but close behind was rookie Musson aboard *Hawaii Kai III* at 109.267. During its cooling-off lap the *Kai* threw a rod, ending Musson's day. Another time was the 1960 Apple Cup, where *Wahoo* won heat 1A as Musson blew the *Kai*'s supercharger. The last time was the 1963 Gold Cup final heat, where Musson took second and Slovak fourth.

"I have to be careful what I say because Ron was liked by many, many people," said Slovak. "And I have also been disliked by many, many people. But I don't remember driving against him, I don't remember associating with him. He's the only guy I just couldn't see eye to eye, and it was the incident in Buffalo. I couldn't figure out why he was upset with me. I never had a fight with him on the racecourse. I think it was a misunderstanding.

"So, I really didn't know the man. I cannot say good for him or bad against him. We just hit it off on the wrong foot. I hurt his feelings probably, and he hurt mine."

* * * *

Jerry Zuvich worked alongside Musson for years, first as a parts-chaser on the 1961 team, then as a fellow Bardahl corporate employee, and remembers him with fondness.

"Great guy. He was neat. Bubbly personality – he had a twinkle in his eye when he was going to be mischievous," Zuvich said. "He was like a little cat. You could tell when he was going to be up to something. He'd talk really fast, his eyes would start to blink, and he'd start making quick little moves. He would always try to get away with some shenanigans, and then kind of look at you like, 'Oh, did I do that?'

"Ron was a pretty jovial guy," he continued. "Very playful, approachable, friendly, and extremely low key. He was a funny character. He had an ego, maybe a little bit of the little-man complex. He was always kind of cocky."

Zuvich said Musson lacked what he calls the "nervous complex" that some drivers exhibit – some literally sweat and shake getting into the boat, and some you can't talk to. But Zuvich said Musson was "pretty easy" in those areas.

When asked in 2012 if Musson's personality was like any subsequent unlimited drivers, Zuvich quickly named Nate Brown, the 2004 Gold Cup winner.

"His temperament is a little like Ron's was, easy-go-lucky, always smiling," Zuvich said. "He didn't seem to worry when he got in the boat like some of them do. He's always jovial and fun. If anything happens he's not pissy."

Zuvich recalled Musson did a good job with public relations and also seemed to get along well with Bill Muncey.

"Sometimes he projected a little bad-boy image, like riding motorcycles down the hallway in motels and into bars and stuff. But otherwise, he was okay. Ron and Bill were friends, but they were different personalities. Bill didn't drink or party, and Ron did. So it wasn't like they were out socializing together, but in an auditorium they'd sit at the same table."

Renowned sportscaster Keith Jackson was hired at Seattle's KOMO-TV after graduating from Washington State University in 1954 with a degree in speech communications. He later became KOMO's sports director before moving to ABC in 1964, where he gained fame on "Wide World of Sports" and as the voice of college football. But for a decade, starting with the 1954 Gold Cup, Jackson covered hydroplanes.

"Musson was like *all* those guys, he was like all race drivers," Jackson said in 2011. "I don't care whether you're on the water or on land, he thought he was bulletproof. He had some derring-do in his soul, he was a tough guy. I thought he was very good, frankly, and he was very cooperative with us and with the rest of the media.

"I remember one instance where somebody made him mad, one of the media boys asked him an untoward question, and he ripped him pretty good. So he had some rooster in him, too!"

Jackson did a memorable interview of Bill Muncey for ABC-TV's coverage of the 1979 Gold Cup in Madison, during which Muncey steered Jackson around the Ohio River racecourse in a runabout. Jackson recited to Muncey the names of several deceased competitors, including Musson, each one triggering a solemn nod. Muncey had said in prior interviews that he thought Musson was the premiere chauffeur of his time, and when asked in 2011 if Muncey ever had shared that with him, Jackson said not specifically.

"But I know that was Muncey's way. Bill had a lot of humility, and he didn't mind paying tribute to other competitors if he respected them, and obviously he respected Ron. He thought Slovak was crazy as hell, but we all did!" Jackson said, laughing.

Jackson's contemporaries remember Musson as a keen competitor, though perhaps less colorful than drivers like Muncey, Slovak, and Jack Regas. John Owen of the *Seattle P-I* said, "I remember Ron as a personable, professional figure in the sport and I was saddened at his death." Rod Belcher recalled, "Ron was not nearly the hotdog nor self-promoter that some of the hydro people were. I think he was rather laid-back and happy to let Ole Bardahl be up front. He was a tend-to-business driver, but an aggressive competitor."

Vanden Berg was careful to note that although he didn't care for Musson's persona, he respected him greatly as a driver – as long as Musson was clear-headed.

"The problem was that booze," Vanden Berg said. "I don't care what you say, it changes your way of thinking, your judgment. And if you've got an aggressive mind and you're using common sense and you're aggressive, you shouldn't have booze to make you more aggressive, which some of those guys think they need. Their judgment goes off. It ain't on a straight line, and they make the wrong decisions."

When asked, "booze" aside, if he thought Musson was generally a friendly person, Vanden Berg described him as not really moody, just not talkative sometimes.

"There were two sides to him. Sometimes he'd treat people nice, and sometimes he wouldn't. Sometimes he'd treat kids nice, and sometimes he wouldn't."

Tony Lamontia was close friends with Musson in the 1950s when, along with fellow Akron resident Jack Force, they raced outboard and inboard hydros, Tony's wife recalled.

"We went out to dinner together a few times, but I have to tell you, charming as he was, Ron never talked about anything but racing. Absolutely nothing," said Jeanne Lamontia in 2011. "Ron wasn't a social person as far as I was concerned, and I'm relatively easy to get along with. I didn't think he was aloof, he seemed pleasant. But they certainly did talk boats and engines."

Evelyn Bardahl McNeil saw Musson in a different light.

"He had a great sense of humor. We used to call him 'Mighty Mouse,' and he just laughed. Because, you know, he was built like a fire plug. He had *big* thighs and he was really strong. He was always planning practical jokes, too. Oh, he was full of hell, he did all kinds of nutty things. He was great fun, we had so many good times with him. He was wonderful."

Gary Breakfield worked with Musson for just one year, but the stout little driver made a big impression on him.

"He was quite a guy, he really was," he recalled. "He liked to joke around a lot. He liked to party, he was always partying. Race day, that was a different story – he was serious. On race day he would disappear, kind of go off and get his thoughts. He would settle down and know he had a job to do. But he was friendly, very much so. The PR guy, jolly, caring, and he cared about us. He liked the crew. He was pretty proud of us for what we did for him.

"He hung around with Bernie Little a lot, and I think Rex Manchester was the other guy," Breakfield added. "Ron called him 'sexy Rexy.' He hung out with the big owners and where the parties were all the time."

Jerry Schoenith was a rookie driver in 1964 who knew Musson on and off the racecourse when Jerry's family owned the *Gale* boats and The Roostertail restaurant overlooking the Detroit River. "He was a big kid with a big heart," he said of Musson. "One line I liked when Ron lost a race once, he came in and laughed and said, 'That's what I get for not driving hung over.'"

Schoenith oversaw marketing and promotion for the Unlimited Racing Commission in 1980, and the following year another man who grew up around hydroplanes handled that role – Sam Cole, son of publicist, promoter, and 1966-74 URC Executive Secretary Phil Cole. Sam's Musson memories are those of a pre-teen.

"Ron was a lot like Dean Chenoweth in personality – a very intense competitor, quiet and reserved," Sam Cole said. "He had a dry sense of humor when you got past racing. He pretty much kept to himself, and he liked to smoke. He had the sharpest driver's uniforms from Hinchman and was one of the first drivers, along with Muncey, to don the leather boots. They actually would buy them in Madison at Hertz Shoes, walk down to the river and wade in to get the boots wet so they would form to their feet.

"Had Ron stayed with us, Bill may have never achieved what he did," Cole added. "Ron was as good a competitor as the sport ever had."

Dax Smith's memory of Musson is colored by their age difference and roles.

"I didn't know him real well. It's kind of like he's a senior-management guy and I'm a worker guy. He didn't specifically make it that way, he wasn't aloof. At the races we didn't do a whole lot of socializing with him. We didn't have a whole lot of time, and we're 20- and 21-year-old kids, and Musson is another 15 years older. We're kind of in different social spheres. At that time in boat racing, there was a fair amount of owner-driver social activity that did not include the crew.

"Pleasant enough guy. You could talk to him; no difficulty there," Dax said. "But he's the driver, and a driver's got a little magical aura around him, at least from my standpoint. He was a little bit temperamental or moody at times. But I want to temper that – that goes along with a lot of drivers. If things aren't going well, there's a lot of pressure on the driver as well as on the crew, particularly if you're throwing darts at each other. Like: 'You asshole, you broke my motor.' 'No I didn't, you didn't build a motor that was strong enough.' We had some discussions about, 'How hard are you pushing on the pedal?' But a lot of that went through Leo."

Ron Jones spent time with Musson over the years, first rebuilding *Bardahl*'s sponsons and later fine-tuning them to correct wear and tear, and he often found Musson funny. "He was well-spoken when he had to be. He knew how to command an audience. He was humorous, it was fun to be around him a lot. And at the most inopportune times, he'd get everybody cracked up when you're trying to get somewhere. He was very friendly, and it was not hard to get to know him.

"I never got the impression boat racing per se scared Ronnie or gave him a little bit of a shock when he was getting ready," Jones said. "I don't think that ever bothered him. I think he was well at home in a hydroplane, and I do believe that's because of his extensive background in *fast* limiteds. He got chosen as the driver of the better limited boats in his day."

Jones paused, then added, "Sometimes he, uhh … what can I say? Sometimes he had to sleep in."

Despite their age difference, David Smith developed rapport with Musson, who eventually made David one of the rare passengers to ride aboard the Green Dragon.

"He was nice to us, he was considerate, he never yelled at us, he never said we screwed up," David recalled. "He wouldn't hang around us a lot. He was more with Bernie and the big guys, and the crew was separate. When I first started, I didn't interact much with Ron. But later I got to work in the cockpit, which was his home, so he would talk to me and I would talk to him. And we got to a pretty good relationship that way. But I didn't ever know Ron real well."

Like many who knew and admired Ron the driver, David hesitates before sharing further insight into Ron the person. But some of Musson's proclivities were so evident to so many of those around him that David eventually elaborated, recognizing he's not exactly revealing secrets.

"Ron would come down to the dock sometimes in the morning, and he'd look like he was still blasted. Because he drank, and he looked like he was still at the party," David said. "I never saw him drink wine or beer. He drank hard stuff. I don't think it was scotch, I think it was whiskey. And he used to eat a lot of Tums, and he loved Camel cigarettes.

Zuvich concurred, "Ron was a hard liquor guy, he wasn't a beer or wine guy."

"But once he got in the boat, he'd make magic out of that thing," David said. "He was pretty quiet. He was always very calm. He was even calm on race day. And he seemed to be in good shape, he never got out of the boat tired."

Roger Kruse joined the *Bardahl* team in May 1964 and met Musson. "We socialized very little. Ron socialized with us at parties after the race a little bit. And, like the times we were in Detroit, he loosened up. He took us to the Playboy Club.

"He had a pretty dry sense of humor," Kruse continued. "He was a very good speaker, and he was outgoing, but not to the point of being boisterous. He was articulate, very intelligent, company-minded. When he was with just a half dozen of us he was very friendly. Ron socialized with the high-class teams. He really didn't want to hang out with some of the guys that had to sleep in their trucks because they couldn't afford a motel, or were always coming over to borrow fuel, and on and on. He didn't have much time for them."

As a *Miss Spokane* mechanic, Skip Schott observed Musson as a rival for several years before joining him on the *Bardahl* team.

"He was kind of a 'man's man,' and he never passed up a cocktail," Schott said. "Probably had the classic short-guy complex. And he had interesting friends, like the guy who owned Mittelstadt Mortuary in Ballard. Musson was articulate, and funny at times. He had an office in the building, he was a sharp dresser, and he'd come in the boat shop and say, 'Hey, how are you guys doing?' We were all on a first-name basis with him. I don't remember him as being demanding because we were the workers and he was the guy who wore the tie."

In 1986, Wild Bill Cantrell told the *Madison Courier*'s Dave Taylor that Musson "was quite a personality. He had a lot of fun with the kids. He was very popular all the time. He was small, he reminded me of a banty rooster. In fact, we sometimes called him Mighty Mouse. But there was nothing too big or too hard

Musson often was kind to kids, like young Jim Osborne, shown here at Portage Lakes near Akron, Ohio, in the early 1950s.
– photographer unknown, used with permission of Jim Osborne

Musson with his 1965 *Bardahl* crew at Coeur d'Alene. L to R, standing: Jerry Zuvich, Roger Kruse, Dax Smith; crouched, David Smith, Skip Schott.
– Marg Smith photo, used with permission of Dixon Smith

Midwest racers and 1953 champions, L to R: Tony Lamontia, Jack Force, Ron Musson.
– photographer unknown, used with permission of Mark Lamontia

Betty and Ron Musson, Ole and Inga Bardahl celebrate another Green Dragon victory.
© *Seattle Times* photo 1964 by Vic Condiotty

for him. He was small but he made up for that by having a big, heavy right foot."

Billy Schumacher was an 18-year-old rookie driving *Miss Tool Crib* when Musson won Seafair in 1961 aboard the second *Miss Bardahl*. Like Musson, he was a champion limited-class driver, but unlike Musson, he had to wait six years before getting a competitive ride in the big boats.

"I'm proud to say that Ron Musson was a very good friend of mine," Schumacher said in 2010. "He was a good businessman and a terrific person as well as one of the best hydroplane drivers in the sport's history. I was a few years younger than Ron and new to the unlimiteds, but he had a big influence on me and I learned a great deal about driving from him.

"Ron had a keen sense of humor and loved to play jokes on his competitors," he continued. "I think that was his way of throwing you off-course from your thoughts, so you didn't concentrate on the race itself. He was very good at that type of mental game. Ron was a handsome guy, so needless to say the ladies enjoyed him, and I think he loved the attention. Some of us were a bit jealous.

"Out of all the people I've raced with and against, Ron Musson and Bill Muncey are missed the most," Schumacher said.

Longtime *Seattle Post-Intellingencer* columnist Royal Brougham's epitaph for Musson summed it up: "Musson was a skillful driver, modest winner and gracious loser, although losing was a rare experience."

Chapter 15

New boats, new players

In the months that followed the 1963 racing season, *Miss Bardahl*'s team makeup continued to evolve. The Freeman brothers, age 44 and 42, left. Joining the core group were Gary "Reb" Breakfield, 21, Zuvich's friend; Roger Kruse, 25, a truck mechanic for Los Angeles – Seattle Motor Express who maintained the team's rolling stock; and 17-year-old Dave Smith, who was in his junior year at Cleveland High School on Seattle's Beacon Hill. Dixon was now 20, Zuvich was 23, and Vanden Berg was the grizzled veteran at age 46.

Breakfield and Zuvich had first crossed paths at the Chevron gas station near Seattle's Fremont Bridge, where they'd hang out and talk about cars. Breakfield was the assistant manager at the Blue Mouse and Music Box theaters in downtown Seattle, and he recalls joining the *Bardahl* crew in late 1963, when Burns Smith was transitioning away.

"I was the fuel man and the oil man," Breakfield said. "As soon as the boat came in they'd throw me the bow rope, I'd walk the boat up to the front, put the fuel in and check the oil, and then I'd wipe it down."

"Bill Marshall was my foreman at LASME at that time, and he was on the *Bardahl*," said Kruse. "And his wife said, 'Either the boat leaves or I leave.' Bill asked me if I was interested in working on the boat, and I said sure. They were looking for somebody to take care of the rolling stock, and my first job in May of 1964 was to get the trucks and trailers lined up and ready to go."

Kruse did the work right in the Ballard Bardahl shop while the others got the boat ready.

"Once the rolling stock was fixed, I'd ride with the team to the races, or fly in and out to places like Detroit and Madison," said Kruse. "From the day I started, I was part of the team. Even though I was a newcomer, they didn't treat me as the new kid. And any money I lost from my full-time job in wages, they made up for me."

"Roger could have worked on the boat itself very easily," said Schott, who joined the team in the fall of 1964. "He was a very skilled mechanic, the kind of person who would pitch right in and help change engines or whatever needed doing."

Aside from Vanden Berg, *Miss Bardahl*'s crew averaged a mere 21 years old. As in earlier years, with youth came boundless energy, but also some challenging traits.

"Leo was definitely the stabilizing force," said Dax. "Had Leo not been there, we wouldn't have lasted 10 minutes in the same room together. Think about it: Here you've got three or four fairly young people, probably all of them not really very mature. All are pretty aggressive, all want to win. Everybody's got their own idea. And if it isn't their idea, it's no good. None of us had grown up to the point where we could accept somebody else's original idea. Think about that age – you're not very receptive to suggestions: 'It's my idea, it's gotta be good; if it's your idea, it's gotta be bad.'

"We all got along extremely well considering the circumstances," Dax continued. "Our chemistry was really good, because we all were interested in winning boat races. And even if we had severe disagreements inside the camp, it was because 'my idea of how to make the raceboat go faster is better than your idea of how to make the raceboat go faster.' Once we got it settled out and decided how to do something, we all would go in the same direction."

When David joined the crew mid-season in 1964, he recalled seeing Vanden Berg as the unquestioned father figure who directed what to do and how to do it. Because of the crew's youth they rebelled at times against their crew chief's "my way or the highway" approach, which likely stemmed from Vanden Berg's strict upbringing as well as his career working for the military.

"Leo was very rigid with us, but he had to be," said David. "Little by little, all of us got to thinking Leo wasn't as bright as we first thought he was. We got a little bit smarter, and more cocky."

"Leo was a good leader, but he was very much one who would demand this is the way it's gonna be, it's gonna be my way, or else," Kruse recalled. "Leo had a tough time with it, keeping track of us. He had such a big generation gap. I was a pretty quiet person, supposed to be respectful of my elders, and I was. Leo and I never clashed over anything; our personalities were pretty close compared with David and Jerry. But we all had good chemistry, and we were a good team."

Skip Schott had a simple assessment of the team chemistry during his later tenure: "We were smart-ass kids!"

When asked if his crew members were fairly responsible for their age and if there were challenges, Vanden Berg said, "Naturally, there were a few problems. They'd try to do something their own way when I wasn't looking. In fact, I think Jerry was the culprit who caused most of the trouble. I'd do something he didn't like, and then he'd get the kids to go along with him: 'Let's give Leo the silent treatment today.' But they were generally pretty good."

* * * *

On Good Friday, March 27, 1964, a 9.2-magnitude earthquake centered in Prince William Sound ravaged Alaska and British Columbia, killing 131 people and triggering a tsunami that claimed lives as far away as Oregon and California. While the Pacific Northwest was rumbling, *Miss Bardahl* sat safely on display at the National Boat Show in the New York City Coliseum. Musson told attendees driving his hydro "is like being in a milkshake machine. A pilot can't do much without a good crew, so give them all the credit. I never dreamed of driving such a fine craft. A few years ago I would have settled for a good outboard."

Unlimited hydroplane racing was healthy and growing in 1964. New Town, N.D., and San Diego became new race sites on the circuit, and several new boats were nearing completion.

Notre Dame was a Rolls-powered Les Staudacher creation, apparently built on speculation and sold to Shirley Mendelson McDonald to replace the 1962 hull that had burned on Lake Washington in the December '63 test run. Unlike the previous hull that employed "drop" sponsons, the new U-7 featured a continuous deck, sleek engine cowling, and a swept-back tail that evoked memories of *Hawaii Kai III*.

Notre Dame also had a new driver, Bill Muncey – "perhaps out of embarrassment" wrote *The Seattle Times'* Georg Meyers, noting Muncey had been driving when the previous U-7 caught fire. Muncey brought along part of his former *Thriftway* crew.

Another new Staudacher hull was, he said, nearly an exact *Kai* copy – George Simon's *Miss U.S.5*. It had one key difference: Simon's scarlet speedster was built largely out of magnesium, a lightweight metal intended to provide sufficient strength but with a higher horsepower-to-weight ratio. Don Wilson would helm the 5,200-pound Detroit craft.

Owner Jim Herrington's team built a new *Mariner Too* from Ted Jones drawings and wooed former *Notre Dame* pilot Col. Warner Gardner to drive. Like *Notre Dame* and *U.S.5,* the red and white *Mariner* would be Rolls-powered. It was launched May 13, 1964, on the Detroit River.

Bill Harrah and crew, though pleased to finish third nationally in 1963 with their new *Tahoe Miss*, were unhappy with the heavy boat's wild handling. So Staudacher got yet another order to design and build a new hydro, and by late winter a sparkling gunmetal gray *Tahoe Miss* with a uniquely shaped tail was under construction. *Tahoe* again would use a two-stage Allison, but without the guidance of engine expert Bill Newman, who had moved on.

Staudacher said that on Saginaw Bay in the fall of 1963, Chuck Thompson "came up and drove the *Notre Dame* – the one with the Rolls – and he liked it." So *Tahoe* was built identical to *Notre Dame*, except it was 11 inches longer to accommodate *Tahoe*'s lengthy aux-stage Allison, and it was "all aluminum, no wood in it at all," according to Staudacher. Joining the *Tahoe* crew for 1964 were Andy Anderson and Herb Witherspoon. The new boat was christened by Scherry Harrah, Bill's wife, on June 5.

Bill Newman's new role was crew chief of Bernie Little's *Miss Budweiser* camp. The *Bud* previously had raced as the 1962 *Tahoe Miss* and before that, *Miss Reno* and *Maverick*.

"Bernie and I got $10,000 from August Busch the first year we put 'Miss Budweiser' on that boat," longtime publicist Phil Cole told the *Unlimited NewsJournal* in 1995. "Bernie met August when August came in to rent an airplane from him."

The Schoenith family's *Gale V* was growing tired after six years of hard racing, so Bill Cantrell and Gale Enterprises built a new hydro. It resembled its Detroit riverboat predecessors – stout, thick, a little heavy. It wore different livery, though – mahogany, plus the blue and red of new sponsor Smirnoff vodka – and *Miss Smirnoff* sported U-90 on its deck. (Reportedly, the sponsor wanted U-80, to signify Smirnoff's 80-proof alcohol content, but *Blue Chip* already had the U-80 number. *Smirnoff* did switch to U-80 in 1966 after *Blue Chip* stopped racing.) Like the *Gale*s, *Miss Smirnoff* was Allison-powered.

Gale V was not ready for mothballs, however. Former driver Lee Schoenith placed his young brother Jerry in the cockpit, and Bill Cantrell commenced with intense tutoring on the Detroit River. Jerry and his identical twin brother Tom had been born July 4, 1943, making Jerry a 20-year-old rookie at his first race of the 1964 season.

Amid new boats and drivers, a new face replaced a familiar one in the hydro broadcast booth. Keith Jackson, a fixture for 10 years at Seattle's KOMO-TV and Radio, left his sports director post in June 1964 to join ABC Radio and TV Sports in Hollywood. Jackson promised to return in August for KOMO's day-long Seafair Regatta broadcast, which he ultimately did in what also became the debut of KOMO's new sports director, George Ray from Zanesville, Wisc.

* * * *

Adventure beckoned from all corners of our neighborhood. Within five blocks in any direction, my friends and I had a mix of attractions: woods, where we'd play army with air rifles, or fight with dirt clods and sword-fern spears. Ponds, for catching frogs and polliwogs, and for launching rafts. New housing developments, which we'd scrounge for scrap wood. The cemetery reservoir, where we'd float our Revell plastic model battleships, then retreat 100 paces and bombard them with stone "bombs."

The air rifles also made good weapons. Plunge the end of the barrel into a lawn, lift it out, and a turf plug remained inside. Cock the gun, pull the trigger, and the plug sailed about 15 feet.

The playground at my elementary school was just a block away, where we'd play football, shoot hoops, and fly kites. But most of our time was spent playing in the residential streets in front of our homes – touch football, whiffle ball, fly up, and of course pulling plywood hydros with our bikes.

Bike hydro races were such a big deal that sometimes more than a dozen kids competed – kids on coaster-brake Murrays and Huffys, 3-speed J.C. Higgins, and of course the rich kids on their 10-speed Schwinns. We'd stage time trials. Racers pedaled furiously around the block, dragging their plywood *Tahoes, Slo-mos, Gales, Wahoos, Mavericks, Hawaii Kais*, and *Exides*. We timed each racer and charted a qualifying ladder.

Some kids added sound effects by fastening baseball cards to their bike's wheel fenders with clothes pins. The spinning spokes snapped the cards loudly, mimicking a motor. Many now-priceless Mickey Mantle, Warren Spahn, and Willie Mays cards were destroyed in that short-sighted stunt.

There was much strategy to ponder. Build your boat with thick plywood, or thin? Sponsons, or no sponsons? Rub the bottom with bar soap, or not? Most kids towed their boats with kite string, which sometimes snapped. Some used 20-pound-test fishing line. Many tied the string to their rear fender, while others tied it to their seat post, which caused problems when the string touched the rear tire and quickly wound around the axle.

Sometimes we'd swing wide around a corner to minimize centrifugal force and the chance of a flip. But if you veered too wide, you could swing your boat right under the tire of a parked car. Snapped string, DNF.

Plywood hydros could flip anytime, but usually it happened rounding a corner. The dreaded spot on our block was "The Church Turn." For some reason, the corner in front of Lake Hills Community Church was always strewn with gravel. It was that way for years. Guys rounding the church turn always fretted about their boats flipping, because they often did. And we had a dumb rule that if your hydro flipped, you had to stop, dismount, and turn it right-side up before racing on.

The first hydro – not bike – to cross the finish line won. One time my neighbor was in a tight battle nearing the finish. Following the "letter of the law" rather than the "spirit of the law," he reached behind his seat, grabbed the tow string and yanked his boat forward across the line just ahead of the other kid's boat. A devious move, for sure.

Those bicycle races lasted only through sixth grade. We had a rule that kids could "drive" up through age 12, but once you became a teenager, you couldn't pull a hydro. However, you could become an "owner" and recruit a younger kid to pull your boat, so we did that for a couple of years. In 1968, at age 14, I made an 18-inch checkerboard *Bardahl* that a 10-year-old named Ricky pulled. Then we outgrew playing with plywood hydros.

Notre Dame was a new boat in 1964, along with *Miss Smirnoff* (right) and *Miss U.S.5* (in distance). *Gale V* (left) was nearing retirement.
– Jon Osterberg collection

Don Wilson aboard the magnesium, 5,200-pound *U.S.5* at Seattle.
– Jon Osterberg collection

Part of 1964 crew, L to R: Dax Smith, Roger Kruse, Gary "Reb" Breakfield.
– used with permission of Roger Kruse

It took *Mariner Too* all of 1964 to mature, but the new U-99 eventually cracked the winner's circle at San Diego.
– Richard Hall photo, used with his permission

Dueling riverboats: mentor Bill Cantrell in *Smirnoff* chases understudy Jerry Schoenith in *Gale V* on Lake Washington, 1964.
© Eileen Crimmin photo 1964, used with permission of The Crimmin Collection

The new Gray Ghost battles the Green Dragon through Seattle's south turn, Seafair 1964.
© Eileen Crimmin photo 1964, used with permission of The Crimmin Collection

* * * *

Thirteen thunderboats gathered in Guntersville, Ala., for the June 21, 1964, Dixie Cup Regatta. Perhaps in a game of psychological gamesmanship, Muncey told everyone who would listen, "I don't know how *Bardahl* can lose this year. It should win every race." In contrast, he offered low expectations for his own *Notre Dame*, saying he had hopes of making it "competitive by midseason, maybe."

America hummed along with a new soundtrack that winter and spring. The British Invasion was well underway, and as race week began in Guntersville, Seattle radio station KJR's "Fabulous 50" was topped by the Dave Clark Five's "Can't You See That She's Mine." Other Mersey Beat artists topping the charts included The Searchers, "Don't Throw Your Love Away" at No. 5, and Jerry & The Pacemakers at No. 9 with "Don't Let the Sun Catch You Crying." Peter and Gordon debuted with a Paul McCartney composition, "World Without Love," but a few American bands still held fast – the Beach Boys' "I Get Around" had been No. 1 for weeks, the Four Seasons' "Rag Doll" was racing up the charts, and the Dixie Cups showed the popularity of girl groups with their "Chapel of Love." On television, the top three shows were "Bonanza," "Bewitched," and "Gomer Pyle, U.S.M.C."

Gary Breakfield found the deep South to be a whole new world.

"In Guntersville we'd go into the restaurant, and the restroom signs said 'men,' 'women,' and the 'n' word pointing around the backside," he said. "I'll never forget that as long as I live. And the racecourse was inside a gigantic fenced area labeled 'whites only.' As Jerry and I were driving through this area through the towns, we'd see this and say, my God, look at this place we're going through. Signs everywhere that said 'whites only.'"

In April 2012, *Oh Boy! Oberto* driver Steve David recalled a story told to him by John Humes, a black *Miss Madison* crewman, about racing in Guntersville in the mid-'60s.

"John and our team walked into a restaurant and he was told, 'Your team can eat here, but you can't.' The team said no thanks, and they were about to leave. That's when several other boat teams who were there all said in unison, 'If you don't serve Big John, you don't serve any of us.' As he told me that story he beamed with the knowledge that sport, whatever sport it is, has a way of breaking down barriers and bringing us closer together. A lot has changed since 1963 in the deep South, and a lot hasn't," David observed. "In the case of Big John, I have a feeling the workers at that restaurant maybe had a change in their thinking."

On Thursday, June 18, Musson circled the 2½-mile Guntersville Lake course at 106.635 mph. Bob Schroeder qualified Bernie Little's "new" hydroplane, *Miss Budweiser*, at 101.580. Billy Schumacher squeezed 97.721 mph out of *$ Bill*, and two new boats got in the show, *Mariner Too* and Warner Gardner at 97.721 and *Miss Smirnoff* with Bill Cantrell, 98.792.

Unlimited rookie Buddy Byers impressed everyone by qualifying *Miss Madison* at 105.882 mph. Another rookie, Jerry Schoenith, didn't fare as well. He rammed *Gale V* onto the rocks while returning to the pits, smashing the boat's lime nose and prompting an all-night repair effort. Cantrell qualified the *V* the following day, and Muncey steered his new *Notre Dame* to the top qualifying speed of 108.434 mph. Altogether, 12 boats qualified. *Tahoe Miss* with Chuck Thompson arrived late, and *St. Regis* and Jimmy Fyle failed to qualify.

In stifling 100-degree heat, *Miss Budweiser* averaged better than 100 mph to win heat 1A. At the time no one dreamed that Bernie Little's boat had just started the winningest saga in hydroplane history. Heat 1B went to *Notre Dame* at 106 mph to beat *Bardahl*'s 104, and rookie Byers aboard *Madison* won heat 1C. *Bardahl* took heat 2A with the day's fastest average speed of 106.719 mph, and *Notre Dame* won 2B at 102.466. The final featured *Notre Dame*, 800 points; *Bardahl* and *Madison*, 700; *Tempo*, 525; and *Mariner Too*, 469.

A crowd of 40,000 cheered as the boats thundered toward the start, where all five jumped the gun. *Madison* held lane one flanked by *Bardahl*, *Notre Dame*, and front-running *Tempo* and *Mariner Too*. Muncey and Musson took a roostertail bath in turn one, with *Bardahl* getting the brunt of it and stopping momentarily. Musson recovered, but not before Muncey had zoomed off after leader *Miss Madison*. Byers held off Muncey to win the heat, and Musson picked off Schroeder and Gardner to snatch third.

Although *Madison* and *Notre Dame* tied with 1,100 total points, Muncey earned the victory over his rookie rival by averaging 99.122 mph for the race compared with Byers' 95.833. Muncey praised his crew chief, Bud Meldrum, and thanked his longtime *Thriftway* team leader Jack Ramsey for advising the new team.

"There were special problems in Alabama," said Dr. Fraser McDonald, co-owner of *Notre Dame* with his wife Shirley. "It was 104 degrees in the pits and the water temperature was about 80 degrees. This made it somewhat difficult to water-cool the engines." McDonald thanked Meldrum, Jim Kerth, Ray Ballard and crew for doing a splendid job with their new hull, and the U-7 team journeyed north to Detroit.

Chapter 16

By the slimmest of margins

Two more Washington state boats joined the Dixie Cup competitors in the Motor City for the 1964 APBA Gold Cup, *Miss Eagle Electric* of Spokane, and Seattle's *Miss Exide*, which now sported a mandarin red deck and blue cowling. Making its debut was *Miss U.S.5*. Muncey and *Notre Dame* topped all qualifiers with a 115.302-mph three-lap average on Monday, June 29. Byers turned a few heads by averaging 113.246 in the stock-Allison powered *Miss Madison*. For the time being, rookie Jerry Schoenith was back on the beach in favor of Rex Manchester, who had the required driving experience to qualify for Gold Cup action.

Tempo did not appear in Detroit after suffering damage in a highway accident following the Dixie Cup. Reportedly, while being towed to Detroit in a severe rainstorm, the boat, trailer, and truck plunged over a cliff. Les Staudacher repaired the hull, and Bernie Little later repurchased it from Ed Cantrell, who had owned it just a short time.

Ron Musson scorched around the historic Detroit River course Tuesday at a three-lap average of 117.647 mph. Within minutes, Bill Brow powered *Miss Exide* onto the river and shattered Musson's mark with a blazing 119.557 mph. Both speeds surpassed the previous course record of 116.463 set the year before by Muncey and *Thriftway*.

Musson's first lap was 118.551, and observers stood transfixed as the Green Dragon kicked up a full roostertail throughout the Belle Isle turn. Of his own run, Brow said he hit 170 mph on the backstretch as he fell just short of Bill Stead's Gold Cup qualifying record of 119.998 mph set aboard *Maverick* in 1958. Noting Detroit's tight Roostertail turn, Muncey guessed Brow's speed would have been 121 or 122 mph on Lake Washington.

Musson was eager to surpass *Exide*'s speed, but Vanden Berg and another key stakeholder reminded him qualifying records were not the goal.

"That was one thing I really didn't believe in," Ole Bardahl said years later. "I remember at the 1964 Detroit Gold Cup when *Miss Exide* qualified at 119 mph, and Musson wanted to go out and beat him. He wanted 120. He said to Leo, 'Drop the boat in the water.' I said, 'No way, you wait until race day.'"

Exide's run topped the front page of *The Seattle Times* Tuesday afternoon along with a report not uncommon for its day: "A 60½-pound King, largest salmon of the year, was boated off Hope Island this morning by a 12-year-old girl, Terri Ensign, a 70-pounder."

Through the rest of the week, Bob Schroeder squeezed quick laps out of *Miss Budweiser*, averaging 110.580. Cantrell caused a commotion by blowing the supercharger off of *Gale V*, which caught fire, and Bill Schumacher passed his Gold Cup driver's test by making a perfect start and turning three laps over 100 mph in *$ Bill*. Much "bumping" ensued as boats scrambled to stay among the 12 qualifiers. *Budweiser* upped its speed to 113.406. Norm Evans and the Lilac Lady *Miss Eagle Electric* roared through a 116.254 lap and averaged 114.284 altogether, pleasing crew chief Kent Simonson and giving Washington state the top-four qualifiers. Don Wilson put *Miss U.S.5* into the show at 110.656, while Thompson and *Tahoe Miss* anchored the bottom of the time-trial ladder before raising their speed to 108.652. A new odd-looking square-nosed boat, *Miss Liberty*, failed to qualify.

Seattle hydro fans tuned their radios to KOL and KING at 10 o'clock Sunday morning, July 5, to hear live Gold Cup coverage. Ron Jones called the action on KOL and described a wind-whipped Detroit River, which on Friday had been blasted by a storm strong enough to cancel qualifying. Heat 1A brought *Exide, Notre Dame, Eagle Electric, Budweiser, Smirnoff,* and *Blue Chip* onto the course. Brow led across the start line and through the first turn with Muncey close behind, but *Notre Dame* roared ahead up the back chute and gradually opened a comfortable lead. Rough water hammered chunks off of *Blue Chip*'s sponson in lap five but Fred Alter steamed onward. Schroeder in *Budweiser* tried to overtake *Exide* in the final turn, but *Bud* hooked, tossing Schroeder into the river. *Bud* coasted on, crashed into the sea wall, and started taking on water before it was retrieved. Meanwhile, *Notre Dame* won at 100.880 followed by *Exide, Smirnoff, Blue Chip,* and a sluggish *Eagle Electric*.

Bardahl, Madison, U.S.5, Tahoe Miss, and *$ Bill* clashed in 1B; *Gale V* did not start. Wilson and *U.S.5* led *Madison* and *Bardahl* across the line, but Thompson poured on the coals and *Tahoe* surged to the front entering turn one. *Bardahl* hooked in the tight Roostertail turn and lost ground, while *Tahoe* finished its first lap at 107.175 mph on lumpy water to lead *Bardahl* by five seconds, followed by *Madison*. The unstable and untested *U.S.5* struggled with the wind and rollers but managed to stay ahead of *$ Bill*. *Tahoe* won at 104.964 mph followed by *Bardahl, Madison, U.S.5,* and *$ Bill*.

Thompson snatched lane one in heat 2A but found himself chasing Muncey and Manchester toward the first turn. Muncey veered *Notre Dame* to the inside and led by two seconds at the end of lap one, but *Tahoe* caught and passed *Notre Dame* in lap two. Determined to regain the lead, Muncey charged hard into the Roostertail turn but smashed a buoy, earning a one-lap penalty. Thompson finished the lap at 112.688 mph, fastest of the heat, and went on to win at 106.755 followed by *Exide, Gale V, U.S.5,* and the penalized *Notre Dame*.

Heat 2B appeared to be an easy draw for *Bardahl* and Musson, who arrived early for the start along with *Madison, Smirnoff, Eagle Electric,* and *$ Bill. Madison* led the field but *Bardahl* powered ahead approaching the turn and maintained the lead throughout the heat, averaging 103.036 mph. Next came *Madison, Smirnoff, $ Bill, and Eagle Electric,* which suffered from an ailing aftercooler in the hot, humid air.

Bardahl, Notre Dame, and *Exide* fought in heat 3A along with *Smirnoff* and *$ Bill*. Muncey won the pole position and led the field through the first turn with *Bardahl* and *Exide* close behind, but *Bardahl* roared past *Notre Dame* on the outside up the backstretch before both boats hit a large swell approaching the turn. *Bardahl* launched skyward and slammed to the river in a burst of spray.

"We were both completely airborne going up the back chute," said Musson. "Both of us were going entirely too fast. I passed him on the outside, but when I hit that big swell I was thrown to the left. I was going almost sideways there for a second. The same thing happened to Muncey."

Officials fired a red flare, halting the race. Some observers thought an overly cautious course judge got trigger-happy over the leaping hydros, but officials said a wayward cruiser had encroached on the racecourse. It perhaps was fortunate for Muncey, who at that exact moment had found no room between *Bardahl* and the entrance pin and swerved to the infield. Since the flare halted they heat, no penalty was called for missing a buoy.

Notre Dame's crew put fresh batteries in for the rerun of heat 3A, but unknown to them, two cells were dead. Muncey could not get *Notre Dame* started; glum, he watched as *Bardahl* ran the fastest heat of the day at 108.106 to beat *Exide, Smirnoff,* and *$ Bill* in that order. Schumacher enjoyed a glorious moment in the spotlight when he led the field through the first turn and held off Brow in *Exide* until lap three, and not until the final lap did Cantrell push *Smirnoff* past the 21-year-old baker's son.

Eagle Electric led at the start of heat 3B but soon was passed by *Tahoe Miss, Madison,* and *U.S.5*. Manchester and *Gale V* lagged behind and averaged just 92 mph for lap one, but Rex gained speed and passed three contenders by lap four, in which he averaged 110. Only *Tahoe* remained ahead, but *Gale*'s Allison blew on the backstretch and Thompson won at 104.767 mph, followed by *Madison* and *U.S.5*. Evans was disqualified by officials for rough driving in lap three, where he pushed the onrushing Manchester wide and nearly onto the beach exiting the Roostertail turn. Manchester floored the throttle and narrowly squeezed through, and he later said the burst of full power likely weakened *Gale*'s motor.

Six boats prepared to race in the final heat of the Gold Cup: *Tahoe Miss*, with three heat wins and a perfect 1,200 points; *Bardahl* with 1,100; *Exide*, 900; *Madison*, 825; *Smirnoff*, 675; and *U.S.5*, 563. *Notre Dame* and Muncey missed the cut with 527 points. *Tahoe* held a 14-second advantage over *Bardahl* in total elapsed time, so Musson needed to win by at least that much to retain the Gold Cup.

The combatants roared out of the pits and began milling around the lumpy river. Just three minutes before the starting gun, Thompson detected low oil pressure and hustled *Tahoe* back to the pits. His crew jumped aboard, swarmed over the motor, and pointed his boat back toward the river, but precious time had passed. *Tahoe* got underway barely before the one-minute gun and trailed the field by a vast distance, three-quarters of a lap.

Five boats screamed across the start line. *Exide* shot into the corner along with *Madison* and *Bardahl* with *Smirnoff* and *U.S.5* in pursuit. *Tahoe* lagged far behind, its raspy motor finally surging to life.

"I got wet in the first turn, and by the time I got it cleaned out, I was third," said Musson. "When I saw that Chuck was in trouble, I changed my strategy. I had figured to race him all the way and it would have been a real tussle. But with him out, I just played it safe. I didn't want to take a chance of burning out my engine. I decided to stay where I was and gamble that *Tahoe Miss* wouldn't pass *Miss U.S.*"

Exide stretched its lead followed by *Madison*, with *Bardahl* settling comfortably into third as Musson did some quick arithmetic and figured he would win the race on points if everyone held their positions: *Bardahl* would outscore *Tahoe*, 1,325 points to 1,295.

But that was a shaky assumption. Wilson and *U.S.5* were hobbled and running poorly in fifth, while gritty Thompson was muscling his Gray Ghost around the heaving river at a frantic pace and steadily closed the gap. When Musson saw this unfolding, he stood on the gas in lap four and tried to run down *Madison*, but the gap was too wide. *Tahoe* appeared poised to catch *U.S.5* and edge past *Bardahl* on points, 1327 to 1325!

The field entered the fifth and final lap. *Tahoe* gobbled ground on *U.S.5* even as Wilson quickened his pace, aware of Thompson stalking him. *Bardahl* charged futilely after second-place *Madison*, which trailed *Exide*. The leaders bounced and slammed around the rough course, rounded the final turn, and took the checkered flag: *Exide* at 103.296 mph, *Madison, Bardahl, Smirnoff*. But all eyes were on the fight at the rear, 30 seconds back.

Tahoe closed quickly on *U.S.5* up the backstretch and disappeared behind Wilson's roostertail approaching the final turn. The boats bucked over swells, leaped, and churned through the corner. Thompson stomped his foot to the floorboard entering the home stretch and *Tahoe* surged on the outside, drawing closer, closer, closer … and crossed the finish line half a boat length behind Wilson and *U.S.5*. Exactly 15 feet separated Thompson from victory. *U.S.5* averaged 90.274 mph to *Tahoe*'s 90.103.

Musson and *Bardahl* had won their second-straight APBA Gold Cup.

Asked if he recognized the developing scenario while battling Thompson, Wilson said with a smile, "You bet I did. And remember, I used to drive for Ole Bardahl."

"We were all taking a beating out there," said an exhausted but elated Musson. "The course was just terrible. I wish we could get this race back to Seattle, where it belongs.

"*Tahoe Miss* had a big advantage over the rest of us, because of its added length," he said, referring to the Nevada boat's 32-foot dimensions. Most of the field ranged in length from *Bardahl*'s 30 feet to *Exide*'s and *Eagle Electric*'s 28 feet 6 inches. "The rest of us were just falling in those holes out there."

The final order of finish showed *Bardahl* first with 1,325 points followed by *Exide*, 1,300; *Tahoe Miss*, 1,295; *Madison*, 1,125; *Smirnoff*, 844; and *U.S.5*, 690.

* * * *

Though reliable on the water, *Miss Bardahl* suffered a mechanical breakdown of sorts while rolling west on U.S. Highway 10.

"We blew the motor on the tractor truck towing the boat," said Breakfield, "and Jerry and I went to Notre Dame in South Bend, Indiana. They put our truck in the shop and we worked overnight and put a new motor in."

North Dakota welcomed the unlimiteds for the first time when the remote outpost of New Town, population 1,586, hosted the $15,000 Dakota Cup Regatta on Garrison Reservoir, the impounded waters of the Missouri River.

"New Town, it was weird to see it," recalled Breakfield. "They had the racecourse on one side, and you look across on the edge of a hillside and there were Indian tepees all over the place. But it was cool seeing that."

Dakotans would not be treated to another Muncey-Musson duel. The *Notre Dame* team announced July 17 that its chauffeur was in Seattle's Swedish Hospital with a back injury and bronchitis, and the Shamrock Lady would skip the July 25-26 race.

"I'll have about 10 days to build myself back up into driving condition," Muncey said, looking ahead to the Aug. 1-2 Diamond Cup, "but I think I can do it."

Also skipping the Dakota Cup was *Miss U.S.5*, which was trailered to Ron Jones' shop in Mountain View,

Calif., for much-needed sponson work to correct its wild ride.

The week before the Dakota Cup, Seattle newspapers ran ads with a photo of Britain's Fab Four over the headline, "Beatle tickets for Royal Crown Cola bottle caps." Contestants submitting the most caps would earn the best chance at 100 tickets to the Beatles' Aug. 21 concert at the Seattle Center Coliseum. That same week, the Beatles held No. 1 on KJR's Fabulous 50 with the title track from their new movie, "A Hard Day's Night," which topped the No. 2 hit "Everybody Loves Somebody," crooned by Dean Martin.

The Garrison Reservoir race site was located at Four Bears Park, 71 miles from Williston, 74 miles from Minot, and 148 miles from Bismarck. Race fans drove long distances for their first glimpse of the thunderboats.

Ron Musson flew his own Cessna airplane 120 air miles each day from his Bismarck motel to the race site. "Every morning, Ole Bardahl, Bernie Little, Lee Schoenith and I pop into my plane and fly to New Town," he said. "Then back again, of course, in the evening." Ole Bardahl said of New Town's grass landing strip, "It's pretty bumpy."

Chuck Thompson stayed in Minot, more than an hour's drive to the pits. Bill Brow stayed in Williston. Many crew members found lodging in trailers towed to the race site especially for the Dakota Cup.

"We stayed in New Town," Vanden Berg said of his *Bardahl* team. "I think we were about the only boat crew that stayed in New Town. You should have seen the motel. You've seen pictures of these little motels in little towns?"

"Some of the *Tahoe* guys flew in, and man, were we envious!" said Dax. "Harry Volpi and Andy Anderson were both pilots."

Jerry Schoenith vividly recalled his own unique accommodations. "New Town, North Dakota, was one of my first races," he recalled while at the 1983 Columbia Cup. "Minot was the *big* city. All the rich people flew in from Minot every day; us poor people had to drive 49 miles to our motel. My room, believe it or not, was a garage made over into a bedroom, just for the race. The garage door just shut," he said, gesturing to indicate a full-size tilt-down door. "And I'm sitting in bed saying to Leo Macutsa, our crew chief, 'This is glamorous racing?!'"

But the racing between *Bardahl* and *Tahoe* was tremendous.

Testing and qualifying took place Friday, July 24, when *Eagle Electric* became the first unlimited to run in North Dakota. Norm Evans circled the 3-mile course at around 110 mph, showing that perhaps crew chief Simonson had solved the Lilac Lady's aftercooler problem. Rookie Schoenith, back aboard his family-owned *Gale V*, didn't qualify until Saturday morning at 100.186.

Race action began Saturday at 2 p.m. near the Four Bears Bridge that funneled 12,000 paying spectators to the viewing areas with fiscal efficiency: Fans paid $1.50 admission when they crossed the bridge heading from New Town, and from the other direction eastbound cars paid $1.50 to turn off North Dakota Highway 23 toward the pits.

Partly cloudy skies and pleasant temperatures in the 80s greeted the heat 1A contestants. Bill Brow squirted ahead in *Miss Exide* and held his lead the entire heat, averaging 105.037 mph to beat Buddy Byers in *Miss Madison* by four seconds, followed closely by Bob Schroeder in *Miss Budweiser*, a distant Evans aboard the still-sputtering *Miss Eagle Electric*, Warner Gardner in *Mariner Too*, and Schoenith aboard

Gale V, which ran a sick 70.643 mph.

Miss Bardahl and *Tahoe Miss* clashed in 1B along with Bill Cantrell in *Miss Smirnoff*, *$ Bill* with Bill Schumacher, and Ed O'Halloran piloting *Savair's Mist*, formerly *Miss Michigan* and *Miss Lumberville*, now owned by Mike Wolfbauer of Savair Products Company. Musson and Thompson battled for five full laps with *Bardahl*, on the inside, showing superior speed through and out of the corners and *Tahoe* proving faster at the end of the chutes. But Thompson's breakneck speed carried him too deep into the turns, which he rounded far outside while Musson shaved the buoys.

"He'd pass us on the chutes and then we'd go through the turns and pass him, and then he'd pass us again on the chute," Vanden Berg recalled. "It went around and around and around. It was the craziest thing. I laughed the whole time."

Bardahl won at a blazing 113.900-mph heat speed, with *Tahoe* just five seconds behind at 112.734, aided by a 117.391-mph third lap. *Smirnoff*, *$ Bill,* and *Savair's Mist* followed. Remarkably, all 11 boats finished their Saturday heats – not one mechanical failure among them.

An angry Musson claimed Thompson cut him off entering a corner on lap four, where Thompson charged hard and tried to gain enough overlap to seal Musson off.

"The official was blind," Musson fumed. "He (Thompson) missed me by inches. And he did the same thing at the Gold Cup in Detroit."

"Aw, he's nuts," Thompson replied. "I had the inside when I reached the deceleration buoy. I had the right of way."

Brow took *Exide* out on Sunday morning for a practice run but blew his Rolls-Merlin, ending his weekend since rules allowed just one engine change, which the crew had performed the day before. Thompson's sweet-riding Gray Ghost continued its torrid pace in heat 2A, averaging 111.754 mph to beat *Miss Madison* by 28 seconds. *Eagle Electric, Gale V,* and *$ Bill* followed, while *Budweiser* did not finish. *Bardahl* ran even faster in winning heat 2B by averaging 112.970 mph, including one lap at 114.894, to trounce *Smirnoff* by 24 seconds; *Mariner Too* and *Savair's Mist* finished third and fourth.

Stiff afternoon winds whipped Garrison Reservoir into a thick chop for the 4:30 p.m. final heat, a Musson-Thompson face-off to determine the overall Dakota Cup victor. Other combatants were *Madison, Eagle Electric, Mariner Too,* and *Smirnoff*. The perfectly-balanced *Bardahl*, though shorter and lighter than *Tahoe*, was considered *Tahoe*'s equal in rough water, and because the two were generally regarded as the fleet's best-riding and best-handling hulls, it stood to reason Garrison's sloppy surface would not deter Musson's or Thompson's aggressiveness.

Six boats charged the starting line, and all arrived early and jumped the gun. Musson tried to hold back and slowed so severely that the Green Dragon bogged down and trailed the field in dead last, while Thompson rocketed *Tahoe* to the front and established a commanding lead, turning a lap at 111.340.

Bardahl was still last finishing lap one, but Musson ground it out and picked off the boats ahead of him one by one – *Smirnoff, Eagle Electric, Madison,* and finally *Mariner Too* entering lap four. Musson set his sights on *Tahoe Miss* and was gaining ground when *Tahoe* emitted a loud "pop," blew its supercharger in the first turn, and coasted to a stop. Musson moved into first and won the heat, averaging 104.408 mph to finish 21 seconds ahead of *Mariner Too* at 100.353, *Madison* at 97.472, and an ailing *Eagle Electric* at

86.928. *Smirnoff* blew its supercharger and did not finish.

Final Dakota Cup standings showed *Bardahl* on top with 1,200 points, *Madison* second with 825, *Tahoe* third with 700, *Mariner* fourth with 652, *Eagle Electric* in fifth with 563, and *Smirnoff* sixth, 525. *Bardahl* collected the $6,000 first-place prize.

In hindsight, it was at New Town that *Tahoe Miss* secured its budding nickname as hydro racing's Hard Luck Boat.

* * * *

Thirteen hydros crowded into the pits near Coeur d'Alene's public boat launch for the Diamond Cup. Because 1964 rules stated a boat needed to run at better than 90 mph just once at any race site to be qualified for the entire season, only Bob Gilliam's *Fascination* needed to qualify, which it did on Friday, July 31, at 97.122 mph.

The hydros took untimed test runs throughout the week, including Spokane's *Miss Eagle Electric*, which was hoisted in and out of the water several times Thursday without running because driver Norm Evans kept detecting a persistent leak. Crew chief Kent Simonson and team finally put the U-25 on the trailer and replaced all the screws on the left rear side of the hull. Earlier that day, *Miss Budweiser* owner Bernie Little had been first on the lake when he drove his beerwagon for a few fast laps.

Bill Muncey was back, aiming for his fourth-straight Diamond Cup win, although he looked pale and thin after 10 days in the hospital. And something stealthy apparently was developing with *Miss Exide*, whose owner Milo Stoen had crowed a few days earlier, "If conditions are right, we're gonna show 'em something new when we get to Idaho."

Gary Breakfield remembered police used tear gas in 1964 to control the Coeur d'Alene party animals near Templin's waterfront motel, where the *Bardahl* team stayed.

"They shot this tear gas bomb that went up and bounced off the front door of my room, and the gas went inside the room," he said. "We came out, and I've never seen men so mad in my whole life as Ole, Ron Musson, and Bernie Little. They went after the cop that did the shooting, and the cop apologized. So they gave us a different room and all kinds of stuff. I'd never seen anything like that happen where Ole was so pissed."

Seven-litre hydros preceded the unlimiteds onto Lake Coeur d'Alene Saturday with the running of the Little Diamond Cup. Entrants included *Challenger*, *Tahitian Miss*, local driver Dr. Ed Johnston aboard *Annie's Dodge,* and Spokane's Earl Wham, who won with his new supercharged, fuel-injected *Miss Merion Blue Grass*.

Norm Evans got the Diamond Cup underway by throttling Spokane's *Miss Eagle Electric* past *Mariner Too* to victory in heat 1A, averaging 102.837 and drawing partisan cheers. It was the Lilac Lady's first heat triumph since 1961, when she ran as *Miss Spokane*. *Mariner, Gale V,* and *Savair's Mist*, now driven by Jim Fyle, followed, while *$ Bill* blew its supercharger trying to overtake *Mariner* on the final lap and did not finish.

Racing continued between thunderstorms. *Bardahl* in lane one and *Exide* hit the starting line side by side in heat 1B, but the Burien milkman pulled away before they reached the first turn, and *Exide* ran its first two laps at 111 and 110 mph in route to a comfortable 106.508-mph heat win. *Bardahl* finished second at 104.006, ahead of *Budweiser* and *Fascination*. It was a redemptive start for the *Exide* camp, which a year earlier had won its Saturday heat only to watch its new boat explode on Sunday.

Stoen, Brow, and crew chief George McKernan hinted at a "secret formula" but wouldn't divulge its nature. Later in the day they revealed Brow hit a button to squirt nitrous oxide – laughing gas – into *Exide*'s Merlin engine, boosting horsepower.

"We had tried out that laughing gas in Bill Brow's limited hydro, *Miss Vitamilk*, before using it in the *Exide*," owner Milo Stoen told John Owen of the *Seattle Post-Intelligencer*.

Notre Dame and *Tahoe Miss* charged to the front to start heat 1C followed closely by *Madison* and *Smirnoff*, but Cantrell soon lost power. The gray-haired crewcut Thompson, on the outside, closed the door and hosed Muncey with his roostertail, helping *Tahoe* hold the lead for three laps – or so Thompson thought. The true leader was Byers in *Madison*, as both front-runners had jumped the gun. No matter. *Tahoe* soon conked, *Notre Dame* lost speed, and *Madison* roared past on a 109-mph final lap to win at a speedy 106.656-mph average. Muncey hobbled home second and immediately buzzed past Thompson, who sat aboard the disabled *Tahoe,* and drenched him with *Notre Dame*'s roostertail, apparently to settle their score. Observers said Muncey shook his fist at Thompson as he whizzed by before returning to the pits, where he seemed wobbly as he extracted himself from the cockpit.

On a bright sunny Sunday morning, Muncey dismissed himself, saying he didn't feel strong enough to drive. "We have a fine piece of racing machinery. The crew has it in good shape and as far as I'm concerned, I've been holding them back," he said. Muncey quickly recruited Rex Manchester to helm *Notre Dame*, which was matched against *Budweiser, Madison, $ Bill, Savair's Mist,* and *Tahoe* in heat 2A; *Smirnoff* withdrew. Thompson charged around the 3-mile Lake Coeur d'Alene course at a record 111.801 five-lap average to win the heat over *Madison, $ Bill, Bud, Notre Dame,* and *Savair*. *Tahoe*'s amazing speed eclipsed the old record held by Muncey and *Thriftway*,109.267.

Musson and *Bardahl* out-accelerated the field exiting the first turn and ran 107.100 to win heat 2B over *Exide, Eagle Electric,* and *Mariner Too*, while *Gale V* conked and *Fascination* returned to the pits. A post-heat squabble ensued when Brow and Evans claimed Musson chopped them off while changing lanes in the dash for the start, but referee Bill Newton waved off the protest after checking with his course judges.

Clouds returned for the final heat, with three boats poised to win the Diamond Cup, each tied with 700 points – *Bardahl, Exide,* and *Madison*. *Eagle Electric,* with 625 points, also could win by taking the final. *Notre Dame* and *Mariner Too* rounded out the field.

The crowd perched on Tubbs Hill watched six hydros charge down the chute, past the official barge and into the north turn, with Evans and *Eagle Electric* narrowly out front. When *Eagle* sputtered at the exit pin, *Bardahl* and *Exide* roared past onto the back chute where they poured on the power, blasting along the log boom at blazing speed, fighting for first. *Bardahl* held a slim lead but coughed in the south turn, giving *Exide* the slack it needed to slide into first on the inside.

For three laps the two Seattle boats scorched around the lake, their Merlins blaring, Musson nipping at Brow's roostertail the entire time, Brow sporadically thumbing the nitrous button and hugging the buoys. *Eagle* held third until Byers and *Madison* surged past in lap three. *Mariner Too* and *Notre Dame* trailed. Rounding the final turn, the incessant Musson mashed the gas and shot wide up the final stretch in a bold bid for the win. *Bardahl* cut the gap but crossed the line four boat lengths behind *Exide*, which won the

Diamond Cup and earned $2,000 first-prize money out of the $10,000 total. *Exide* averaged 108.783, *Bardahl* 108.346. Brow and *Exide* had now won three races in a relatively short span, dating to the 1963 Governor's and President's Cups, solidifying their status as top contenders.

Madison took third at 101.446 followed by *Eagle Electric*, 97.649; *Mariner Too*, 92.134; and *Notre Dame*, a sluggish 75.418. "I wasn't at all sure of myself, and I wanted to bring the boat back in one piece," Manchester said of his unfamiliar new ride.

The jubilant *Exide* team took a ceremonial dunking at the pits, and soon everyone was abuzz over their now-*un*secret weapon, nitrous oxide. "We'll only use it when we need to, and it doesn't guarantee that we'll win," co-owner Milo Stoen told the *P-I*. "But it sure seems to help. Bill really had her jumping in that final heat."

Unknown to Stoen, his nitrous pioneer Bernie Van Cleave – a metallurgist at Airco whom Burns Smith once described as "a very intelligent, inquisitive mechanic" – and McKernan and crew, their *Bardahl* rivals had secretly been doing their own nitrous oxide research and development, which they would test that offseason and fully implement in the U-40 in 1965.

* * * *

As the Diamond Cup unfolded in Coeur d'Alene, America had its eyes on far-away North Vietnam, where the destroyer *USS Maddox* came under attack from three communist torpedo boats in international waters. The *Maddox* and Navy jets returned fire and damaged all three boats in what became known as "the Tonkin Gulf incident," which escalated America's involvement in the Vietnam war. Two days later six torpedo boats launched a second attack, and the Navy sank two in a counter-attack.

In Cincinnati, Seattle's hometown sports hero Fred Hutchinson underwent a week of testing and treatment for chest cancer at Christ Hospital. The Cincinnati Reds manager had been diagnosed earlier in Seattle.

President Lyndon B. Johnson announced he had ruled out six men, including U.S. Attorney General Robert Kennedy, as his vice-president candidates for the November election. Among those not eliminated was cherubic Minnesota Senator Hubert H. Humphrey.

And 228,000 miles beyond the Earth, American spacecraft Ranger 7 snapped the first close-up images of the moon's surface. NASA said more than 4,000 photos showed objects as small as a car in remarkable detail, helping to determine the eventual Apollo lunar landing site.

* * * *

"I'm going down to the Washington Athletic Club and try to work myself into shape," said Bill Muncey. "I'm embarrassed about the Diamond Cup."

It was the start of race week in Seattle, and Seafair was the last of three 1964 regattas held on three consecutive weekends.

"I got out front in that first heat Saturday, but then everything went out on me. I just couldn't hold on and had to let him pass me," Muncey said of Chuck Thompson. Muncey also received a $100 fine from referee Bill Newton for unsportsmanlike conduct at Coeur d'Alene, where he gave a roostertail bath to not only the idled *Tahoe* and Thompson ("I thought his boat was on fire," Muncey deadpanned) but to a

Coast Guard patrol boat as well.

Tempest owner Peter Woeck announced on Tuesday he had sold his white and red U-4 to Bernie Little and Lee Schoenith. Built in 1960 as *Miss Burien* and dry-docked in 1964, it would run at Seafair as *Miss Michelob*. Little reported he would keep the boat, with Schoenith keeping the spare engines and equipment. Also returning was *Miss U.S.5*, fresh from Ron Jones' shop with shorter, lower sponsons, and minus its bow spoiler.

Race officials moved the official barge 650 feet south from its prior location and again erected grandstands on the eastern edge of Stan Sayres Pits, giving fans a less-obstructed view. To access the barge, Fort Lewis Army engineers built a 472-foot walkway that floated on pontoons extending from shore south of the pits.

Seafair time trials began Wednesday, and with nearly all of the field already qualified for the year, race officials offered $3,000 as incentive for hot test laps over the next four days. Bob Schroeder and *Budweiser* ran three circuits at 112.735 mph to earn the first day's top prize, while Muncey pushed *Notre Dame* to the fastest single lap at 115.385.

Bill Brow offered this pre-race assessment. "*Tahoe Miss* is the quickest. The question is whether she can last. *Notre Dame* is still a question mark. The solid boat that we worry about is *Bardahl*."

Brow stood on *Exide*'s throttle for three laps Thursday, averaging 117.391 in the warm sunshine. Former *Maverick* pilot Bill Stead spun a test lap of 109.765 in his former Gold Cup-winning *Maverick*, now named *Budweiser*, but it was just for fun. Musson turned three laps at 116.798 in *Bardahl*, while Muncey averaged 111.493 aboard *Notre Dame*. Chuck Hickling steered *Tempest*-turned-*Michelob* onto the course but blew his engine before completing a lap.

Bob Schroeder ran three respectable laps on Friday in *Bud* at 113.208, followed by Norm Evans in *Miss Eagle Electric* – whose Rolls-Merlin valve covers bore the script "SKIPSCHOTTSUPERSTOCK" – at 111.878; he later ran a fast lap of 113.445. Hickling made *Miss Michelob* the 15th and final entry on Friday, turning a lap at 107.570 mph. Before qualifying ended at 5 p.m., Warner Gardner pushed *Mariner Too* to the day's fastest lap of 115.139, tying Stead's fastest circuit aboard *Bud*.

Eagle Electric hit something during a late-Saturday test run and punched a hole in its bottom, requiring the crew to spend all night patching it at *Miss Exide*'s shop, which had moved from Seattle's Cascade neighborhood to an M-G-S Distributors warehouse for Exide batteries and Dunlop tires, near the ship canal just east of the Ballard Bridge at 1121 N.W. 45th.

Seattle broadcast media chronicled Seafair as events unfolded. KING-5, anchored by Rod Belcher, touted its seven cameras that included a 100-inch lens. KOMO-4 brought back Keith Jackson, teamed him with new sports director George Ray, and also hyped seven cameras, plus videotape replay, and one-upped KING with a 150-inch lens. KIRO-7, which decades later provided the sole annual Seafair telecast, broke tradition and opted to show a Yankees-Orioles game followed by a John Wayne movie. However, KIRO Radio, along with KOL, KVI, KING, and KFKF, all broadcast Seafair in 1964.

Sunday brought sketchy weather, thanks to the infamous "Puget Sound convergence zone." Atypical northerly winds collided over Lake Washington with southerly winds, peaking for a time at 21 mph, all amid cloudy skies that heated to only 67 degrees. Paperboys walked the boulevard outside the pits pedaling *Seattle Post-Intelligencer*s, families reclined on lakeside beach blankets, and teenagers' transistors blasted KJR's No. 1 hit, the Animals' "House Of The Rising Sun."

Heat 1A pitted Muncey *(Notre Dame)* against Musson *(Bardahl)* along with Hickling *(Michelob)* and Gardner *(Mariner Too)*; Wilson and *U.S.5* withdrew before the race with steering problems. Muncey squeezed ahead on the inside at the start, but Musson in lane two pulled *Bardahl* ahead in the south turn and led by two boat lengths through much of the lap before gradually extending his lead, which eventually exceeded 15 seconds. *Michelob* and *Mariner* trailed. *Bardahl* won with a heat average of 111.065 mph while *Notre Dame* took second at 107.620.

Tahoe Miss led 1B before *Gale V* caught fire when its blower exploded in the north turn on lap two, stopping the heat. Jerry Schoenith escaped uninjured by climbing aboard a helicopter's rescue basket. In the rerun, following a 90-minute delay caused by gusts and rough water, *Tahoe* passed *Madison* in the first turn of lap one but stalled at the exit pin. Recovering quickly, Thompson chased and caught Byers in the north turn, then stretched his lead while averaging 110.429 for the heat. *Madison* finished second ahead of Jimmy Fyle in *Savair's Mist; Fascination* did not start.

Leadfoot Norm Evans throttled *Eagle* ahead at the start of heat 1C and pulled away throughout lap one from *Smirnoff*, with *$ Bill*, *Budweiser*, and *Exide* battling for third. Brow charged hard, faded, then charged again in lap two to roar past *Eagle* into first. Evans pressed for the remaining laps but *Exide* won at 104.570 over *Eagle*, 101.694, followed by *Smirnoff*, *$ Bill*, and *Bud*. Bob Schroeder, still sore from his Detroit dunking, recruited Chuck Hickling to finish driving *Bud* the rest of the race.

Bardahl dodged the other hot boats in the draw for heat 2A and, after scrapping with *Eagle* through the first turn, pulled away on the outside to win at 105.222 mph. *Madison* ran 101.656 to take second followed by *Eagle, Bud, Fascination,* and *$ Bill*. Three speedsters clashed in 2B, where *Exide* held the inside and sprinted to the south turn alongside *Tahoe Miss* with *Notre Dame* nipping at their heels. Thompson powered the Gray Ghost ahead entering the backstretch and gradually widened his lead, while Muncey pressed Brow. *Mariner* died in lap three. At the finish it was *Tahoe* first at 109.914 mph, then *Exide* at 105.551, *Notre Dame* at 104.327, *Michelob*, and *Savair's Mist*.

Bardahl and *Tahoe* entered the final with 800 points each. *Exide* had 700, *Madison* 600, *Notre Dame* and *Eagle Electric* 525 each.

All six boats arrived early and crossed the line nearly abreast in a slow start. From the inside out it was *Tahoe, Notre Dame, Exide, Bardahl,* and *Madison; Eagle* trailed. Brow goosed his nitrous button to push *Exide* ahead, but entering the south turn Muncey pulled *Notre Dame* nearly even. *Bardahl* and *Tahoe* followed, then *Madison* and *Eagle*. Musson charged and drove around Muncey on the outside in the north turn, but *Exide* now had the inside and open water as Brow finished lap one in front by four seconds.

Thompson, driving his typical gritty, win-it-or-break-it race, rocketed over the lumpy, rough chop on the outside to pass *Notre Dame* in the south turn, then passed *Bardahl* on the backstretch of lap two. The 32-foot-long *Tahoe*, riding smoothly on rough water, ran the heat's fastest lap at 114 mph.

Thompson could have settled for second and won Seafair on overall points, but instead he pounded after *Exide*, closed the gap, and nudged into first a lap later. As *Tahoe* rounded the north turn it fell slightly behind, edged too close to *Exide*'s wash and veered left into a roostertail bath, losing power at the exit buoy. Thompson swung his dead mount to the infield. *Exide* roared onward to the checkered flag at 109.533 mph, 28 seconds ahead of a struggling, black-smoke-puffing *Bardahl* at 103.567, followed by *Madison, Notre Dame,* and *Eagle Electric*.

The *Exide* and *Bardahl* teams, knotted at 1,100 points apiece, tensely waited for officials to sort out total elapsed time for the 45-mile race. "I tried to close the gap on him," Musson said of Brow, "but I lost a couple of cylinders when *Tahoe* was beside me. That's all I could get out of my engine. I dropped into a wake and over-revved it."

After an excruciating 15-minute wait, the announcement came: *Miss Bardahl* won the 1964 Seafair Trophy Race by two-tenths of a second over *Miss Exide*. The team that lost Seafair by a narrow 6-second margin one year earlier now had won in the same manner, and did so by running all three heats on one motor. *Madison* took third in the overall standings followed by *Tahoe, Notre Dame,* and *Eagle Electric*.

The *Bardahl* crew gave Musson a belated victory dunking in chilly Lake Washington. "I don't like to win races that way, but it kind of makes up for last year," Musson said while toweling off, then credited his reliable equipment for the victory.

"Two years ago, they said I would never be able to do anything with this young crew," said Vanden Berg. "They called them my teenagers."

* * * *

As the hydros broke camp at Stan Sayres Pits, Seattle prepared for an invasion of another sort. The Beatles' first movie, "A Hard Day's Night," opened Aug. 12 at the Paramount Theater amid hordes of screaming girls, and tickets quickly disappeared for the band's upcoming concert at the Seattle Center Coliseum.

The Beatles played to a raucous, sold-out crowd on Aug. 21, 1964, culminating weeks of hype. "A Hard Day's Night" topped the album charts, four songs from it climbed the 45-rpm Top 50 charts, and the movie earned critical acclaim. My friends and I spent the weeks after Seafair listening to the Fab Four's "Something New" Capitol Records album while racing our Eldon Road Race slot cars.

The day before the Beatles had performed, road construction crews closed off our Lake Hills street to replace storm drains – the same ones we'd crawled through years earlier – and two young neighborhood kids, perhaps age 6 or 7, rode up on their bikes asking what the "Road Closed" barricades were for. Someone made up a whopper and said, "Haven't you heard? The Beatles' helicopter is landing right here, in the street!" The little kids bought the tall tale. We said, "Run home quickly and get something for the Beatles to autograph, they'll be here any minute!"

The gullible little guys scurried off on their bikes. Shortly they returned, cresting the hill, pedaling furiously back our way down S.E. 14th Street. We ducked inside my house and locked the screen door but left the main front door wide open, then quickly cranked up "Meet the Beatles" on our mono record player and waited for the doorbell to ring. When it did, I strapped on my brother's Alamo Titan electric guitar and stuck its neck beyond the entryway wall into view of the kids at the screen door, bobbing the guitar up and down like it was being played by a Beatle. The illusion completed our ruse. We ignored the doorbell and the kids' urgent pleas to let them in, and eventually they left.

I'm not certain those youngsters truly believed our scam, but it's a childhood prank that I now feel sheepish about. At the time we thought it was hilarious. My CEO, Stan McNaughton, says there are two types of humor: the good type that gives, and the bad type that takes away. We were bad that day, deceiving little kids and dashing their hopes.

* * * *

Lifelong *Bardahl* fan Dave Peterson of Seattle met his hydro idol in the days following Seafair '64.

Coeur d'Alene's 3rd Street public boat launch served as the Diamond Cup pits from 1958–68, except for 1965.
© Eileen Crimmin photo 1964, used with permission of The Crimmin Collection

Musson reviews Vanden Berg's checklist after qualifying for Seafair at 116.798 mph.
– Jon Osterberg collection

Musson got the best of Muncey in this "M&M Boys" duel, passing him to win heat 1A of the 1964 Seafair Trophy Race. *Bardahl* averaged 111.065 mph.
© Eileen Crimmin photo 1964, used with permission of The Crimmin Collection

Driver Norm Evans confers with Skip Schott before qualifying the former *Miss Spokane*, now sponsored by retailer Dave Heerensperger.
– Jon Osterberg collection

Musson steers "the buoy tender" around Madison's racecourse, oblivious to his blunder. Said the *Bardahl* driver, "I've never been so embarrassed in my whole life."
– used with permission of Sandy Ross

Bill Brow docks his speedy *Miss Exide*, the first unlimited to use nitrous oxide, and winner of the 1964 Diamond Cup.
– Jon Osterberg collection

Col. Warner Gardner finished first aboard *Mariner Too* in 1964's last race of the year, despite *Bardahl* earlier setting a heat record of 113.660 mph.
– used with permission of David Newton, the Roger Newton collection

"Outside of getting his autograph every year, my 'Musson moment' was riding the bus down to Frederick & Nelson with my mom after the 1964 Seafair race," Peterson said. "I still remember seeing as part of the full-page Frederick & Nelson ad, 'Come meet Ron Musson, Seafair Trophy Race winner.' Very cordial, great smile. He was busy signing those cardboard cutout boats and he signed one of my *Bardahl* postcards. It was early morning, hardly anyone there. I would have been 9 years old and also very shy."

I could relate to the "shy" aspect, having blown my only opportunity to meet Musson. In the spring of that year, Dad and I swung by the Bardahl plant in Ballard on our way from his Richmond Beach home to Lake Hills. The roll-up shop door was open, and there standing outside in front of the Green Dragon were three men, including Musson. Dad said, 'Would you like me to park so you can go meet him?' For some crazy reason I was too shy or awe-struck, and meeting Musson seemed intimidating. I said no. *What was I thinking?* Rather than talk me into it, Dad kept driving.

Beyond the hydro realm, New York Yankees rookie Mel Stottlemyre pitched nine full innings Aug. 12 to win his first major league start over the Chicago White Sox, 7-3. The 22-year-old Mabton, Wash., native got help from Mickey Mantle, who belted two home runs.

Seattle 225-class limited hydro driver John Ryan, 25, was killed Aug. 13 when his *Shillelagh II* flipped in a test run on Lake Washington near Kenmore. Ryan was a winning driver and a national contender in his class.

Less than two weeks after Seafair, former *Tempest* owner Peter Woeck had a change of heart and bought his old boat back from Bernie Little. Only the renamed *Miss Michelob* was to be returned, though, as Lee Schoenith retained the U-4's Allison motors and equipment. And then Woeck flip-flopped yet again: He sold the craft before the Governor's Cup to Lee Schoenith, who needed a replacement hull for younger brother Jerry while his burned *Gale V* underwent repairs. Now without a ride, Chuck Hickling was wooed to the *Budweiser* camp to drive Bernie's beerwagon.

Chapter 17

"Never been so embarrassed"

Miss Bardahl was showing wear and tear from the 1964 circuit. Rough water had pounded her to where the sponson frames were starting to lift the deck, and the sponsons themselves showed fatigue and were breaking loose from the center section of the hull. Ron Jones' busy schedule precluded his doing the repairs, so Dax Smith lobbied for his younger brother to do the work. David had helped his dad, Burns, build three runabouts at home and was becoming a decent "wood butcher," Dax said. So Vanden Berg phoned the teenage Smith and invited him to the shop.

"The sponson frames were starting to shear, the glue and the bolts were moving back and forth," David recalled. "The way to fix it is you have to open up the deck, put angles in there and reattach the sponsons to the side of the boat. Leo said, 'Can you do it?' And I said, 'Oh sure, I can do it.' Leo gave me the job.

"I went home and had no idea what to do. I asked my dad and he said, 'You know how to do it. You cut out the deck, put the angles in there, glue everything really good, tighten it all back up good, butt-block the deck, scab the deck back on, glass over it and get it painted and you're good to go.' So that's what I did using Bardahl's equipment, plus tools borrowed from my dad."

Impressed with David's work, Vanden Berg invited him to accompany the team on the second Eastern swing of the 1964 circuit. Skip Schott asserts that David *earned* his way onto the *Bardahl* team. "He was a very hard worker, always. And he was talented beyond his years."

Because of his inexperience and age, David was an "unofficial" crew member auditioning for full status. Bardahl covered his expenses but paid him no wages. David wore his brother's team attire, covering Dax's name with a *Bardahl* pin, and hit the road for Madison, Ind.

"My first trip back east with the *Bardahl* was memorable," David said. "I was relegated to ride in the van, the Ford C-750, with Leo. There was one problem: This would be his wife, Mylrea. And Mylrea was large. So they stuck me in between those two. No air conditioning, in the heat, and everyone's sweating and dripping … the doors would open and I would bolt out of there, the guys all laughing at me."

David maintained *Bardahl*'s hull, helped the mechanics a little with the motors, and handled the stern rope. Soon he found himself the man responsible for the back of the boat.

"I don't know who handled the back before me, but it soon became mine," David said. "And it stayed that way, right through *Pay 'n Pak*. The person in the back of the boat learns quickly to check the rudder, do the propeller, and then jump up into the cockpit and help. So I was always the back-end guy."

Gary Breakfield recalls crisscrossing the country that summer of 1964, traveling two-lane highways before the advent of four-lane interstates like I-70 and I-80.

"The first time Bob Gilliam ever went back East racing, he flipped his boat off the trailer upside down on the highway," he said. "That was in Kansas, out in the middle of nowhere. They had to get a crane from town come out there and pick it up, put it back on the trailer."

He also recalled how unlimited hydroplanes were such a novelty to many motorists sharing the road.

"We're coming up Highway 6 near Omaha, a two-lane highway," said Breakfield. "This car is driving alongside of the boat because they'd never seen a hydroplane before. They were taking pictures of the boat. Leo's driving the truck with the boat on it, and he had to whip that trailer back and forth to get the cars off the highway because they're gonna have a head-on collision. It was a really scary situation."

The *Bardahl* team arrived in Madison the end of August along with *Notre Dame* and Muncey; the third Seattle boat, *Exide*, pulled into town Sept. 1. Hoosiers held high hopes for *Miss Madison*, ranked second behind only *Bardahl* in national high points entering the Governor's Cup Regatta.

On Wednesday, Sept. 2, Muncey abruptly left the *Notre Dame* team, citing what he called an aura of mistrust and poor communication between himself, crew chief Bud Meldrum, and the boat's owners. He also said the Shamrock Lady wasn't handling well, that it kited occasionally and needed further modifications before racing again. The McDonalds, determined to race in Madison anyway, pressed forward.

"I very definitely want to drive again and I'm willing to sit down and discuss it with anybody who is seriously interested in me," Muncey said. Meanwhile, Dr. Fraser McDonald announced that Rex Manchester would take over the U-7 seat immediately.

Apparently, McDonald and wife Shirley Mendelson McDonald also took precautionary measures.

"When she fired a driver, she changed the locks on all her buildings," said Breakfield. "So Muncey couldn't get in the building. Well, he had bought a Buick Riviera, but couldn't get it. So Muncey flew back to Seattle, and he had Jerry and I take turns driving that Buick back for him."

Thirteen unlimiteds crowded Madison's riverbank Sept. 6, where race fans anticipated another slugfest between the big three – *Bardahl*, *Exide*, and *Tahoe* – and hoped for an upset by the community-owned *Miss Madison*.

Fans lining both sides of the Ohio River enjoyed good racing and a few surprises. *Tahoe* led *Exide*, *Budweiser*, *Smirnoff*, and *Savair's Mist* to the first turn in heat 1A, but too much speed carried *Tahoe* outside. *Exide* edged in front and ran a 112-mph lap before dying in the first turn on lap two, and she remained sidelined the rest of the day with mechanical trouble. *Tahoe* resumed the lead and won at 108.216 mph.

Heat 1B featured a duel between *U.S. 5*, *Bardahl*, and *Madison* before Don Wilson throttled the *5* to a surprising lead. Then Musson, racing in Madison for the first time since his flip a year earlier, blundered badly: He miscounted his laps and slowed entering lap five, thinking his heat was finished. Buddy Byers closed the gap and passed *Bardahl* to claim second behind winner *U.S. 5*, as Musson managed to finish ahead of only *Such Crust*.

In heat 1C *Blue Chip* did not start, *Mariner Too* conked in lap four, and Manchester powered his new ride

Notre Dame home first at 98.021 mph followed by Jerry Schoenith in U-44 *The Roostertail*, formerly *Miss Michelob/Tempest*.

Tahoe, *Bardahl*, and *Budweiser* battled in heat 2A through a 110-mph first lap in which Musson committed Governor's Cup blunder No. 2: he speared an orange buoy, which glued itself to *Bardahl*'s bow and refused to budge for the rest of the heat. Somehow Musson wrangled his boat around the long, narrow 3-mile course in second place behind winner *Tahoe*, which ran 106.132 mph, and ahead of *Budweiser*, *Notre Dame*, and *Roostertail*. Because it struck and dislodged a buoy, officials penalized *Bardahl* an extra lap, dropping the Green Dragon to fifth, good for just 352 cumulative points – too few to earn a slot in the final heat. The Dragon was done for the day.

Musson tried but couldn't deny his blunder, because the buoy clung to *Bardahl* all the way back to the pits, where it was removed.

"I've never been so embarrassed in my whole life," Musson grumbled.

"That's when they started calling the boat 'the buoy tender,'" said Breakfield. "He always leaned to the left and the right looking out the side of the motor, because he couldn't see over it. He couldn't say he didn't hit the buoy because when he came in to shore the buoy was still stuck to the bow of the boat."

Bill Cantrell throttled *Smirnoff* to a wire-to-wire win in heat 2B at 104.570 to beat *Madison* and *Savair's Mist*. *Such Crust* did not finish, and *U.S.5* returned early to the pits after taking a giant leap that left Wilson with a cut brow and deep bruises. Five final heat combatants would vie for the trophy: *Tahoe Miss*, *Notre Dame*, *Smirnoff*, *Madison*, and *Budweiser*.

The two grizzled veterans, Cantrell and Thompson, fought furiously for the lead in lap one as *Madison* battled *Notre Dame* for third and *Budweiser* hooked. But unlike prior races where Thompson won his preliminary heats only to break in the final while needlessly chasing the leader, this time he settled *Tahoe* into second and on track to earn 1,100 points, enough to win the Governor's Cup. Cantrell and *Smirnoff* won the heat at 105.633 mph followed by regatta-winner *Tahoe*, *Madison*, *Notre Dame*, and *Budweiser*.

Seventeen hydros showed up later that week later for the 1964 President's Cup in Washington, D.C., with four of the rookie hulls – *Tahoe*, *Smirnoff*, *Notre Dame*, and *U.S.5* – hitting their stride, and *Mariner Too* soon to follow. The season-long qualification rule left prerace testing less than scintillating, but the action picked up with the first heats of racing on Saturday.

Tahoe Miss led wire-to-wire in heat 1A at a mere 98.253 mph thanks to rough water on the wind-swept Potomac. *Notre Dame*, *U.S.5*, and *Savair's Mist* followed, while *Mariner Too* did not start. Heat 1B was halted when *Miss Budweiser* spun out briefly in lap one and an overanxious official fired a flare. The former 1959 champion *Maverick* hull had proven to be a "hooker" throughout its career. *Bud* was allowed to run in the restart and battled *Bardahl* side-by-side on smoother water until the second turn of lap one, where *Budweiser* swung wide and lost ground. Musson surged onward to win at 108.958 mph followed by a raspy *Madison*, *Budweiser*, and Jerry Schoenith in the repaired *Gale V*. *Smirnoff* picked up where it left off in Madison as Cantrell sped to victory in heat 1C at 104.186 mph to beat *Such Crust* and *Tempo*; *Blue Chip* did not finish.

Cold showers and more wind greeted racers Sunday morning, prompting *Notre Dame* to withdraw because of the rough water, leaving the field at 16 boats. *Budweiser* led heat 2A but officials announced in lap four that Hickling had jumped the gun. *Madison* and *Gale V* battled back and forth for second with the

Hurrying Hoosier eventually winning at 103.349 mph over *Gale, Blue Chip, Budweiser, Savair's Mist,* and *Mariner Too*. In heat 2B *Tahoe* led at the start and averaged a quick 109.644 mph to barely edge *Smirnoff*, which averaged 109.400, then *Bardahl* at 105.571, *U.S.5,* and *Tempo*; *Such Crust* did not start.

Tahoe entered the final heat with 800 perfect points, while *Madison* and *Smirnoff* tallied 700 each. *Bardahl* was in with 625, and the fives – *Gale* and *U.S.* – rounded out the field. Wind and rain pounded the Potomac as Cantrell and *Smirnoff* roared out of the first turn in the lead with *Bardahl* close behind. Thompson and *Tahoe* were mired in fourth behind Schoenith and *Gale V* but quickly sped past, then overhauled *Bardahl* for second and charged after *Smirnoff*. Cantrell, however, found plenty of beans in his two-stage Allison and whipped off impressive laps of 112 and 113.326 to stay in front.

Thompson kept his foot in the throttle but smoke started pouring from *Tahoe*'s stacks in lap four, and the hard luck Gray Ghost once again coughed and died, in the first turn of lap five. Now in second place, *Bardahl* gained on *Smirnoff* and seemed poised to challenge for the lead and the Cup when, inexplicably, Musson missed a buoy, penalizing him an extra lap. Wild Bill Cantrell, 56, took the checkered flag in his big riverboat.

The final President's Cup standings showed *Miss Smirnoff* the winner with 1,100 points; *Miss Madison*, 1,000; *Tahoe Miss*, 800; *Miss Bardahl*, 752; *Gale V*, 638; and *Miss U.S.5*, 619. *Bardahl* clung to its narrow national high-point lead with 2,284 points over *Madison*'s 2,094.

Dixon Smith was asked years later if something was hampering or distracting Musson during the two-race bout of driving errors.

"I don't think anything was going on with him. Hitting the buoy, missing one, you're going to do that once in a while. When he hit the buoy, it just happened that it got hung up on the nose of the boat, and he said, 'I didn't hit anything!'" Dixon recalled, laughing. Musson was too short to see over the engine, which blocked his view of the evidence.

The 1964 fleet was proving to be one of the strongest ever, with seven boats showing sufficient speed and savvy at times to win: *Tahoe, Exide, Bardahl, Notre Dame,* and now *Smirnoff. Madison* was nearly as quick and rock-solid consistent, while even the flighty *U.S.5* showed sporadic flashes of brilliance, and yet another new hull soon would emerge as top dog for one weekend before the year ended.

Within the hydro fraternity, *Tahoe* had been the consensus pick all year for fastest boat – when it held together. *Exide*'s team had good reason to dispute that, saying the U-75 was fleetest of the fleet. But the boat camps agreed, only *Bardahl* had fused sheer speed with reliability, making her the boat to beat.

* * * *

During the Madison-Washington, D.C. swing of the hydro circuit, weighty events dominated the news. A newspaper headline read, "2 clansmen acquitted in Negro's slaying," reporting a white Georgia jury's acquittal of a white man in the death of an African American educator.

The Warren Commission continued its investigation of President Kennedy's assassination, while nationally syndicated columnist Dorothy Kilgallen wrote that a week before JFK's murder, a mysterious meeting took place at Jack Ruby's nightclub between Ruby, officer J.D. Tippit, Bernard Weismann, and a rich Texas oilman. And in Washington state, Republicans nominated Rep. Daniel J. Evans to run for governor against incumbent Albert Rosellini in November.

The Seattle Totems announced that a Sept. 30 exhibition hockey game against the Toronto Maple Leafs would christen the 12,300-seat Seattle Center Coliseum as a sports venue, newly remodeled from the World's Fair. The Washington Huskies, coming off a Rose Bowl year, were ranked 8th nationally in the 1964 preseason poll. Hydro jockeys Mira Slovak and Chuck Lyford, a renowned inboard racer, announced they would pilot piston fighter planes in the National Air Races at Reno.

And at the Lake Sammamish Inboard Regatta, Bill Muncey – now without an unlimited-class ride – raced his 225- and 266-class limited hydros. He won the 266 class aboard *Best Wishes*, sharing driving duties with future unlimited racer Leif Borgersen. Other top finishers at Sammamish that day were Earl Wham, George Babcock, and a smiling 280-class driver named George Henley.

* * * *

The *Bardahl* team trekked west across the American heartland bound for Lake Tahoe, Nevada. Sometimes Vanden Berg and crew stayed in comfortable lodging, while other times they made do with whatever they found after grinding across hundreds of miles of blacktop.

"One time we had been driving all night long," said Breakfield. "We were worn out and tired. Leo jumped out of the truck and went and got a motel room, and Jerry and I thought we had the same kind of room. So we started walking, Leo, Millie, Jerry and I, but they went to one place and said, 'No, your guys' room is over there.' We walked through these trees to this *dump*. And Jerry and I had to sleep in the same bed together. It sloped – it was a big 'U.' I swear to God, somebody had just got out of that bed before we did."

Chapter 18

Back on top

Miss Bardahl rolled cross-country to 6,225-foot Lake Tahoe with a 190-point lead in the 1964 season-long points race. If the Green Dragon failed to finish a heat at Tahoe, *Miss Madison* could move into first by finishing hers. But the *Bardahl* team was confident in its boat, equipment, high-altitude setup, and personnel – until Musson came down with a virus. He flew in with a fever, all bundled up, but drove regardless.

The $25,000 Harrah's Tahoe Regatta offered daily prize money to the fastest qualifier, and the fleet ran slower than usual. *Bardahl* topped Thursday's runs with a mere 108.361 three-lap average, *Tahoe* took Friday honors at 106.369, and Musson sped up to 111.417 on Saturday, including a course-record 113.208-mph lap, before stiff winds cut qualifying short.

Sunday's action proved to be no contest – not because of wind, but because *Bardahl* dominated the field so easily. Under warm clear-blue skies, 13 boats gathered off U.S. 50 along the southeast shore of the pristine Sierra Nevada lake to race in light chop around the 3-mile course. *U.S.5* was not among the competitors, having withdrawn after an engine was dropped on its hull.

Rex Manchester shot *Notre Dame* to the front in heat 1A and won at 102.350 over *Smirnoff*, 100.259; *Budweiser*, 100.000; *Eagle Electric*; and *Savair's Mist*. The still-ailing Musson sprinted through heat 1B at 109.756, his *Bardahl* seemingly oblivious to the thin air, to beat *Tahoe Miss*, which blew its engine while crossing the finish line at 101.580; *Exide*, 101.389; *Madison*, 100.111; and *Fascination* followed. Heat 1C saw *Mariner Too* and *Tempo* conk out in lap two, leaving 21-year-olds Billy Schumacher in *$ Bill* and Jerry Schoenith in *Gale V* to finish one-two.

Bardahl again showed its roostertail to the field in heat 2A, churning the lake at 105.840 to beat *Smirnoff* at 102.272, *Madison*, *Exide*, and *Savair's Mist*. Amazingly, the well-funded host hydro *Tahoe Miss* was out of engines and did not start. Hickling steered *Bud* to first in 2B at 102.739 while a back-and-forth duel between *$ Bill* and *Gale V* ended when *$ Bill* died on lap three, leaving second to *Gale V* followed by *Notre Dame, Eagle Electric,* and *Fascination*.

Fast and formidable *Tahoe, Exide,* and *Madison* failed to earn slots in the championship heat, foiled by breakdowns and low finishes. *Bardahl* entered the final with *Notre Dame, Smirnoff, Budweiser, Gale V,* and *$ Bill*.

Musson trailed Hickling and Cantrell at the start by 100 yards, but *Smirnoff* died in the first turn, and *Bardahl* shot past *Bud* entering the backstretch and widened its gap throughout the heat. *Bardahl* won at a leisurely 101.848 in heavy chop and bright sunshine to beat *Budweiser, Gale V, $ Bill,* and *Notre Dame* in that order. It was *Bardahl's* fourth regatta win in 1964.

Bardahl's perfect day of racing also earned her enough points to clinch the National Championship for the second year, perhaps a tonic of sorts for the coughing and wheezing Musson, who one year earlier had yielded the cockpit to Don Wilson after the Madison flip and lost the 1963 driver's title to Bill Cantrell.

In 2002, at a banquet where he announced his retirement from air racing, revered "Master of the Merlin" Dwight Thorn reminisced about the *Bardahl* team's ingenuity at Tahoe.

"The Seattle race teams guarded their secrets closely," Thorn said. "Ole had a mature crew chief, Leo Vanden Berg. The rest of the crew was a bunch of wild teenagers. They could sure thrash!

"One of their more-daring, on-the-spot modifications was at the Lake Tahoe race in '64 or '65. They felt that more boost was needed from the Merlin to win that high-altitude race, as *Harrah's Tahoe Miss* was very close in qualifying times. So race day morning, the crew decides to decrease the clearance of the first stage supercharger impeller, as this would increase the output. But too close, and the impeller brushes the inlet when it heats up. KABOOM!"

Thorn thought that was a "dicey decision for race-day morning" and recalled the *Bardahl* crew's deliberations.

"What to use for shim material? The sheet metal from a five-gallon Bardahl oil can is about .015 thick. The shim was cut out with tin snips, and they won the race. True story!" Thorn said. "I have witnesses, and I think I have the shim somewhere. That's how things were done in boat racing. Merlins were plentiful and fairly cheap in the early '60s, $500 used, $800 to $1,000 new."

Bardahl won the Tahoe final heat using a motor that had been slightly damaged in heat 2A, so Roger Kruse flew home to Seattle to fetch a fresh Rolls-Merlin for the following weekend's San Diego Cup. In his absence the team ran into a little trouble with its rolling stock.

"They let Reb drive the truck," Kruse said. "Well, Reb wasn't a truck driver, and coming down the mountain from Lake Tahoe, he didn't know you're supposed to shift down and use gears. He just came down the mountain on the brakes. Got to the bottom, and he was lucky he made it without rolling."

"I wasn't towing the boat, I drove the truck that had all the motors, tools, and everything else in it," Breakfield recalled. "I lost the breaks, burned them up we were going so fast down this gigantic hill. I passed the truck that had the boat on the back of it! I got it stopped, but boy…."

"There wasn't a brake left on the truck," said Kruse. "They had to pull into Reno and have everything rebuilt. It's amazing that he survived."

* * * *

On April 10, 1963, the nuclear submarine *Thresher* had sunk in 8,500 feet of water while making test dives in the Atlantic Ocean 220 miles east of Boston, killing all 129 men aboard. On Oct. 1, 1964, the U.S. Navy announced it had pinpointed and photographed remains of the *Thresher* using advanced search techniques. While plunging to the ocean floor the sub presumably suffered a ruptured pipe and imploded into pieces from the immense water pressure.

In Seattle, hopes of wooing the Cleveland Indians baseball team were dashed when the Indians' directors voted against moving to the Jet City, opting to resolve their problems in Cleveland instead.

As those events unfolded, KJR listeners were grooving to Manfred Mann's No. 1 hit, "Do Wah Diddy Diddy" and the Four Tops' "Baby, I Need Your Loving."

KJR Radio, 950 AM, sat at or near the top of the Seattle ratings heap throughout the 1960s and '70s, thanks in large part to drive-time disc jockey Pat O'Day, who eventually became program director and station manager. KJR dominated local radio with an astounding market share. In January 2012, the top radio station in the Seattle market earned a 6.0 share – the percentage of radio listeners. In March 1960, KJR became the top-rated Seattle station with 37% of the audience, and KJR typically earned a share in the high-teens and 20s throughout the decade.

O'Day gained fame as a radio man and teen-dance sponsor, and in 1967 he co-founded Concerts West, promoter of world-class rock artists like Jimi Hendrix and Led Zeppelin. O'Day remains known to hydro fans as an enduring voice of boat racing who helped anchor KIRO-TV's Seafair telecast in 2011, continuing his long string of hydro broadcasts dating to Seafair 1968.

For baby boomers who grew up around Seattle, O'Day helped define our culture. He brought prominent rock bands to unlikely neighborhood venues like Lake Hills Roller Rink in the Crossroads neighborhood of Bellevue. He guided "♪ KJR, Seattle, Channel 95 ♪," whose listeners *still* consider Seattle the Jet City, not the Emerald City. He played a role in fielding racing's first turbine-powered hydro, the *U-95*. He brought us talented and amusing on-air personalities like Larry Lujack, Dick Curtis, Chuck Boland, Lan Roberts, World Famous Tom Murphy, Norm Gregory, and Burl Barer, the brash "boss jock" from Walla Walla who anchored O'Day's KYYX-FM in the late 1970s – or as Barer voiced it, "*KAY*-why-why-ex!"

O'Day knows promotion, and as the owner of KYYX-FM he found a way to cut through the advertising clutter and differentiate his product. He bought the former turbo-Allison powered *Squire Shop* hydro, renamed it *Miss KYYX* in 1981, and hired a woman to drive it. Brenda Jones became the first female to drive a hydroplane in the modern era. Never mind that she had zero experience; O'Day sent her out on the smaller limited-class hydro circuit to earn the prerequisite time behind the wheel to be eligible to drive his U-96.5.

Jones eventually won a heat of racing, in the 1982 Emerald Cup in Seattle, before fading into hydro obscurity after KYYX folded.

* * * *

As the inaugural San Diego Cup approached, Roger Kruse hitched a U-Haul trailer to the back of his new 1964 Ford Thunderbird, drove to the Bardahl shop in Ballard, and had one of the warehouse workers help load the fresh Merlin into the trailer and bolt it down.

"I drove to San Diego towing that trailer, and my wife went along," Kruse said. "Reb's wife rode with us, and she didn't quit talking for the 22 hours it took us to get there. She talked and talked and talked, and so we always remembered that and gave her a bad time about it."

David Smith missed out on the 1964 San Diego race. He was still attending Cleveland High School, starting his senior year – as senior class president of 1965, no less – and his parents insisted he stay home and attend school.

"I was supposed to go to retreats and learn how to be a president, but I was boat racing," David recalled. "I didn't have a clue. I got to school and had to stand up in front of the whole student body and give a nice speech, and I was just petrified. I had been boat racing; I had no skills whatsoever. But it ended up all working out."

Because of hydro racing's popularity in the 1960s, David enjoyed star status on campus at times.

"I could wear my National Championship jacket to school when everybody else had a letterman's coat," he said with a smile. "I had a letterman's coat too, but if I wanted to kind of duke 'em a little bit, I'd just throw on my *Bardahl* National Championship jacket."

Unlimited hydroplanes had never raced on salt water, and the 13 teams that converged at San Diego's Mission Bay were wary of how salt might hamper their motors, systems, and hard-to-reach (and rinse) nooks and crannies of their hulls. Unlimiteds also had never raced in Southern California. The site awaiting them was soon to be embraced by many as the finest racecourse ever devised for hydroplanes.

Mission Bay Park traces its origin to 1948, when work began on jetties to divert the San Diego River to the south. Dredging of the tidal basin, once called False Bay, later created depths ranging from 8 to 20 feet and yielded millions of cubic yards of sand that eventually produced Vacation and Fiesta islands. Formerly called Cabrillo Island, Fiesta Island was completed in 1961.

Mission Bay Park comprised 4,600 acres and 32 miles of shoreline when the unlimiteds arrived to race in 1964. The gently sloping sandy beaches surrounding the 3-mile course dissipated boat wakes and offered superb viewing. The late-afternoon autumn sun lit the hydros from a low angle that soon made the San Diego race a photographer's delight. For the initial race only, the pits were located at Perez Cove next to SeaWorld, which had opened March 21, 1964.

Like Tahoe and Seattle, San Diego offered daily prize money for fast laps. Bill Brow blistered the 3-mile oval aboard *Miss Exide* at 119.495 mph Friday to edge Norm Evans, nearly as impressive with a 117.647 lap in the modestly funded *Miss Eagle Electric*. *Smirnoff* and Bill Cantrell took the $250 prize Saturday with a 114.164-mph lap to top *Mariner Too*'s 111.455.

Among those watching from the beach was a 30-year-old Los Angeles attorney witnessing his first unlimited hydroplane event. Bob Fendler was hooked, and he vowed to return the following year piloting his own boat.

Exide screamed around Mission Bay for a 117.647 lap in heat 1A but strained his motor and slowed to nurse it, allowing Col. Warner Gardner and *Mariner* to squeeze past and win, 104.845 mph to *Exide*'s 103.726. *Tempo* took third at a respectable 101.560 with *Savair's Mist* fourth, while *Tahoe Miss* did not finish and was done for the day. In a swift heat 1B, *Budweiser* turned 109.577 to beat *Madison* at 107.698, *Fascination* at 105.058, and *Gale V* at 103.926. *Bardahl* blasted around the buoys in 1C at 111.963 mph to beat *Eagle Electric, Smirnoff,* and *$ Bill*.

Byers coaxed *Madison* home first in heat 2A at 103.886 ahead of *Exide, Smirnoff,* and *Tempo*; *Eagle* and *Savair* did not start. Musson and *Bardahl* roared onto the course for heat 2B and scorched through five laps at an all-time record 113.660 mph, well ahead of *Mariner Too* at 108.739 and *Fascination*, 102.544; *Gale V* and *$ Bill* did not finish. *Bardahl*'s 15-mile heat bested the old mark of 112.500 set by Bill Muncey aboard *Thriftway* at the 1963 Seafair race.

One other boat didn't finish heat 2B – *Miss Budweiser*. As had become almost customary for the craft, it hooked violently. Driver Chuck Hickling, unhurt, tried to straighten out and resume racing but couldn't accelerate, then noticed the left sponson was entirely gone. It had sheared off when *Bud* hooked while zooming down the back chute. A patrol boat towed the gold and red craft to shore and beached it, where a bizarre sight unfolded as frenzied fans scavenged the semi-submerged *Bud* for souvenirs. An ignoble end, indeed, for the 1959 Gold Cup winner and high-point champ.

Five boats – not the customary six, because of snug clearance on the racecourse – earned spots in the final heat: *Bardahl,* 800 points; *Mariner Too,* 700; *Madison,* 700; *Exide,* 600; and *Fascination,* 450. Gardner pushed hard on the throttle, and as it had all day, the red and white *Mariner* ran fast and steady. *Bardahl* and *Exide* gave chase while fending off Bob Gilliam in his suddenly spunky *Fascination,* which led *Madison.*

Musson hoped to finish close enough to *Mariner* to take second, earn 300 points, and win the race on shorter elapsed time. But in lap four a faulty magneto crippled *Bardahl,* which could only chug around the course, barely churning a roostertail. Gardner took the checkered flag at an impressive 111.156 average, making *Mariner Too* the fourth novice hull to mature into a regatta winner in 1964. *Exide* finished second at 104.732 to narrowly beat *Fascination,* which turned 104.400 and averaged more than 100 mph in all three of its heats, perhaps the high mark of Bob Gilliam's hydro career. *Madison* took fourth at 101.960, while *Bardahl* limped home fifth at 71.370.

Final standings for the inaugural San Diego Cup: *Mariner Too, Miss Bardahl, Miss Exide, Miss Madison, Fascination.* By earning 927 points for the day, Musson clinched the 1964 boat and driver championship. The final 1964 national high points standings: *Bardahl, Madison, Tahoe Miss, Exide, Smirnoff, Notre Dame, Mariner Too, Budweiser, Gale V, Eagle Electric,* and 10 others.

* * * *

Spokane lost its beloved Lilac Lady after the San Diego race. Despite Dave Heerensperger's Eagle Electric sponsorship, running the former *Miss Spokane* was costly and laborious for representative owner Kent Simonson and his volunteer crew. So there at the Mission Bay race site, Simonson struck a deal to sell the boat, equipment, trailer, and 1953 GMC cabover box truck to *Mariner Too* owner Jim Herrington.

"Heerensperger wanted to buy the boat, but by this time he and Kent were kind of in a pissing match," said Skip Schott, *Eagle Electric*'s engine mechanic. "Kent had dinner with Jim Herrington and Herrington bought the boat, and we didn't even know it until the next morning."

Now without a truck to drive home, Schott implored Vanden Berg to load his toolbox and Honda 90 motorcycle in the *Bardahl* van and take them to Ballard. Schott had hauled the bike from Spokane to San Diego on the back of the *Eagle Electric* trailer, for race-site transportation.

"I had to get it home, and I wasn't going to *ride* it home, because I only had enough money to come home on the bus," Schott said. "So I begged Leo, but he was convinced the *Bardahl* truck was way overweight, and there's no way he could take that motorcycle. I think Jerry finally intervened and said, 'We can take it.' I planned to pick it up in Seattle and take it home to Spokane."

According to Simonson's son, Kent "Pancho" Simonson Jr., Herrington's 18-year-old driver left San Diego with the *Eagle* truck, towing the U-25, bound for Michigan. Somewhere in the Southwest – California, Arizona, or New Mexico – the young man crashed, wrecking the truck. *Miss Eagle Electric* slid off the trailer and crunched its sponsons, which were rebuilt with aluminum frames in the offseason. The following year the boat would run as U-9 *Miss Lapeer.* Pancho said the truck's box was seen years later in a Southwest junkyard with the fading "Miss Eagle Electric" lettering still visible on its side.

As a sidenote, in August 1965 at the Gold Cup in Seattle, Kent Simonson was sad to see *Miss Lapeer* painted blue and white, especially its distinctive tail. "That was rough," his son Pancho said, "because Herrington was not real friendly, and we had a tough time even getting pit passes."

* * * *

I acquired every piece of hydro literature I could find as a kid – race programs, newspaper clippings, and treasured magazines like *Boating News* and *Hot Boat*, which ran stories and photos from the talented duo of scribe Eileen Crimmin and photographer Bob Carver. The narrative of this book owes much to Crimmin's detailed, lively race reports.

Sometime during fifth grade, my friend Mikey discovered he could make perfect renderings of hydros by slipping sheets of carbon paper and typing paper underneath hydro photos, then tracing the hydro outlines with a pen or pencil. In this way he and I systematically went through a good portion of our hydro collections, tracing every photo at his kitchen table, effectively ruining the magazines. Then we'd staple the carbon tracings together into our own "programs," which we perceived as valuable at the time. Go figure.

I later spent a few dollars as an adult backfilling my collection of hydro literature with replacement copies of what I'd wrecked in elementary school.

Chapter 19

Harnessing nitrous

Miss Exide's use of nitrous oxide – laughing gas – kindled excitement among journalists hungry for colorful story angles in 1964. The Stoen team enjoyed dropping hints about its "secret weapon" before divulging why they had nicknamed *Exide* the Happy Hydro.

Concurrently, while *Bardahl*'s Dax Smith was studying in the Engineering Library at the University of Washington, he found a 1945 report from the National Advisory Committee for Aeronautics – NACA, the parent organization of NASA – about tests during World War II. The report was titled "Nitrous Oxide Supercharging of an Aircraft Engine Cylinder," and it described work done on a single-cylinder Allison engine. The young physics and math major knew he was on to something.

"I read this article, and I read it again, and I read it a few more times … I didn't know what nitrous oxide does, but that title tells me they're looking for horsepower," Dixon recalled in 1987. "I thought, 'This is neat stuff,' and I took the report down to the boat shop. The first reaction I got was, 'Aw, people have tried everything that you pour in a gas tank.' I said, no, wait a minute, this isn't something you pour in a gas tank.'"

Dixon explained to Leo and crew that nitrous oxide has twice the oxygen per volume, about 40 percent, than regular atmosphere. Nitrous oxide's advantage is it injects more oxygen into the engine, allowing proportionately more fuel to burn, which makes more fire and more horsepower. The horsepower comes not from more oxygen, but from the additional fuel the oxygen allows you to burn.

"So it took a while, and I finally talked enough and, probably to shut me up, Leo condescended to let me try it on the boat in testing," Dixon said.

Former *Exide* crewman Bob Woolms suspects Dixon learned about nitrous via different means, despite Dixon, Vanden Berg, and crew consistently and independently recounting for decades the same UW library sequence of events.

"There was a conflict of interest between Dax and his dad," said Woolms in 2012. "Burns was on our *Exide* crew. And it was always suspected that his dad was giving Dax a lot of our secrets. We were the first ones to ever use nitrous in a hydroplane. And so one day we were going down to try out the nitrous at the lake. Guess who showed up? The *Bardahl* crew. And nobody was supposed to know about it. Well, who do you think told Dax? Burns did."

Woolms, a longtime Stoen brothers associate, said he started with hydros in 1960, serving on the *Miss Seattle* and *Miss Seattle Too* crews. He places his recollection of working with Burns at the Harrison and Minor Street shop, home base for *Seattle Too* and the Karelsen-built *Exide*. Dixon Smith, David Smith, and Doug Brow say that Burns never worked on any *Exide* crew. It's possible that Woolms' recollection is blurred between *Seattle Too* and *Exide*, both Stoen-owned boats.

Further, since hydroplane test sessions are not secret affairs, and since hydro teams have always attended their competitors' tests, it seems a stretch to deduce that the *Bardahl* crew's mere presence meant nitrous secrets were being shared between father and son, even if Burns *had* worked on *Exide* and known of its nitrous. Also, *Exide* and *Bardahl* were fierce racing rivals, with no member of either team likely to spill secrets. Bad blood existed between *Exide* crew chief George McKernan and Ole Bardahl – ever since Ole had fired McKernan as his crew chief in 1960.

"George did not like Ole," Woolms said. "And I stayed out of that because I liked them all, Leo and everybody in the *Bardahl* group.

"But anyway, we were down at the pits, and I'm not gonna say it was a top secret, but only the crew members knew about the nitrous. So here comes the *Bardahl* crew. And what we did was, we snuck the bottles up into the boat in a Navy sea bag."

Woolms recalled *Exide*'s nitrous was mounted behind the driver's seat in 1964, inside the rear cowling under the tail. This matches what crew chief George McKernan told *The Seattle Times* in a July 16, 1965 article, which said *Exide*'s nitrous is "stored in the stern" in what looks like "miniature acetylene tanks."

Milo Stoen was cited in a 2001 *NewsJournal* article as having said, "There was a tank of nitrous mounted in front of the engine, behind the small cowling," and the same author wrote in 2012 that *Exide*'s nitrous was mounted *Bardahl*-style, inverted up front ahead of the blower.

"That confused me. But I'm not gonna call him a liar, that's for sure," Woolms said. "Because that wasn't my ballyhoo. Everyone had their specific job, and that wasn't one of mine. I specialized in camshafts and valve trains."

Based on McKernan's 1965 statements, Woolms recollection, and what *Bardahl* crewmembers observed at the time, it's likely that *Exide* ran in 1964, and perhaps part or all of 1965, with its nitrous bottles under the tail, then moved them to the front of the motor later. What's certain is that *Bardahl* placed its large, inverted tanks in front of the blower from the beginning, and that application became standard among subsequent hydros.

When told that Dixon acknowledges *Miss Exide* was the first unlimited to use nitrous, but that Dixon believes he and Van Cleave learned about and experimented with nitrous concurrently and independently, Woolms growled, "I don't believe it.

"For us, it was a secret," he said. "Mira Slovak was our driver in 1963, and he told Bernie and us one day at lunch that in World War II, the Messerschmitt used nitrous oxide."

When asked about that in February 2012, Slovak responded via email. "I am not interested in credit for introducing the laughing gas of Hermann Goring's," he wrote. "In 1948, I was assigned to fighter school. At that time the Czech Air Force was flying a modified Me-109. … This Me-109 according to regulation had to be exercised every month, so I managed to get quite a few rides in the front seat. One time when sitting in single seater, an old Me-109, I went through the check list and noticed by the throttle a special lever which had an 'inoperative' sign on it. Later I found that it was an engaging lever for nitrous oxide injection system only in emergency, time limit was five minutes.

"Around 1959, I brought this subject about nitro to June Czech and Les Eide, *Miss Wahoo* chiefs. June asked me if I need more power in *Miss Wahoo*, I said no and the conversation about oxide was finished. When I drove *Exide*, I again mentioned the same story to Bernie who was interested in the story, and for me it was the end.

"Later I have heard that Bill Brow in his limited-class hydro was successfully using nitrous. … I am sure that Dixon and Bernie were looking into it, but I think that Bill Brow was the first successful operator. I have no credits to it," Slovak concluded.

Told that this book would credit Bernie Van Cleave as developing the nitrous system for *Miss Exide*, and that in 1964 the news media reported *Exide* was the first unlimited to race with nitrous oxide, Woolms seemed satisfied.

"Yeah, good. Bernie was probably one of the best in the business," Woolms said. "He designed and built that system from day one, he and his kid. And nobody can take that away from him. I didn't want to have anybody lose sight of that. He's passed away, of course."

* * * *

The 1964 race schedule afforded little time for experimentation, but "Dax's science project" finally was put to test aboard *Bardahl* in the offseason.

"That may have been in the fall of 1964, because after that the Dragon was stashed in the corner, and we were focused on the cabover. And by the time we had to go racing we didn't have time to sort out that stuff," Dixon said, referring to the last-minute thrash to recommission the mothballed Green Dragon in spring 1965.

"We did some screwing around, experimenting, and the initial couple of times we tested it at Sand Point, it was real intermittent and sporadic," he continued. "Musson was way, way out there, way up the lake, as he liked to do when we were testing instead of being close. As he's coming towards us you see this horrible amount of black smoke, and the motor sounds crappy. Then it cleans up, and then a horrible amount of black smoke again, and then it cleans up. I thought it looked like it was burning soft coal. I didn't understand some of the properties of nitrous, and the valving we had was completely wrong for what we were doing."

Nitrous oxide is a gas under normal pressure. When compressed to 750 pounds per square inch under standard conditions, it turns into liquid. When nitrous escapes compressed-air bottles, it gets very cold as it transforms from liquid to gas, absorbing much heat to make that transformation.

"Finding the correct kind of valve was a major difficulty, because when nitrous goes through a valve it's very cold, and it leaves residue on valves that makes them a little sticky," Dixon explained. "Because of the extreme cold, it creates a problem of freezing valves half open, half closed, all the way open, somewhat closed."

The NACA nitrous-test report detailed what was strictly a controlled laboratory situation, not an operational test, of gaseous nitrous. The American military never used nitrous in the war, so all of the mechanical applications such as the type of valves to use, where specifically the nitrous should be squirted into the engine, how long it can be used before it harms an engine, how much additional fuel you can burn, and how to balance those variables, were not prescribed. In practice, how to use nitrous in a Rolls-Merlin was unknown. In addition, Dixon was determined to use more-potent *liquid* nitrous, not gaseous.

"The piloted valve I used in testing was such that it would freeze up real easily," said Dixon. "We had problems where we'd go out and run it once, and Musson would say, 'Boy, that really works!' He'd go out and run the next time and it didn't do anything. We went through half a dozen types of valves before we found something that worked really well."

David Smith recalled the first time *Bardahl* tested nitrous in the boat, at Sand Point.

"Ron pushed the nitrous button on his steering wheel and the boat just flew. The next time he pushed the button, it froze. Ron came in and said, 'I don't know what the hell that stuff is, but whatever it did the first time, that's what we're gonna do again.'"

Dixon knew he wanted a stout, direct-acting valve that, when open, you could look straight through – like a guillotine. He asked Spencer Aircraft to find him one, and after some research, they did.

"We ended up with the Barksdale valve, which is the big one," David said. "You could hear them. In the pits we'd have to oil them between heats, it would go *thunk! Thunk!* It was a big valve with a humongous spring in it, and it's stainless steel with a guillotine in the thing, and it was made for transferring very cold liquid, like liquid oxygen. They're real expensive."

"They don't fail," Dixon said. "It weighed about six pounds, and that thing shook the boat when it opened and closed."

Not until Coeur d'Alene in 1965 did *Miss Bardahl* use nitrous oxide in competition. *Bardahl*'s system, Dixon later learned, was quite different from *Exide*'s. The rival teams guarded their secrets carefully and developed their nitrous programs quite independently. In the early 1980s, Dixon was hired to improve the Griffon *Miss Budweiser*'s nitrous system. Owner Bernie Little had purchased Hydroplanes Inc. – the *Exide* operation – after the 1965 race season, including the team's documentation. While consulting on the Griffon *Bud*, Dixon learned *Miss Bardahl* had been using three times more nitrous than *Exide*, and that would have translated into more horsepower for the Green Dragon.

"There was a big difference in the approach, because we had *big* bottles," David said. "*Exide* had little bottles like you'd see in the dentist's office, the size of those oxygen bottles that people take with them in their wheelchairs. Coeur d'Alene was the first time you saw the big red bottles on our boat, the size of big fire extinguishers. And if you notice, in the pits we covered them so you couldn't see what it was, but when the boat went out you saw the red bottles upside down, up front by the blower."

"The *Exide* guys, they were only putting it in with little bottles right-side up, gaseous," said Schott. "They weren't putting liquid nitrous in like we were, with the big red upside-down tanks. And liquid nitrous is like drinking really good whiskey instead of 3.2 beer. That's the difference right there. So we put it in, liquid, with a whole lot more fuel and got a lot more out of it."

"*Exide* used the same nitrous bottles all day," said David. "We used ours up and had to change them after each heat. We were definitely using more, and we needed every bit of it – our boat was at least a thousand pounds heavier than theirs."

If *Exide* crew chief George McKernan's assertion to reporters was accurate – that *Exide* used "about five gallons" of nitrous, enough for 45 miles of racing with 90 gallons of regular fuel aboard – *Bardahl* indeed used much more.

Before *Bardahl* actually raced with nitrous, the crew recognized it needed a safety cushion of sorts.

"Squirting the wrong amount of fuel and nitrous can make an engine fly apart," Dixon said. "There's this little equation that says, 'Horsepower times reliability is a constant.' So when the horsepower goes up, the reliability goes down. We were real concerned about how long you can use nitrous. And we knew from past history with Musson that, if you gave him an extra 300 or 400 horsepower, he'd use that as far as he could.

"So we designed an electrical system where, if he pushed the button, he would get nitrous for four or five seconds, and then it would shut off. And when he got off the button, he had to *stay* off the button for like three seconds before it would reset, and then smash it again."

Dixon also added a built-in safety cushion by metering just a little extra fuel and nitrous, which was injected into the base of the supercharger, ensuring good distribution. Enriching the mixture guarded against detonation, which harms engines. The rich mixture also produced telltale black smoke that belched out of *Bardahl*'s stacks whenever Musson squeezed the nitrous button.

Nitrous oxide was a significant innovation in hydroplane racing, soon adopted by other camps. While serving in the Navy from 1966 to 1972, Dax turned it into a cottage industry of sorts, selling his perfected nitrous system – first in 1968 to *Notre Dame* and *Miss Eagle Electric*, and later to other teams – via brother David, whom he paid a commission.

Dax didn't sell the hardware; rather, he sold a single-sheet "recipe" that told the buyer precisely what to buy, where to buy it, and how and where to install it. He literally was selling intellectual property.

"Whatever the price was – it was either $1,000 or $1,500 – for that money, you got one piece of paper. And that piece of paper told you everything you needed to know about a nitrous system," Dixon said. "I think I talked to Jack Cochrane of *Eagle Electric* about it and gave him the horsepower-times-reliability lecture, and also, 'If you've got a fourth-place boat, putting nitrous on it won't make it a first-place boat.' But that went right over most people's heads. They figured, we put nitrous on, we'll be just like the *Bardahl* and win races.

"Nitrous is not my idea. It's NACA's idea, and we just implemented it into the race boat," Dixon said, holding up the NACA report. "But you can see what we worked from. We took this information and built a working nitrous system."

* * * *

Skip Schott's Honda 90 motorcycle never made it home to Spokane.

Schott, 23, served in the Air National Guard in Spokane and wanted to stay with its fighter interceptor group, which required him to live near enough to Spokane to serve one weekend a month and two weeks in the summer. He had finished aircraft and powerplant school, had an airframe and engine (A&E) license, and was approached by Harrah's, which was recreating a Ford tri-motor and a World War I Jenny biplane and asked him to work in Reno.

Schott also knew *Miss Bardahl* would have an opening, because Gary Breakfield was leaving the team. Not wanting to move to Nevada, Schott drove to Seattle soon after returning from San Diego and "kind of camped at the Bardahl office," lobbying Vanden Berg for a job. The two knew each other as friendly *Bardahl* and *Miss Spokane/Eagle Electric* rivals, plus Schott and Dixon had been friends since their teenage model-hydro days.

"I told Leo he needed me," Schott said. "They needed a fairly experienced person to help them, and they hired me because I was available and eager, for $2.25 an hour. So I ended up working for them, and I never took my motorcycle back to Spokane. It stayed in the *Bardahl* shop, and I rode it around Seattle."

Schott began his job as a full-time Bardahl Chemical Corporation employee two weeks before Thanksgiving in November 1964, around the time Ole Bardahl was finalizing plans to order a new cabover hydro from Ron Jones, now based in Mountain View, Calif.

The Seattle Times had reported on Aug. 9 that on the previous day, John (Joe) Brown, president of Seattle's Spot Oil Corp, ordered a rear-engine, low-profile unlimited from Ron Jones. Limited driver Tom Snyder was announced as driver, with *Exide* and *Fascination* veteran E.W. Gustafson named crew chief. "If we can match the conventional boats on the straightaways, we hope to pick up speed and time in the turns," said Jones, whose *Tiger Too* cabover enjoyed great success in the limited 225 class.

Brown's Rolls-powered cabover never materialized. But on Jan. 5, 1965, a Bardahl news release said Ole Bardahl had officially ordered what sounded like an identical hull "designed and currently under construction by Ron Jones." The release described it as "much lighter, slightly wider and longer, more aerodynamic, and able to accelerate and turn faster than last year's boat."

The venerable Green Dragon, deemed too worn and tired after logging 52 hours, 51 minutes of running time in its three-year career, would be retired.

Chapter 20

New and improved: the cabover cometh

It's inexact to say that Ole Bardahl simply thought his Green Dragon was worn out. The reigning two-time Gold Cup and National Champion obviously remained competitive. The deciding factors for building a new boat were wear and tear, but also the chance to try something better.

"It kept falling apart," said Vanden Berg. "The frames kept breaking, the battens kept breaking, and all the glue joints were busted. They used hard wood glue at that time, and they were all loose."

"The boat was a little worn, and the longer you keep it, the more chance you have of some major structural damage happening," said Dixon. "It takes more maintenance and repair just because it's getting older and beat up. At some point you say, okay, we've used this boat three years and learned some stuff. We can keep changing it, making the motors better. Or in lieu of that, we can better spend our time, money, and effort by building a new boat that will maybe give us a significant leap forward."

In this case, the leap was embodied in Ron Jones' cabover design. The veteran *Miss Bardahl* was no slouch, but competition had stiffened in 1964. Sweet-riding *Tahoe Miss* was perhaps the fastest boat in the fleet when it held together. *Exide*, already significantly lighter than *Bardahl* and fast, was now even quicker with nitrous. *Notre Dame* had speed, potential to improve, and had wooed revered engine expert Bill Newman to its team for 1965, replacing Bud Meldrum. *Smirnoff* blossomed and had big bucks at its disposal, *Mariner Too* had matured into an occasional speedster, and some still believed the feather-light *U.S.5* would hit its stride once balanced properly.

"Ron Jones felt and presented, apparently, a very strong case that he could build a boat that was significantly faster," Dixon said. "At some point it was decided we can go a lot faster if we build a new boat. We can do things with the new design that we can't do with our existing boat. And we can make it lighter."

In an article he wrote for the March 1966 *Popular Mechanics* magazine, Ron Musson said of the 1962 *Bardahl*, "like all other conventional unlimiteds her speed drops to around 90 mph in a turn. We wanted a boat that could go through a turn at 100 mph or more. To get it, Ole Bardahl commissioned Ron Jones to design the world's fastest unlimited hydroplane."

To stay in prime condition after three hard years of racing, wood hulls like *Bardahl* require much work as the finish on the inside breaks down and starts soaking up water and oil. A Merlin explodes, and chunks of metal roll around on the bottom, dinging the varnish finish. Every time that happens it leaves an area where water and oil can soak in.

"Then you punch a hole in the boat and do a quicky repair, and maybe you don't do it *exactly* the way you should," Dixon said. "So you end up with wood that's soaked with oil and water and losing some structural integrity, and it's heavier. Plus the plumbing's getting old and having problems, and the wiring's corroded from running in salt, so now you really ought to fix the wiring. Each year you run it, a boat gains weight. It's almost impossible to make a boat lose weight. And now you're three years behind in technology. All of that combined says, time for a new boat."

Schott recalled a similar sequence of reflection, analysis, and decision making.

"Ron Jones wanted to build an unlimited cabover because he was convinced it would work," Schott said. "Musson saw that this new technology could be the next step in boat racing. And Ole wanted to win. I'm pretty sure Jim Raisbeck and Ron Jones were collaborators in some of the design of the boat, the aero part of it. He came out a couple times and gave us dog and pony shows, because as the smart-ass young crew, we wanted to know, 'How is this boat going to work?'"

Musson confirmed Raisbeck's involvement in his *Popular Mechanics* article. "Jim Raisbeck, a Seattle aerodynamicist, made use of a NASA airfoil section to design a stabilizer of minimum drag."

David Smith wasn't involved in conversations deliberating about a new boat, but he cites the same key factors: old and worn versus new and improved.

"The Green Dragon was tired," he said. "You could see the deck was starting to move, the sponsons were starting to come up. We also knew the boat was heavier. And I think at the time, because of the Jones' relationship in building the two boats, we were being romanced by a Jones, and this time it was Ron: 'I've got this new innovation that's going to set the world on fire. Why don't I build you this boat?'

"I didn't even know they'd ordered the boat, didn't know it was being built," David recalled. "Bill Voorhees, Bardahl's graphic designer who worked upstairs at the plant, said to me, 'Hey, this is the new boat,' and he had the artist's conception of it."

Jones and crew constructed the cabover in their Mountain View shop, near Palo Alto in the Bay Area. Slated to debut at Guntersville in June 1965, the new hull was 14 inches longer, 3 inches wider, had a thinner deck than the 1962 hull (3/16" birch plywood versus ¼" mahogany plywood), and was planned to weigh 6,000 pounds race-ready, according to Bardahl's press book. Because its aft engine would result in a short prop shaft with an overly steep angle, the engine was mounted backwards and the hull was fitted with a V-drive gearbox, atypical for unlimiteds.

"That boat has quite a history for me," said Ron Jones in 2007. "And you know, it was *so far* ahead of its time. I thought I had arrived. It was going to stir up the business, and I was going to get new boat orders. I mean, I thought it was all there for me."

But the cabover fell behind schedule. Up in Seattle, the *Bardahl* crew kept hard at work, building and honing secret mechanical improvements to squeeze more power and reliability out of its motors. Company chemist VanSteenvoort refined a performance-enhancing mixture. All of it was innovative – and experimental. But the new hull lagged behind.

As March and April came and went, the team grew restless. Jones had not completed the cabover, there was difficulty procuring a V-drive gearbox, and Vanden Berg knew the unfamiliar hull and design would require ample testing.

"If I could have taken the bull by the horns and followed through with it, I probably could have gotten things going," Vanden Berg said in 1989. "But finding a gearbox at the price that Musson and Ole agreed on, I had to go to Casale, which I really didn't want to do."

"The boat was late," said Dixon. "Casale was building the gearbox, and he had lots of experience building limited gearboxes. He had a real good reputation and actually built a pretty good gearbox. But there were difficulties getting ours built on time."

Schott recalled Musson had flown to California to check on the gearbox at one point, and Casale gave him what Schott called a "snow job."

"Then Leo and Jerry and I went down to Mountain View to do some stuff to the boat, and we thought we were going to bring the boat back, because we took the truck and trailer," Schott said. "Well, the boat wasn't ready to come back, it was about 80 percent done. So we went to Mickey Thompson's in Los Angeles, talked to him about pistons, and then went to Casale. We were expecting to see gearbox castings being machined and stuff, but we never actually saw any patterns. They were way, way behind. It wasn't going to happen. At some point someone said, 'Are you going to have this ready or not?' 'Well, probably not.'"

Jones finished the cabover, then faced an interesting dilemma: how to remove it from the shop through a door that only had a half-inch of clearance.

"I measured the full-size drawing, and I measured the door opening of the shop I was renting in Mountain View," Jones recalled. "I did not change the boat. I decided I can get it out, but it ain't gonna be easy. It took about four hours to get it through the door. We just kept inching it. Didn't scratch anything, it just made it. That was the last hydro and the only unlimited I made in that shop. I moved to Costa Mesa not long after."

Vanden Berg fetched the boat by himself from Jones and, aside from a chilly nap in Northern California's Siskiyou Mountains, towed it home virtually nonstop with the Ford C-750 tractor, arriving in Ballard on May 7, 1965.

"It was still freezing at night," Vanden Berg said. "I went down and got it, and I had to take a nap in a rest stop, and I woke up and everything was ice. I remember we publicized it; the papers had pictures of it coming in. I know we were under the gun to get it ready."

Schott recalls the boat was pretty, all painted, and it "looked like a racebaot." But in reality it was essentially a shell, a long way from being ready to run.

"It wasn't even close," said Zuvich. "There was nothing in it. There was a cowl on it and a driver's cockpit, and that was it."

"It was supposed to be pretty well done," said David. "Well, it wasn't done. There was nothing in the boat, it was just a raw hull. We had made the decision, don't take parts out of the old boat and put them into the cabover. So we had to get all new instruments, I had to build the dashboard, the steering. It didn't even have water pickups. It didn't have the engine stringers in, the gearbox, didn't have any plumbing, hadn't been wired. It was just a pretty boat sitting on a trailer with an empty cowling.

"I remember seeing that thing come in. It was a sunny day. Dixon and I both said, 'How are we going to finish a full offseason's worth of work in six weeks and make the first race?' That gearbox was a small issue compared to all the rest of the stuff. I know, because I built most of that other stuff, and I would have had to drop out of school to do it.

"Something else," David added. "All of us weren't really excited about it because the crew had no input into it. We were just given it. We were just the crew, and everybody else was an expert."

Dixon recalls the team was discouraged when they discovered the cabover was not the light hull they had been promised. In fact, it was heavier than the Green Dragon. Regardless, the team plunged ahead, striving to complete final assembly. And then one day late in May 1965, reality set in.

"Everything kind of piled up to where it became pretty obvious that, if we did make it to the first race, it was going to be a last-minute thrash," said Dixon. "Here we have a boat that's a *significant* design change. It's also significantly heavier than it was supposed to be. I think the old boat raced at around 7,200 pounds; that cabover was going to be well over 8,000. Not only is it heavy, but the weight distribution is in question. The gearbox is going to be late. When you stack all that together, at some point you say, hey, this isn't going to work. We just flat-out don't have time. We need an extra month in here that we don't have, and there's a serious commitment that we *will* be at all the races, and we *will* go fast.

"Around a month before the first race," he continued, "I don't know who exactly made the decision, but we all concurred: 'Put that sucker over in the corner and drag the other one out. We know we've got something that's a known quantity. It goes fast. We're going to have to do some work on it, and we may not have a hands-down winner, but we're not going to have a dog. This new one, without some serious work, potentially could be a dog.' There was too much risk with not enough time."

The good news was, the crew already had built its arsenal of engines for the 1965 race circuit. And in '65, *Bardahl*'s engines packed some surprises.

Musson and Ole Bardahl admire their new Dragon outside Bardahl Manufacturing Corporation headquarters.
– *Seattle P-I* collection, used with permission of the Museum of History and Industry

Vanden Berg arrives in Ballard May 7, 1965, with the much-delayed cabover *Miss Bardahl*. "There was nothing in the boat, it was just a raw hull," said David Smith.
© *Seattle Times* photo 1965, Leo Vanden Berg collection

Vanden Berg said the team was "under the gun" to get the cabover ready to race, and in the end the team decided, "Put that sucker over in the corner and drag the other one out."
– *Seattle P-I* collection, used with permission of the Museum of History and Industry

Chapter 21

Tricks and innovations

Miss Bardahl wasn't the only racing machine sponsored by the oil-additive company. Bardahl had sponsored Indianapolis 500 cars since 1950, and in 1964 it began sponsoring a Rolls-Merlin-powered P-51 fighter plane driven by Chuck Lyford, 22, a Seattle limited-hydro whiz kid who had no interest in driving dangerous unlimited-class hydros. He turned to airplanes instead.

"I raced boats for fun," Lyford told *The Seattle Times*' Bud Livesley. "It ceases to be fun when you move up to the unlimiteds."

Part of the agreement between Ole Bardahl and Lyford was that the hydro and airplane crews would exchange engine technology. Dwight Thorn was crew chief on the P-51, and when informed of the new "partnership," a wary Dixon wanted no part of sharing *Miss Bardahl*'s secrets.

"That agreement caused a little heated discussion in the camp, like, 'Over my dead body you will!' At first Dwight and I did not talk to each other, even though we were forced to work together," Dixon said. "Essentially, we became very good friends, close friends. But that was real hard for me to swallow, because here we had developed all this neat engine technology over several years, and we're basically directed, 'Give it to these airplane guys.'"

Eventually that sentiment was smoothed over, and one of the things Thorn provided was a rudimentary water-injection system. At that point the boat crew knew almost nothing about water injection, or water-alcohol injection, also called ADI (anti-detonation injection). Vanden Berg was somewhat familiar with it because his *Maverick* teammate Bill Newman had perfected its use in *Maverick*'s two-stage Allison, to solve a detonation problem inherent with that motor.

Detonation occurs when, instead of having a controlled burn in a cylinder, there's an explosion, which kicks rods out of engines. "Engine knock" is the same thing as detonation. If a car is built to run on premium gasoline, it has a higher compression ratio, and if you don't use premium, it knocks – "ping-ping-ping."

"In a hydroplane that sound is more like 'bang-bang-bang,' and after about three of those you hear 'BOOM,' and a rod kicks through the side. That's what detonation is," Dixon explained.

"My initial reaction was, 'That water injection might work in the airplane, but it sure as hell won't work in this race boat.' Well, it wasn't my idea! Remember what I said earlier?" Dixon said, turning up his palms and laughing, noting his pre-adult view that "if it's not my idea, it's no good."

Water injection/ADI provides significant benefits. It cools the fuel mixture and the motor, increases engine power, and also can increase engine reliability. It allows you to lean the carburetor and get more power out of it. If you don't have water injection, you must run the carburetor a little rich to cool it and keep from melting the motor, losing perhaps 5 percent power.

The easiest place to inject water or water-alcohol in a Rolls-Merlin is just below the carburetor. Fuel enters the carburetor; a little below that, water is squirted in and gets stirred up with the air. Water literally enters the engine's induction system and vaporizes, which cools the mixture.

"We ran it a little bit when testing the boat, and we didn't see any immediate improvement because that's not the kind of thing where you see a quantum leap," Dixon said. "But it turns out that it does, in fact, make some significant differences. It took me about four months to calm down and decide, 'Maybe these guys aren't complete jerks, maybe they *do* know something I don't know,' so I hiked back over to the UW library and started digging around. Sure enough, water injection is a neat deal. It really is.

"Had Chuck Lyford and his airplane-racing operation not walked it into our shop with it, saying 'Here's something that will make your race boat go faster and make your engines live longer,' we probably never would have tried it. It's to their credit, and Leo's credit, or whoever basically made the command decision, 'You *will* put this on the race boat.'"

Lyford told the *Bardahl* team that *Miss Thriftway*'s crew had experimented with water injection after stumbling across it by accident. One of their engines ran a lot better than the others and they couldn't figure out why. They finally narrowed it down to one of their aftercoolers – the black box that works like a radiator, mounted on top of the front of a Rolls-Merlin. Lake or river water runs through one side of the aftercooler, induction air through the other, and it cools the intake mixture.

"The *Thriftway* guys discovered this particular aftercooler had a leak and was squirting a little bit of water into the engine," Dixon said. "They wondered what they could use as a regulator, and being truck guys with a lot of refrigerated trucks around, they looked at a Freon refrigeration regulator and figured it would probably work, and they used one of those. And in fact, Lyford came to us with a refrigeration regulator. Now, I don't know how he managed to get that, but he had one."

Miss Bardahl used water injection late in 1964, modifying Thorn's system. Initially the boat picked up water out of the lake with a tube below the sponson that ran to a small can, a pump, and what Dixon called "a little Mickey Mouse regulator" that squirted water into the engine. The team conducted flow tests to improve the system in the offseason and used it regularly in 1965. Eventually, before the Oct. 3 San Diego race, the team bought two surplus 10-gallon stainless steel tanks at a Reno junkyard, cut and welded them together, and strapped the tank inside the back of the boat and filled it with a 50-50 blend of fresh water and alcohol, which Dixon had learned performed better than plain water. Because salt encrusts spark plugs, salt water couldn't be picked up out of the bay and squirted into the motor, as pretty soon it wouldn't run.

"We were one of the first people to run a Merlin motor with alcohol," said Zuvich. "We left the aftercooler on, but we ran water-alcohol along with the aftercooler."

In fact, *Bardahl* likely was the first Merlin-powered hydro to ever run water-alcohol in racing. It's believed alcohol was first used in a Merlin by Bill Newman, who in 1965 pre-season experiments removed *Notre Dame*'s aftercooler in favor of a chrome tube. Sadly, Newman collapsed and died April 9, 1965, at age 48 while onboard the boat following a Lake Washington test session.

"We made several fast runs and Bill was very excited," driver Rex Manchester told the *Seattle P-I*. "Then suddenly he said 'Uh, oh' and slumped down."

"Bill walked up to look at things," Burns Smith told the *Unlimited NewsJournal*. "All of a sudden he fell down, slid into the water. Rex went in after him, but he was dead. He'd had a heart attack right on the boat."

The self-contained water-alcohol system later used in San Diego was *Bardahl*'s final significant refinement, increasing boat speed and engine longevity. But other "skunkworks" projects were under development in early 1965 that gave the Dragon more muscle.

* * * *

In search of power, the *Bardahl* team secretly experimented with flat-top pistons, also called "pop-ups" or "high-domes," starting in the fall of 1964. Previously tried only in Allisons, the crew welded aluminum into the concave top of Rolls pistons to increase combustion. The compression ratio increased, boosting horsepower, but at a price.

"I kind of had a sneaking hunch that was going to be more problems than it was worth," said Vanden Berg, "Nobody tried them in a Merlin before. Sure, we outdid everybody with them, but it cost us. We bent rods, and there was so much pressure, it 'tuliped' the valves. And it was the same way with nitrous. I knew that we had to come up with something to keep up with the other guys – we had to go ahead, to advance."

"The problems you inherit go up faster than the horsepower you get, so there's a big trade-off," Dixon said about the pistons. "Things like the mechanical loads on the rods and bearings increase a lot faster than the horsepower goes up."

The team's first efforts were rudimentary. A stock Rolls-Merlin piston has a 3/8-inch dished-out gap on top, engineered that way to spread the flame uniformly. If that concave gap were filled in, compression and horsepower would increase a little. So that's what the team did – by simply filling the gap to make the top of the piston flat. The accurate term for what *Miss Bardahl* used is "flat-top" pistons. The term "high dome" is often used interchangeably, and although some motors do in fact have cylinders designed to accommodate a domed piston, Rolls-Merlins do not.

"The flat top gives you more compression and more power, but the gas in there gives you problems with hot spots," Vanden Berg said. "It's not a nice round fireball; it's real hot here and cooler there. So we did those pistons right here in the shop. Argon welding. We filled them in with 6061-grade aluminum."

Schott vividly recalls details of the flat-top project, because he did the machine work himself shortly after joining the *Bardahl* team, along with local welding expert Bill "Flash" Gauntlett.

"I took the stock pistons and chucked them up on the lathe," he explained. "I cut an angle in and faced off the top of the piston. Then Bill the welder and I cut out aluminum circles that I would hold and pass to Bill, who welded them on top of the piston. Then we would face off the pistons, and they'd be flat on top instead of concave.

"The first time I helped do that, we'd weld them on a big steel plate," Schott continued. "I had a welding hood on, and Bill had a welding hood on, but later on I found out why he had what looked like a dish rag hanging from the bottom of the welding hood. It was to block the reflection on this steel plate from coming up underneath, because at 2 o'clock in the morning in my apartment in Burien, I woke myself up screaming. I had sunburned my eyes."

After getting the pistons dimensionally correct, holes were drilled in the bottom to lighten them to their original weight.

"Those flat-tops created all kinds of problems," Schott said. "They created a lot of detonation, pre-ignition, and then at a certain point the welded-on lids decided to come off. We started looking down the spark plug hole with kind of a home-made boroscope to see if the lids were coming off."

When Vanden Berg, Zuvich, and Schott visited Mickey Thompson's machine shop in early 1965, they did so to check out his forged flat-top pistons, believed to be superior to *Bardahl*'s home-made welded contraptions.

"They had some slugs, and they were trying to make some pistons, but we never got them in the boat during the '65 season," Schott said. "Mickey Thompson forged some high-domes from scratch for *Bardahl* later, and I think they ran them in the Karelsen boat, but I was gone by then."

The first sign of trouble with the flat-tops came when *Miss Bardahl* tested on Lake Washington and Musson complained about the engine running rough. Amazed, the crew found the ceramic portion of two spark plugs entirely missing. The Green Dragon was literally spitting spark plugs. The team didn't fully understand cause and effect until much later, after frustrating and even comical trial and error.

"I can remember Zuvich had just put together a brand new ignition harness," said Dixon. "Musson went out and it goes, *pop pop, bang bang*, and a couple of spark plugs launch out and take about a third of this electrical harness with it. He comes back in and Zuvich jumps on the boat and looks at Musson and says, 'You dumbshit, I just spent all day building that harness, and you screwed it up again!' And Musson simply shrugs and says, 'That's the way it goes sometimes.' Everybody laughed because we were to the point of, 'What'll we do?' We didn't know."

When *Bardahl* raced in 1965, blown-out spark plugs became a severe consequence of the increased pressure and hot spots from running welded flat-tops. Dixon said altogether *Miss Bardahl* popped more than 20 plugs that year – blew the porcelain core right out of them. Not until later in the season did they solve the problem when Champion Spark Plug custom-built a plug with a lower heat range and a better crimp that held up.

"Before that, our spark plug heat range was wrong for the pistons we were running," said Dixon. "We needed colder plugs, which they weren't making at the time. They finally made us some, and that was another thing we had that other people didn't, thanks to Champion."

Schott had become one of the team's "spark plug guys" as the 1965 season progressed, and he worked with Bobby Strahlman and Skip Mason, Champion Spark Plug's master field techs/representatives. Strahlman was revered for his ability to diagnose problems just by "reading" plugs. As one of his contemporaries said, "Bobby Strahlman can tell you your momma's maiden name by the look of the plugs." Champion wouldn't outright give its customized plugs to the *Bardahl* team but instead made 50 of them, heavy-duty platinum, screwed together – not crimped – that Strahlman retrieved after each race.

"Bobby brought them and said, 'You will *not* blow these out,'" Schott recalled. "They were kind of beefy, and I said, 'These look expensive.' He said, 'You don't want to know.' They made a special tool for gapping them. We'd pull the plugs each heat, we'd look at them with a spark plug viewer, measure the gap, use this tool to reset the gap, put them back in. At the end of the last race we took them all out, and I wanted one as a souvenir, but Strahlman took them back to Toledo. But they gave us a lot of T-shirts and Champion jewelry, which my wife still wears."

The subsequent *Bardahl* team eliminated its spark-plug woes once they were able to get real flat-top pistons, made from scratch, out of Los Angeles in 1967-68.

"There's about 1,500 degrees in a cylinder," Dixon explained. "A piston with an aluminum donut on it doesn't transfer heat correctly, only through the welds. So the compression and temperature there was higher, extremely hot. Those are the pistons that blew the spark plugs out. We did that one year, and later *Bardahl* ran the Mickey Thompsons and didn't knock out any more spark plugs. They were full-cast pistons, real pistons, and they transferred the heat."

* * * *

Vanden Berg took advantage of Bardahl Chemical Corporation's access to a performance-enhancing – and extremely toxic – liquid substance not available to the general public: tetraethyl lead, or TEL. General Motors researchers developed it in 1921 along with Standard Oil and DuPont, and soon GM and Standard partnered to market it under its commercial name, "Ethyl," after forming Ethyl Corporation. When diluted in gasoline, Ethyl became the term synonymous with premium automobile fuel. Baby boomers might recall their parents pulling up to now-vanished service stations like Flying A, Enco, Mobil, Richfield, or Standard, and telling the attendant, "Fill it up with Ethyl."

Miss Bardahl's use of TEL was, like the flat-top pistons, highly secret. The team absolutely did not want anyone to know about it, and crew members remained guarded when discussing it more than 20 years later.

TEL prolongs engine life. Again, the big problem in a piston engine is detonation, which in racing engines can break rods. Like water-alcohol, and even nitrous oxide to a degree, TEL allows a motor to indirectly generate more horsepower without detonation, or engine knock. Directly, TEL improves reliability. Lead coats pistons and cushions them, and it also boosts octane.

TEL also is poisonous. In 1965, because the scope of TEL's health and environmental impacts weren't fully recognized or acknowledged, environmental laws weren't nearly as strict. Today, leaded gas is banned from use in road vehicles because of TEL's dangerous pollutants. The Environmental Protection Agency finished phasing TEL out of the U.S. market in 1996 under the Clean Air Act, and consumer gas stations now sell only unleaded fuel.

Donald VanSteenvoort, Bardahl's chief chemist, worked in the division of the company that did research and development, manufactured Bardahl products, and distributed them to canning plants. VanSteenvoort was able to obtain TEL.

"One of the problems with tetraethyl lead is, if you breathe the fumes, you potentially get lead poisoning," said Dixon. "It's nasty stuff, and that's essentially why you can't get it now. Once you dilute it heavily in gasoline, it's not as bad."

In 1924, GM told distributors to add 3 grams of Ethyl fluid per gallon of gasoline, a ratio of roughly 1 to 1,000.

After everyone had gone home from the pits the night before a race, Vanden Berg and a helper would return in the early morning hours to mix TEL with their fuel. They would don a protective suit, mask, and heavy rubber gloves to protect their hands.

"Usually, Jerry and I were the ones who mixed it, pure lead," said Vanden Berg. "We'd put so many ounces in a drum. Later on, we had it mixed with fuel at the plant in top-oil cans so we wouldn't have to handle it straight, and then we added it to our drums of fuel at the race sites. For some reason I remember doing it in Coeur d'Alene in particular, where Templin's motel was right next to the pits."

VanSteenvoort directed Bardahl's canning plant in Ballard to mix a diluted sum of TEL with a petroleum product and seal it in 4-ounce cans resembling Bardahl Top Oil. The truck carried a case or two, which to observers looked like a standard Bardahl product, but in fact was a potent dose of tetraethyl lead. The amount was calculated so that one can was just right for mixing with fuel in a 55-gallon drum.

"When we first started using it, there was *big sweat* that only one or two guys can do it, and they're going to have to go take a piss test once a month to see if there's any lead in their urine," Dixon said. "If someone does, he's in trouble."

"Dixon said to me, 'Don't ever get close to that crap. It'll kill you,'" said David. "So we made sure we were totally away from it. I saw Jerry do it a couple of times, but most of the time it was Leo. I wouldn't get near that stuff. Dixon said to make sure you're busy so you never have to touch it."

"They dumped the little can in there, put the bung back on the drum, and rolled it back and forth in the 55-gallon drum to mix it up," said Schott. "It was done at night surreptitiously. Nobody knew what we were doing, and that really helped a lot. Nobody had a clue that we were doing that."

"We could run real steep timing," said Zuvich in 1988. "We used it only one year, probably the last year, and it was decided that it was just too dangerous. And there was no way of getting rid of the contaminated can. I was the one having to add it. We had a vest to put on and gloves and the whole thing, and I had to take a blood test before and after. We also had manganese like they have now. That's okay; that's not bad. Then we used toluene, or toluol, to be a carrier. But that other stuff was pretty dangerous shit."

* * * *

Striving for more horsepower and an edge over his rivals, Musson located a source for the Rolls-Merlin 620, the final British-built model of the Merlin engine used by hydroplanes. Rolls engineers strengthened the 620's internal components for long-range commercial airline routes flown by the North Star, a DC-4 variant built by Canadair, starting in 1946. Rolls-powered hydro teams used the dash 9, or the earlier dash 7 that had shorter water jackets that didn't cool as well. *Miss Bardahl* always used dash 9 motors; the crew typically rebuilt a dozen each winter to use throughout the racing season.

"We had four of those 620 engines," said Vanden Berg. "We bought four nacelles to get them. We never got around to racing them in '65, we just ran dash 9s. We only got the 620s half torn apart."

Schott disassembled the 620s in early 1965, and the team soon recognized 620s had a few differences that required more time to adapt them for racing.

"Nobody had ever had one of those apart before," Schott said. "The internal parts were the same, but externally, I don't think the 620 crankcase would bolt to the gearbox. But we knew there's got to be some good stuff there. That's where we got those really great round exhaust stacks that we ran in '65. The standard stacks are oval; we were the first people to run the round ones, the best stacks ever made for a Merlin. I sandblasted them, painted them with VHT white paint, bolted them on, and they never cracked."

* * * *

In January of my fifth-grade year at Lake Hills Elementary my teacher, Mrs. Bellos, gave me a clipping from one of the local newspapers. She knew I loved hydros, and the clipping bore a hydro illustration with the headline, "Green Dragon Has A New Look." The caption announced a new *Miss Bardahl* would replace my favorite boat in 1965. Above the caption was Bardahl staff artist Bill Voorhees' rendering of the new *Bardahl* – an odd-looking cabover hydro, with the driver seated in front of the motor.

I disliked the drawing of the weird boat with its long cowling and clunky tail. It was ugly, not sleek. This was not good. Why replace *Miss Bardahl*, the best boat of all? Disappointment sank in.

Happily for me the cabover *Bardahl* was slow to develop, and the iconic Green Dragon eventually was rushed back into service for her 1965 farewell campaign.

Mrs. Bellos made quite an impression. She kept her brown hair short, wore neat and tidy skirts every day, and retained a mild Southern drawl from her native locale. A few of us lively boys kept her hands full, and she awarded "conduct cuts" to anyone who disrupted class. My report card typically said, "Lots of potential, but must stop disturbing others with socializing."

Mrs. Bellos kept a ledger booklet with all the students' names listed in alphabetical order, written in her neat, distinctive backslanted printing. Horizontally across the page, she'd mark a capital "C" next to a name when she levied that person a conduct cut.

The C's next to my name ran past the saddlestitch, more than halfway across the page.

A few times Mrs. Bellos' patience wore thin, and this was a time when schools still allowed corporal punishment. One of the guys did something that really got her stoked, so she steered him by the arm outside the classroom and fetched Mr. Steiling from the sixth-grade class next door. Paul Steiling was a tall, stout man who looked a bit like JFK, and – whether as a favor or perhaps per school regulations – Mrs. Bellos asked Mr. Steiling to apply the penalty.

Our classmate was told to grab his ankles. Steiling whacked his rump with a wood paddle, and we all giggled at the sound, clearly audible indoors even though the door was closed. Mrs. Bellos then steered the pink-faced boy back inside to his seat; he looked a bit sheepish but also wore a hint of a smile. He later bragged about that swatting like it was a badge of honor.

Ann Bellos was the teacher who introduced us to the principles we now call "green" and "sustainable." She took us on field trips to tree farms, watersheds, and lumber mills, where we learned about renewable resources. And she was our surrogate mother for a memorable week when our entire fifth-grade class rode a school bus to conservation camp (schools now call it outdoor education) at Camp Lutherland, east of Federal Way on the north end of Lake Killarney. Camp Lutherland has since been torn down, and international relief organization World Vision now occupies its former site.

Conservation camp was a blast! We were paired with students from another elementary school, perhaps Sherwood Forest or Ivanhoe, and among the many enduring memories from that week, three stand out. One, a kid was homesick and cried in his bunk the entire first night, so the poor guy's parents came and got him the next day. Two, we were divided into squads – boys were named after cool cars like Mustangs and Sting Rays, while my squad was named for the new and very *un*cool Marlin. Girls were named after flowers – Daisies, Posies, Pansies. Third, all squads competed for points each day, and the Marlins were penalized at dinner when a teacher monitoring our table manners caught me nudging peas onto my fork with my thumb.

Around the time we went to conservation camp, my friend Mikey came by my house one spring morning so we could walk to school together. Suddenly the floor shook, the walls creaked, and Mom yelled "Earthquake! Stand in the doorway!" This was the April 29, 1965, Seattle temblor that hit 6.5 on the Richter scale and caused moderate damage around Puget Sound. Mom grew up in Los Angeles and recognized the sensation. Mikey and I weren't really scared, just fascinated with the whole thing.

* * * *

Over in Ballard, Skip Schott lay under the '62 *Miss Bardahl*, removing hardware. The boat sat on four empty 55-gallon Bardahl oil drums. Schott felt movement and yelled to Jerry Zuvich, who had been using a forklift, "Quit ramming the boat, Jerry! I'm still underneath it!"

"I'm not on the forklift," Zuvich said.

Schott noticed a tall stack of engine crates rocking back and forth, a bit unnerving because the crates contained heavy Rolls-Merlin superchargers. Somebody yelled, "We're having an earthquake!" and Schott scampered out from under the boat. Standing in the outside doorway he heard a strange slapping noise, like the sound of hands clapping, and looked up to see the N.W. 52nd telephone-pole wires swaying wildly, slapping together.

"All the secretaries from the building across the street came out and stood in the middle of the road," Schott recalled, "and the wires were still slapping each other. One of the guys from our plant was driving a Bardahl delivery truck on the Alaska Way viaduct, and he later said it was like a snake. It was undulating."

Chapter 22

Recommissioning the Dragon

Once the team had decided, in Dixon's words, to "Put that sucker over in the corner and drag the other one out," a frantic thrash began to revive the Green Dragon and prepare it for racing. The hull hadn't been touched since post-season nitrous and ADI testing, and it needed attention, but mechanically it was in fairly good shape. The good news was, all of its engines had been rebuilt, although modifications already made to accommodate the cabover now needed reversing.

"The engine package that we had would not fit in the cabover with all of the oil pumps on the bottom of the pan, where they're normally mounted," said Schott. "You have to drive the oil pumps off of different accessory points on the engine. So I had cut the oil-pump shafts off of the bottom of the pans, so the engine could sit lower in the cabover. When we decided not to run the cabover, we needed oil-pump shafts, but we had enough parts to come up with that. That's why we missed Guntersville. The boat wasn't put together."

Miss Bardahl had gained weight over the previous three years, partly because of repairs made with added hardware like aluminum plates, partly because of oil-soaked wood, and also because of extra weight from hardware and tanks for the add-on nitrous oxide and (later) ADI systems. The hull was stuffed with styrofoam, which boat camps at the time hoped would keep their wooden hulls afloat if they flipped or broke apart.

"I went through the hull, tightened up some stuff, moved some stuff," David said. "We got rid of the styrofoam and flotation that made it heavy. It was all oil-soaked because it was open-cell, not closed-cell. So all this heavy, sloppy crap was in the wrong places – stuffed up in the nose, everywhere else. I'd say we probably took out 200 pounds."

The crew identified other overweight areas, but there was too little time to tackle the task. By now the first race in Guntersville, on June 27, was less than a month away. Simply hauling the boat there was a three-day journey.

"We had a fire system in the boat that was all steel," said David. "We had a huge CO2 bottle mounted behind the driver, and that was really heavy. The other thing that was enormously heavy was the cowling. They made it out of three sections of what's called 'roving.' It's really thick, and it had a full piece of marine plywood for the tail. It took two or three of us to pick the damn thing up to get it off the boat. We also had enough tanks to run the Harmsworth in that thing. I think it could carry about 110 gallons."

Dax replaced all of the Dragon's wiring, and the hull was replumbed. Schott recalled groping into voids for styrofoam and removing obsolete hoses from years past that never had been taken out.

"That boat was worn," he said. "The boat was not supposed to run in 1965. It had been taken care of, but it got fat, it leaked, and it had been run. *Hard*."

Fiberglass now peeled from *Bardahl's* deck around the edges and curled up, and the only thing holding it in place was the aluminum trim. David removed it, cut the fiberglass off, ground the deck, applied new fiberglass, and reapplied the trim.

"I had to do that because we thought we were gonna blow off the deck," he said. "There was a bunch of other little nit-nack stuff I had to do because the boat had bashed the dock a few times."

Somehow during this busy race against the clock, 18-year-old David also found time to take final exams and graduate with the Cleveland High School class of 1965.

Schott recalled there were some "questionable spots" that they reinforced with aluminum plates inside the boat, despite their desire to trim weight. "It was a case of, 'This is what we got, this is what we're gonna run,'" he said. "There wasn't any time. We were already going to miss Guntersville, and there's no way we were going to miss the second race too."

The entire boat needed painting, not just because of repairs, but because Voorhees had changed one of the brand colors on Bardahl's canned products, and the font on the corporate logo had changed the year before – Voorhees replaced the traditional font that featured pointy "A's" with block lettering. The rolling stock had been changed the previous summer, and the cabover already bore the lighter shade of yellow.

"Voorhees had changed the graphics on the cans and gone to a lighter, brighter yellow, so we decided to do that on the boat, too," David said. "And we had to paint the boat quickly. Took it to the Heiser Body Company on 6th Avenue South, and before they painted it, they wanted somebody to check it off. Leo said, 'You're a designer, you go to school, you go down there and make sure they tape it off correctly.'

"Because we had to paint the boat quickly, we never even put the metalflake on it," David continued. "We couldn't get the metallic green paint because it was a custom mix that had to be specially ordered, and we were out of time. Metallic is also harder to shoot. It wasn't catalyzed paint in the day, it was a paint that was lacquer, so it just dried. We said, let's just put some green on the thing, nobody will know the difference.

"If I remember right, we got something really close, and I think I picked it, and it was a John Deere green something. They had some there, the choices were limited, and I said, 'Just go for it.' So they slapped on some green paint, no clearcoat. Heiser truck painters painted it."

* * * *

Roy Duby returned to drive for George Simon's team in 1965, and on June 24 he set a course record of 115.385 mph aboard the one-year-old *Miss U.S. 5* to qualify for the Dixie Cup Regatta on Guntersville Lake, Ala. *Notre Dame*, which had tested extensively over the winter, was the lone Seattle representative among the 12 combatants, with *Bardahl* busy being revived and *Exide* staying home as well. *Exide*'s pilot, Bill Brow, stayed busy by winning the 7-litre British Columbia race aboard *Miss Vitamilk*.

Jerry Schoenith drove the brand-new *Gale's Roostertail* to 107.5 mph, just behind *Miss Madison*'s 107.7, on the enlarged 3-mile course. Also among the qualifiers was *Savair's Probe*, a new name on a familiar boat – the former *Burien/Tempest/Michelob*, now a stablemate of *Savair's Mist* and also owned by Michigan's Mike Wolfbauer. And Chuck Thompson turned a modest 106.615 mph aboard *Tahoe Miss*, newly equipped with an immense General Electric C-23 turbocharger dubbed the "trashburner," developed under 1965 *Tahoe* crew chief Everett Adams, a former Air Force C-124 Globemaster crew chief.

"*Tahoe* probably was the first hydro to use a turbocharger," Dax said. "Turbocharger technology was developed during World War II. The turbo that *Tahoe* used was straight off a P-47D-10 – unbolted off a Thuderbolt and bolted onto *Tahoe*'s Allison. That thing was just huge."

Meanwhile, halfway around the globe, on June 22 American F-105 Thunder Chiefs had dropped 17 tons of bombs beyond the "Hanoi line" in North Vietnam for the first time, signaling further escalation of the war. In serene Seattle that week, music lovers could choose between Dave Brubeck and Peter, Paul and Mary at the Seattle Center Arena, Mel Tormé at the Edgewater Inn, or a big band orchestra at the newly renovated Vasa Park Ballroom near Lake Sammamish's southwest shore.

In Guntersville, everyone sweltered under bright sunshine and 100-degree heat. Warner Gardner picked up where he left off in San Diego the year before by winning his first two heats aboard *Mariner Too*, including a speedy 110.787 mph in taking heat 1A. The much-improved *Miss U.S.5* ran a strong second in 1A at 106.930 and won heat 2B at 109.756 mph. Manchester and *Notre Dame* won a tight 1B duel with *Madison* but conked in its second heat with water in the fuel. Buddy Byers and *Miss Madison*, reliable as always, garnered 600 points by twice taking second, posting 103.646 and 104.590.

Approaching the line in the final heat, Thompson, Duby, and Manchester had trouble seeing the starting clock, which Manchester said was hidden behind a water shed. All three jumped the gun. Gardner and *Mariner Too* shot to the front but suffered engine trouble and sputtered home fifth. Byers stuck *Madison* in front and averaged 100.111 for five laps to beat *Gale's Roostertail*, *U.S.5*, *Notre Dame*, and *Mariner*. *Tahoe Miss* did not finish. The final standings showed *Miss Madison* winning the 1965 Dixie Cup with 1,000 overall points, the first-ever victory for the Hurrying Hoosier team, followed by *Mariner Too*, *U.S.5*, *Gale's Roostertail*, and *Notre Dame*.

While the rest of the hydro fleet raced for Guntersville's Dixie Cup, the weary *Bardahl* team was fighting time just to join them in north Idaho. Ole Bardahl said in the June 16 *Seattle Times* that his cabover was now wired and plumbed but still awaited its special gearbox. "We've had the old boat painted and fixed up, and we'll be in Coeur d'Alene," he said.

"I think we tested the boat once before we went to Coeur d'Alene, to run the nitrous," Schott said in 2007.

Indeed, the *Seattle P-I* reported on Sunday, July 4, 1965, that Musson had taken *Miss Bardahl* out for a spin the previous week and announced, "We're ready. It performed very well. The boat will leave for Idaho Monday or Tuesday and we'll be on the water for tests Wednesday." Obviously, Musson was maintaining a poker face in light of *Bardahl*'s teething problems with the new nitrous system and flat-top pistons.

The Seattle Times reported *Bardahl*'s June 28 test near Sand Point prompted nearby residents to complain to Harbor Police, which in turn told the *Bardahl* team "to get back to the prescribed course" already set up for the Gold Cup near Stan Sayres Pits.

Coeur d'Alene's race officials had endured a rocky offseason. On April 5, the city council voted 5-4 not to renew its Diamond Cup lease for use of the traditional dock facilities and Tubbs Hill. The council objected to charging admission for access to public property, and it cited problems with youth rowdiness in prior years. There even was talk of moving the race to Lake Pend Oreille at Sandpoint, but in the end Bob Templin provided pit facilities at his newly expanded hotel, and the Diamond Cup was rescheduled for

July 11, yielding its Aug. 15 date to the new Utah race.

David Smith smiled as he recalled feeling affirmation at that harried time of his *Miss Bardahl* career. "The first year I was Dixon's little brother, but by then I was a full crew member, so I actually had a uniform with my own name on it," he said. "And, I got paid."

* * * *

The *Exide* team was scrambling, too. The U-75 crew had extensively renovated the hull in the offseason and Brow said it was "nip and tuck" whether the Happy Hydro would be ready for the rescheduled Diamond Cup even if they thrashed through the long July 4 weekend.

The *Bardahl* team's Ford C-750s chugged across Washington towing the Green Dragon and equipment to Coeur d'Alene, where they parked in the new pit area along with early arrivals *Notre Dame* and *$ Bill*. For 1965, the fleet occupied a newly paved parking lot – surrounded by two temporary metal fences – immediately west of Templin's new North Shore Motor Inn, which was built west of the public boat launch. The new asphalt for the substitute pits had barely cooled when the hydros arrived.

Also new was a one-day race format, with all Diamond Cup heats taking place on Sunday. Without Saturday racing, officials hoped to curtail much of the now-customary Saturday night revelry. For added measure Idaho Governor Robert Smiley sent units of the National Guard to protect the Lake City in case hooliganism again broke out.

Bardahl crew member Roger Kruse recalled the pit area and a pathway to the adjacent Templin's motel were encircled by a fence. He assumed it was for protection from revelers, though it simply might have been to cordon off Templin's new-construction zone.

"They locked us in the pits inside that chain-link fence, during the high time of the riots," said Kruse. "They chain-linked the whole place in, and we couldn't leave the motel. But we snuck out to drive up to Wolf Lodge for sandwiches and beer. Jumped in my blue '64 Thunderbird, gave the guard at the gate a *Bardahl* T-shirt or something, and we drove up there and had dinner."

Musson and Manchester flew together into Coeur d'Alene, where Musson and team looked forward to several days of testing to get *Bardahl*'s new tricks sorted out. "We got to Coeur d'Alene, and Dixon and I ran back to Industrial Air in Spokane and bought nitrous oxide because we didn't have any, or didn't have enough," said Schott. "They interrogated us about what we were going to do with it."

By now, news reporters had sniffed out the fact that *Bardahl* would employ nitrous oxide, yet their focus remained on *Exide*, whose crew talked freely about its once-secret weapon. George McKernan told Georg Meyers, sports editor of *The Seattle Times*, that *Exide* carried three nitrous jugs in the stern, 4 inches in diameter by 24 inches high, a total of five gallons to run with 90 gallons of fuel, enough for 45 miles.

Newcomer Bob Fendler, the L.A. attorney and former B Stock outboard-hydro driver who had fallen in love with unlimiteds at Mission Bay the previous year, was on hand with *Miss San Diego*. The U-19 was the former *Coral Reef*, which Fendler had purchased in January and driven for the first time June 26 on Mission Bay. Fendler had some veterans with him including "driving tutor" Mira Slovak and seasoned hydro mechanic Rudy Boppel, from the 1958 *Bardahl* team.

Exide's team finished its work and sped east on U.S. 10 early Friday, with the hydro equipped with just one race-ready Rolls and minus a complete paint job. Short on time, *Exide* sported fresh red paint and a white (replacing blue) cowling, but no lightning stripes across its deck. Shortly after setting up camp in the new pits McKernan sent Brow out, and the defending Diamond Cup champ circled the 3-mile oval at 109.321 mph to qualify. That easily surpassed the new 100-mph qualifying minimum, raised from the previous year's 90 mph. Musson spun *Bardahl* around at 112.971.

Rookie *$ Bill* driver Rex Bixby squeaked into the race by qualifying with laps of 100.935 and 101.313 but blew two superchargers in the process. Fendler failed to qualify *Miss San Diego*, turning only 89 mph. Bernie Little ferried passengers around the course in his four-seat *Miss Budweiser*, the former *Tempo*. And after a troubled performance in Guntersville, *Tahoe Miss* reverted to its two-stage Allison minus the turbocharger to run 110.883. Driver Chuck Thompson employed another new wrinkle – two-way radio communication with his crew, who watched the action from a new penthouse atop the *Tahoe* truck.

Twelve boats had arrived, but *U.S.5, Such Crust IV, Savair's Probe*, and what the media called "Mariner Three" – the former *Miss Spokane/Eagle Electric* now owned by Jim Herrington – were not among them. Norm Evans was on hand to drive, just in case Herrington's No. 2 hull appeared. And on July 10, Ken Murphy of Sacramento announced he had bought the aging *Miss Seattle* from the Stoen brothers and planned to race it in the Gold Cup.

* * * *

Other big sports news around that time included the NFL hiring the first-ever African American on-field official for a USA major-league sport. Burl Abron Toler would be a head linesman for the 1965 NFL season. "There are no rules that would keep a Negro out of the majors," said Baseball Commissioner Ford Frick. "We have several in the minors now, and I'm sure some will be in the majors in a matter of a few years."

Zebra brand fireworks had been on sale throughout the region before July 4, and newspaper ads touted "tested and approved" kits containing fountains, smoke bombs, pinwheels, snakes, and sparklers for as little as $3.95 – "Old Glory" – or as extravagant as the $9.95 "Family Lawn Display."

Namu the killer whale, already a rising media star, began his highly publicized journey to Seattle on July 8. The orca bull estimated to be age 4 or 5 had been accidentally caught in a salmon net near his namesake British Columbia town. Seattle Marine Aquarium owner Ted Griffin bought Namu and, accompanied by radio personality Bob Hardwick, towed Namu 400 miles south in a floating pen. Shortly after embarking, Namu's kin – later learned to be Northern Resident C1 pod – passed nearby. Namu squealed and thrashed wildly, a sad sight for many.

And in Coeur d'Alene, after a serene and orderly Saturday night, two *Bardahl* crewmen tiptoed down to the pits in the early morning darkness on July 11, donned protective gear, and mixed a dose of tetraethyl lead with their racing fuel. Running a tired old boat against a fast fleet, they wanted every advantage available. When the sun came up and *Bardahl* raced later that Sunday, she would secretly employ TEL, flat-top pistons, and nitrous oxide.

* * * *

Forecasters predicted thundershowers for Sunday, but sunshine warmed the crowd of 60,000 as six boats pulled onto the choppy lake for heat 1A. Wily veteran Bill Cantrell and Warner Gardner hooked up in a close duel, and Cantrell came from behind to nip Gardner by three boat lengths at the finish: *Smirnoff*,

98.666 mph to *Mariner Too*'s 98.306. Rookie Rex Bixby drove *$ Bill* to a perfectly timed start and a commendable third over Byers in *Madison*, Hickling in *Budweiser*, and Red Loomis aboard *Savair's Mist* in that order.

The water settled for heat 1B, and four hot dogs battled – Musson in *Bardahl*, Brow in *Exide*, Manchester in *Notre Dame*, and Thompson in *Tahoe Miss*, along with Jerry Schoenith aboard *Gale's Roostertail*. *Notre Dame* was first to the turn but bounced and hooked, got hosed by a roostertail and died. Manchester lit a giant stackfire before the U-7 roared to life, but an overanxious official presumed "Fire!" and shot a flare, stopping the heat.

In the 1B rerun *Notre Dame* again jumped into the lead, but *Exide* smoked ahead entering the backstretch in lap two as Brow squeezed the nitrous button. *Bardahl* also passed *Notre Dame* and then challenged *Exide*, but Brow hit the nitrous again to fend Musson off. Like Cantrell earlier, Manchester closed fast at the finish. He took a wide final turn to keep his speed up and squeaked past *Bardahl* on the outside to barely snatch second. *Exide* averaged a near-record 110.882 mph to win, including one lap at 114.165, with *Notre Dame* second at 108.173, and *Bardahl* third at 108.129. *Gale's Roostertail* died on lap two and *Tahoe* did not start with a crippled blower.

Musson motored back to the new pit area and coasted to the dock, which floated 12 feet below the freshly paved pits alongside a concrete seawall. Frustrated, he debriefed with Vanden Berg and Dax about his uncommon third-place finish. An old crane plucked the Green Dragon from the lake with Schott holding the bow rope, David the stern rope, and Zuvich eyeing the skid fin. The boat eased downward, and when the rudder was within reach overhead, David grabbed it to guide it into the rudder box on the trailer.

Suddenly *Miss Bardahl* fell. Her bow whacked Schott on the head, knocking him to the ground. David yanked his hand away just as the rudder crashed through plywood flooring on the trailer. *Bardahl* bounced a few times and came to rest, a 15-inch hole punched through her bottom.

"It could have taken my whole hand off," David said. "The back of the trailer was all a big piece of plywood except where the rudder sat in a metal box."

Bardahl had fallen four or five feet onto the steel vertical arm that keeps the hull from sliding off the trailer while in transit. The arm poked clear through *Bardahl*'s aluminum-skinned bottom.

"Luckily, the boat landed on part of the trailer, and the other sponson landed on some fuel drums," said Zuvich. "Otherwise, it would have been a real mess."

"The boom-brake stuck, he moved the lever too far, and all of a sudden it unreeled," Vanden Berg recalled. "Like a fishing reel. It was an old Army crane if I remember correctly, an old wreck of a thing. And the operator wasn't that sharp.

"Then we put a patch on it," he continued. "That's when we had Dave Smith inside, putting nuts on the back. His arms were reaching that far. Put that plate in, put the nuts on, and held it. We had 45 minutes to do it, we did it with the boat on the trailer, and we had to move a lot of stuff out of the way to get the bolts and nuts on. We only had a narrow space to get your arms in. Chuck Hickling helped me."

Hickling had been observing the entire commotion from close range, since his *Budweiser* team was parked alongside *Bardahl*, immediately to its left. Vanden Berg said Hickling had skinny arms and was able to squeeze them through a tight gap in the trailer.

The ends of *Bardahl*'s two nitrous oxide tanks are visible in front of the engine. Lake Coeur d'Alene, July 1965.
© Jim Larsen 1965, Leo Vanden Berg collection

Chuck Thompson (left), Ron Musson, and Fred Alter in 1965.
– used with permission of Sandy Ross

Dax (left), Burns, and David – the Smith hydro legacy stretches from *Miss Seattle* in 1956 to the 2004 turbine *Budweiser*, and on to the restored *Miss Bardahl*.
– Marg Smith photo, used with permission of Dixon Smith

Dixon Smith found a 1945 U.S. government report on nitrous in the UW Engineering Library and developed *Miss Bardahl*'s nitrous system, first used by her in a race at the 1965 Diamond Cup.
© Jim Larsen 1965, Leo Vanden Berg collection

Bill Stead (left) and Vanden Berg assess *Bardahl*'s damage after it was dropped by a crane, July 11, 1965.
– used with permission of David Newton, the Roger Newton collection

Team Dragon awaits its next heat at the 1965 Diamond Cup. L to R: Skip Schott, Leo Vanden Berg, Jerry Zuvich, Ron Musson.
© Eileen Crimmin photo 1965, used with permission of The Crimmin Collection

"We were all friends that year," recalled Schott. "Chuck was the truck driver, engine man, crew member, and driver of the four-seater. Bernie was getting Budweiser to sponsor, and Chuck always had a case of Budweiser beer for us at the motel."

Being the team's woodbutcher, David always made sure he packed spare materials to fix the hull – wood, glue, screws, nuts, bolts, and aluminum. Kruse remembers David cutting the aluminum patch and beveling the edge.

"I ripped open the deck, got in there and put the patch on the thing, and we went out and ran," said David.

Exide and *Bardahl* battled again in heat 2A. Musson needed 400 points, and *Bardahl* led *Exide* for more than four laps until the final turn of the lap five when Brow nudged ahead on the outside, then cut to lane one. Musson nicked a buoy and claimed Brow chopped him off. The officials disagreed, leaving *Exide* with 800 points for the day and *Bardahl* a mere 525. Brow averaged 108.564 for the heat; Musson checked in at 107.100 followed by a distant *Mariner Too* and *Savair's Mist*. *Gale's Roostertail* and *$ Bill* did not start.

"Those were the days you could cut people off," David said. "You could just hose 'em and be done with it and nobody would care. There was no overlap rule."

Smirnoff broke down while leading in lap two of heat 2B. *Notre Dame* won, and again racing was close: the Shamrock Lady clocked 103.369, *Budweiser* 101.809, and *Madison* 100.896. *Tahoe Miss*, suffering blower woes, failed to start and scored zero points for the day. The hard luck Nevada entry of 1964 seemed to be no different in '65.

Bardahl stood little chance of winning the Diamond Cup, even by earning 400 points in the final. She already had spotted the fleet a head start by missing Guntersville, and losing more ground in Idaho would make it even tougher to repeat as high-point champ. 1965 points leader *Madison* was one of six finalists that roared onto Lake Coeur d'Alene for the final heat along with *Exide, Notre Dame, Bardahl, Budweiser,* and *Mariner Too.*

Bardahl charged to an early lead and never looked back. *Exide* followed until lap two when her engine backfired, and Manchester powered *Notre Dame* all the way from fifth into second. But third place was all Brow needed to secure his second consecutive Diamond Cup victory. At the finish it was *Bardahl* at 105.820, *Notre Dame* at 103.633, *Exide* at 101.694, then *Madison, Bud,* and *Mariner*. All in all, a day of close, terrific racing.

Miss Exide was an unlikely winner of the $15,000 Diamond Cup, having scrambled – like *Bardahl* – to even participate at Coeur d'Alene. Seattle's hometown fleet finished one-two-three in the final standings: *Exide*, 1,025 points; *Notre Dame*, 1,000; and *Bardahl*, 925, plus the fastest race average of 107.008.

"We weren't ready to race, but we came anyway because we were the defending champions," said a giddy Glen Stoen. "The first time we put the boat in the water this year was when we arrived Friday. And we only had one engine ready."

The "world's fastest milkman" Brow acknowledged, "I guess we were all a little bit surprised."

The Diamond Cup stirred excitement for the upcoming North Dakota and Seattle races. Sportswriters covering it reported the Idaho race as "the greatest Diamond Cup ever … the racing was superb."

* * * *

July 1965 was a vital, momentous time in my life. My sister was engaged to marry a man I soon regarded as my best friend, an Idaho rancher named Gordon Sylte from Rathdrum, a town of 710 people 14 miles northwest of Coeur d'Alene. Judy had plenty to do leading up to their Aug. 1 wedding, and Mom thought it would be good if I visited Sylte Ranch for awhile and stayed out of everyone's hair. Or maybe it was Gordon's idea.

Around July 4 Gordon and I drove east in his beige Studebaker Lark VIII from Lake Hills to the ranch. I spent the next few weeks doing things that most 11-year-old kids from the suburbs only dream of, or saw on TV: I drove a creaky flatbed truck around hay fields. I learned to ride a black and white pinto horse named Salty (who unexpectedly jumped over obstacles at times, pitching me off). I helped with roundup, when on horseback we herded 200 Sylte steer – "cutting cattle," they call it – to the corral for branding, dehorning, and crimping. My crude job: pulling the calves' rear legs taut while Gordon's dad, Jack, seared a putrid-smelling flying "S" brand into their hide (which I recall with nostalgic fondness, for some sick reason).

There is absolutely nothing on earth as foul as the stench of burning cattle hair and flesh.

I fished for rainbow trout in the creek that flowed cool and clear through the ranch, attended a Grange picnic, stacked hay bales, went to church, ate like royalty each day (when she wasn't making pancakes for the cats, Gordon's sweet mom Evelyn often served meat and potatoes, my favorite), played with ranch dogs, rode horses to a rocky gap where we watched Golden Eagles soar, and challenged Gordon to basketball games of H-O-R-S-E and 21, played on an old hoop and wood-plank backboard that he'd fastened to a Ponderosa pine.

One day Gordon came home from an errand in Spokane and handed me a brand new BB gun, said "it's yours," and instructed me to shoot all the tin cans and gophers I wanted, but never to shoot any other animals or birds.

I spent July 11, 1965, on the front lawn of the Sylte ranch house listening to a large transistor radio, perched atop a white log fencepost, that aired day-long KVNI Radio coverage of the Diamond Cup. As sportscasters described the excitement – a crane dropping *Bardahl* on its trailer, *Bardahl* coming back to win the final heat, *Exide* winning the race – I gazed across Rathdrum Prairie at Canfield Mountain on the horizon, knowing all of this action took place not far below it, so tantalizingly close. Three years later in August 1968, I finally would see a Diamond Cup in person.

* * * *

While most of the fleet left Coeur d'Alene and headed 877 miles east for the July 18 Dakota Cup, *Exide* returned home to Seattle to prepare for the Aug. 8 Gold Cup, and *Bardahl* stayed in the Lake City a few extra days to lick its wounds.

"The patch over the hole worked loose in the final heat," Musson told reporters. "That's a dangerous situation, and we have to correct it."

Truthfully, the team needed to further lighten the hull, which remained too heavy even after being trimmed in Ballard.

"We stayed in Coeur d'Alene for a couple of days at the Desert Hotel, took the engine out, had the oil tank out, and started pulling stuff out of that boat because it was a slug," Schott recalled. "We were running water injection, nitrous, tetraethyl lead in the fuel, and we were doing everything we could to make as much horsepower as we could, but the boat needed to be lighter. So we took as much weight as we could. Anything that wasn't being used was taken out."

The team drove the long haul east via U.S. 10 and U.S. 2 to Minot, a memorable destination for Zuvich.

"Ahh, Minot, North Dakota – we stayed there, but we raced at New Town, 60 miles southwest. The first year we tried to stay in New Town, and it was a two-horse town. It had two bars, not even a stop sign. I think it just had a four-way stop. I mean, it was a little town in the middle of nowhere. You ever heard of New Town, North Dakota? It's hard to *find* North Dakota. We raced on an Indian reservation." Zuvich referred to Fort Berthold, home of the Mandan, Hidatsa, and Arikara Nations.

Perhaps the *Exide* team had a premonition. Eleven boats, including *Miss Bardahl*, gathered in New Town later that week and found Garrison Reservoir in disturbing condition. Floods and high winds had left the racecourse strewn with logs and debris, and the 1964 pit area sat under water. Dumbfounded race teams wondered, why are we even here?

Undeterred, the race committee moved 32,000 tons of soil to build a new pit area, installed temporary utilities, and patrol boats combed the racecourse for debris. But there was simply too much to overcome. On Sunday winds stiffened beyond 25 mph and rising water refloated beached driftwood, causing a series of 30-minute postponements beginning at noon. Finally, at 5 p.m., the Dakota Cup was called off.

Who canceled the race? No one confessed. Not the race committee, not the sponsor, not the race teams. It seems likely that Bill Newton, referee, gave the final word. No matter. APBA Unlimited Commissioner Lee Schoenith said, "I think this ends unlimited powerboat racing in North Dakota, unless something miraculous comes up in the future."

As of 2012, no miracle had appeared.

* * * *

From 1962 to 1965 Dad and his wife, Evelyn, lived in a new house in the north Seattle suburb of Richmond Beach, right on the King-Snohomish County line. I frequently spent Saturdays or entire weekends with Dad, and the week after the canceled Dakota Cup – likely Saturday, July 24, a day or two after I'd returned from Sylte Ranch – we drove to Ballard in his maroon 1965 Impala Super Sport to see if we could get a peek at the *Bardahl*.

Yes! The boat was visible through the open roll-up door to the shop, and Vanden Berg and crew swarmed over it in frantic preparation. We got out of the car and Dad asked if we could take a quick look, and Leo graciously allowed us inside. I could hardly contain my excitement, standing next to and *actually touching Miss Bardahl*.

Something else caught my eye. To the left, sitting just above the floor, was the shiny new cabover *Bardahl*, minus an engine. Dad had brought his trusty 35mm Leica camera and snapped an underexposed Kodachrome slide of the cabover in natural light. (A year later I dropped that slide in the mud at school and, trying to clean it with a tissue, I scraped off much of the emulsion and ruined what little image existed.) Then we walked outside and Dad photographed the Green Dragon head-on. The image shows Leo and David eyeing us and Zuvich's red Honda 250 motorcycle parked to the side.

The thrills continued as we walked to the fenced-in side yard, where I inspected three visiting hydros awaiting the setup of Stan Sayres Pits: *Miss Madison*, *Miss Budweiser*, and *Miss San Diego*. Dad photographed me standing next to each, and the shot of me standing next to *Budweiser* currently is posted on missbardahl.com.

We also drove to the *Exide* shop about seven blocks away, south of Leary Way near the ship canal. I could see the Happy Hydro inside, but the crew was not happy to have visitors, so we left.

"The *Exide* was kept about a block east of the Ballard Bridge," said Bob Woolms. "Exide Batteries had a warehouse there, and the other half of it was our shop. We were just a few blocks south of the *Bardahl* shop."

Dad enjoyed listening to AM radio, usually tuned to contemporary music stations that played crooners like Jack Jones and Andy Williams. He did *not* indulge his kids' taste for Top 40 music, which he called "jump and jive." In fact I clearly recall riding with Dad, Judy, and Dave when I was just 4 or 5, and we wanted Dad to tune in KJR. Dad furrowed his brow and said in a grave tone that his car radio was wired so that if anyone ever pushed the KJR button (950 AM), that person would get an electrical shock. Dad's teasing humor went over my head, and I believed his warning.

Had he allowed me that July 1965 day to tune his car radio to KJR, I would have heard chart-toppers like the Beach Boys' "California Girls," the Rolling Stones playing their first huge American hit "Satisfaction," a new Beatles song called "Help!" and the fast-rising hit "Gloria" by Them, a British band featuring vocalist Van Morrison.

The next day, President Johnson said in an interview about the Vietnam conflict, "We cannot just get out," noting that success demands "power. Power on land, power in the air, power wherever it's necessary." On a lighter note, Seattle media ballyhooed the now-famous killer whale Namu's arrival on Monday, while Vancouver, B.C.'s, aquarium curator warned, "This is a live animal, not a parade float."

The following week our Lake Hills home buzzed with activity while Seattle sizzled in a mid-90s heat wave. My sister Judy and Gordon were to marry Aug.1, and we hosted a houseful of family from out of town. I was too young to be an usher in the wedding but was tasked with hosting the guest-book table, and I wore a tux just like the adult groomsmen. Heady stuff for a lanky 11-year-old. Mom was amused that in the group photos, I was a mere inch shorter than one of the guys in Gordon's wedding party.

Chapter 23

Three Gold Cups

The hydro camps rested, patched hulls, and repaired equipment for the 58th APBA Gold Cup, to be held Aug. 8 on Lake Washington.

Exide's crew built more engines and returned the hull to its usual appearance by painting white lightning bolts across her deck. The *Tahoe* team pieced its turbocharger back together. Jim Herrington's team arrived with his second hull, the blue and white U-9 *Miss Lapeer*, no longer the lilac "Queen of the Inland Empire." Other hulls missing the previous two events also arrived: the new *Blue Chip, Savair's Probe, Such Crust IV, Tri-City Sun, Miss U.S.5,* and Ken Murphy's former *Slo-mo V / Miss Seattle*, now named *Beryessa Belle*. However, *$ Bill* returned to California. With the Dakota Cup called off, rookie driver Rex Bixby had not compiled sufficient experience to qualify as a Gold Cup driver.

Roy Duby and *U.S.5* pulled into town on July 30 as Seattle thermometers hit a record 93 degrees. Duby told reporters his boat, which tested extensively during the winter at Cypress Gardens, Fla., and Guntersville, now was using nitrous oxide.

1965 Gold Cup qualifying opened with a roar. On Tuesday, Aug. 3, Buddy Byers powered *Miss Madison* around Lake Washington's three-mile course to a three-lap average of 115.139 – the boat's fastest speed ever. Warner Gardner put *Mariner Too* into the race at a respectable 111.340. Six other boats qualified, including *Notre Dame* (now the national leader by 6 points over *Madison*; *Bardahl* held sixth place), *Savair's Mist, Miss Budweiser,* and *Such Crust IV*. Bill Muncey qualified the *IV* as a favor to owner Jack Schafer and later turned the wheel over to Red Loomis on race day.

"I think Muncey and Musson had good respect for each other, because when Muncey drove the *Such Crust* here at Seattle – he did that as a favor for Jack Schaefer, an old family friend – Muncey came and changed his clothes in the back of our van," Schott said. "He and Ron would go in there and smoke because the fire department couldn't see them. Muncey hung around us a lot because we knew him and he wasn't driving then. But he always had his helmet bag."

Chuck Thompson provided most of Tuesday's thrills. Setting *Tahoe Miss* up for a qualifying run, he swept wide around the north turn, his eyes fixed on the cockpit gauges. *Tahoe* straightened out, Thompson stomped on the throttle – and charged directly toward the log boom that hugged the shoreline. Quickly he saw his mistake and backed off, swung behind the log boom and patrol boats, circled the north turn, and continued his qualifying run. He averaged 111.035.

Pre-race excitement peaked on Wednesday when Bill Brow blasted *Miss Exide* around the course at a world-record speed of 120.356 for three laps, including one scorcher at 120.536. The old mark, set on

Lake Washington in 1958 by Bill Stead driving the *Maverick*, was 119.956, with a fast lap of 120.267.

Brow told reporters that damp weather, flat water, and quick cornering earned him the record.

"I hit about 165 mph going into the first turn," he explained. "After that, I never hit more than 160 in the chutes."

Exide's record reportedly was set using a Rolls-Merlin that had been discarded by *Tri-City Sun* owner Bob Gilliam. *Exide*'s crew – George McKernan, Bernie Van Cleave, Nelson Kinney, Scotty Freeman, Tommy Frankhouser, George Elijah, Phil Bishop, and Bob Woolms – welded the cracked block and told Brow to go for broke, since there was nothing to lose.

Bill Stead ambled up to congratulate Brow, then pretended to strangle him for "running off with my record." Brow and his crewmembers laughed. They were happy and confident – so confident that later, before Sunday's final heat, they gave their wallets to a friend for safekeeping so their money wouldn't get wet in the victory dunking.

Musson was asked if he would try to beat Brow's speed. "I want to get the boat running right. That's all I'm concerned about right now," he said, having taken only test runs for two days.

The rest of qualifying, though less spectacular, was dramatic. *Miss Bardahl* joined the field Thursday after suffering mechanical malfunctions for two days. That morning, Musson took aim at *Exide*'s record but broke his only qualifying engine. Late Thursday afternoon he made a conservative run with his race-day engine but lost a magneto. *Bardahl* limped home with a three-lap average of 110.279 – slow, perhaps, but fast enough to qualify.

"It's too late in the game to go for 120 now," said crew chief Vanden Berg. "You don't win races in qualifying."

* * * *

Unknown to shorebirds, the *Bardahl* crew felt immense psychological pressure that week, and failing to match *Exide*'s record run added to the strain. It took trial and error to sort through the new nitrous system and flat-top pistons, and wanting to keep the pistons secret the team didn't publicly cite them as factors.

"We were in deep trouble then," said David. "There was a lot of pressure on us, because we were the team everybody thought they needed to beat, because we had the winning record. We were the young guys and everybody's out to beat us, and they kept telling us they're gonna beat us, because we were real cocky about the whole thing," he said, laughing.

"Ron came in just disgusted saying, 'I can't go any faster,' and Ole says you gotta go faster," David said. "*Exide* did about 120, I believe. We didn't go 120. We were so far off everybody gave up on us, and that's when Leo and Ole and everybody else was in our face saying, 'You guys gotta do better because we gotta win this race, you guys have a bad attitude, you've got to figure it out.' And the press is saying, why isn't the *Bardahl* winning? Most of the time when we raced we had very little pressure, or we put pressure on ourselves. But that race was in Seattle, it was the Gold Cup, and it was a big deal. We had already proven we could do it, and everybody was kind of laughing at us because now we couldn't.

"And then on top of that, *Exide* ran really fast," David continued. "They had a light boat, big motor, and we're thinking, 'We're gonna get it handed to us.' I mean, we were just barely beating the *Madison*. We were really struggling, and nobody was happy."

Friday morning the *Bardahl* crew arrived at Stan Sayres Pits in a sour mood. Ole and Inga soon arrived, and Schott, David, and perhaps Dax failed to greet her.

"We almost got fired because we didn't say 'Good morning' to Inga," Schott said. "Well, we hadn't *seen* Inga yet to say good morning to her, and we didn't know we were supposed to. We got into a lot of trouble, because apparently Ole mentioned it to Ron."

Seattle Times photographer Vic Condiotty had arranged to take a photo of Seattle's hometown boats – *Bardahl, Exide, Notre Dame* – and their crews for the front page of the Sunday newspaper. He choreographed the shot at the end of a dock at Lakewood Moorage, a marina ¾ of a mile south of the pits.

"We all got put on the boat and they towed us down the beach," Schott said, "and as we're being towed, our asses got reamed by Ron. Because we hadn't said good morning to Mrs. Bardahl. But from then on, we said good morning to Mrs. Bardahl. We would go find her and say good morning."

Zuvich perceived Schott, in particular, as being in Inga's crosshairs. "You know, when you're dealing with old-country people, people like my parents and Mr. Bardahl, politeness doesn't hurt. That's how I felt about it, anyway. And Mrs. Bardahl couldn't figure out why he would not say 'hi' or 'good morning.'"

"That was tough," David said. "They chewed us out. We got talked to because we had bad attitudes. They had towed us down to the little yacht club south of Stan Sayres pits, but Ron didn't want to be towed back, so he started the boat up and we all rode on the *Bardahl*. He got it up on a plane, and we all just hung on and motored back up to the pits."

* * * *

Eighteen boats now crowded Stan Sayres Memorial Pits, requiring the east side of the pits to host hydroplanes for the first time. Another first: There would be no restrictions on the number of race-day engine changes in the 1965 Gold Cup.

Thirteen hydros had managed 104 mph or better for three laps, and five others waited for their chance to make the final 12. Some boats were sure to be "bumped" on Friday.

Budweiser fell first, then *Savair's Mist*: Norm Evans pushed *Miss Lapeer* around the course at 109.238, *Mariner Too* driver Warner Gardner qualified *Miss San Diego* at 108.506, and there sat *Bud* and *Mist* on the outside looking in – with speeds of only 105 and 107 mph.

Other boats upped their speeds, including *Gale's Roostertail* at 111.187, *Bardahl* at 113.524, and *Miss U.S.5*, which bounced and leaped around the course at 114.407 mph.

Chuck Thompson played mind games with the other drivers before making a run on Saturday. He told KING-TV sportscaster Rod Belcher that *Tahoe* was faster than any boat in the pits and, what's more, he would prove it by qualifying the Gray Ghost at 130 mph. In the end, however, referee Bill Newton ordered him off the course for "wasting time" and robbing unqualified boats of their chance to run.

A Friday announcement reminded *Bardahl* fans, in case they'd forgotten, that 1965 was indeed the Green Dragon's farewell tour: Bernie Little would buy the boat after the Oct. 3 San Diego regatta and race it in 1966 as *Miss Budweiser*.

"I guess you've heard the saying that if you can't beat them, buy them. Well, that's what I did," Little later told the *Tampa Tribune*. "It's got power. It rides beautifully and has speed coming out of the turns."

The final Gold Cup qualifiers weren't decided until 3:59 p.m. Saturday, when the outdoor thermometer hit 87 degrees as Gardner raised *Miss San Diego*'s speed to 109.091. That put 61-year-old Walt Kade and *Savair's Mist*, which had requalified at 108.724, on the beach for Sunday's race. Joining the *Mist* were *Miss Budweiser, Savair's Probe, Tri-City Sun, Berryessa Belle*, and the new *Blue Chip*.

The fastest Gold Cup field in history was set: *Miss Exide* (Bill Brow), 120.356; *Miss Madison* (Buddy Byers), 115.139; *Miss U.S.5* (Roy Duby), 114.407; *Miss Bardahl* (Ron Musson), 113.524; *Notre Dame* (Rex Manchester), 112.971; *Mariner Too* (Warner Gardner), 111.340; *Gale's Roostertail* (Jerry Schoenith), 111.187; *Tahoe Miss* (Chuck Thompson), 111.035; *Miss Lapeer* (Norm Evans), 109.238; *Miss Smirnoff* (Bill Cantrell), 109.164; *Miss San Diego* (Gardner again), 109.091; and *Such Crust IV* (qualified by Bill Muncey), 108.871.

Collectively, the qualifiers averaged a record 112.194 mph, surpassing the 1964 Gold Cuppers' average of 111.500 mph. (At the 1966 Gold Cup in Detroit, a decimated field of 12 boats would muster only 106.910 mph collectively; the 1966 Seafair race, where qualifying wasn't mandatory, featured a top test run of just 113.356. One final comparison: *Such Crust IV*, slowest of the 1965 Gold Cup entries at 108.871 mph, would have been the third-fastest qualifier at Detroit the following year.)

A throng of 125,000 gathered downtown on Saturday night along Fourth Avenue for the annual Seafair Torchlight Parade, led by Honorary Grand Marshal James Drury, star of the popular NBC-TV Western "The Virginian." Forecasters called for clouds the next morning with a sunny afternoon.

One of the largest crowds in Seattle's 15 years of hydro racing lined Lake Washington under sunny skies Sunday, Aug. 8, 1965, when the gun fired at noon for heat 1A of the $50,150 Gold Cup. *Mariner Too* hit the line first in lane three and led *Exide* by 100 yards exiting the south turn. *Tahoe, Madison, U.S.5*, and *Gale's Roostertail* trailed.

Brow, on the inside, careened past Gardner in the first turn of lap two. Thompson followed suit at the exit pin and charged after Brow, cutting *Exide*'s lead to four seconds at the end of the lap. *Tahoe* got no closer, though, as Brow throttled his mount to a blistering pace that earned him victory. *Exide* finished with a record 15-mile Gold Cup heat average of 112.172, breaking *Bardahl*'s 1963 mark of 109.489. *Tahoe* finished second at 109.800 followed by *Madison, U.S.5,* and *Gale's Roostertail. Mariner Too* conked out in the north turn of lap three and did not finish.

When *Mariner* conked, *Miss San Diego* owner Bob Fendler chafed even more than *Mariner* owner Jim Herrington: Gardner was slated to drive both boats but, because of his long tow back to the pits, arrived too late to pilot *San Diego* in heat 1B. Fendler withdrew his boat, putting Walt Kade and *Savair's Mist* back in the Gold Cup as the 12th entry.

The next heat saw *Smirnoff* roar to an early lead followed by *Bardahl, Lapeer, Notre Dame*, and *Savair's Mist. Such Crust*, Red Loomis now driving, lagged far behind. *Bardahl* powered ahead at the exit pin of turn one and quickly opened a big gap over *Lapeer* and *Notre Dame*, while *Smirnoff* faded to fourth.

Manchester overtook Evans on the backstretch of lap two. Then Cantrell made his move, passing Evans on lap four. At the finish it was *Bardahl*, 108.651; *Notre Dame*, 105.099, *Smirnoff*, 100.259; then *Lapeer, Savair's Mist*, and *Such Crust IV*.

Heat 2A provided bizarre excitement as two boats collided while dicing for the start. Halfway through the north turn, Norm Evans in *Miss Lapeer* veered in front of Roy Duby and *Miss U.S.5*, causing the latter to climb over *Lapeer*'s stern and whack Evans' shoulder. *U.S.5* suffered a punctured left sponson, while six feet of *Lapeer*'s rear deck was ripped away.

For a moment the two vessels rode piggyback. Duby promptly killed his engine, but *Lapeer* kept running and the boats pulled apart. Evans, his shoulder badly bruised, steered an erratic course toward the official barge and signaled that his leaking boat needed a crane – quickly. After judging the *U.S.5* still seaworthy, Duby restarted and joined the race.

Meanwhile, *Notre Dame* slid past *Exide* and into the lead at the south turn, followed by *Such Crust, U.S.5*, and *Lapeer*, which pulled into the pits after making one circuit. Brow, his motor misfiring, struggled to fend off Loomis and Duby and eventually fell to fourth on lap two. Manchester had a close call in the north turn on lap one when *Notre Dame* hooked badly, but he later ran away from the field and came within 1,000 feet of lapping *Exide* at the finish. The final order was *Notre Dame* at 100.037, then *Such Crust, U.S.5*, and *Exide*. *Gale's Roostertail* did not start.

* * * *

Mark Evans was 8 when his dad Norm drove *Miss Lapeer* that day, and when Norm steered the damaged craft to the pits it left quite an impression.

"At that age I remember getting Ron, Rex, Bill, and the others mixed up. I didn't know who was who," Mark said. "The only thing I remember about that Seattle race is when Dad drove by the barge, somebody screamed, 'Oh shit, he's gonna beach it!'

"I was sitting up on the side of the crane, and in a panic, Mom grabbed my pant leg and pulled me off. I was quite a ways off the ground and hit hard. Mom thought she broke my leg and was very upset. Imagine Mom thinking, 'Norm is hurt,' and then thinking she just broke her kid's leg! Poor Mom. She went through a lot, but laughs about it now."

Doug Brow, age 9 at the time, also recalls the 1965 Gold Cup. Despite Musson being his dad's racing foe, Doug knew Ron as a friendly, approachable man.

"Back then it was more like family," Doug said. "Mark and Mitch Evans and me and any of the kids could run and jump up on the competitors' boats. I remember doing that with the *Bardahl*, and Ron would come up and slap me on the back and say, 'Hey Doug, how you doing?'

"Our family had a big party every year at our house in Burien, and all the hydro drivers would come. Bill Cantrell, in particular, was Dad's good friend."

Doug recalled that though Musson was friendly, once the racing started he became serious and focused.

* * * *

As was her custom throughout 1965, *Miss Bardahl* was the last boat lowered into the water for her next heat. That was at Vanden Berg's request. "The boat had turned into a pretty good leaker," he said. "We'd wait to be the last one in the water."

"We'd put the boat in the lake and water leaked up through the center of the keel," Zuvich recalled, laughing.

"Yeah, that thing was getting to be a pretty good sieve," said Dax. "Gettin' old. Any water that leaks in a boat, you're obviously going to carry around, so we'd like to be the last in the water. It wasn't where, if you put it in an extra five minutes, it would sink. But if you let it sit in the water 15 minutes, it would add weight."

Everyone made a near-perfect start in heat 2B as *Tahoe*, on the inside, led *Bardahl* and *Mariner Too* around the south turn. Byers in *Madison* charged after Gardner, passed him in the north turn, then set his sights on *Bardahl*. Meanwhile, Thompson pounded out a 111-mph lap to stretch his lead to three roostertails over Musson. The Gray Ghost was on a tear, sizzling down the chutes, its big turbocharger whistling and banging as Thompson backed off to set up for the turns.

Suddenly, *Tahoe* slowed to a crawl entering the backstretch on lap four. *Bardahl* quickly roared by on the outside and built a sizeable lead before *Tahoe* surged to life and took off in pursuit. But Musson throttled his boat to a 110-mph lap and maintained his lead to the finish. *Bardahl* averaged 107.355 to *Tahoe*'s 105.882. *Madison* finished a close third at 104.813, and *Mariner Too* nipped *Smirnoff* by less than a boat length to take fourth. *Savair's Mist* blew an oil cooler on lap three and did not finish.

Only five boats started heat 3A as the *Mist* crew couldn't finish repairs in time. Cantrell in *Smirnoff* led the field through the south turn and up the backstretch with *Notre Dame* charging hard in second. At the end of lap one Cantrell held a five-second lead over Manchester, *U.S.5* edged past *Madison* to briefly take third, and *Such Crust* lumbered along at the rear.

Notre Dame swung wide through the north turn on lap two, poured on the power, and nosed past *Smirnoff* to take the lead entering lap three. Then *Madison* and *U.S.5* closed on Cantrell until *Madison* sliced inside and gained second exiting the north turn. *U.S.5* and *Such Crust* did the same thing one lap later when *Smirnoff* bounced badly entering the turn and bogged down. At the finish, *Notre Dame* posted 107.057 to win, followed by a fast-closing *Miss Madison* at 106.592, *U.S. 5* at 103.966, *Such Crust* at 99.852, and *Smirnoff* at 97.826.

Three of the hot dogs squared off in 3B: *Exide*, *Bardahl*, and *Tahoe Miss*. *Mariner*, *Gale's Roostertail*, and *Budweiser* – a late replacement for the crippled *Lapeer* – filled out the field. Race fans rubbed their hands in anticipation of a full-blown battle.

All six boats thundered toward the line in a tight pack. *Mariner* streaked across first on the outside – but too soon. Indeed, everyone jumped the gun except *Exide*. Brow backed off the pedal at the last moment to make a perfect start and assume a one-lap lead over his rivals, although none of them knew it yet.

Six abreast, they dove into the turn. *Exide* and *Bardahl* tore through it and sprinted up the back chute with *Tahoe* close behind. Brow, on the inside, kept *Bardahl* on his hip and led by two boat lengths at the end of lap one.

Musson noticed the clock on the official barge was partially blacked out, signaling someone had jumped the gun. Not knowing who was penalized and who wasn't, he squeezed the nitrous button and kept his foot to the floorboard.

Together, Brow and Musson ran away from the field. Again they rounded the south turn and pounded up the backstretch, Rolls-Merlins blaring, their roostertails arcing high and white against the blue sky; again they charged toward the line with *Exide* still holding a slim lead.

Suddenly, *Bardahl*'s engine popped and went raspy. Musson eased off the throttle and watched Brow pull away, hoping *Exide*'s engine might blow from the strain. It didn't. As *Bardahl* exited the north turn on lap five, Brow took the checkered flag. Musson and the others took a green flag and ran a penalty lap. *Exide* turned 109.223 to win the heat; *Bardahl* averaged 89.050 because of the extra lap. *Tahoe* finished third, followed by *Gale's Roostertail*, Chuck Hickling in *Budweiser*, and *Mariner Too*.

When Musson returned to the dock, his crew again discovered an increasingly familiar sight: Some of *Bardahl*'s spark-plug cores were missing. Musson took the blame, telling reporters he hadn't yet mastered the art of using laughing gas.

"I found out today you just can't push the nitrous button and run," he said. "It blows spark plugs right out of the boat."

But Ron knew the true cause of the spark plug failure had nothing to do with nitrous. Rather, it was the flat-top high-compression pistons. Intended to provide a competitive edge, the pistons were sometimes a hindrance instead. Not until later in the season would they be fully diagnosed and counteracted by the custom-tailored Champion plugs that *Bardahl*'s mighty Merlins couldn't destroy.

Vanden Berg and crew changed *Bardahl*'s engine for the final heat, putting in the one they had qualified with on Thursday. With 1,100 points, Musson was in good shape to defend his title. Eager to dethrone him were *Notre Dame*, also with 1,100 points; *Exide*, 969; *Tahoe Miss*, 825; *Madison*, 750; and *U.S.5*, 619.

Because they were tied on points, Musson knew he had to beat Manchester to win, and vice-versa. Brow could steal the Cup if Musson and Manchester finished third or worse. Thompson and Byers had to hope the others would break. Only Roy Duby and *U.S.5* were mathematically out of the running.

The sun-soaked crowd cheered as the three Seattle boats led the pack across the line and piled into the first turn. *Miss Exide* cranked around the exit pin on the inside and scorched into the backstretch to open a lead over *Notre Dame*, lane two, and *Bardahl* in lane three. Suddenly, near the middle of the chute, *Exide*'s Rolls-Merlin backfired loudly and burst into flames, the victim of a ruptured fabric fuel line. Brow steered his red charger to the infield and coasted to a stop. He hopped up, took one look at the fire and waved for help.

Meanwhile, *Notre Dame* roared by and into the lead with *Bardahl* and *Madison* trailing. *Exide* continued to burn. Brow tried to fight the blaze with a small extinguisher, but when that didn't work he waved his right arm in a frantic "come on!" gesture. Patrol boats nearby couldn't move, however, as long as the race continued.

Manchester, out front and in control of the course, opened a commanding lead over Musson and *Bardahl*. The Shamrock Lady seemed on her way to a Gold Cup win. At last, Manchester thought, he would savor victory. Five years earlier he had *Miss Spokane* just 17 seconds from winning the Seafair Trophy Race when Don Wilson jumped from a burning *Miss U.S.1* to halt the race. Bill Muncey piloted the *Thriftway* to victory in the rerun, and Rex had to settle for second. But not this time....

Splash! Brow jumped into the lake, automatically stopping the heat. *Notre Dame* rocketed across the line to complete lap two just as red flares pierced the sky. The boats slowed, circled, and returned to the pits. Much of *Exide*'s deck was ablaze when the fireboat *Alki* and Coast Guard patrol boats finally arrived. Though it later went unmentioned in most accounts of the race, much of the fault was Brow's: Rules stated that a driver requesting immediate help must "wave a visible object" such as a helmet or life jacket;

a driver waving his hands meant that "everything is under control." Unfortunately, Brow waved only his bare hands as he gestured for help.

"He was waving his hands not at the official barge, he was waving his hands at those guys up above him in the helicopter," said *Exide* crewman Bob Woolms. "He was trying to get their attention to drop him a fire extinguisher."

Fifteen minutes after it started (and after what critics called ill-advised attempts to douse the gas-fueled flames with water rather than foam retardant), the blaze aboard *Miss Exide* flickered out. A patrol boat towed the badly charred hull to the pits where *Exide* owners Milo and Glen Stoen exchanged heated words with race officials over the handling of the fire. Meanwhile, the other camps prepared their boats for the rerun of the final heat.

* * * *

Before *Exide* blew, Brow was running away in the final heat with Manchester solidly in second; Musson was off the pace in third. *Bardahl* fans assumed their boat had a mechanical problem and prepared themselves for disappointment.

"No, he just screwed up. It was driver error," said David Smith. "Ron had his own watch that he set himself. I always set the clock in the boat, that was my job. Ron would set the one he wore on his wrist, and it wasn't one of the big ones, it was a smaller watch. And that first Gold Cup final, he just missed it. You think *we* had pressure, *he* had pressure! He had to win the race, and on top of that he was working full-time for Bardahl, and Bardahl wanted the Gold Cup, and the race was here in Seattle. Ron was carrying the Space Needle on his shoulders that day.

"We were getting pushed on," David continued. "The competition had caught us and was passing us. We had an old and tired boat that we hadn't spent any time with – it had been put away while we had spent all our energy getting the cabover ready. So it was a very tough time and we were behind the eight ball in a big way. Thank goodness we had the pop-up pistons and nitrous, because without that advantage we would have had it handed to us on a plate."

Race photos during the 1965 season don't always show *Bardahl*'s red tell-tale nitrous tanks. When asked why in 2012, Dixon said he didn't know, because the team never switched the type of tanks or their location. He acknowledged the tanks don't appear in all photos and said it's likely that "if we ran out of nitrous at a race, we wouldn't have run heats with empty tanks." 1965 Gold Cup photos of *Bardahl* appear to show no red tanks, so the Dragon may have run some heats – including the final – without it.

* * * *

Six hydros entered the course for the final in 80-degree sunshine, with *Such Crust IV* taking *Exide*'s place. In a mild surprise, Musson shied away from his customary spot – lane two – while dicing for the start, and instead moved *Bardahl* to lane one. The field approached the line a bit early, held back, and then Musson shot the *Bardahl* across it and into the lead. *Notre Dame*, *Madison*, and *Tahoe* charged after him, while *U.S. 5* and a sick *Such Crust* trailed.

The Green Dragon ripped through the south turn, then screamed up the backstretch all alone as Musson poured on the power. *Notre Dame* ran at breakneck speed trying to close the gap, but couldn't. *Tahoe* held down third, while *Madison* expired near the end of the backstretch.

At the end of lap two Musson held a three-second lead, thanks largely to *Bardahl*'s superior acceleration out of the turns. Manchester managed to gain ground the following lap but said he "fell in a hole" in the north turn. Musson, feeling the pressure, throttled *Bardahl* to 112+ mph to further secure his position. *Notre Dame* refused to quit, though, and thundered close behind.

Musson ran hard the final two laps to outdistance the field and even lapped *Such Crust* near the end of lap five. *Bardahl*'s green and yellow paint glistened in the hot sun, her Merlin barked steadily, and she cast a long, low roostertail indicating steady balance and a smooth ride. Musson had exceeded 112 mph on laps two, three, and four.

Finally, after 69 fast, grueling miles (including the penalty lap in 3B and two laps in the aborted first final), Musson and *Miss Bardahl* streaked past the official barge to take the checkered flag and earn their third consecutive Gold Cup. *Bardahl* averaged 110.655 mph to win the heat, followed by *Notre Dame* at 107.612, *Tahoe Miss* at 94.869, *Miss U.S.5* at 92.879, and *Such Crust IV* at 77.967. *Madison* did not finish.

An elated Musson flashed a wide smile as he coasted into the pits. Despite racing a boat that was supposed to be in mothballs – a boat he described as "running sick" that blew two or three spark plugs in every heat and still showed the scars of its Diamond Cup accident – Musson made modern-day hydro history in winning the 1965 Gold Cup. And this time he did it in front of the hometown Jet City fans.

The Big Event was over. A snarling Green Dragon, tamed by a diminutive jockey wearing yellow and black coveralls and a crafty smile, still reigned supreme in the premier class of powerboat racing. The Gold Cup would stay in Ballard.

Leo Vanden Berg grinned as Musson climbed out of the lake following the traditional victory dunking. A much-used, battle-worn engine again had powered the Green Dragon to first place, and the crew couldn't wait to tell its driver.

"We've got an engine I don't like to use and the crew keeps sneaking it in on me – number 22," said a dripping wet Musson after hearing the news. "They did it again today."

"That's the engine Ron hates," Vanden Berg added with a smile. "He always gripes about it, but he always runs well with it."

"I've been trying to get rid of that engine for three years," Musson complained.

"All that engine does is win," countered Vanden Berg.

In 1983, Vanden Berg recalled Musson's notions about certain motors. "He always said number 22 had no power, and we'd put it in and he'd win races with it. 'We changed engines for you, Ron.' We'd taken it out and put the same engine right back in. 'Oh, it's great!' he'd say.

"We had to work on his mind," Vanden Berg said, laughing. "Oh, we did that many times. I think Ron hated number 13, too."

* * * *

The smiles that permeated the *Bardahl* camp reflected complex feelings, not mere elation.

"At the end of the race, everybody was so tired and worn out," said David. "It was a big deal and they gave us the gold '65 Mustang, the governor was there, and if you look at us we're happy because we won, but we're totally exhausted. Everybody was just spent.

"We were flogging. We changed props, we changed motors, we popped out spark plugs, we changed everything. We had a tough race, and that was one of those races that we won because we really worked our butts off," he said.

When asked if the team was perhaps more relieved to win than happy, David said, "I think so. There was way, way too much pressure. Maybe that pressure made us work really, really hard? I don't know. I do know that there were very few times in all my career that there was a lot of pressure. *That* day was the biggest pressure pot I ever worked in. When I worked on the *Pay 'n Pak*, *Notre Dame*, the checkerboard *Bardahl*, when I've done other jobs, we never had that."

* * * *

The final 1965 Gold Cup standings showed *Bardahl* posting 1,500 points to win, followed by *Notre Dame*, 1,400; *Tahoe Miss*, 1,050; *Miss Exide*, 969; *Miss U.S.5*, 788; and *Miss Madison*, 750. *Notre Dame* had the fastest 60-mile race average – 104.864 – while *Bardahl*, because of her penalty lap, averaged only 103.132. Had Musson not jumped the gun in 3B, *Bardahl*'s average projects to about 107 mph for the race.

By winning that day, Musson, Vanden Berg, and the *Miss Bardahl* team achieved something unheard of since the Depression-era days of George Reis and *El Lagarto*: three consecutive Gold Cup victories. Despite racing with a patched-up boat and temperamental equipment, and despite facing the fastest fleet in Gold Cup history, Musson had successfully defended his title against the best in the sport – Brow, Thompson, Cantrell, Byers, Manchester, Gardner.

Musson told a *Time* magazine reporter, "If I can win five Gold Cups to tie Gar Wood and then win one more for myself, it's doubtful that anyone at any time can beat that record." He's halfway there, *Time* noted.

News media, competing teams, and fans on the beach were quite aware of the significance of a boat winning three consecutive Gold Cups. But when asked years later what he remembered about it, crew chief Vanden Berg said, "Oh, it's nice to have, but I can't even remember where the race was."

Reminded that it took place in Seattle, he said, "I remember the first Gold Cup. I thought that was pretty good. But a lot of races we won, it was just another race: 'Let's get ready for the next one.'"

Twenty-two years after the 1965 Gold Cup, Dixon was asked what he recalled and if three in a row was a big deal. He paused and thought.

"Yeah, but it doesn't really stick out in my mind," he said. "After you win a bunch, you maybe get a little bit calloused. You've been working at it, you're essentially a professional racer, and your job is to win races. It's very important to win. But if you win today, what you almost immediately start worrying about is, 'How am I going to win the next one?'"

Schott's perspective differed, coming from a winless *Miss Spokane* team that felt like the 1960 Seattle race had been taken from them, a team that also appeared to be winning the 1961 Gold Cup before Manchester flipped. Close, but no reward.

"The '65 Gold Cup was the first race I ever won," Schott said. "That was very satisfying. I was doing the carburetor changes, and we went through three engines but only used one carburetor, the only good one we had left. And I think we only had one good blower for three engines. But all I remember is changing the carburetor all day, and working *really* hard, and being totally exhausted but very satisfied that we'd won the race. Dan Evans was governor then, and he came over to the boat and he shook all our hands. The governor of the state of Washington was very proud that we'd won, and the Detroit boats hadn't won."

Following the Gold Cup awards ceremony, where Chuck Thompson collapsed from a cracked rib suffered earlier when *Tahoe Miss* bounced badly in heat 1A, *Miss Exide*'s owners talked of retiring from the sport after losing their third hull in four years: *Miss Seattle Too* nosedived and blew apart during Seattle's 1962 Gold Cup; the first *Exide*, a new boat, disintegrated at the 1963 Diamond Cup; and now this.

"You can only come back so many times," said a despondent Milo Stoen.

The warm August sun dropped behind Mount Baker Ridge. Die-hard race fans, weary from a week of excitement, plodded toward the Genesee parking lot toting lawn chairs, ice chests, and transistor radios. For Seattleites, hydro week was over.

For *Miss Bardahl*, winner of the $10,500 first-place money plus the gold 1965 Mustang, it was on to Ogden, Utah, and a new race the following weekend on Willard Bay. Manchester and *Notre Dame* led Musson and *Bardahl* in the national points race, 2,969 to 2,425.

"We started rebuilding engines and blowers early the next morning," Schott said.

* * * *

Rocky Fridell is another baby boomer who rooted for Ron Musson and *Miss Bardahl*. He grew up at Bitter Lake in north Seattle, and in 2008 he recalled when, as a sixth-grader, he met Musson.

I must have been 11 or 12 years old when I met Ronnie. I made little balsa wood pins and sold them, and I was real excited when I heard they were going to race a cabover boat. I didn't have a paint scheme at that point, it was 1965, and so I called down to the Bardahl *shop. They said we could come in, and I got my mom to take me down there.*

So I met Ronnie Musson and showed him the little 1962-65 Bardahl *I'd built for him. He took me into the shop, and that's where I got to see the cabover sitting over on the left-hand side of the shop. He spent some time with me there. Got some pictures with him and me there in front of the boat.*

He was very, very nice and spent lots of time with us. I promised him I'd make him a little cabover Bardahl *pin. I had already made it, I just didn't have it painted yet, because all I needed to know was what tail was put on it and the paint job. And I made another appointment with him and went down a second time and gave him the pin, and he gave me a tour through the shop again. Spent lots of time, and I was very impressed.*

We actually sat in his office. He put his pins, one on each corner of the desk. He was always dressed in a suit, very dressed up. He showed me the Bardahl *model out in the lobby. This was before the racing season, the cabover wasn't even done. I don't even think the motor was in it at that point. And the whole tail wasn't on there – I remember the two pieces of the tail sitting there, and it was a three-piece tail.*

One of my fondest memories was qualifying for the Gold Cup. I'm sitting with my Mom and Dad down in the pits, watching Exide *qualify. And I remember Ronnie and his wife came over and saw us, and they sat down; he introduced himself to my Dad. They could have gone anywhere and they sat by us. And I remember Ronnie*

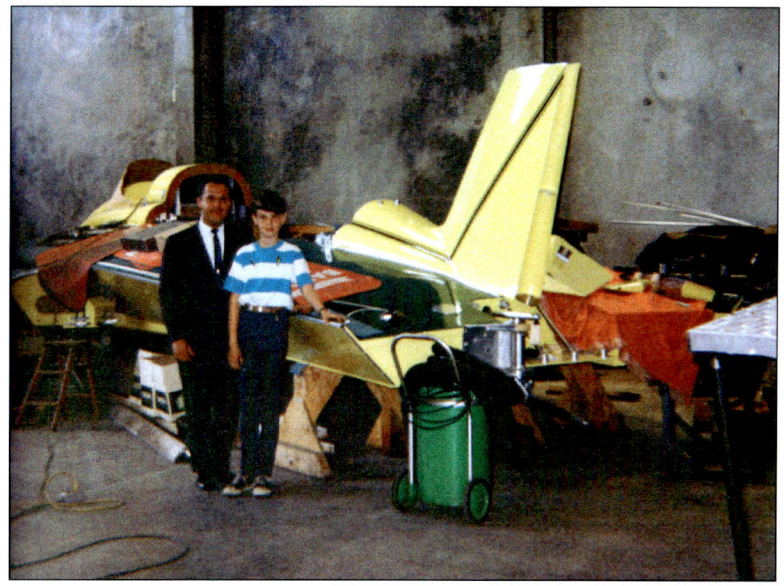

12-year-old Rocky Fridell was treated kindly by Ron Musson, shown here alongside the unraced cabover *Bardahl* in Ballard, 1965.
– used with permission of Rocky Fridell

Bill Brow's "Happy Hydro" qualified at a record 120.356 mph for three laps at the Gold Cup, with one scorcher at 120.536.
– photographer unknown, from Nostalgic Thunderboats Unlimited

Exide held a solid lead in the final heat when it blew, caught fire, and burned for several minutes. *Bardahl* won the restart, and its third Gold Cup.
– photographer unknown, from Nostalgic Thunderboats Unlimited

Tahoe Miss had mixed success using its "trashburner" turbocharger at the 1965 Gold Cup in Seattle.
© Eileen Crimmin photo 1965, used with permission of The Crimmin Collection

to this day saying, 'Boy, he is really going,' about the Exide. *He was very impressed with* Exide's *run. So I was pretty honored that he would even come sit by me. That was a great thrill.*

Years later, Leo was working on Budweiser *at the time at Tri-Cities. He was working on a propeller, and I talked to him about Ronnie and told him that I was the one that went to the shop and gave Ronnie the models, and Leo remembered me exactly. He said, 'You were that kid?' He said Ronnie hardly ever toured anybody through the shop, especially any kids, so he was interested why Ronnie liked me so much, and how did I do that? That made me feel even more special!*

* * * *

In the summer of 1965, my friends and I journeyed on bikes much farther than Mom would have allowed. She worked full time as a pastor's secretary at University Presbyterian Church, so I was by necessity unsupervised on summer weekdays, a latchkey kid. Of course, Mom left me with firm instructions and boundaries, but the lure of adventure sometimes pulled my self-discipline askew.

Peewee and Mikey's parents were more lenient, and my friends figured that even though their parents might frown on our bike journeys, getting caught would earn them relatively mild punishment. For me the stakes were bigger. Mom typically punished me by grounding me, meaning I couldn't leave our yard for days or weeks. But peer pressure and thrill-seeking often won out over obedience.

In preceding summers we had ventured two miles down 140th Avenue past present-day Bellevue College to Eastgate, which aside from Lake Hills Shopping Center was the only local hub of commerce and retail at the time. It also was home to Graystone Sand and Gravel, where we'd climb three-story-high dirt mounds and do other harmless boy stuff.

By fifth grade we'd gotten bold, and when we heard the roar of a Merlin or Allison echoing in the distance – signaling a hydro test run or, in August, Seafair qualifying – we'd ride our bikes all the way to Lake Washington, a journey of 10.2 miles.

On a typical bike trip we'd stop at gas stations along the way to fill our tires with air (free in those days), pilfer the ice-maker for ice cubes to suck on, and maybe grab a road map (again, they were free). In 1965 I had a red, one-speed Murray bike with coaster brakes, and I struggled at times to keep up with Peewee and Mikey on their 3-speeds. I also had a stripped bolt on my front axle, which required that I stop frequently to tighten the two nuts that held the wheel and tire to the fork.

The most unforgettable bike trip of my youth sprang from Peewee's idea to see the recently built IBM Building, a tower on 5th Avenue in downtown Seattle designed by Minoru Yamasaki. We left on a weekday morning and followed our usual route: past the entrance to Sunset Hills cemetery, down Kamber Road to Richards Road and south to U.S. 10, where we turned west and rode its walkway across Mercer Slough and the East Channel Bridge to Mercer Island. There we'd exit past Island Motors, take an overpass and follow local roads through the island's little business district, past the Roanoke Inn (Peewee wanted to show us its outdoor fountain-statue of a little boy peeing in a pool), and onto the Lake Washington Floating Bridge, which had a pedestrian shoulder.

On previous trips we had looped under the west end of the floating bridge and ridden south along the lake to watch the hydros. This time we entered the Mount Baker tunnel, which had a narrow walkway that allowed precisely two inches of clearance on either side of my handlebars between the railing (left side) and the concrete wall (right side). This required nerve-wracking precision steering.

Once through the tunnel we made our way into downtown Seattle, where after 12 miles we arrived at the IBM Building, gawked for a few minutes, and turned for home. While riding alongside a busy downtown street my front wheel suddenly rolled off the fork, veering me toward traffic. Horns blared as I quickly wrestled my bike to the shoulder, unscathed but jolted. My friends frowned and hollered at me like I'd done it on purpose. Having no wrench I tightened the axle nuts with my bare fingers and cautiously continued homeward.

We rode past the Goodwill store on Dearborn Street to Rainier Avenue, the most-direct route to U.S. 10. But with my stripped axle I wanted no part of another busy arterial, so while Peewee and Mikey turned south on Rainer, I crossed it and pedaled east on Dearborn, continuing into a residential area.

One block later I decided to turn right onto Hiawatha Place, hoping to eventually intersect with U.S. 10. As I approached the corner I saw a large group of youths gathered in the front yard of the southwest-corner house. This was the Central District, at the time primarily an African American neighborhood, and all of the youths ahead were black, some eyeing me suspiciously as I drew near. Three older kids in their mid-teens were working on a bicycle and the biggest one yelled, "Hey, honkey!"

Not yet certain they were talking to me – what's a honkey, I thought? – I pedaled on and started rounding the corner where they all were gathered.

"Hey, *HONKEY!*" the older boy again yelled.

"Who, me?" I said, slowing a bit.

"Yeah, you! What the hell you doin' here? Pull over!" he barked in a threatening tone. Fear surged through me. Pedaling faster, I said, "I'm not doing anything." As I rode past, the teenagers charged after me, and I yelped, "I'm getting out of here!"

Pumping the pedals furiously I saw a screwdriver flash by, spinning end-over-end mere inches from my head, and it skidded along the pavement ahead of my bike. I raced on without looking back until Hiawatha intercepted Rainier Avenue, where I was relieved to find Peewee and Mikey just a short ways ahead. Shaken, I told them what happened, and we rode through the Mount Baker tunnel without stopping, after which we felt safe and continued home. I dared not tell Mom what had happened.

I must have been a naïve Eastside kid. I had been aware of racial tension elsewhere, especially in the South, because I saw it often on NBC's "Huntley-Brinkley Report." But I'd never experienced such hostility in Lake Hills or thought of it as a local reality. My neighborhood friends included an African American family that lived at the end of our block. We all played together and towed hydros.

Chapter 24

Green roostertails

The Tuesday after the Gold Cup, referee Bill Newton suspended *Miss Lapeer* driver Norm Evans from driving unlimited hydroplanes for one year for unsportsmanlike driving and "cutting blindly" into *Miss U.S.5*'s path, causing their collision. It was the second rebuke for Evans, who a year earlier had been disqualified at Detroit for "rough driving" in the Gold Cup. Both *Lapeer* and *U.S.5* returned to Detroit for repairs and would skip the next race.

On that same day, Boeing announced Northeast Airlines of Boston had ordered a dozen 727 jetliners. Northeast also bought ten DC-9s from Boeing's chief rival at the time, Douglas Aircraft Co.

Happily for the *Exide* team, its charred hull had not been burned beyond repair. "There's not nearly as much damage as we first thought," Brow said, adding it should be repaired in time for the Lake Tahoe race Sept. 25. Seattle's Fire Chief Gordon Vickery pointed out the *Alki* crew sprayed water only on *Exide*'s engine, to cool it, while dry powder and carbon dioxide were applied to the flames that burned stubbornly on the hull from being fed nitrous oxide by an electric fuel pump.

"When Brow came back to the pits, oh my goodness, he was livid. He was so upset," recalled Bob Woolms. "We all met at the trailer, and he apologized. He said, 'I forgot to turn the switch off.'"

Vanden Berg and Zuvich towed *Miss Bardahl* southeast to Utah for the inaugural Bonneville Regatta, held on a freshwater reservoir nine miles northwest of Ogden named Willard Bay, built in 1964. They brought one Rolls-Merlin with them.

Dax, David, and Schott stayed behind in Ballard to continue rebuilding additional engines and repair a carburetor, then drove straight through to Utah. The young crew approached Ogden with the truck radio on, listening to familiar new hits like Barry McGuire's "Eve of Destruction," Sonny and Cher's "I Got You, Babe," and Bob Dylan's "Like a Rolling Stone." But they found some things in Utah distinctly unfamiliar.

Willard Bay, which averages just 19 feet deep, sits at an elevation of 4,223 feet, requiring a high-altitude setup for hulls and carburetors. The novice race committee hadn't assembled the pit area when teams first arrived Wednesday, alarming Referee Harry Woods and Chuck Thompson, who described race facilities as "unbelievably bad." Volunteers worked feverishly to install utilities and create a suitable pit area by the time *Bardahl* arrived on Friday. And there would be no libations for those wanting.

"The guys couldn't believe we couldn't drink, because we were in Mormon country," said David.

The hastily prepared pits sat on an inlet connected by a narrow passage to the bay and its 3-mile racecourse. Musson qualified Saturday in clear, hot weather on flat water, circling the course at 112.15

mph, the day's top speed, followed by Manchester and *Notre Dame* at 108.01. Schoenith ran some test laps in *Gale's Roostertail*, which ultimately would score zero points for the weekend.

"We had to tow the boat out into the lake because it was so shallow," David said. "I remember saying, 'I bet we can get Jerry Schoenith to wave to us when he goes into a corner.' So we'd get up on the boat and wave, and he'd go into the corner and wave to us and then grab the wheel, and we were just laughing our heads off saying, 'I can't believe he just did that.'"

Bardahl looked slightly different for the Utah race, running with light yellow valve covers atop its engine instead of the customary black ones, a preview of *Bardahl*'s 1966-69 look.

With 13 qualifiers altogether, officials decided to run Sunday's heats in three sections comprising five, four, and four boats each. Sticky water and searing sun greeted the fleet when racing began. Rookie driver Bob Fendler outlasted early leaders *Roostertail* and *Savair's Mist* to win heat 1A aboard *Miss San Diego*, followed by *Such Crust* and an ailing *Tahoe Miss* that popped and clanked at the rear.

Smirnoff led start to finish in heat 1B with *Madison* outdueling *Budweiser* for second; *$ Bill* died in lap two. *Bardahl* also led start to finish in 1C, although *Notre Dame* pressed hard and finished just a roostertail behind, far ahead of *Savair's Probe*; *Mariner Too* did not start. *Bardahl*'s best lap was 111.801 mph with a heat average of 108.695.

Smirnoff again led a parade to win heat 2A over *Madison*, *Such Crust*, and *Savair's Mist*; *$ Bill* expired before reaching the first turn and was finished for the day. *Bardahl* passed the fast-starting *Mariner Too* in the first turn of heat 2B, ran a lap at 110.204, and averaged 107.142 to outdistance *Budweiser* and *Mariner*. Hot dog *Tahoe Miss* did not start, ending its day and furthering its 1965 disappointment. *San Diego* and *Roostertail* died in heat 2C, leaving *Notre Dame* and *Savair's Probe* to circle the bay in such boring fashion that some Utah fans griped, "They call this racing?"

The top six point-earners battled in the final heat, expected to be a brawl between *Smirnoff* and *Bardahl* (800 points each) and *Notre Dame* (700). *Madison* always merited respect with crafty Buddy Byers aboard, and *Budweiser* and *Savair's Probe* rounded out the field.

Sadly for Utah's novice hydro crowd of 12,000 – deprived of close racing most of the day – *Notre Dame* failed to start. Musson snatched the inside lane and outsprinted the field to the first turn followed closely by *Madison* on the outside, with *Bud* in third in the middle. *Bardahl* pulled away from the field and by the second turn held a comfortable lead of more than a roostertail over *Madison* and *Bud*. *Smirnoff* and *Probe* fought for fourth, with the blue and red vodka vessel prevailing. And that's how they finished, somewhat unspectacularly, with Musson averaging 100.037 mph.

Miss Bardahl earned a perfect 1,200 points to claim the first-prize Utah Cup, presented by Utah Governor Calvin Rampton. Following *Bardahl* in the final standings were *Smirnoff*, 969 points; *Madison*, 900; *Bud*, 750; *Notre Dame*, 700; *Savair's Probe*, 652; *Such Crust*, 525; *San Diego*, 400; *Tahoe*, 225; *Savair's Mist*, 225; *Mariner*, 225; *Roostertail* and *$ Bill*, zero points.

Bardahl also moved into second in national high points, narrowing the gap between the Green Dragon and leader *Notre Dame* to 44 points.

Musson wore his familiar smile as a pleasure boat towed the Green Dragon through the narrow channel to the pits. His and the crew's smiles later turned to frowns.

"We're still owed prize money from Ogden, Utah," Schott said in 2007. "They never paid. They owe me money, they owe everybody money. Everybody lost on that deal."

"You know what I remember most about Utah? Green roostertails," said Dixon. "There was an algae bloom or something in the lake, and the roostertails had a definite green tint."

That night, Zuvich likely tuned in Wolfman Jack while driving back to the motel. And most likely, Wolfman Jack told his listeners how that very evening, the Beatles were playing to 55,000 frenzied fans at Shea Stadium in New York City.

Chapter 25

Tahoe Miss *regains her stride*

The *Bardahl* caravan headed east from Utah to the next stop on the 1965 hydro tour, Detroit. Zuvich and David Smith paired up for this trek in the Ford cabover tractor that towed *Miss Bardahl*. David saw this as a step up, since the previous year he'd ridden cross-country in the *Bardahl* box van squeezed in between Leo and his wife, Mylrea.

"Because I was young, I didn't have the responsibility or the knowledge or whatever to drive the truck towing the boat," David said. "But on that '65 trip east, Jerry said, 'You're gonna drive.' Leo didn't want me to, and I drove for two days. Jerry said, 'Sit here and drive, I want to sleep. You can drive, you've been watching me long enough, and I'm not gonna drive the whole way back east.'"

David told Zuvich he didn't know how to shift, so Zuvich gave him on-the-job training, and soon David was zooming east on U.S. 30 at the helm of a Ford C-750 tractor truck. Not until the caravan stopped a day and a half later did Vanden Berg notice something odd, David recalled.

"Leo said, 'You're coming out of the wrong side of the truck,' and I said, 'No I'm not, the driver always comes out that side of the truck.' Leo said, 'Why the hell are you driving?' 'Because Jerry told me to.'" David laughed at the memory.

Although *Miss Bardahl* had won two races in a row, the team fretted that the Dragon had lost a bit of its edge, a combination of loosing a little speed and the competition getting faster.

"We were getting beat," David said, noting tough Coeur d'Alene and Seattle battles with *Exide, Notre Dame,* and *Tahoe,* when the latter didn't break. "*Exide* was coming on strong with nitrous oxide, *Tahoe* was running faster, *Smirnoff* had the aux-stage Allison – it was getting real competitive."

The team also noticed *Bardahl* was plowing water and discussed how to deal with it. After Dax calculated some numbers they figured the hull was running "downhill" on its sponsons about an inch and a quarter.

"We said, jeez, that's really bad because the way Ted Jones designed it, the sponsons are supposed to barely touch the water, yet they're always slamming the water in race-day conditions," said David. "We had this old dog that was heavy and tired, and we needed to lighten her up. So we decided to lower the main runners of the sponsons an inch in Detroit, before the race. Made the sponsons taller. That way when it comes off the corner there's more lift, and going down the straight Ron could fly the boat a little bit. And he said fine, let's go for it."

The *Gale* team offered its shop on 15 Mile Road and Barrett to *Bardahl*. Vanden Berg and Musson called Ron Jones in Costa Mesa and asked him to fly to Detroit.

"Ronnie would call me up once in a while and say, 'Get an airplane ticket and meet us in such and such, the boat's starting to drop down in the corner and I need you to work on it,' said Ron Jones. "So I'd fly there a couple days ahead of the race and shim the sponsons or whatever they needed. So I went to the Detroit race."

David scrounged up some materials, then drove to the airport to pick up Jones and Bob Mackey.

"Mackey walks off the plane, and instead of having a billfold in his back pocket he has a block plane," David said, chuckling. "He always carried his block plane. Back at the *Gale* shop the way we set it up is, Dixon and Jerry worked on engines, Leo and Jones would do the left-hand sponson, and Mackey and I did the right-hand sponson. For Mackey and I, it was a race!

"I think we did the work with the boat on the trailer," David continued. "You've got Jones 'the master' and Leo against Mackey and I. Leo thought he was a great wood butcher, and he actually was pretty good. But Mackey was great, and he and I worked really well together. He said, 'We've gotta show those guys who can build a fricking boat.' So we get under there and go like crazy, and we've already got the battens up while they're just pulling the other side apart, and we finished way before those guys. Ron Jones and Leo were saying, 'I can't believe they did it that fast, it must be wrong.' And they checked it, and of course Mackey was so good it was dead-on."

"Ronnie made one test run and came back in, and boy, his eyes were big," Jones recalled. "'That's the best that thing's ever run!' he said. 'It's faster than it was before!' And what I remember about it was the river was so rough that day, and he went right over that stuff."

"Once we dropped those sponsons, we didn't lose," David said. "It was the best thing we ever did for the boat. With that modification, all of a sudden we added 5 or 10 mph on the top end. It was a big deal. And Ron said it was great — came off the corners better, down the end of the chute it set up better."

In actuality *Bardahl* did lose a few more heats in 1965, but she also ran faster. Musson didn't show his hand in qualifying for the $35,000 Spirit of Detroit Regatta, in which Duby pushed *Miss U.S. 5* to the top speed of the 13-boat field at 113.924 mph. Several camps protested when race officials bent the rules to allow two Detroit boats that didn't qualify into the race, *Smirnoff* and *Such Crust IV*.

Tahoe Miss ran with its turbocharger Wednesday for what proved to be the final time in 1965 after the aluminum hull caught fire from the turbo's hot exhaust. Although Chuck Thompson told *The Detroit News*, "We'll use it in Madison," the Gray Ghost ultimately ran only its aux-stage Allisons the rest of the year.

An interesting "new" boat appeared at Detroit but failed to qualify: U-5 *Shu-Shu*, the rebuilt 1962 *Notre Dame*. Still owned by Shirley Mendelson McDonald (whose childhood nickname was Shu-Shu), the burned white and blue hull had been given a new mahogany deck, a new U-number, and was managed by an all-volunteer Detroit crew. Rookie Jim Miller drove the stock-Allison-powered craft but failed to qualify at the 100 mph minimum.

While hydros qualified on the Detroit River, astronauts Gordon Cooper — an occasional boat racer and one-time *Tempo* driver — and Pete Conrad battled power-cell and thruster problems aboard their Gemini 5 capsule, which eventually stayed aloft eight days to set a spaceflight endurance record. In Seattle, the Boren Avenue crossing above the new Interstate 5 freeway opened. Local Mayfair supermarkets advertised U.S.D.A choice rib steaks for 89¢ per pound.

Bardahl and *U.S.5* sped to the front in heat 1A before Musson took command down the backstretch, eventually running the fastest lap (112.500) and heat (110.921) of the day. *U.S.5* took second, *Savair's Mist* third, while *Madison* did not finish and *Such Crust* did not start. The river turned lumpy for heat 1B, won by Fred Alter in *Blue Chip* followed by *Gale's Roostertail*, *Savair's Probe*, and a fading *Mariner Too*. Heat 1C saw *Notre Dame*, *Bud*, *Tahoe*, and *Smirnoff* circle the first turn in a pack. *Tahoe* powered into second and gnawed at *Notre Dame*'s lead for four laps, then snuck inside on the final turn of lap five and sprinted to the finish, where the Gray Ghost clipped the Shamrock Lady by two boat lengths, 106.508 mph to 106.090, followed by *Smirnoff* and *Bud*.

As *Miss Madison* won heat 2A at 99.594 mph, Bill Muncey drove *Such Crust* past *Roostertail* to a second-place finish; *Mist* and *Mariner* died. *Bardahl* was last at the start of heat 2B behind *Tahoe*, *Budweiser*, and *Blue Chip*. Musson passed *Blue Chip* on lap two and *Bud* on lap three but couldn't catch Thompson, who throttled *Tahoe* home first at 108.346 to *Bardahl*'s 103.408. *U.S.5* won heat 2C at 107.484 to beat *Notre Dame* at 104.166 and a distant *Savair's Probe*.

The Horace Dodge Memorial consolation race featured a full six-boat field, and Chuck Hickling steered *Miss Budweiser* into first to beat Muncey driving *Such Crust*, Byers in *Madison*, Gardner in *Mariner*, and Red Loomis aboard *Savair's Probe*. Cantrell and *Smirnoff* did not finish.

Musson, with 700 points, squared off in the final heat against a field that included hot dogs *Tahoe Miss* with 800, *U.S.5* with 700, and *Notre Dame*, 600. *Blue Chip* and *Roostertail* rounded out the field.

Tahoe jumped to an early lead with *Bardahl* and *Notre Dame* in pursuit. *Bardahl* slowed after three laps and struggled to hold position. Finally, on the fifth and final lap, *Notre Dame* caught *Bardahl* in the upper turn and roared past the checkered flag in second place at 101.104 mph behind winners *Tahoe Miss* and Thompson, who averaged 108.805 mph to take the trophy with 1,200 perfect points. Musson and the ailing *Bardahl* averaged 99.944.

Bardahl earned second overall with 925 points ahead of *Notre Dame*, 900, and *U.S.5* with 869. Duby's craft had lost some aluminum sheathing near the propeller shaft in winning heat 2C and ran the final without it, finished fourth, then sank after returning to the dock.

Musson chugged back to the pits and said, "Something broke on lap three. I don't know how it kept running."

"We knew something was wrong," said Schott. "We had a big red light on the dash to show low oil pressure, and it was on for two full laps – we could see it all the way from the pits."

When the crew returned to the pits late that night, they found *Bardahl*'s engine *still* was hot. Dax Smith later helped dissect the engine to learn what happened. What he found shocked him.

"We kicked a rod, and the vibration knocked out a plug between the valve chamber and the water section of the head," he said. "Water drained into the pan, and the scavenge pump put it into the oil tank. After all the oil ran out, the oil pump sucked nothing but water.

"That engine ran two or three laps with nothing but water in the oil system," Smith said. "We shouldn't have even finished! When he turned the engine off it seized solid, because everything in it was garbage by then."

"That was one of those times where the through-bolts, or the heat-treated bolts, or something else we had done kept that thing together," said Zuvich.

By finishing ahead of *Bardahl* in the final heat, *Notre Dame* maintained a slim 19-point lead in the season standings heading into Madison for the Governor's Cup Regatta, 4,569 points to *Bardahl*'s 4,550.

* * * *

"Madison probably gets the gold star for being the most welcoming town," said Zuvich. "You go to Madison, and you're treated like good guys – 'You're here to entertain us, and you're here to put on a show.' Go-cart races for the crews, fun times. Madison always makes you feel good."

"I always liked Madison because we were the circus that came to town, and everybody treated us like we were royalty there," recalled David.

But for Musson the previous two years in Madison had been harsh, flipping in 1963, then making blunders in '64 and missing the final. He vowed to reverse that in 1965. His boat was quick again, his equipment hadn't broken down since 1963, and he felt another national title was within his reach.

David Smith got an unexpected invitation, and the thrill of his life, during testing for the race.

"Ron asked me if I wanted to go for a ride in the boat, and I said, absolutely!" David recalled with a smile. "That's what's really strange. Nobody else got a ride in that boat. He never asked Dixon, never asked Jerry. He said, 'David, you need to go and have a ride with me. Put the double seat in, we're going.'

"I was never more impressed with an individual because of what he could do with that boat," David recalled. "We weren't out on the course by ourselves – *Smirnoff* was out, *Tahoe Miss* was out, and we were out, and he'd put that boat within two or three feet of the others, in the corner, sliding, with me in the boat with him. I was totally amazed with what he did. Slid that thing, snapped that thing, reverse-steered that thing. I was just awed. It was one of the best things I ever did because after that ride, when I got out of the *Bardahl*, all of a sudden boats were magic. Before that, they weren't."

Shu-Shu followed the fleet to Madison but rookie driver Miller again was unable to qualify, mustering a top lap of only 93.248 mph. (The craft never again attempted to race as *Shu-Shu*, but it later re-emerged under a bevy of monikers over the years – including *Evergreen Roofing*, Mark Evans' first unlimited ride, in 1979 – and eventually became a mainstay of The Hydroplane & Raceboat Museum's fleet as the restored 1967 *Miss Budweiser*.) Owner Jim Herrington beached his *Mariner Too* and sent the repaired *Miss Lapeer*, sporting a new all-white tail and cowl, to Madison along with driver Warner Gardner.

Under gray, threatening skies, heat 1A got underway Sept. 5, 1965, on the Ohio River. Cantrell powered to the front aboard *Smirnoff*; *Savair's Mist* passed *Such Crust*, which later spun out but finished; and *Lapeer* died while running second. *Smirnoff* won at 98.110 mph. *Bardahl* breezed to victory in 1B at 106.867 mph, fastest heat of the day, easily outrunning *Gale's Roostertail*, *Blue Chip*, and *Savair's Probe*, which nearly nipped *Chip* for third.

Thompson herded *Tahoe Miss* to a wire-to-wire win in heat 1C, averaging 106.698 to beat *Notre Dame*, *Budweiser*, and *Madison*, which held second until losing a blower and limping home at 65.052 mph.

Heat 2A brought three boats charging toward the first turn – *Bud* on the inside, *Smirnoff* in lane two, and *Probe* in lane three; *Lapeer* had fired up late and lagged far behind. *Smirnoff* hit the deep wake left by the late-starting *Lapeer* and leaped high in the air, tossed Cantrell overboard as it leaned left with its bow high, touched down stern first and landed rightside up in the middle of the turn, bashing *Bud* in the process. *Smirnoff*'s motor continued to idle and patrol boats nudged the craft ashore downriver. Rescuers gingerly fished Cantrell out of the water and sent him to the hospital with several broken ribs.

With *Smirnoff* driver-less and sporting a dented sponson, and with *Bud* banged up, officials redrew the remaining boats into just two heats. *Bardahl* again blasted to the front and led heat 2A the entire way to beat *Probe*, a late-fading *Lapeer*, and *Such Crust*; Musson averaged 105.799. *Tahoe* was nearly as dominant in 2B and ran 104.610 to outrun *Notre Dame*, *Madison*, *Blue Chip*, and *Savair's Mist*.

Musson and Thompson entered the final heat tied with 800 points each. It would be *Miss Bardahl* versus *Tahoe Miss* for the Governor's Cup: Rolls-Merlin versus Allison, youthful crew versus World War II vets, pint-sized dark-haired Buckeye versus pint-sized gray-crewcut Michigander. With just 600 points, *Notre Dame* stood little chance of winning unless the green and gray boats broke down. Other finalists were *Probe* and *Mist*.

Musson and Thompson diced for position before the start, with Musson securing the inside lane while at some point Thompson steered inside a buoy. The field charged to the line under the Madison-Milton bridge, their blaring motors echoing off the wooded Kentucky and Indiana hillsides. *Bardahl* pounded into the tight turn, scooted swiftly around the buoys with her characteristic tilt that placed much of her balance on the front of her right sponson, and screamed up the backstretch in the lead. *Tahoe* charged after her in lane two, pressing hard.

For five laps the two boats battled in lockstep around the long and narrow 3-mile course, *Bardahl* forcing *Tahoe* wide on the turns and out-accelerating her into the straightaways, *Tahoe* gaining ground on the latter half of the chutes. Meanwhile, behind third-place *Notre Dame*, *Savair's Probe* and *Savair's Mist* doggedly fought. Red Loomis used the shorter inside lane to close the gap on Walt Kade, only to lose ground as Kade in *Mist* out-accelerated *Probe*. Loomis finally pushed *Probe* into fourth for good on lap five.

Half a lap ahead, *Bardahl* screamed down the Madison shoreline toward the checkered flag. But Musson didn't see black and white – instead he saw a green flag, indicating he had to run a sixth lap. Behind him Thompson took the checkered flag, the 400 points that went with it, and claimed his second straight Governor's Cup for the *Tahoe Miss* camp with a 105.222-mph heat average. *Notre Dame* finished second at 97.297, *Probe* took third, *Mist* fourth, and the disbelieving Musson loped home last in fifth place aboard *Bardahl* for just 127 points, at an 87.110 mph average that reflected his penalty lap.

Referee Bill Newton ruled that Musson had illegally forced *Tahoe* inside the course after establishing lanes before the start. Musson protested, yet despite uncertainty among many about how to interpret the APBA rulebook, it was to no avail. Newton's decree was a judgment call, and it stood.

Despite their disappointment, each member of the *Bardahl* camp felt buoyed by the resurgent Green Dragon's strong performance, having never trailed all day. *Bardahl* took second overall in the Governor's Cup with 927 points, followed by *Notre Dame* with 900. The other consolation prize: *Miss Bardahl* edged ahead of *Notre Dame* in the season-long standings, 5,477 points to 5,469. By blowing its supercharger and scoring just 169 points all day, *Madison* relinquished third place in the national standings to *Tahoe Miss*.

* * * *

During the time between the Madison and Lake Tahoe regattas, Reno hosted the National Championship

Air Races at Sky Ranch Airfield, where Chuck Lyford was favored to win the unlimited-class division aboard his *Bardahl Special* P-51 fighter plane. Lyford won the first two heats on Sept. 10 and 11 as Mira Slovak finished third, but in the final race on Sunday the favored Lyford lost, finishing 10 seconds behind an F8F Bearcat piloted by Darryl Greenamyer. Slovak, also piloting a Bearcat, finished fourth before making an emergency landing after fire broke out in his cockpit.

On Sept. 18, *Miss Exide* tested on Lake Washington following repairs from her disastrous Gold Cup fire. Much of the work had been contracted to former *Slo-mo-shun* crewman Marsh McCann and Ken Eline, who teamed with the *Exide* crew to restore the charred Happy Hydro in 29 days. Brow hit 140 mph on choppy water and declared his like-new hydro ready to resume battle.

That weekend, George Babcock was favored to win the 7-litre division at the Seattle Inboard Regatta held near Alexander's Resort on Lake Sammamish. Babcock's *Wildcat I* was formerly *Challenger*, Chuck Lyford's 1960-61 national champion. George Henley was favored to win the 280 class aboard *Calypso Too*; both Babcock and Henley won their divisions.

Big dollars and a rare format, last used in the 1961 Seafair World's Championship, lured 17 unlimiteds to Stateline, Nev., for the Lake Tahoe World Championship Regatta and its record-high $60,000 purse, surpassing the 1965 Gold Cup's $50,150 payout. Lanes would be assigned based on qualifying speeds, with the six fastest hydros racing for the top title. The next six-fastest hydros would compete for the Ponderosa Trophy, with any remaining boats vying for the South Shore Trophy.

Miss Bardahl crewmembers' wives and families loved going to Lake Tahoe each year. Not only did Bill Harrah and his race committee stage the regatta in style, all of the teams' wives were pampered with first-class activities and entertainment while the hydro crews toiled. One year they met Liberace and toured his venue and dressing room. In 1965, Fats Domino roomed next door to them.

"We looked forward to the Tahoe race, and Bill Harrah basically owned and ran the town," Kruse said, remembering Harrah's fleet of neat and tidy gray garbage trucks. "They always treated us well. I could call Harrah by his first name. He gave me a ride into Reno in his Jaguar to pick up a part. We were running 120 mph and got to Reno in no time, and coming back we were driving up the mountain full bore and went through a radar trap. The trooper didn't even try to catch us, so they just sent him a bill."

Postcards mailed home noted hot days, cool nights, and short breath caused by Tahoe's thin air. At the Sahara Tahoe, Kruse put a quarter in a slot machine and won $25 before sitting down to a prime rib dinner. Although the postcard didn't say, Leo Vanden Berg almost certainly ordered his well done with baked potato, tossed salad, and Thousand Island.

"We worked on the boat before the race, at Harrah's shop in Sparks, and we had such a good time because they treated us like we were kings," said David. "I got to walk through the car collection and see all this stuff that nobody ever got to see, and it was magical for me."

Qualifying got underway Tuesday, Sept. 21, and Roy Duby surprised onlookers by scorching around the 3-mile course in *Miss U.S.5* at a two-lap average of 119.986 mph. Musson and *Bardahl* ran second fastest at 116.114, and on Wednesday *Notre Dame* posted 115.574 to top Bill Brow's 114.574 in the rebuilt *Exide*. *Miss Madison* made it into the fast flight on Thursday with a 111.631 speed, and host boat *Tahoe Miss* finally overcame gremlins to run 112.271 mph on Friday, sans turbocharger. That bumped Danny Foster, who had come out of retirement to replace broken-ribbed Bill Cantrell, into the second-tier race in *Miss Smirnoff*.

At Willard Bay, Utah, hydros were towed to and from the racecourse by runabouts via a narrow channel.
© Eileen Crimmin photo 1965, used with permission of The Crimmin Collection

Start of heat 1A at Lake Tahoe, before *U.S.5* ran over *Notre Dame*'s stern and crunched its tail. L to R: *Exide, Notre Dame, Bardahl, U.S.5*.
© Eileen Crimmin photo 1965, used with permission of The Crimmin Collection

Bardahl fried an engine midway through the final heat at Detroit but still held off *Notre Dame* until the fifth lap. *Bardahl* finished the heat.
– used with permission of Sandy Ross

Thompson returns to the pits on pristine Lake Tahoe, where the Gray Ghost won the final heat and earned second overall in the $60,000 World Championship Regatta.
– used with permission of David Newton, the Roger Newton collection

Miss Bardahl won the Lake Tahoe race four straight years, 1962 through 1965.
© Eileen Crimmin photo 1965, used with permission of The Crimmin Collection

Like *Miss Exide* at the Gold Cup, *Tahoe Miss* suffered a devastating fire, on Mission Bay. But *Bardahl* stole the headlines with her record-shattering swan song.
– used with permission of the *San Diego Union-Tribune*

By the time qualifying ended, race officials were praising the top-six boats for posting the highest average qualifying speed ever – 115.020 mph aggregate, topping the 114.622 average for the six speediest Gold Cup qualifiers the month before. Altogether, 15 boats qualified with only *Tri-City Sun* and *Miss Sacramento* (the former 1956 *Miss B&I*) falling short.

With an estimated 35,000 spectators on hand, six thunderboats roared onto pristine Lake Tahoe for heat 1A at 11 a.m. on Saturday and queued up between numbered buoys into their assigned lanes, Indy 500 style: *U.S.5* in lane one, then *Bardahl*, *Notre Dame*, *Exide*, *Tahoe Miss*, and *Madison*. They stormed up the lake and into the first turn where Brow in *Exide* – slightly ahead, along with Musson in *Bardahl* – pinched Manchester in *Notre Dame*, who veered left. Roy Duby aboard *U.S.5* climbed over *Notre Dame*'s stern, shearing off the Shamrock Lady's tailfin, smashing its rear cowling, and narrowly missing driver Manchester. *Notre Dame* stalled while *U.S.5* got underway and limped after the frontrunners.

Musson exited the turn in first, ripped up the backstretch, and ran away for a wire-to-wire victory. *Exide* finished second, *Madison* third, *Tahoe* a sick fourth with a damaged supercharger, and *U.S.5* did not finish along with *Notre Dame*. *Bardahl* averaged 104.976, fastest heat of the day.

Between heats several crewmen from other camps swarmed over *Notre Dame* to help make her seaworthy again. They stripped what remained of the rear cowling, secured Manchester's cockpit and seat, and the U-7 entered the course for heat 2A, looking painfully awkward minus her aft superstructure.

Miss Bardahl was equally dominant in heat 2A, where the three hot dogs blasted into and around the first turn nearly abreast – Green Dragon, Happy Hydro, and Gray Ghost. *Bardahl* screamed up the backstretch and pulled away to lead all five laps, winning decisively at 102.118 mph. Thompson brought *Tahoe* home second at 98.450 followed by Brow in *Exide*, Buddy Byers in *Madison*, and Duby in *U.S.5*. *Notre Dame* was washed down before the start but restarted to finish last.

With 800 perfect points, *Bardahl* needed no better than a fourth-place finish in the final heat to win the World's Championship Regatta. Musson stuck the Green Dragon's nose out front yet again and led until they approached the second turn of lap one, where *Tahoe Miss* powered past into the lead. Musson settled into second, and at the finish it was *Tahoe* first with a 104.834-mph average followed by *Bardahl*, 101.771; *U.S.5*, 99.264; *Madison*, 95.795; and an ill *Exide*, 88.321; *Notre Dame* did not finish.

Bardahl won the regatta with 1,100 points, while *Tahoe* tallied 869 to earn second ahead of *Exide*, *Madison*, *U.S.5*, and *Notre Dame*, which tallied a paltry 95 points to all but kill its chances at a National Championship. The Shamrock Lady now trailed *Bardahl* by 1,013 points. United Press International reported *Miss Bardahl* "would have to sink to lose the title" at San Diego, the final 1965 race.

"Our boat never did poorly at Lake Tahoe," said David Smith. "Never lost up there. Do you know why? We changed the air traps. We had two setups, big ones for altitude and regular ones, and we'd do it before we ever rolled into town. And Dixon changed the carburetion. Everybody was dying out there and we were going like hell. Nobody ever figured that out. They didn't understand thin air."

The 1965 Lake Tahoe event earned rave reviews. Spectators liked the Indy 500-style starts and constant action. Altogether, nine heats were staged – three each in the World's Championship, Ponderosa Trophy, and South Shore Trophy races – spaced only 30 minutes apart. Danny Foster and *Miss Smirnoff* dominated the Ponderosa event, winning all three heats to beat *Budweiser*, *Savair's Mist*, *Savair's Probe*, and *Berryessa Belle*. Fearless Freddy Alter won the South Shore Trophy aboard *Such Crust IV*, beating Bob Fendler in *Miss San Diego* and rookie Rex Bixby piloting *$ Bill*; *Mariner Too* did not score a point all day.

Yet despite critical acclaim, 1965 proved to be the final year of the Lake Tahoe event. The *Bardahl* team members must have been disappointed. Their U-40 won all four races, 1962 through 1965, and their first-place share of 1965's $60,000 purse was a handsome $13,000.

"That's something else unique – in 1965, we were the first crew that ever got a percentage of the action, 2.5 percent of what the boat won," said David. "And that was huge because we won a lot of money, especially the World Championship and Gold Cup. That was wonderful because after boat racing, that's the race winnings that bought my piece of property that I built my first house on after the *Pay 'n Pak* years."

Vanden Berg explained how the lure of prize money helped to further temper Musson's lead foot and mold him into a seasoned, savvy driver. Even after Guntersville 1963, where Vanden Berg said "the light came on" for Musson connecting engine life with success, the little Ohioan disliked following the leader to conserve equipment.

"Ron still wanted to be out front," said Vanden Berg. "So we told him, 'This race is a money race. We want the money. We have to win this one. Play it cool, just get enough points to get in the winner's circle.' Or, 'This race is a low-money race. You go do what you want out there, we'll experiment. We'll run different ratios and try this or that.' We did that many times. We always experimented on the low-money races.

"That was the last couple of years. The crew got part of the purse then; we never did before. I got 5 percent, each crew member got 2.5 percent, and Ron got 25 percent. So it was an incentive for him, too."

Zuvich also witnessed the change in Musson's driving style.

"At first, yeah, he needed to be reminded not to break stuff," he said. "I wasn't around that much in '61, but I know from stories I heard that when he drove the *Hawaii Kai* he blew all those motors. He'd say, 'Hey, this is easy' as he'd pass somebody up. He'd say, 'I've got all this throttle left,' and proceeded to use more throttle and blow a motor. He'd think something was wrong with the motor since he had all this throttle. So it took him a long time to figure out that, when you use a blower, you can't use the throttle like you do without a blower. And Ronnie, you know, would strive to be number one.

"Later, he understood," Zuvich added. "It helped his payroll and helped his publicity and helped to win races not to be towed in."

Ron Jones attended the Tahoe race and the post-race awards banquet. Something had gnawed at him over the years – he said that despite his periodic sponson modifications and tune-ups that contributed to *Miss Bardahl*'s success from 1963-65, he wasn't mentioned by the team as having a role or having touched the boat.

"It always was advertised as a Ted Jones boat, and that's all they said," Jones said. "I kept thinking, well, one day they'll put it all together.

"Liberace was the star of the program, I was in the audience, and finally the trophy-presentation time came. When Ron Musson accepted the winning trophy, he said, 'Before I say too much more, there's someone who has worked on this boat that we have never mentioned.' And I sat up in my chair and I thought this was going to be my big moment. And Ron began to tell about this guy who worked on the boat, and that it went from a dog to a winner, and the guy is one of the best in the business, and he's done this and that. He went on for a long time and, boy, I was feeling pretty good! And he said, 'I'd like to introduce him to you right now. Would Chuck Lyford please come forward?' Well, I about died right in my chair. I just couldn't believe it.

"So, you know, I came real close, but it wasn't me after all." Jones laughed. "Oh, well."

* * * *

That same week, anglers in Washington state reeled in some big salmon – big, but not uncommon for that era. Jim Kerns of Seattle landed a 60-pound king near Sekiu while "mooching" with herring, while others nearby caught lunkers weighing 42 to 45 pounds.

Chapter 26

Exiting in a blaze of glory

Water injection had served *Miss Bardahl* well, limiting detonation and optimizing the power of her Merlins. The team knew salt water awaited them at Mission Bay, and knowing salt would encrust their spark plugs, they went on a scavenger hunt at a Reno junkyard for a container that could hold fresh water, and more. For the San Diego Cup, thanks to Dwight Thorn's advice and Dax's further research in the UW engineering library, *Miss Bardahl* would run a 50/50 mixture of water and alcohol for even better performance.

Two 10-gallon stainless-steel tanks were purchased for $10.50 each, cut, welded together into one 20-gallon tank, and strapped inside *Bardahl*'s aft hull with bungee cords at the Sparks *Tahoe Miss* shop.

"We had driven straight from Madison to Nevada and did the modifications before Lake Tahoe with the water-alcohol tank in the back," said David. "It put more weight on the strut, so we picked up the nose a little bit and made the propeller more efficient. We didn't understand that at the time, but it sure as hell worked.

"We also took the radiator guts out of an aftercooler and ran it like that," he continued. "The *Bardahl* was the first one to do it. We just said, screw it, because we had water-alcohol and didn't need all that mass and weight. You lose about 50 pounds. It was a predecessor to the big chrome tube, which is much more efficient."

Dax's nitrous system now was ready to deliver in a big way. The heavy duty Barksdale valves would not gum up and stick in racing conditions, and the team brought lots of nitrous oxide to San Diego – enough to refill the tanks after each heat with plenty to spare. *Miss Bardahl* now was ready for Musson to inject nitrous practically at will, in five-second bursts for added speed.

The combination of nitrous oxide, water-alcohol injection, flat-top pistons, heavy-duty spark plugs, taller sponsons, tetraethyl lead, countless engine modifications, and Musson's ever-increasing skill and familiarity with his craft created a formidable arsenal. *Miss Bardahl* was poised to conclude her career in an astounding, crushing climax.

San Diego would be no cakewalk, however. Musson's friendly foe, Bill Muncey, stepped back into the cockpit of a competitive ride the week of the San Diego Cup, replacing Roy Duby as driver of Detroit's *Miss U.S.5*. The light, 5,200-pound magnesium hydro had shown impressive speed sporadically, and owner George Simon decided Muncey was the best man to optimize his scarlet speedster.

"I don't want people to think I'm forsaking Seattle or the West Coast," Muncey said. "But, heck, I sat on the beach all year. The fact is that none of the West Coast owners needed a chauffeur. I don't have too many years left for competitive driving. And I don't want to waste them."

The fleet found gorgeous new pit facilities awaiting them on Vacation Island, just east of Ingraham Street south of Ski Beach. Light standards lit the roomy asphalt area that was plumbed with fresh water and 110v/120v electricity, and spacious docks extended below a rock retaining wall.

Muncey immediately began squeezing the potential out of *U.S.5* on Friday, Oct. 1, when he stepped into its cockpit for the first time and ran the week's fastest lap at 119.469 mph. "I'm mighty excited about the boat," he said afterward.

Musson averaged 117.519 mph around the 3-mile course, and Danny Foster coaxed an impressive 116.379 out of *Smirnoff*. The *Tahoe Miss* crew again eschewed its problematic turbocharger and installed an aux-stage Allison motor, and Harry Volpi tested at 108.651 mph. *Notre Dame*, with a new white tail minus its blue trim paint, qualified fastest on Saturday at 115.879 mph. The pits then buzzed with excitement when the M&M boys were drawn to face each other in heat 1D.

A crowd of 40,000, larger than in 1964, turned out Sunday for the second San Diego Cup. Officials drew the 16 qualifiers into four heat sections of four boats each. Heat 1A saw Chuck Thompson guide *Tahoe* to the pole position flanked by Warner Gardner in *Mariner Too*, Fred Alter in *Such Crust*, and Walt Kade aboard *Savair's Mist*. Gardner led across the line, pinched Thompson in the first turn and washed him down, leaving *Tahoe* disabled. The maneuver disqualified Gardner, and Alter won at a lumbering 95.846 mph with *Such Crust*.

Heat 1B saw Manchester and *Notre Dame* speed away from *Budweiser* (Chuck Hickling), *$ Bill* (Rex Bixby), and *Tri-City Sun* (Bob Gilliam) to win at a swift 110.882. Bill Brow and *Exide* led wire-to-wire in 1C but jumped the gun by a mere two feet, handing Buddy Byers and *Madison* the victory at 107.441 over *Smirnoff* (Danny Foster). *Exide* ran a penalty lap but still beat fourth-place *Miss San Diego* (Bob Fendler); subtracting its penalty lap, *Exide* averaged a quick 110.457 mph for the first five circuits.

Musson and *Bardahl* roared onto Mission Bay to battle Muncey and *U.S.5* in heat 1D along with *Berryessa Belle* (Bob Miller) and *Savair's Probe* (Red Loomis). However, *U.S.5* was ailing and never started. It might not have mattered: *Bardahl* scorched around the 3-mile saltwater course for five laps at an inconceivable 116.079 mph, with a fast third lap of 117.870, to trounce the field. Observers said the Green Dragon not only looked fast, it *sounded* fast, its wound-out Merlin blaring at a high pitch.

Astounded fans speculated that Musson must have been instructed to take it to the limit and close *Miss Bardahl*'s career in a blaze of glory.

"I don't think he was told to go out and dust everybody off – at least, I wasn't aware of that," said Dax. "That was one of those days when the water was just right for the boat, the temperature was just right, we had fairly fresh motors. We really had the nitrous system sorted out, we had the water injection system sorted out, and a lot of stuff we'd been doing earlier in the season came together."

Zuvich thinks Musson did, in fact, push harder that day.

"Ronnie knew the boat was being retired, and I think he gave it a little extra on his own," Zuvich said. "He wasn't told to, but he went all out. It was a good day; he was smiling and laughing the whole afternoon. When he felt naughty and nice, he had a little twinkle in his eye. And that was one of those days."

Heat 2A brought *U.S.5*, *Notre Dame*, *Berryessa Belle*, and *Savair's Probe* together. Once again, the fastest qualifier couldn't bring her 119-mph speed to bear. Muncey managed to start the heat but *U.S.5* soon conked out after one lap at 94.158, and owner George Simon's team was done for the day. Manchester throttled *Notre Dame* past *Berryessa Belle* into first at 107.741 with *Probe* taking third.

Tahoe and *Exide* met in heat 2B along with *Budweiser* and *Savair's Mist*. Thompson and Brow pounded down the back chute toward the south turn when suddenly *Tahoe*'s blower exploded, and its engine erupted in huge flames. Thompson bailed overboard but didn't have time to activate *Tahoe*'s built-in fire extinguishers, and soon the Gray Ghost was engulfed in an inferno, billowing thick black smoke. Thompson suffered minor burns and was plucked from the water. A patrol boat nudged *Tahoe* aground at Fiesta Island and, after 20 minutes, doused the flames. Badly scorched, *Tahoe Miss* was done racing. Brow steered *Exide* to victory in the restart, averaging 109.577 to beat *Budweiser* and *Mist*.

Having clinched the 1965 driver and boat national titles in heat 1D, Musson and *Bardahl* had little to lose in heat 2C, and they again streaked around sunny Mission Bay at a torrid pace to thrash their rivals. *Bardahl* averaged 115.335 mph in beating *Smirnoff*, which ran 108.173, *$ Bill*, and *Tri-City Sun*. *Bardahl*'s slowest lap was 114.771.

"I can remember Musson coming in after one of those preliminary heats with a great big grin on his face," said Dax. "He said, 'Boy, that was really fun!' He had pulled right up next to somebody, looked over and waved bye-bye, and pulled away. By that time we had the nitrous system figured out, and we had engines that really would take a lot of abuse.

"In one of those little episodes, he ate an engine in one heat," Dax said. "He essentially took a brand new engine and almost made garbage out of it. He didn't bust it, but when we took it apart later, the thing was trash inside. He had taken a fresh overhauled engine that only had break-in time, which was usually about two or three laps, and in five laps of hard running used it up. We had to yank it after one heat. But it lived as long as it had to live."

Byers and *Madison* won heat 2D at 98.684 mph over *Such Crust* and *San Diego*, while *Mariner Too* died just past the start. *Madison*, *Notre Dame*, and *Bardahl* each had two heat victories and 800 points, placing them in the final with *Exide* and *Such Crust*.

The 1965 season had come down to one final heat of racing. Brow and his rebuilt *Exide* were fast that day, but Musson and *Bardahl* were faster. The Green Dragon roared by *Exide* in the first turn and churned past *Notre Dame* into the lead, skimming lightly across the water and casting a long, steady roostertail. Musson averaged 114.890 on lap one to Manchester's 112.734, then steadily pulled away from the Shamrock Lady. *Bardahl*'s nitrous and ADI worked flawlessly as she danced lightly on her sponsons, and for five laps Musson roared around Mission Bay at a 113.780-mph average to clobber the field. *Exide* finished second at 109.823, then *Madison* at 100.539 and *Such Crust*, 97.174. *Notre Dame* blew a supercharger in lap four and did not finish.

Musson guided the Green Dragon to the dock wearing his victory grin. The *Bardahl* team was all smiles, too. Their tired old boat had dazzled everyone with its dominating, perfect performance, revealing the speed they believed it always had been capable of, but which hadn't been fully unleashed while pursuing the durability record. Now the race and season were over, *Miss Bardahl* owned the National Championship for the third straight year, and she had raced an astounding 57 consecutive heats without a mechanical failure. The last time Musson's mount had failed to finish a heat was July 1963, in the Diamond Cup at Coeur d'Alene.

Musson now had won 16 races in his unlimited career, second only to Bill Muncey, who had 19 victories.

Bardahl also shattered world records by setting all three major competition marks: fastest lap, 117.870 (previous record, 1964 *Exide*, 117.647); fastest heat, 116.079 (1964 *Bardahl*, 113.660); and fastest 45-mile race, 115.064 (1963 *Tahoe Miss*, 109.459) – records that eventually stood until 1972 and 1973, well into the picklefork-hull era.

"We'd done really well at Tahoe and hadn't hurt anything," said David. "So it was like, okay, this is the last time the boat's ever going to run. That was Ron's boat, and I'm sure he wanted to show everybody the old boat could really do it. We had really good equipment. We also had the advantage, because we could pull more manifold pressure than anybody because we had water-alcohol. We were at sea level, in salt water, so we ran the most manifold pressure we'd ever run, with popup pistons, with nitrous oxide. He just ran the daylights out of that thing. A new engine every heat."

It was late Sunday afternoon on Oct. 3, 1965, when *Miss Bardahl*'s crewmembers hooked their boat to the sling, attached ropes, and lifted it out of the water for the last time. Skip Schott held the bow rope, Dax Smith directed the crane, David Smith held the aft rope, Jerry Zuvich aligned the boat on its trailer, and Leo Vanden Berg marked his checklist.

Final results for the 1965 San Diego Cup showed *Miss Bardahl* the winner with a perfect 1,200 points, followed by *Miss Madison*, 1,025; *Miss Exide*, 925; *Such Crust*, 869; *Notre Dame*, 800; *Miss Smirnoff*, 600; *Miss Budweiser*, 600; *Berryessa Belle*, 600; *Savair's Mist*, 525; *$ Bill*, 450; *Savair's Probe*, 450; *Miss San Diego*, 394; and *Miss Tri-City Sun*, 338.

Final standings for the 1965 season: 1. *Miss Bardahl*, 7,777 points; 2. *Notre Dame*, 6,364; 3. *Miss Madison*, 5,595; 4. *Tahoe Miss*, 5,069; 5. *Smirnoff*, 4,142; 6. *Miss Exide*, 3,571; 7. *Miss Budweiser*, 3,565; 8. *Such Crust IV*, 3,342; 9. *Miss U.S.5*, 2,934; 10. *Savair's Mist*, 2,652; 11. *Savair's Probe*, 2,415; 12. *Mariner Too*, 2,261; 13. *Gale's Roostertail*, 1,966; 14. *Miss San Diego*, 1,217; 15. *Blue Chip*, 1,090; 16. *$ Bill*, 1,069; 17. *Berryessa Belle*, 695; 18. *Miss Lapeer*, 394; 19. *Miss Tri-City Sun*, 338.

"San Diego was very, very satisfying, because we earned it," Schott said. "We *knew* we were the class of the field. You don't set lap, heat, and race records – and not break – by accident. Musson used every bit of what we gave him."

"The last time that boat ran, the keel was leaking," said Zuvich. "We had to put a carpet on the floor of the cockpit that we changed in between heats to keep the salt water from jumping up and getting under Ronnie's visor. That's how badly the boat was leaking and falling apart, and it still ran faster than it ever ran before."

San Diego marked *Miss Bardahl*'s fourth victory of the year and 12th overall, dating to the last race of 1962. She retired as a rarity among unlimiteds, a hydroplane that ran her entire career under one name.

Miss Bardahl's caravan motored north on U.S. 99 through Los Angeles, up the San Joaquin Valley and past Lake Berryessa, site of the season-ending Oct. 10 Champagne Cup exhibition race that had been canceled just the week before, and eventually home to Ballard. There the Green Dragon, the fastest competition hydro of all time, was parked off to the side, relegated to display duty as the cabover *Bardahl* again took center stage.

The cabover *Bardahl* wouldn't benefit from Schott's services, however. Shortly after returning home, Schott resigned from the team.

"I was engaged by then," he said, referring to his Spokane-born, Montana-schooled sweetheart Karin Renwick. "I guess I was kind of moralistic. I grew up in a home where my mother and father didn't even know anybody who was divorced. But it was different in boat racing – it was the same men and women each year, but each year they were married to different people. I knew I couldn't be a boat racer and be married. The two just didn't seem compatible."

In many ways, 1965 marked the end of unlimited racing's age of innocence. Never again would race fans watch nonchalantly as thunderboats rocked on their sponsons or nosed skyward. Not for years would drivers again throttle their mounts beyond the 120-mph barrier or consistently race at pre-1966 speeds.

The participants and fans didn't know it at the time, but as 1965 waned, so too did unlimited hydroplane racing.

Chapter 27

Reflecting on excellence

Miss Bardahl's crew members shared their thoughts years later on how their boat stacks up against the all-time greats, and which boats and drivers posed the biggest challenge to the Green Dragon. All agreed that *Bardahl* was the top boat of its day, yet not all agreed on descriptors like "dominant."

David Smith, for example, sees dominant hydros as those that lose only when they break, and which demonstrate clear superiority over the competition when all boats run their best. He cited examples like the *Slo-mo-shun*s, 1957-58 *Hawaii Kai III*, 1962 *Miss Century 21*, 1977-78 *Atlas Van Lines*, and several of the latter-day *Miss Budweiser*s.

Between 1962 and 1965, three competitors consistently are named as *Bardahl*'s biggest threats: *Thriftway*, *Exide*, and *Tahoe Miss*.

"I'd say *Exide*," recalled Zuvich. "And *Tahoe Miss* was *always* there. Of course, the first couple of years it was *Thriftway* or *Century 21*, the same hull. *Gale V* was there when they got all their stuff together, but it wasn't that often enough where you had to spend time fretting about them. By the time they got all their ABCs together, we were at another race site, a whole new course, and then they had to try everything all over again.

"Later, *Notre Dame* was in that league of being within two to three miles per hour," he added. "They just didn't have all their apples in the same basket, that's all. But they could strike."

Vanden Berg's list begins with the team that *Bardahl* "dethroned" in 1963.

"*Thriftway*," he said. "And *Tahoe* was the one that used to be right on our tail all the time, but they weren't consistent. That was their big problem. I think they were trying too many things at once. They didn't know which one was benefiting them and which one wasn't. *Exide* was quite competitive. But again, they weren't consistent, either. That consistency is a big payoff.

"But I would say we were just as fast as anybody," Vanden Berg continued. "For its time, *Bardahl* was tops. I'd say so. And we got a little more out of the engines than anybody, reliability and power."

When asked about *Notre Dame* in 1964-65 and the *Gale* boats, Vanden Berg said with a chuckle, "Never even thought of them. Never."

Ron Jones' perspective is interesting because of his role in either building or modifying many of the top boats in that era.

"I would have to say *Bardahl* was better than *Thriftway* around the corner, and I believe it out-accelerated all the other boats," Jones said. "The *Tahoe* and *Exide* people spent more time and effort on getting more horsepower. Leo wasn't real big into, 'Let's see if we can get 3,000 horsepower out of this thing.' No, that wasn't his thing. He said, 'What good does it do to have 3,000 horsepower and have a piston and a rod hanging out the side of the block? It just doesn't work. We want to get there and finish and come back and do it again tomorrow.' And that's what he did."

David Smith again emphasized the importance of durability, of collecting the most points. He also concedes that other boats were faster when their equipment held together and the water and weather complemented their particular setups.

"When other boats ran at their peak, they were faster," David said. "But we were consistent all the time. And we strategized, we wanted to win the race. Winning the race was more important than winning the heat. So if we had to, we'd take a second. There was a lot of strategy. We used to tell people all the time, 'We can beat them in the pits, we don't have to beat them on the water.'

"*Bardahl* was good but wasn't dominant," he said. "We won races with points, we didn't beat everybody. What's dominant is the *Thriftway*, the white boat. It only lost when it broke. It blew everybody away. The *Hawaii Kai* was dominant, *Slo-mo* was dominant.

"*Exide*, *Tahoe*, the *Gale-Smirnoff* team, they were the big threats," David continued. "Byers and *Madison* were always there, but we knew we could beat him whenever we wanted, though he would fly the boat and do really well. Those are the guys you were always watching. *Notre Dame*, they were nothing. They spent a lot of money just going sideways. We knew we could blow 'em off. The guys that were really tough was the *Exide*, because we knew if they got it right, we were screwed.

"And the *U.S.* was so sporadic," he added. "We'd drive by that thing all the time. They never got it right. It's like nobody ever tested, they'd just show up."

Gary Breakfield's perspective spanned just the 1964 racing season, but he didn't hesitate to identify the top threat.

"*Miss Exide*," he said. And the *Gale* boats, of course, they were real competition – the *Smirnoff*. But *Miss Exide* was a real fast boat. They came out with that nitrous oxide and made their boat go like a bat out of hell. And the *Tahoe* Gray Ghost, you betcha. They were a hell of a competitor – oh, they were fast! *Notre Dame* wasn't a real powerful boat, they didn't do too much. It was never really competition hardly at all."

Schott, who competed against *Bardahl* until joining the team for 1965, describes a stronger U-40 when comparing it with other top hydros.

"It really *was* good," Schott said. "It won three Gold Cups, three National Championships, 57 consecutive heats, and to that point nobody had done that. The '65 Gold Cup, we earned it. Every bit of it. We worked our asses off and beat the best at that time.

"That boat ran against the best of the field in its day – the *Thriftway* and the *Tahoe Miss,* and when *Exide* was running good," he continued. "I'd rate it pretty high. In its time, it was the class of the field. *Tahoe Miss* always looked better, because they had people just polishing chrome wheels on their trucks. But we did more with less. And they didn't like that.

"Our biggest threat? The *Exide*," said Schott. "They didn't go to all the races, but at their peak they were running gaseous nitrous oxide, their boat was light, and Bill Brow was an excellent driver. And I think they were pulling a lot of inches and a lot of rpms. But they broke; we didn't break.

"*Tahoe Miss*," he added, "because when they were running good, they had good people, they had good motors, and Chuck Thompson – he had two foot positions, either on or off it. If you beat Chuck Thompson, it was not because he gave you anything. He didn't. And *Tahoe* had money. Mr. Harrah had a copper roof and copper gutters on his house!" he said, laughing.

"In '65 we thought there was going to be a problem," Schott recalled, "because Billy Newman, who had been the engine man for the *Maverick*, came to work for Shirley as the crew chief on the *Notre Dame*, and he was *the* Mr. Allison. But at their first test session he dropped dead down at Lake Washington. As for *Gale* and *Smirnoff*, they were neat guys to be around, they spent tons of money, and you knew they were going to break. But Cantrell was a marvelous guy, and if they kept things under him, he was gonna getcha."

Schott then noted a boat and driver not mentioned by others, the 1964 San Diego Cup winners.

"Warner Gardner wasn't shy about putting the pedal to the metal," he said. "He was driving *Mariner Too* and he was retired from the military at that point. He drove the truck, built the motors, drove the boat. They used kind of a pickup crew, his kids helped, and they had some guys from Jim Herrington's factory come in and help. But as long as it stayed together, it was a threat."

Dixon's assessment of *Bardahl* and its competitors resembles those of his teammates.

"*Bardahl* was a top runner. It was not two steps above everybody else, but it was right there on top," he said. "It's got the record to back it up. In its day, it was a really good boat, top of the line, one of the very best for its era. At that time, I don't think you could have done significantly better.

"*Thriftway* was *always* good competition," said Dixon. "Those guys were no slouches, they really had all their stuff in one bag. We got beat by other guys on occasion. The *Tahoe* guys were *tough*. They had the horsepower, the boat was pretty decent, they had a good driver. The *Exide*, those guys were tough, too. We could keep up with any of them, and we could beat most of them most of the time. But on any particular given day, there were probably about three boats that, under ideal situations, could probably beat us. I don't think it was a case that anybody was significantly faster than us, but under any given set of circumstances, yes, we definitely could be beat, and we were at times."

When asked about the No. 2 boat on the 1965 national circuit, Dixon gave a familiar assessment of *Notre Dame*.

"They were good competition, but they weren't consistent," he said. "The guys that we considered the biggest threat were the *Exide* troops, at least from my standpoint. *Tahoe* was not consistent. They'd go out and blow everybody's doors off, and the next heat they'd go down to the starting line and launch blower parts all over the course. But *Exide* was consistent and always seemed to be there. *Notre Dame* seemed close to putting it all together, but they could never quite make it happen, and I don't know why."

* * * *

Debates about the top unlimited driver of all time typically include three names: Muncey, Hanauer, and Dave Villwock. Those three top the list for most race victories – Villwock, 65 and counting entering the 2012 season; Muncey, 62; and Hanauer, 61. Other winning drivers often cited in those debates include Dean Chenoweth (25 wins), Jim Kropfeld (22), Billy Schumacher (17), George Henley (12), and

Ron Musson (16).

Other fine drivers merit inclusion in those talks. But one factor often cited as a good measure of skill (versus the opportunity to drive a clearly superior boat) is the ratio of race wins to races entered. Topping that list at a .500 ratio is the savvy Villwock, yet detractors quickly dismiss him because he drove dominant *Budweiser* and *E-lam* enclosed-cockpit turbine boats. Likewise, Muncey detractors note his winning ratio of .325 reflects a mid-career "slump" of several years.

Hanauer (.381) and Henley (.353) score higher. Henley drove the elite *Pride of Pay 'n Pak*, a near-dominant boat in 1974-75. Hanauer claimed many 1990s victories aboard the dominant *Miss Budweiser*, but he also won with good-but-not-elite boats like *Squire Shop*, *Miller American*, and *Miss Pico*, and his 1982-83 open cockpit *Atlas Van Lines* raced against the formidable Griffon-powered *Miss Budweiser*.

Ron Musson, too, drove an elite hydro. But through the eyes of its crew (if not its fans and competitors), *Miss Bardahl* was not an overwhelmingly dominant boat. The refrain "on any given day" comes up often in describing that era of tighter competition. Musson's race-winning ratio of .340 includes his *Bardahl* years, preceded by wins aboard the stock-Allison-powered *Nitrogen Too* and *Hawaii Kai III*, a fast but diminished boat under Joe Mascari's ownership compared with its Edgar Kaiser days. Musson's entire unlimited career spanned just seven years.

Another criterion is to gauge drivers by heats won. In March 1974, the *Unlimited NewsJournal* calculated all drivers who had started at least 75 heats since World War II and won more than 30 percent of them. Only 10 drivers made that elite list, and Ron Musson topped it. Musson won 61 of 118 heats entered for a .517 winning percentage, far ahead of Jack Regas, .467; Guy Lombardo, .461; Danny Foster, .430; and Bill Muncey, .420, good for fifth place.

So how does Musson stack up against the all-time great unlimited drivers?

"Musson was as good as any of them," said Zuvich. "Really. I think the drivers had to be more cunning back then, and that's where Muncey got good. And Ronnie *was* good. I think saying he's with Muncey is in good company. There were a lot more boats running at the same speeds, so he who was cagiest would win."

"I'd say he was right up there with all the top drivers," said Vanden Berg. "At the time, I'd say he was just as good as Muncey or any of the others."

But what about those who say Muncey is clearly the all-time best?

"Because of his years," Vanden Berg said. "That's not comparing, say, Muncey at five years and Musson at five years. Musson didn't do much winning in that 'yucky' *Bardahl*, one or two races," he said, referring to the 1958 hull and its poor riding characteristics. "And then the first year, in 1962, he didn't do very good with the new boat. So most of his winning was done, actually, in about three years."

Ron Jones was there from the start of unlimited racing in Seattle, watching all the greats from 1951 onward. His comments in 2007 reflected half a century of involvement.

"It's very hard to say one guy was absolutely the best," Jones said. "But there were few, if any, any better than Ronnie Musson. Muncey had his times. His early career was tremendous, the middle of his career was not so good, and his latter days he was back on top again. There was a time in the middle there, Muncey did very poorly. But Ronnie Musson was on it, all the time. It would be really hard for me to think of anyone any better than he, other than Muncey. In the limited hydros, I think Ronnie in his day was the best. I don't know that anybody in limiteds ever came close to him.

"This is just my opinion, and other people will certainly disagree, but I don't think Bill Brow was a real cagey driver," Jones added. "But he was real willing to get after it and go fast."

"I would put Musson as one of the all-time great drivers," David Smith said. "He would be up there with Chip if he'd been here longer. I think the all-time best driver is probably Chip, for what he's done and the crap he drove. Some of it was really good and some of it wasn't; he made it all look pretty good. Muncey was an incredibly good driver. All you had to do was see the day when he qualified the *Such Crust*," he said, referring to the 1965 Gold Cup.

Schott picks a familiar trio.

"Musson has got to be in the top three," he said. "All-time, you gotta go Muncey, Musson, and Hanauer. And Hanauer has proved to be smart, because he got out before he got killed."

"Musson was very good, probably as good as the really good drivers," Dixon said in 1987. "He would stack up with people like Chenoweth and Muncey and Thompson, Kropfeld and those guys."

Dixon is the first to mention *Tahoe Miss* driver Chuck Thompson among the all-time greats. Thompson won two National Championships (1951-52) and 15 races and in his career, many aboard the twin-Allison step-hull *Miss Pepsi* that he first drove in 1950. He also owned and drove his own *Miss Detroit* and *Short Circuit* for several lean years.

"That guy was a balls-out driver," Dixon said. "He didn't drive good equipment very much. He wasn't one of those guys fortunate enough to get into good equipment for any real length of time. He drove some real trash. But, boy, when he was in good equipment, I saw him do some *really* good driving.

"I'd be hard-pressed if you asked who was *the* best unlimited race driver," he continued. "Muncey went through some sieges when he kind of sunk, and then he did good. Musson was really good, no doubt about it. He went fast, he had a good feel for the boat. Looking back, I don't think we could have asked for anything better. I don't think we could have done better by changing drivers. There were a few times when, on the spur of the moment, I probably would have said, 'Yeah, *anybody*.'

"But I would much rather work with a driver that occasionally you have to yank on his choke chain to slow him down than somebody you have to kick in the fanny to get going. If you've got a guy who's going really hard and fast and busting equipment, you can eventually build something that he won't break, and he'll go fast. You've got a guy who isn't going fast enough, it's almost impossible to light a fire under him to make him go. If we build the safest boat in the world, the guy isn't going to go fast unless he's inclined to. And the guys that really go fast are going to bust stuff occasionally by nature of the game. So, Musson was good," Dixon said.

The overseers of Seattle's Man of the Year sports-star award agreed, nominating Musson for its top honor following both the 1964 and 1965 hydro seasons. Musson lost in 1964 to Rick Redman, All-Coast linebacker for the UW Huskies, and the following year to John Goodwin, successful Seattle Metro League football coach. Perhaps that earned Musson some playful teasing from Bill Muncey, who won the 1962 Man of the Year award.

Musson described his own driving style in an August 1965 interview with John Owen of the *Seattle P-I*.

"When I first started out, I really blasted it," Musson said. "The *Kai* blew engines right and left. I led a lot of heats, but I won only one race. Now I drive to stay alive. I know what speed I can live with, and I stick with it. And each year the crew tries to give me a little more. In the last two years I haven't lost an engine. And we managed to beat a lot of boats that were running faster than I did, but couldn't last."

David chuckled at the reference to Musson's rookie year driving *Hawaii Kai*. His father, Burns, was part of the *Kai* crew and told his son about Musson's struggles.

"Ron had to apologize to the *Hawaii Kai* crew because he was so drunk one time he blew the hell out of the thing," David recalled. "And my dad said, 'You're gonna be fired if you don't figure out, it's serious on race day.' Ron said 'I apologize,' and the next race he drove around Muncey on the outside with the *Hawaii Kai*, and everybody said, 'You're a good guy now.'"

Chapter 28

Finishing the cabover

David Smith had developed rapport with Musson while modifying the Green Dragon's dashboard to the driver's liking. Musson had complained about instrument location, and David said he could improve the dash by seating Musson in the cockpit and learning which gauges he relies on most when racing, then mocking up a new dash.

David moved the Dragon's key instruments upward into Musson's field of view, onto a panel that ran perpendicular to Musson's face at the top of the dash, so that instead of tilting his head to read them Musson needed only to roll his eyes slightly downward. The stopwatch was moved toward the center of the dash and the less-important gauges moved to the perimeter, where the new panel bent inward toward Musson's eyes.

"Ron said it was a great idea," said David, "so Leo agreed I could build it that way, and I did a couple of other little mods on the boat for Ron."

In mid-October 1965, all attention turned to preparing the cabover for the 1966 season, and as with the Green Dragon, David again tailored the cabover's cockpit to Musson's liking.

"When the cabover first arrived at the shop, it basically wasn't finished," David said. "It had a cowling on it. Steering was in, but it wasn't really working correctly, and there was nothing else. It was just a dry hull. So I started working on it. The only thing I remember that we used out of the old boat is Ron's seat. He said, 'I want my seat,' and because he sat so far forward where the hull didn't have depth, I leaned the seat back to get his feet up, like a Formula One car. It got him lower in the boat because he didn't have to look over the motor. I did the whole cockpit installation, dashboard, pedals and all that stuff, because I'd done it on the old boat, and Ron and I worked really well together. And Leo worked on the steering."

Newspapers reported on Halloween that the *Tahoe Miss* team had ousted driver Chuck Thompson in favor of *Miss Madison* pilot Buddy Byers. "In the interest of the best operation of the boat, we are changing drivers. We think it's an ideal match of boat and driver," said *Tahoe* team manager Harry Volpi. "The *Tahoe* is the best race boat in the world," Byers pronounced.

As the holidays drew near, Ron Musson endured personal tragedy. His mother, Gayle Musson, boarded the *SS Yarmouth Castle* cruise ship in Miami with a friend and other retirees for a four-day cruise to Nassau in the Bahamas. Ron's dad, Glenn, was still battling pneumonia and opted to stay home.

In the early morning hours of Nov. 13, 1965, mattresses stacked too close to a ceiling light on the *Castle* caught fire, igniting paint cans and triggering a fast-spreading inferno. Fire alarms and sprinklers failed, and 88 of the 376 passengers died, including 23 of the 60 senior citizen club travelers. An Associated Press story reported, "Gayle Musson usually took a sleeping pill. Perhaps she died of asphyxiation in her sleep, and never awoke to the terror around her."

The *Castle* sank at 6:03 a.m. 120 miles east of Miami. Ron Musson had lost his mother.

* * * *

The sale of the 1962-65 *Miss Bardahl* to Bernie Little never materialized. Little flew to Seattle in early December 1965 to take delivery of the Green Dragon, but Ole Bardahl expressed concern that his boat had been run hard and required extensive repair. Ole and Bernie agreed to cancel the sale, and in a Dec. 8 *Seattle Times* article Bud Livesley reported *Miss Bardahl* no longer was for sale and instead would be retired to a life of display duty, much like Little's 1964 *Bud*, which was undergoing repair for promotional displays.

"We had planned to retire the *Bardahl* last year," Musson said. "There were no repairs made last season and the boat simply is not in racing condition."

Little struck a deal to instead buy the recently rebuilt *Miss Exide*, to be run in 1966 as *Miss Budweiser*. In fact, Little bought the entire Stoen brothers operation – boat, motors, trailer, equipment, tools, and crew. Bernie Van Cleave was named boat manager, to be joined by veterans George McKernan, Scott Freeman, Nelson Kinney, and Tommy Frankhouser. The new *Bud* remained housed in Seattle, now at a Boeing Field hangar, but would be registered with the St. Petersburg, Fla., Yacht Club.

Milo and Glen Stoen were done with unlimited hydroplane racing, this time for good.

In Nevada, the South Tahoe Regatta Association made it known that Bill Harrah and colleagues intended to bid big bucks for the 1966 Gold Cup, or perhaps another World Championship Regatta, and would run the race under the "Tahoe Format," which largely duplicated the Stan Donogh "fan plan" format used at Seattle in 1961. As it did in 1965, the Tahoe Format again would include assigned-lane starts, a sticking point for some hydro kingpins.

The May 2007 *Unlimited NewsJournal* contained a story written two years earlier by former Tahoe race promoter Phil Cole, who wrote that at the sport's 1965-66 winter meetings, Bernie Little called the lane starts the most dangerous thing he'd ever seen. When asked why, Little said, "All the boats got to the turn at the same time!" Harry Volpi of the Harrah organization replied, "Isn't that what we want, close competition?"

When the Tahoe group returned home and told Bill Harrah about the disparaging remarks made by Little, Lee Schoenith, Bill Brow, and Bill Muncey, a discouraged Harrah said, "I don't think we want to play under their rules anymore. Let's just cancel the 1966 race and find other ways to invest our promotional money."

An Associated Press story that ran Jan. 3, 1966, said the $77,777.77 Lake Tahoe World Championship Regatta scheduled for Sept. 17, 1966, was canceled.

Greater Seattle Inc. officials ran into trouble as well in the fall of 1965 when they announced the 1966 Seafair Trophy Race would follow the Donogh fan plan, with a winner-take-all final heat. The APBA sanctioning committee said it wouldn't approve a fan-plan race for only a $25,000 purse, citing Seattle's prize-money distribution plan that was out of step with APBA practice and a point system at odds with the rule book. Ron Musson, in his role as Western Region Unlimited Commissioner, said, "I will not approve a special race for Seattle, not for $25,000."

* * * *

Seattleites got a good look at the new *Miss Bardahl* Feb. 3 when it debuted publicly at Seattle Center as the star attraction at the Custom Auto, Hot Boat and Speed Show. One week later, on Thursday, Feb. 10, 1966, the cabover was christened by Inga Bardahl and launched at Sand Point on a typically gray Seattle winter day.

"We knew the captain out there and took him for a ride once," Vanden Berg said, referring to Captain William "Bull" Dawson, Commanding Officer of Sand Point Naval Air Station. Vanden Berg explained that the naval base was more convenient for testing than a public facility like Stan Sayres Pits, which required city permits to run there. "Just a little brown-nosing," he added, "and there were less people at Sand Point."

On the day of *Bardahl*'s launch, a who's who of hydroplaning showed up including designer-builder Ron Jones, Bill Muncey, Bernie Little, Milo Stoen, Harry Volpi, Rex Manchester, the extended Bardahl family, and hydro-beat reporters Bud Livesley (*Seattle Times*) and John Owen (*Seattle P-I*).

The new U-40 growled to life on choppy Lake Washington, but Musson cut his first run short when the gearbox misbehaved and spilled oil. He shut down, accepted a tow to the dock, and after Vanden Berg directed some adjustments Musson went out again and briefly hit 145 mph. This time the gearbox overheated and he shut down 4 miles north of Sand Point, off Sheridan Beach near Lake Forest Park.

Publicly, Musson and team voiced pleasure with *Bardahl*'s maiden run. Privately, they worried. The cabover handled well in the turns but drifted on the chutes, and it seemed to labor.

"It's a lot different sensation, sitting up front," Musson said. "You can't hear the engine. All you hear is the gearbox … it sort of sings.

"It's going to be interesting."

"Once we ran it the first time, we figured out what an *awful* pig it was," David said of the cabover. "It was plowing, you could hear the engine just screaming. That boat was big. It was 32 feet, 8,000 pounds, a thousand pounds heavier than it should be. It was beautifully built, but we had so much strut weight on that thing it would go into the corner and drop the transom. And Ron would take bigger corners, and that engine, you'd just hear it. We're thinking, we aren't going to have enough rods in the world, because we're gonna pop every engine. After the first or second time we ran that thing, we wanted to park it."

Vanden Berg voiced similar thoughts about the cabover in a 1989 interview. "The day we started running it, we wanted to build a new one. We were just going to use it for a test boat and build a new one, a picklefork."

Zuvich recalled shifting weight in the boat to lessen the strain on the motors, and many subsequent test sessions, some attended by new *Bardahl* crew member Gary Crawford.

"We moved the motor back and forth, because the boat didn't ride right," Zuvich said. "And the gearbox ran hot because Casale had never built one that size, and no one else had ever built a V-drive yet that we knew of, or could get our hands on."

As Vanden Berg noted, Casale's gearbox was chosen because, though unproven, it fell within the budget decreed by Musson and Ole. Hindsight shows that might have been penny-wise but pound-foolish.

"I know Andy Casale very well, he's a good friend of mine," said Ron Jones. "He's got this idea that gearboxes need to be built as if they're going into a bulldozer or a huge earthmover. They were massive. And that one, he had trouble building the shafts for it and getting the gears correctly heat-treated. He had to throw a couple sets of gears away. From day one, that boat had a vibration problem. It always had this little 'bzzzzzz' going on, and they tried everything to find out what was wrong. Leo told me he finally thought it was in the gearbox. He said, 'We've done everything else to eliminate it, and we can't find it. It's probably in the gearbox.' So they decided to live with it."

The team searched for answers, made changes, tested, tweaked some more, and tested again as winter gave way to spring. Baffled by the vibration, Musson asked Billy Schumacher to drive the boat, describe what he felt, and give his objective opinion about what might be causing the buzz. Schumacher did so – he drove the cabover once – but aside from suggesting it might be "rudder flutter," he also was stumped. The craft had other troubles as well.

"As soon as we started running the boat, we had problems with too much strut weight," said David. "We wondered, how are we going to shift weight? First, the oil tank came forward from the back, and we pushed the engine as far forward as possible."

Jones said, "The Casale gearbox took up like 3½ feet, so they lost a lot of engine compartment by the time they got everything in there. No place for the water-alcohol tank."

The team held meetings to explore further ideas. It wasn't practical to shift the center of gravity by lengthening the sponsons, and David offered a novel solution.

"I said, why don't we put the water-alcohol tank in the cowling? Why don't I move the batteries forward? Why don't I move the nitrous-oxide? So I chopped up the front cowling, which literally became the water-alcohol tank. I made a fiberglass tank inside the cowling," David recalled.

"There was a section right behind it that opened up, and in front we put the two nitrous bottles, and over Ron's legs were three batteries," he said. "That's how I got the weight forward, and I built all of that stuff. Then Ron wanted a headrest, so I built the little black headrest, and then we finished up different bits and pieces."

On May 4, Musson spoke with *P-I* sportswriter John Owen.

"We're making one change at a time," *Miss Bardahl*'s driver told him. "We have the balance worked out. Right now we're concerned with a vibration problem. I don't know if it's in the tail, or where. But we've eliminated about 10 problems, and if we can eliminate this one we'll be about ready to go.

"Of course, I won't really know how ready we are until I get into competition," Musson added. "Then we'll see how it reacts in racing water, surrounded by other boats. I spent 21 years sitting in the rear end of boats, and now suddenly I'm up front. It's an entirely new feeling."

Miss Bardahl graced the cover of the March 1966 *Popular Mechanics* magazine, which contained a four-page feature under Ron Musson's byline that gushed optimism. Conventional hydros, he explained, drop to around 90 mph in a turn, while the new *Bardahl* should turn at 100 mph or more, in part because of a lower center of gravity.

"It's also designed not to kite," Musson wrote. "That is, if the nose rises up, the tail should rise also. Otherwise the boat could flip over on its back or begin a porpoising motion that could end in a nose-first dive that would shatter it into matchsticks." He concluded by saying he, Ole, Jones, and the crew "think we have a real surprise in store for all the other unlimited hydro teams."

Dax thinks Musson was being charitable with his public comments. Everyone on the *Bardahl* team was competitive, all were determined to make their new boat a winner, and everyone worked hard to solve their challenges. But the obstacles were frustrating.

"That sucker was really a pig," Dax said of the cabover. "It was a motor eater. It was heavy, it didn't have enough aerodynamic area – it had a *lot* of problems. Looking back, we definitely made the right decision in '65 to yank the old boat out to go boat racing.

"Now I understand a lot more about hull design than I did back then," Dax said in 1987. "The big problem on that cabover was the center of gravity was way too far aft, and there was too much weight on the prop for the technology at the time. We didn't have props that could handle it. With a surfacing-type propeller, once you load it enough that the top blade starts to get wet, you generate a fantastic amount of lift. What happens is, if you're in a corner and get off the power, or something forces the prop down, as soon as the top blade starts getting wet and you get back on the power, it pops the back end right out. That's almost impossible to cure without a major weight change."

Vanden Berg concurred, noting the only propeller that worked on the cabover was a three-blade that provided more lift, but even that propeller wasn't ideal. The 1962-65 *Bardahl*, like most boats of its era, primarily had run two-blade props.

"We had two three-blade props, you know," Vanden Berg said. "We lost one that cracked right away, and then we had the one that came from *Maverick*. So think of the miles it had on it!"

Vancouver Sun sports columnist Denny Boyd drove south to Ballard in spring 1966 to check out the new *Miss Bardahl*. He wrote that Musson returned from lunch and "didn't look like the right kind of man to handle that much boat. His fingernails weren't dirty … he looked too short and too full of relaxed fun and too dapper. He was wearing an obviously expensive tailored suit that had his initials embroidered on the jacket cuff … he explained the lobster tails at Rossellini's that day were the best he could remember."

When Boyd asked Musson how long he thought he could stay on top in hydroplane racing, Musson noted the cabover required new driving techniques but said, "As for me staying on top, would you believe 10 years."

* * * *

The soundtrack for America's youth in mid-June 1966 was topped by the Beatles' "Paperback Writer" and "Rain," along with "Don't Bring Me Down" by the Animals, "Along Comes Mary" by the Association, "Hey Little Girl" by the Syndicate of Sound, and "Did You Ever Have To Make Up Your Mind?" by the Lovin' Spoonful. Those songs rang out from AM radios on the dashboards of trucks towing hydros to Tampa for the season-opening Suncoast Cup. Other rigs driven by older crew members likely rumbled south tuned to adult-contemporary stations playing vocalists like Frank Sinatra crooning his new hit "Strangers In the Night," or Mel Carter singing "Band of Gold," or Jack Jones belting out "The Impossible Dream," and other popular artists like Andy Williams, Harry Belafonte, and Tony Bennett.

Arriving at Tampa for Florida's first-ever unlimited hydroplane race, the boat fraternity sadly recalled a fallen brother, 1959 Gold Cup winner Bill Stead, who had died April 28 when his 85-horsepower midget airplane lost power and crashed into Tampa Bay. The Nevada cattle rancher had retired from racing years earlier but served as the unlimited drivers' representative in 1964-65. He was 42. Among those who had attended Stead's May 2 funeral in Reno were Manchester, Muncey, and Musson.

The *Notre Dame* team already had been in Tampa for two weeks, "testing and changing things" according to Rex Manchester, who told the Associated Press "the boat is handling well." Sixteen hydroplanes joined the Shamrock Lady at Tampa Bay, including the new *Miss Chrysler Crew*, powered by twin Chrysler hemis and driven by Kentuckian Bill Sterett, pilot of 7-litre champion *Miss Crazy Thing*.

Muncey was there with *Miss U.S.* (now minus the *"5"* moniker), of which he had told the Spokane Greater Sports Association earlier that spring that the boat accelerates from 90 mph to 160 mph faster than any hydro he had ever driven.

Musson told *St. Petersburg Times* reporter Red Marston the *Bardahl* team was still experimenting with the cabover, "trying to work out the bugs. It goes like a bomb in the corners but we're having trouble getting up to speed on the straightaways."

Also new was *My Gypsy*, a Bill Cantrell-Fred Dube creation that "was a low-crowned *Gale*," according to owner-driver Jim Ranger. Mira Slovak returned to racing aboard the repaired *Tahoe Miss*, now painted red and green. Buddy Byers, who had been hired away from *Miss Madison* to replace *Tahoe* pilot Chuck Thompson, never got his chance. Racing in the Jan. 15 Orange Bowl Regatta in Miami, Byers flipped his 7-litre *Chrysler Queen* and suffered serious injuries, prompting his retirement from racing.

Qualifying for the Suncoast Cup was slated to begin Wednesday, June 8, but two days earlier a tropical storm moving northward out of Honduras strengthened to become hurricane Alma, the earliest hurricane to strike U.S. soil since 1908. Winds peaked at 130 mph on Wednesday, then weakened as Alma slid northward past Tampa and crossed the Florida panhandle, but qualifying was scuttled for three days.

"I was out at two o'clock in the morning in front of the hotel, watching the palm trees bending," recalled Slovak. "It was my first hurricane."

Early Saturday morning, Bill Brow climbed aboard *Miss Budweiser*, the former *Exide*, to qualify at 106.143 mph. Musson followed in the cabover *Miss Bardahl*, circling the 2½-mile saltwater course at 103.806 mph, but late that afternoon he ran again and encountered the same troubling gearbox vibration he'd fought all spring. Race officials then waived qualifying for 1965's boats and drivers but required it for rookies and new boats.

Musson told St. Petersburg *Evening Independent* reporter Bob Chick, "We've had the boat in the water twice here and eight times previous. Despite how we finish here there's no chance of bringing the old boat out of mothballs. We're going to give this boat all the rope she needs. We're sticking with it regardless and we will make it work."

Calm weather greeted the fleet Sunday morning. Musson again drove *Bardahl* around Tampa Bay but couldn't get the gearbox to behave. *Bardahl* withdrew.

"The boat could have run but we didn't want to take any chances," Musson said. One of *Bardahl*'s crewmen was less certain, telling Chick of the *Evening Independent* that the motor was overheating to 140

The cabover *Miss Bardahl* tested on Lake Washington eight times before running on Tampa Bay, where a baffling gearbox vibration remained unsolved.
© Eileen Crimmin photo 1966, used with permission of The Crimmin Collection

Reporters described a fast, nimble new boat, but *Bardahl*'s frustrated crew portrayed an overweight, poor-handling "motor eater."
© Eileen Crimmin photo 1966, used with permission of The Crimmin Collection

Ron Musson won the highest percentage of heats entered, .517, of any post-World War II driver, as reported in the March 1974 *Unlimited NewsJournal*.
© Eileen Crimmin photo 1966, used with permission of The Crimmin Collection

Musson tested the cabover twice at Tampa and ran a lap of 103.806 mph, but *Bardahl* withdrew because of gearbox woes.
© Eileen Crimmin photo 1966, used with permission of The Crimmin Collection

degrees centigrade, adding, "There were bits of metal in the oil and the filter was clogged." David Smith recalled years later, "In Tampa, you could see the heat waves and hear that motor screaming. Fortunately, we only blew up a couple motors down there."

Such Crust also withdrew with mechanical problems, and the unraced *Miss Liberty* failed to exceed 60 mph.

Notre Dame won heat 1A at 94.537 mph followed by *My Gypsy* and *Gale's Roostertail*; *Tahoe Miss* blew its supercharger after leading the first lap and did not finish. Bill Muncey won 1B aboard *Miss U.S.* at 100.483 over *Miss Lapeer*, *Busch Bavarian* (formerly the four-seat *Bud*), and *Smirnoff*, while *Chrysler Crew* did not finish.

Smirnoff driver Cantrell suffered burned hands, though the exact cause was difficult to recall years later. "I hope he wasn't cooking breakfast for the crew," Slovak joked in 2011. Cantrell yielded the driving for subsequent heats to Chuck Thompson, an observer at the race.

Rookie Jim McCormick drove *Miss Madison* to a slow 87.195-mph victory in heat 1C over *Savair's Mist*, *$ Bill*, *Budweiser*, and *Wayfarer's Club Lady*, the renamed *Miss San Diego*. Bill Brow broke his right shoulder while driving *Bud* into the lead – and into a deep trough – in the first turn of lap one, so spectator Don Wilson quickly unretired from racing to replace Brow for the rest of the day.

"I decided to settle down after a dozen years on the circuit," Wilson later told the *St. Petersburg Times*. "Now it might be back in my blood."

Section two winners were *Budweiser* (93.360), *Miss U.S.* (100.934), and *Smirnoff* with relief driver Thompson, who ran the day's fastest heat at 103.726. Six boats earned a spot in the final: *U.S.*, 800 points; *Notre Dame* and *Madison*, 700 each; *Savair's Mist*, 600; and *Bud* and *Smirnoff*, 569.

Smirnoff roared to an early lead in choppy water but took a huge leap and smacked down hard, badly cracking its front deck, and Thompson limped home in last place. Manchester throttled *Notre Dame* to the front and won the final at 96.017 mph over *U.S.*, *Budweiser*, *Madison*, and *Savair's Mist*. Muncey's lightweight magnesium hull suffered severe sponson damage in the rough water, yet his *Miss U.S.* won the overall victory on elapsed time, nipping Manchester – whom he tied with 1,100 points – by .208 seconds.

Once again, victory eluded the driver reporters had dubbed "Hard Luck Rex."

Battered and broken, *Miss U.S.* and *Smirnoff* headed straight to Michigan for repairs, bypassing Washington, D.C., and the upcoming President's Cup. Brow also joined Muncey and Thompson on the beach, giving his broken shoulder a chance to mend in time for the Gold Cup. Wilson agreed to continue as *Budweiser*'s relief driver for the President's Cup, which he had won in 1958 driving *Miss U.S. 1*.

Chapter 29

Black Sunday

The *Bardahl* crew packed up and drove north. "I remember we had to do some hull work on the boat in between Tampa and Washington, D.C., so I drove to Fyle's in Baltimore to get some Utily plywood," David recalled, referring to the shop of boatbuilder and former *Miss St. Regis* driver Jimmy Fyle. "I can't remember exactly what we did. Another mod on the damn thing before we went to Washington."

With Muncey skipping the race, *Notre Dame* and Manchester became the favorite to win the two-day regatta on the 2½-mile Potomac River course. Organization and logistics trouble plagued the regatta before boats even got in the water. On Wednesday, Burns Smith complained that officials had no patrol boats available. "They knew we were coming in Tuesday night. There's no water and no electricity to begin with."

Crews toiled in the Hains Point pits under muggy, overcast skies Saturday, June 18, when late in the afternoon the unlimiteds got underway after the undercard limited-class hydros concluded their program.

Bob Fendler steered *Wayfarer's Club Lady* to the front in heat 1A until Bill Sterett pulled ahead in lap two, his *Chrysler Crew* sounding shrill and unlike an unlimited – more like a swarm of hornets – with its twin auto engines. Sterett barely held off Slovak and *Tahoe Miss* to win, 99.337 mph to 99.223. *Wayfarer* was third, *My Gypsy* fourth, and rookie Jim McCormick conked out early in *Miss Madison*.

Miss Madison had tested earlier Saturday morning, and crewman Lloyd Risk told the *Washington Daily News* that she probably picked up some driftwood that caused her to blow four cylinders in heat 1A, despite the crew having backflushed the motor.

Manchester throttled *Notre Dame* into first on the backstretch of lap one in heat 1B and went on to win at 96.826 mph over Jerry Schoenith in *Gale's Roostertail*, Fred Alter in *Miss Dixi Cola*, and Walt Kade, whose *Savair's Mist* died near the start.

Musson powered onto the Potomac for heat 1C in his metallic green and yellow *Miss Bardahl*, which finally ran true to her pedigree. *Bardahl* roared to the front and led all six laps to win, posting the day's fastest heat average of 101.218 mph. *Budweiser* and Don Wilson finished second, 32 seconds behind Musson at 95.238, followed closely by Warner Gardner in *Miss Lapeer*, while Norm Evans took fourth aboard *$ Bill*.

The *Seattle P-I* reported the rear-engine Dragon "showed incredible turning ability, easily the best in the fleet." Designer-builder Jones recalled the same thing, saying in 2007 that it "was probably a light year ahead of its time. It pushed really easy, it took no horsepower to make the thing go. It would go around the corner, it would come off the exit pin 20 mph faster than anyone."

Longtime hydro chronicler Eileen Crimmin wrote in her *Hot Boat* magazine account of the race, "Once again the camps marveled at the smooth turning ability of the vessel. Less impressive were its straightaway characteristics."

"Boy, she was looking at a different boat than I was! It may have looked fast through the corners, but it wasn't," said Dixon.

Crimmin also included a telling quote from Musson, who acknowledged some anxiety with the cabover because he couldn't yet anticipate its behavior like he could the previous Green Dragon.

"Things happen before I feel them and by the time I feel them it's too late to do anything but try to correct the situation," Musson said.

The *Bardahl* crew stayed late Saturday, preparing the U-40 for Sunday's action. David, responsible for the rear of the boat, performed his usual inspection of *Bardahl*'s three-blade propeller with Zyglow and a fluorescent lamp, shaded under a Bardahl car-fender cover he threw over his head.

"I'm sure we used Zyglow back in Washington D.C., because I had a place I ran an extension cord, and sometimes if you got the polarity wrong on the trailer it would bite you," David said, recalling getting shocked. "You're trying to do this and it's all wet, there's always water coming out of the back of the boat."

The propeller checked out fine, and David signed it off on the checklist. It was an old three-blade Cary propeller, made in Italy, with many laps on it. Seldom used on the previous *Bardahl* because Musson disliked it, it had propelled *Maverick* often and was a relic of Vanden Berg's late-1950s stint with that team.

"That day, we won an easy heat and the boat looked pretty good," David said of the cabover. "We got the boat all ready to go and Leo said, okay, you guys can sleep in. We didn't have to race Sunday until 1 o'clock, and we didn't want to be in the hot sweaty pits. So we were kicked back at the Twin Bridges Marriott. And we almost missed the race – we got up late, and there was a huge traffic jam, and we thought, whew! We're gonna miss this one!"

The nation's capital already was an unpleasant stop on the hydro circuit for Zuvich.

"Of all the places to race, Washington, D.C., was the worst," he said. "In that town, 98 percent of the people didn't give a shit if you were there, and they wanted you out. You raced in a sewer – debris is sticks and stuff, but our country's capital has a sewer running through it. And no one really showed up. I've never seen a president or somebody of any stature there. They kept saying it's a prestigious race, but sometimes they wouldn't pay you, sometimes they would. It's not prestigious if the people you want to be there ignore you, and if it didn't make the newspaper."

Burns Smith echoed Zuvich's sentiments in a 1977 *Unlimited NewsJournal* interview. "You name it, and it goes down that river," he said of the Potomac. "I've seen telephone poles, dead cows, rats, and any kind of garbage … normally, the water is quite rough. The patrol boat situation has been poor. The pits are on grass. If it's good weather, it's nice. If the weather is bad, you're in a swamp."

Sunday, June 19, 1966 – Father's Day – was bright and sunny with light winds at East Potomac Park as six unlimiteds entered the course for heat 2A. *Budweiser* and *Chrysler Crew* fought fiercely for five laps, but Wilson held Sterett at bay and pushed *Bud* across the finish line first at 98.468, while *Chrysler* gulped too much roostertail and sagged to sixth. *Tahoe* took second, *Lapeer* third, *$ Bill* fourth, and *My Gypsy* fifth.

"I just had to get enough points so I could qualify for the Gold Cup," said Slovak, "because I didn't race for three years and they had a new regulation."

Musson stepped into *Bardahl*'s cockpit, tightened the strap on his bright red helmet, lowered his visor, and prodded his black Rolls-Merlin to life. It snarled, puffed a little smoke, then the prop churned a foamy wake as the green hull cut a trough and lifted onto plane. Heat 2B of the President's Cup brought five other boats roaring onto the river. *Miss Bardahl*, *Notre Dame*, *Roostertail*, *Wayfarer*, *Dixi Cola*, and *Savair's Mist* maneuvered for position, with Musson snatching lane one flanked by Manchester, Alter, Fendler, and Kade; Schoenith started late and conked out quickly.

The hydros thundered across the start and into the turn with *Bardahl* again leading the way, *Notre Dame* glued to its hip. They roared up the back chute, past Gravelly Point and toward National Airport and into the turn with Musson holding a slim lead. Observers noted that *Bardahl*'s steady roostertail became jagged, and *Notre Dame* closed the gap. Accelerating onto the front chute the boats were dead even, and then *Notre Dame* nosed slightly ahead to finish lap one in first. Musson and *Bardahl* gave chase, pouring on the power at an estimated 160 mph.

At that moment *Bardahl* bounced, leaped skyward, and nosed into the water, stuffing its bow. A vast explosion of water and debris shot high above the river, out of which came the aft section of *Miss Bardahl*, tumbling down the Potomac in front of the judges' stand.

Spectators gasped in disbelief.

"We lost a blade on the propeller, which pulled off the strut and raised the back of the boat way up," Vanden Berg said later. "It nosed in, and there wasn't enough water there, and it went down and pierced the mud. There was only a few feet of water where he hit. Just broke the bow right off."

"Dixon and I were sitting on the end of the dock, those big steel Navy things," said David, "and it literally happens right in front of us. All of a sudden you see the spray and the whole thing coming apart. We looked at each other and said, 'My God, what was that?' I said, 'That's our boat.' We looked at each other. 'But Ron will be okay.' Ron will be okay is the first thing we said."

The other hydros avoided the debris and shut down. Fendler was distraught that rescue craft took so long to come to Musson's aid. Several minutes passed before Musson was brought ashore unconscious. For 10 minutes doctors worked to revive him with mouth-to-mouth resuscitation and heart massage. Dr. Herbert Ramsey said, "there was no pulse, no heartbeat that I could feel. I could find no sign of life."

"It took forever to get him out of the water," David recalled. "He had his life jacket, and he bobbed and bobbed and bobbed. They finally got him in a boat, from the boat to the shore, and then through the traffic jam."

Rex Manchester phoned home and told his wife, Evelyn, that Musson had been badly hurt. He asked her to "get up to Betty's house" to tell Musson's wife before she heard about it on the news.

Reporters wrote that Don Wilson's freckled face was streaked with tears as he knelt onshore beside his gravely injured friend. Medics took Musson to the emergency room at George Washington University Hospital, where the 38-year-old national-champion driver was formally pronounced dead at 5:03 p.m.

Meanwhile, Dax and David sat on the dock, stunned, watching debris surface around the stern of *Miss Bardahl*, which floated in front of them. Vanden Berg and others hopped on a patrol boat to retrieve it as smaller bits and pieces were brought ashore. When *Bardahl*'s hull arrived observers saw it was merely the afterplane, minus the tail but with the engine still in place. The front of the boat was gone, disintegrated.

"In that day, at the age we were, those guys were invincible," David said. "They never die. Grandparents get old and die, but they're supposed to. And then Ole got us all together and said, 'I'm sorry to tell you boys that Ron is dead. He didn't make it.'

"It was like somebody shot us with a cannon, because Ron was never supposed to die. He's our hero."

Burns Smith of the *Notre Dame* crew consoled his sons and asked if they were okay. David didn't know what to say and took a long walk in the adjacent park by himself. Then the crew puttered around the *Bardahl* camp, talked a little, and cleaned things up just to stay busy. A solemn Vanden Berg remained very quiet.

As boat crews received word of Musson's death, out in Seattle Evelyn Bardahl Manchester sped to the nearby Musson home, located on N.W. 97th near Evelyn's North Beach neighborhood. But she arrived too late.

"We were washing the dog, and I heard it on the radio," Betty later told *Seattle P-I* reporter Bill Sieverling. "Nobody called me."

Evelyn comforted her friend as best she could. Betty was in shock and later had trouble recalling the day's events. She was suddenly a single mother of three children – Robert, 18; Josette, 14; and Michelle, 2½. Ron Musson also left behind a son from a previous marriage, Glenn, as well as his retired father in Florida, also named Glenn, who just seven months earlier had lost his wife, Gayle, in the *Castle* fire.

* * * *

No one knows for certain precisely what doomed Musson and *Miss Bardahl*, but those closest to the accident feel they have fairly accurate assumptions.

"Depending on whose opinion you take, Musson getting killed in the cabover may or may not have been a freak incident," said Dixon. "I tend to think it was. I think the boat hit something." Zuvich, too, told reporters it was a strong possibility *Bardahl* hit something.

Clearly, *Bardahl*'s propeller lost a blade prior to or during the accident. After the accident, Dixon scraped his fingernail across residue on the propeller that might have come from wood. The Potomac was notorious for its flotsam.

"Conditions were lousy here," *Notre Dame* mechanic Jim Lucero said at the time. "No patrol boats, the river filthy from debris, and boats running all over the course." A July 1 *Time* magazine story about the accident described the Potomac as "often studded with beer cans, packing crates and half-submerged logs."

Vanden Berg theorized that Musson, frustrated all year by the cabover's stubborn unsolved vibration, felt it worsen when the blade began to shear, and rather than shut down kept his foot hard on the throttle. "He might have thought, 'Enough of this, let's just see where this vibration leads once and for all,'" Vanden Berg said.

Ron Jones' theory includes the gearbox, plus a propeller he thinks might have been questionable to begin with.

"There were a couple of major problems," he said. "One was the gearbox and the vibration. That gearbox was one of the reasons Ronnie died in that boat. Also, they took a propeller somebody else had owned to a guy in Ballard who used to do propeller work for all the unlimiteds. He thinned it down for them to run faster, and after the third time he said it was beyond where he wanted to go. It was too thin. So on Sunday in D.C., Ronnie got out front, and in the movies they have of that day, the first lap the roostertail was nice and long and low and very even. Suddenly, it got jagged.

"Now, the vibration may have always been the gearbox," Jones continued. "When the roostertail went jagged, a chunk of the propeller probably flew off. Now we're seeing this terrible roostertail, and *Notre Dame* starts coming up on him because he's lost speed. Just as Ronnie crossed the finish line *Notre Dame* went by him. And then he crashed. Leo told me Ronnie had run it until the blade finally flew off. The gearbox was so massive, the couplings were so massive, everything about it was just huge and heavy. Any other boat, if the propeller shears off, the first thing it does is make a pretzel out of the shaft, and it pulls the shaft right out.

"But that coupler wouldn't let it go. And the engine was *still running* with this bent piece of junk hanging out the end, whipping around, cutting the whole back end, and it picked the tail up and stuffed the nose down.

"I found out from Bob Carver, who was the great photographer of his day, where *Bardahl* went in the river was only about five feet deep," said Jones. "So the bow went right to the bottom *and stuck there*, while the rest of the hull broke off and tumbled down the river."

David's 2010 assessment of what caused the cabover to crash is similar, aside from the thinned propeller. He believed his team was far too conscientious and precautious to run questionable equipment.

"The prop broke," he said. "The controversy is whether it threw a blade or hit something. I don't know. But the whole thing was caused by the prop. When the prop threw the blade, all that mass dropped in the water and raised the transom. Once it raised the transom, the nose went in. And the nose was in front of the sponsons, and the sponsons were very shallow in the front, not like the current boats. The bow was so far under the water by the time the sponsons had something to pick it back up, it was a torpedo, and it was all over.

"The sad part about it is, Ron never came out," David continued. "He rode it in. So in front of him was a big water-alcohol tank. He had two nitrous bottles above his legs, and he had three car batteries right in front of him. All that stuff hit him. And that's what crushed him, plus the water. If you go in at 160 mph, that's what crushed him, because Ole said his chest was crushed."

Ironically, Musson had dodged disaster in a very similar mishap at Coeur d'Alene in 1960 aboard *Hawaii Kai III*. In position to win the Diamond Cup, the *Kai* threw one of its three blades off the prop in the final heat, creating a severe imbalance that ripped the strut off *Kai*'s bottom and pretzeled the prop shaft. That time, Musson merely lost the race.

* * * *

Though some distraught drivers and crew wanted to cancel the President's Cup in the wake of Musson's death, the hydro camps deliberated, regrouped, and reran heat 2B, won by *Notre Dame* at 97.192 mph ahead of *Savair's Mist*, *Roostertail*, and *Wayfarer*.

Notre Dame earned a spot in the final heat with two heat victories and 800 points, joined by *Budweiser*, 700; *Tahoe Miss*, 600; *Roostertail*, 525; *Chrysler Crew*, 495; and *Lapeer*, 450. Both Manchester and Wilson needed a 400-point victory to win the overall regatta, since *Notre Dame*'s elapsed-time margin over *Bud* was so small, 1.7 seconds.

"Don Wilson and I were really very good friends," said Slovak. "I told the guys, 'Rex and Don are fighting for points, I just want to have enough points to go to the Gold Cup.' I said, 'You guys, I'm going to stay away from you.'"

Shortly before the start of the final heat, the public-address system announced that Ron Musson had died from his injuries, casting a profoundly bleak aura over the pits and shrouding the drivers in gloom.

Well after 7 p.m., the subdued finalists gunned their mounts onto the Potomac. *Chrysler Crew* snagged the inside lane flanked by *Budweiser*, *Notre Dame*, *Tahoe Miss*, and *Lapeer*, while *Roostertail* did not start. "I had a good spot to get that buoy position, but I took the number four line," said Slovak.

Wilson and Manchester blazed into the lead through turn one and pounded up the backstretch toward the pits turn. *Notre Dame* nosed slightly ahead, leaped, settled, but then bounced twice, this time veering left with its bow high and its right sponson tilted down. A horrific sight ensued: *Miss Budweiser*'s bow speared *Notre Dame*'s bottom amid a monstrous explosion of water, debris, mangled hulls, and Wilson's body cartwheeling sickeningly through the air. The disintegrated boats sank.

"As we're getting out of the turn, these guys are fighting like banshees," Slovak said, who had held third place. "Rex was in the middle, I was on the right side, and Donnie was on the left side. If *Notre Dame* had gone to the right, he would go on top of me. I would probably hit him.

"Then I made a U-turn right away, and I jumped in, and I saw Don Wilson face down," he said. "His jacket was ripped off. And I grabbed him and turned him right-side up, holding his face up, but his face was completely oil, blood, and everything in it. And I started sinking with him – I was very sentimental and had an old jacket from many years ago, and we started sinking. Then the Coast Guard jumped in and got him out. Sad memories."

Once onshore Slovak frantically asked, "Where's Rex?" Manchester was tangled up in *Notre Dame*'s wreckage, and it took awhile before rescuers freed him and brought both drivers ashore. As with Musson, medics performed cardio-pulmonary resuscitation, but both Manchester and Wilson were pronounced dead on arrival at George Washington University Hospital.

Some officials speculated a gust of wind nudged *Notre Dame* askew, but *Lapeer* driver Warner Gardner bluntly told the *Washington Daily News*, "They were going much too fast for the water conditions. I was at 3,800 rpms and running on the ragged edge, but they were pulling away from me like I was tied to a post."

The coroner's report said Musson and Manchester died from broken necks, Wilson from a ruptured heart.

Evelyn was still consoling Betty at the Musson home in north Seattle when the phone rang. It was Ole, Evelyn's father, with the shocking news about Rex and Wilson. "They're gone. They're all gone," Ole said.

* * * *

The next day Evelyn spoke with the *Seattle P-I* about hydro racing and Rex. "He loved it. They all love it, and I suppose they will continue it. But it's sheer agony for the people who stand on the shore and watch. There is nothing worse."

Rex, 39, left behind several children including Gary, an adult from a previous marriage; Eric, 11; Kurt, 10; Wade, 8; Nancy, 7; Leslie, 3; and Mark, 1.

"I can't understand why they ran that final heat," said Betty Musson. "They must have been in shock."

Though the participants themselves decided to continue the race, Spokane *Spokesman-Review* columnist Harry Missildine chided, "at the very least you can charge the officials running the President's Cup with deplorable taste and worse judgment." Missildine recalled Musson as someone who "drove with fearless intelligence, trying never to put undue strain on the equipment, but never failing to bear down in the clutch."

"All three were family, and we lost all three of them," said Vanden Berg. Musson was the crew's friend and teammate, Manchester was Ole Bardahl's son-in-law, and Wilson had been their likeable relief driver.

"They ran more of the race," said David, "and I remember at the end we said, let's go … no, we'll watch the final heat. And again, Dixon and I are on the end of the dock watching the *Budweiser* with Donnie Wilson driving it, and Rex trying to take him on the outside. And that thing flies up, and you see the whole bottom of Rex's boat, and you see *Budweiser* stab the bottom of *Notre Dame*, right through the boat. And it all comes flying apart. Oh, God.

"Dad had already come over to console us, and because of what's happened with Ron they've got the county there, the sheriff there, the coroner there. They want to do an investigation because somebody's been killed. So those guys are milling around and then two more people get killed. So we all got sat down and drilled by these guys: 'What do you know?' Because we're right in the midst of the whole thing. It was a real mess, mess, mess."

My Gypsy crew chief Graham Heath had been a close friend of Musson since their days racing limited hydros in the 1950s, describing them as "great buddies." As recounted by APBA Unlimited Historian Fred Farley, Heath struggled to cope with Black Sunday.

"I've been in racing where bad things occurred," Heath said. "But that was the worst blow to me that's ever happened." Afterwards, he did a lot of soul searching. "I thought to myself, 'We've got to be crazy. Sane people don't do this!' But there's just something about racing. It's in your blood."

Ironically, Manchester was declared the winner of the President's Cup based on the 800 points he accumulated before the final. It was Rex's first and only race victory in an unlimited hydroplane.

* * * *

After I finished sixth grade at Lake Hills Elementary School in June 1966, Mom and I took a much-anticipated trip to California to visit my sister Judy and her husband Gordon at their Pasadena apartment. We spent an exciting day at Disneyland on June 19 enjoying rides, good food, and great company, and then left to find the car in the vast parking lot.

Once inside Gordon's trusty Studebaker Lark VIII he turned on the radio, and before he put the car in gear a national news story at the top of the hour jarred us: "Three speedboat racers died today in Washington, D.C., in violent accidents. Champion driver Ron Musson of Seattle died when his *Miss*

Bardahl disintegrated...."

Stunned, disbelieving, I tried to process the horrible news. Rex Manchester – who the newscaster cited as a father of eight – and Don Wilson also had perished. It seemed such a sick paradox: enjoying Disney's "happiest place on earth," only to learn that my childhood hero was dead.

The news cast a pall over the rest of our vacation, and I didn't learn the details of the horrific President's Cup crashes until we returned home to Seattle several days later, where the news story lingered.

* * * *

Jones suffered greatly in the wake of *Miss Bardahl*'s demise. Some critics blamed him and his unconventional cabover design for Musson's death.

"The Bardahl people wouldn't talk to me after Ronnie died, nobody, not even Leo," he said. "Later I got assigned a job as an announcer on one of the radio stations to announce the Seafair race, and I walked in the pits, and nobody would talk to me. It was a very traumatic experience. I had lost 35 pounds after he was killed, feeling that I must have done something wrong.

"But I lived through it," Jones continued. "I'm okay, and everything's fine. It's just that it takes extra time. The years go by before you can prove your point because people are so negative. They don't want you to be ahead, you can't take a big step. Keith Black told me that. When I talked to him about the '66 *Bardahl* he said people do not want you to be able to take a step. Progress in life requires intermediate steps, because people aren't ready to simply step forward. That's why it's taken me so long to get anything across, it's just people won't listen. 'Nobody runs a three-blade propeller, Jones. What's wrong with you?'"

David shared similar angst. He had been the one who configured Musson's cockpit, shifted the batteries and nitrous bottles forward to balance the boat, and proposed that the nose cowling house the water-alcohol tank.

"It didn't hit me until the next day when we started working on the boat, and I felt so bad because we started examining what happened," David said. "I checked the prop; the prop breaks. Ron gets crushed, and all the stuff he gets crushed with, I built. Well, I'm 19. I'm still a kid. And I start analyzing this thing: What happened? Why did it happen? You start looking at this wreckage that comes in, and the seat's all whacked apart. I helped build all that stuff. He's sitting in all the stuff that I built. And all of a sudden, I'm just feeling *horrible*. Me *personally*."

"We had put everything we could get up front in that boat, and the nitrous bottles were up in front of him, in the cockpit," said Dax. "After the accident, the nitrous bottles were out, all floating around, because the whole front of the boat disintegrated."

As hydroplane participants and fans struggled to cope with the deaths of three drivers, it dawned on some that for the first time since *Slo-mo-shun IV* raced in 1950, Seattle had no hometown boats on the race circuit. *Bardahl* and *Notre Dame* were destroyed, as was *Budweiser*, which as *Miss Exide* had been a Seattle boat but became Tampa-based when Bernie Little bought it.

Saddened by the deaths but undeterred, Little phoned hydro builder Les Staudacher on Monday afternoon, June 20, seeking to buy another hull in time for the July 3 Gold Cup in Detroit.

"If I can buy a boat, we'll be back in business," Little told Washington's *The Evening Star*. The next day he did so, buying a new aluminum hull Staudacher already had built on speculation. Bill Brow would drive it.

The bereaved hydro teams secured the wrecked boats' remains to their trailers and towed them home. *Notre Dame* and *Budweiser* had significant portions of their hulls ripped away. The U-7's entire bow, right sponson, cowlings, and tail were gone. Only the afterplane of *Miss Bardahl* remained, as Seattleites saw June 22 when *The Seattle Times* ran Bob Carver's photos of the wreckage. On July 7 the *Seattle P-I* ran photos of Ole Bardahl and Vanden Berg examining their splintered hulk in Ballard.

Musson's and Manchester's bodies were flown by Northwest Orient Airlines to Sea-Tac Airport on June 21, where hearses from Mittelstadt Mortuary – owned by Musson's friend, Gene Mittelstadt – picked them up.

Don Wilson was buried Wednesday, June 22, in Palm Beach, Fla. His friend and Rollins College roommate, Bill Muncey, was among the mourners. Wilson left behind his wife, Sandy, and a preschool son and daughter.

Officials overseeing the remaining 1966 race sites, particularly Greater Seattle Inc., pondered cancelling their races. In the end all decided to continue, dedicating their events to the memories of the deceased drivers.

News media questioned whether hydro racing had become too brutal and dangerous, with several conducting "man on the street" polls that showed the vast majority wanted hydro racing to continue. A common cliché response was, "The drivers would have wanted it that way."

Musson and Manchester were eulogized on Friday, June 24, in a joint memorial service at Ballard First Lutheran Church. More than 600 attendees crowded the sanctuary, including a vast segment of the hydro fraternity and scores of fans. The Rev. Peter Tengesdal described Musson and Manchester as "brave men aware of the risks."

A funeral procession more than a mile long led to Evergreen Cemetery, where the late drivers' teams served as pall bearers: Leo Vanden Berg, Jerry Zuvich, Dax and David Smith, Roger Kruse, and Gary Crawford, *Miss Bardahl*; Burns Smith, Mike Welsch, Jim Kerth, Jack Larson, Wes Kiesling, and Jim Lucero, *Notre Dame*.

"The thing that I thought was horrible is when they made a public spectacle of the funeral," said David Smith. "Oh, it was awful. We were pall bearers, and we were up in front with the family and with our team uniforms on, and I remember KING-TV in our faces. It was all on TV, and we said, my God, isn't this bad enough the way it is? And Betty and Evelyn and the whole thing. It was a horrible time."

In the days that followed, the grieving families and race teams moved forward as best they could. Vanden Berg oversaw the grim task of salvaging and disassembling the cabover's remains, working with David and Zuvich. At some point Vanden Berg removed the twisted prop shaft, strut, and propeller and took it home; years later he gave it to the Hydroplane & Raceboat Museum.

"I worked for a week on the boat at the shop, taking it apart with Leo, cleaning up," said David.

Ole Bardahl soon made public what many had assumed: He was done racing hydros. And not just for the season.

"Ole met with the crew and said we quit," recalled Roger Kruse. "He said we're closing the doors, we're

Rex Manchester and *Notre Dame* were picked by many to be No. 1 in 1966. They arrived at Tampa two weeks before the Suncoast Cup for ample testing.
© Eileen Crimmin photo 1966, used with permission of The Crimmin Collection

Musson told reporters he could not yet anticipate the cabover's handling like he could with the Green Dragon.
© Eileen Crimmin photo 1966, used with permission of The Crimmin Collection

Bardahl's forward cowling housed a built-in water-alcohol tank, with nitrous bottles and Exide batteries visible just in front of the windshield.
– used with permission of Sandy Ross

Likely cause of the fatal crash: *Bardahl*'s prop lost one of its three blades, creating a severe imbalance that ripped out the strut, twisted the shaft, jacked up the stern, and stuffed the bow.
– *Seattle P-I* collection, used with permission of the Museum of History and Industry

done racing, period."

Some speculated that Ole gave some thought to pulling the previous hull out of retirement to finish the 1966 racing season, but David said, "No, Ole was through racing. Ole's done."

Ole confirmed that in a 1980 interview with the *Unlimited NewsJournal*, saying, "No. Under the circumstances, we did not want to race."

By that time Dax already knew he would not continue with the *Bardahl* team. He paid his own way to Detroit to find another job for the balance of the summer and was hired by the *Tahoe Miss* team.

"Before I even went to work for them, I had a commitment to go into the Navy," said Dax, who entered the U.S. Navy in December 1966. "It was either that or dig foxholes, and I wasn't inclined to dig foxholes."

Inside the Ballard boat shop, all that remained of *Miss Bardahl* was a stripped hulk.

"So Leo and I took the boat on the trailer out to the Midway landfill, and we put a rope on the thing and a tractor pulled it off," David said. "The *Bardahl*'s buried there, the back of the cabover. Then he and I drove the rig back, and he fired me.

"He said, 'You're fired,' he didn't say I was laid off, or 'We're not racing anymore.' He just said, 'You have a bad attitude and it's hard to work with you.' I was hurt because of what happened. That was very strange, and I was really mad at Leo. And I thought, 'What am I gonna do?' By the time I drove home, I had a phone call from Dwight Thorn to go work on Chuck Lyford's Bardahl-sponsored airplane. So the next morning I got up and went to work. But instead of driving to Ballard, I drove to Paine Field, and didn't skip a beat," David said.

"By that time I was working at Jet Air with Dwight," said Skip Schott. "They had a Lear Jet dealership, and we were getting Chuck Lyford's P-51 ready for the Reno air races. Dwight, David and I were the crew in Reno."

* * * *

Qualifying for the 1966 APBA Gold Cup got underway Monday, June 27, on the Detroit River. The next day, Greater Seattle Inc. announced the Seafair Regatta indeed would be held Aug. 7 as planned, and the APBA commissioner confirmed all the remaining 1966 race sites also would stage their regattas based on the unanimous decision of the hydro owners and drivers. Whether a Seattle boat would race was uncertain. *Bardahl* and *Notre Dame* had been the last of the long-dominant Seattle fleet. Californian Ken Murphy, owner of the *Berryessa Belle* (formerly *Slo-mo V/Miss Seattle*), announced he was seeking a Seattle sponsor for his 15-year-old hull.

On Wednesday, Chuck Thompson steered his repaired blue and red 7,800-pound *Smirnoff* onto the 3-mile Gold Cup course and averaged 112.500 mph for three laps. Second best was Bill Brow aboard his brand new *Miss Budweiser*, which averaged 108.542. *Smirnoff*'s speed eventually dropped to second-fastest of the week when Muncey qualified the mended *Miss U.S.* at 115.138 mph.

Muncey's success was short-lived. In his opening heat on July 3, *Miss U.S.* plowed into a swell, slinging Muncey part way out of the cockpit, twisting the steering wheel in the process, and battering the hull and its hapless driver. Muncey said *Miss U.S.* turned a complete loop, landing rightside up. "I blew it into a corner and it did a 360 roll, upside down and rightside up again," the *Unlimited NewsJournal* later reported him saying.

Owner George Simon withdrew *Miss U.S.* from the Gold Cup, and the magnesium craft never raced again. "When you were out there by yourself, you could run some fast laps," Roy Duby told reporters of his time in the boat. "But in competition, when the water roughened up, you were just lost with it. Just wouldn't get the job done. It never was a complete, practical race boat."

Smirnoff and *Tahoe Miss* each won their two preliminary heats, Thompson averaging 93.103 and 100.371, Slovak averaging 94.835 and 87.040. In their heat 3A showdown, Thompson drove *Smirnoff* far out front at 110 mph after *Tahoe Miss* conked on lap one, but the heat was stopped when *Chrysler Crew* blew an engine and caught fire. *Chrysler* driver Bill Sterett, his hands slightly burned, jumped into the river. "She just blew up. It got too hot to stay, so I left," Sterett told *The Windsor Star*.

In the rerun, Thompson grabbed lane two inside of *Tahoe* but trailed Slovak slightly at the start. Surging down the front stretch, he squashed the throttle until *Smirnoff* suddenly leaped at full speed, twisted sideways, and dropped its left sponson into the river. *Smirnoff* exploded amid a cascade of spray and fragments that flew 100 feet into the air. A Coast Guard helicopter rescued Thompson, who was rushed to Detroit General Hospital with a crushed chest, broken thigh, and severe leg lacerations. About an hour later, Chuck Thompson died.

The next day Jack Dulmage, *The Windsor Star*'s sports editor, reported *Savair's Probe* driver Red Loomis' grief. "It can't be, it can't be. I was right alongside him. It was just like the *Bardahl*. There was only half his boat there," Loomis lamented, his head in his hands. "How can it be?"

Thompson had been openly bitter over being dismissed after the 1965 season by the *Tahoe Miss* team, which in 1966 was led by team manager Harry Volpi and crew chief Andy Anderson after Everett Adams shifted to another division of Harrah's empire.

"Before Chuck got killed, he comes to me and says, 'Mira, you know, I don't like your people on the Harrah's boat.' I said I know, Chuck. He said, 'Mira, I want to let you know, if you're gonna beat me, you're gonna fight for it.' And I said, 'Chuck, you know something, you're gonna fight, because I don't give up so easily, just like you don't give up so easily.' And then he gets killed."

Officials postponed the remainder of the Gold Cup until the next day. Slovak and *Tahoe* won the heat 3A restart, giving him 1,200 points. He then drove a prudent final heat and finished fifth at a mere 84.295 mph, easily securing enough points – 1,327, compared with second-place *Miss Dixi Cola*'s 1,200 – to win the 1966 APBA Gold Cup.

"It's just not the same because of Chuck," Slovak said. "It couldn't be. But we all know the risks involved."

Just two weeks after the President's Cup triple tragedy, hydro racing had lost its fourth driver. Thompson died with 15 race victories, including three straight President's Cups driving *Miss Pepsi* from 1950 – 1952 and the 1960 President's Cup aboard his self-owned *Miss Detroit*.

Most Seattleites remembered Thompson as the hard-charging gritty threat to the *Slo-mo-shuns* and the leadfoot *Tahoe Miss* jockey. Leo Vanden Berg remembered Chuck as a friend. When many race teams left the pits at the end of the day, bound for local bars, "Chuck and his wife and me and my wife would go get milkshakes together," Leo said.

* * * *

The hydro clan marched forward doggedly for the rest of the 1966 season. Boats generally ran slower than in 1965, due in part – but not entirely – to some courses shrinking from 3 to 2½ miles to condense spectator areas. Slovak and *Tahoe* won four races to earn the National Championship. Besides the Gold Cup, they won the British Columbia Cup in Kelowna, B.C.; the Diamond Cup in Coeur d'Alene; and the Governor's Cup in Madison.

Other post-Detroit 1966 winners were Bill Brow in the new *Miss Budweiser*, which won the inaugural Atomic Cup in the Tri-Cities, Wash., and the San Diego Cup; rookie Jim Ranger and *My Gypsy*, which won Seattle's Seafair Trophy Race; and Warner Gardner aboard *Miss Lapeer*, which as *Miss Spokane* had come close to winning twice, and in 1966 won the Sacramento Cup on Folsom Lake.

On Thursday of Seafair week 1966, Ole Bardahl reversed himself and confirmed he would build a new, conventional *Miss Bardahl* to race in 1967 with new driver Billy Schumacher.

"Ron (Musson) had told Ole he wanted me to replace him in the boat," Schumacher later told the *Unlimited NewsJournal*. "I got it, I'm sure, because of that."

Still reeling from the Potomac disaster, Leo Vanden Berg stepped away from hydro racing entirely and did not rejoin the Ballard team.

One Seattle-based boat did emerge to represent the host city Aug. 7 in the Seafair Trophy Race. Bob Gilliam secured sponsorship from *Hilton Hy-per-Lube* for his U-88, formerly *Fascination*, and led the field for two circuits in heat 1A with a first lap of 107.784 mph before breaking down.

Aside from Seattle, where each heat winner averaged between 100.148 and 108.870 mph, not until San Diego did the fleet approach pre-1966 speeds. *Budweiser* averaged 109.778 for a heat and 106.438 for the entire San Diego Cup regatta, while *Miss Lapeer* ripped through a 114.893-mph lap. Seattle and San Diego stuck with their 3-mile courses for 1966.

At the end of the 1966 season, the *Tahoe Miss* and *Miss Budweiser* teams gathered at Zephyr Cove, about 3 miles north of Stateline on Lake Tahoe's southeast shore, from Oct. 17-31 to assault the world straightaway speed record (Roy Duby's 1962 mark of 200.419 mph aboard *Miss U.S. 1*). Despite army-size support teams, both boats failed.

Slovak escaped serious injury Oct. 26 when the turbocharger on *Tahoe Miss* exploded in a fireball that singed him before he jumped out at 125 mph. Observers said Slovak bounced across the lake "like a skipping stone." Rescuers fished him out of the water and Dr. Cliff Wright examined him ashore, concluding Slovak's shaking was caused by cold water and a little shock. Slovak later wrote, "It's a kind accident that only requires a change of clothes."

And with that, the tragedy-laden 1966 hydroplane season mercifully drew to a close.

Chapter 30

The Checkerboard Comet

Construction on the new *Miss Bardahl* had commenced in Bardahl's Ballard boat shop the week of Oct. 23, 1966. Ole hired Ed Karelsen, a respected builder of limited hydros whose only unlimited-class hydro had been the ill-fated 1963 *Miss Exide*.

"Karelsen is a damn good builder," Ole told the *Unlimited NewsJournal* in 1980. "I had him build the boat here so I could see what he was doing. It's better than having your boat built in some far-away place where you can't keep an eye on what's going on."

With Leo Vanden Berg gone, Ole quickly named Jerry Zuvich the new *Bardahl* crew chief. Veteran crew members David Smith, Roger Kruse, and Gary Crawford would return to campaign the craft for new driver Billy Schumacher. Zuvich also added a newcomer, John Koenig.

"We called John 'Dainty.' Jerry had a nickname for everybody," David said. "Peter Carey hung around all the time, and Jerry named him 'Viola.' The crew was called the Teeny Bopper crew when that whole group came together, because Leo was gone and we were all younger. And we had the young driver, Billy Schumacher."

"I nicknamed everybody," said Zuvich. "My dad always had nicknames for people, and somehow it just seemed to catch. Breakfield was Rapid Reb. Koenig wasn't Dainty, he was Rodney Dangerfield, after the comedian. Pete Carey was Viola Flake, and he'd answer to Viola and to Viola Flake."

The new U-40 employed Karelsen design innovations like full-length nontrips on the afterplane, taller nontrips on the sponsons, and full-width frames instead of detachable sponsons. But the bottom of the hull and sponsons – so critical to performance – were carbon-copies of the 1962 Green Dragon.

"Sure was," said Schumacher. "We copied it. Exactly. If the afterplane was wider, it was only because it had to be in order to put nontrips on. The running surfaces were exactly the same."

"I got the call from Jerry Zuvich around October to go back to work on the boat," said David, who declined until Zuvich explained that Vanden Berg – who had fired David that June – was no longer with the team. "Jerry said, 'I'm the crew chief, and I want you to work here.' And I went in when they were lofting off the old boat. The Green Dragon was sitting inside the shop on barrels, and they were making drawings,"

Karelsen and his assistant, Ed Weiser, finished construction of the basic hull in mid-February 1967, at which point the *Bardahl* crew installed hardware and plumbing and fiberglassed the deck.

"I did the cockpit, the cowling, pedals and stuff, like before," said David. "I put Billy in the boat, set him up, adjusted the seat, asked him where he wanted the instruments and so forth. So I got to know him pretty well like I had with Ron, because I took care of the cockpit, and that's where they spent their time."

On April 8, 1967, *The Seattle Times* ran an article headlined "Bardahls Coming and Going," which said:

Ole Bardahl has unlimited hydroplanes coming and going.

One of Seattle's famed Green Dragons was crated and shipped east yesterday; a new Miss Bardahl will debut next week.

… By this time, the boat that won more races than any other in a long line of Bardahls will be rumbling across the Midwest somewhere on a freight car, headed for Boston and an exhibition tour of New England and the eastern seaboard.

Ron Musson's former charger was taking up residence on the East Coast, basing its exhibition roadshows out of Bardahl's facility in Norwood, a Boston suburb. Little did hydro fans suspect that when the third *Miss Bardahl* left home aboard that eastbound train, it was the last time virtually any of them would see the Green Dragon for 16 years. A strange odyssey was about to unfold.

The new *Miss Bardahl*, the fifth – and last – of its line, was unveiled at Seattle Center April 10, 1967, and launched three days later at Stan Sayres Memorial Pits. Aside from the boat's wider, flatter appearance, the biggest change was its color scheme. Gone was the familiar metallic green; in its place was bright yellow and, where yellow had previously been, pale olive green. Black bow scallops remained. Reporters felt compelled to bestow a new nickname on the boat and contrived aliases like "Gold Dragon," "Blonde Bombshell," and "Gold Lady."

"Voorhees came up with the color scheme," said David, referring to Bardahl's corporate art director who chose the yellow hull with olive-green trim. "That was the new corporate look of Bardahl, the new brand."

Ole's wasn't the only established team constructing a new hydro for 1967. Shirley Mendelson McDonald had announced at Seafair the previous summer that she would campaign a new *Notre Dame*, to be built by Les Staudacher and driven by Jim McCormick. Staudacher got an early start on the hull and delivered it to Seattle before Christmas 1966, pleasing team manager Mike Welsch and crew chief Jim Kerth.

Staudacher also built a new *Miss U.S.* for Detroit owner George Simon. Later nicknamed the "bobtailed" hydro, Simon's new boat had no tailfin, which driver Bill Muncey said was unnecessary on the shorter 2½-mile courses becoming commonplace on the circuit. Dave Seefeldt continued as crew chief with the Seattle-based team.

Muncey ran four times on April 22 out of Stan Sayres Pits on Lake Washington, telling sun-splashed observers he was "awfully pleased. I've never launched a boat that performed as well in its initial tests as this one."

Inexplicably, the Schoenith family built a new twin-Allison step-hull *Gale's Roostertail*, employing a variation on a design rendered obsolete years earlier by the *Slo-mo*s.

The *Budweiser* team had all winter to hone the new boat it launched in July 1966. Owner Bernie Little expected it to handle better, its mahogany deck having been replaced with lighter spruce after the Diamond Cup. In a preseason *Hot Boat* magazine feature, driver Bill Brow told writer Eileen Crimmin how unlimited-class competition compares with the smaller boats. "I find it much different because you are under more pressure when driving for a 'name' company. Also, considering the money involved, you drive harder to win," Brow said.

* * * *

Thirteen hydros converged at Tampa Bay for the June 11 Suncoast Cup, where Bill Brow topped qualifying in *Miss Budweiser*, the favorite to win the 1967 crown. On the first lap of the first heat, Brow lived up to his nickname of "World's fastest milkman" by roaring past *Miss Madison* in the first turn and blasting up the backstretch aboard *Bud*. Brow left the field far behind and sizzled at an estimated 170 mph across choppy water when *Bud* suddenly wobbled, kited, bounced hard, rolled and plunged nose first into the bay. Brow was rescued quickly by chopper and delivered to St. Joseph Hospital just eight minutes later.

Emergency room doctors fought for two hours to save Brow, but he never regained consciousness and was pronounced dead from severe head and internal injuries. The married Burien father of four was 41.

Another elite racer was gone. Bill Brow was the fifth unlimited driver to die in less than 12 months.

The race continued, and Schumacher took two firsts and a second to win the Suncoast Cup in *Miss Bardahl*'s first race, an uncommon feat for a new boat, although the 1958 *Bardahl* had done likewise in the Chelan Apple Cup. Schumacher then qualified the fastest at Detroit, 115.384 mph, but finished just one heat of racing on the day *Chrysler Crew*'s auto engines held together to give Bill Sterett the victory.

Zuvich faced an emergency when *Bardahl*'s wiring burned during testing in Madison, Ind. David Smith phoned the person he knew to be an electrical expert, even though that person now served in the U.S. Navy.

"Dixon was in Pensacola and was able to get a little bit of leave," David said. "I picked him up at Louisville, drove him to Madison. Dixon said to throw all of the wiring in the garbage can and gave me a shopping list. Gary Crawford and I got it, the three of us strung wires, and Dixon put it all together. And the first time it turned on, it worked."

Bardahl won two heats in Madison on July 9, including the final, to give Ole Bardahl his first-ever Governor's Cup victory, beating Chuck Hickling aboard the former *Tahoe Miss*, now renamed *Harrah's Club*. Jim McCormick was unceremoniously replaced in Madison as *Notre Dame*'s driver by veteran Jack Regas, who hadn't raced since crashing the second *Miss Bardahl* in 1959.

Two weeks later in Tri-Cities, *Bardahl* won all three heats, including a come-from-behind thriller over *Chrysler Crew* in the final, to claim the Atomic Cup. *Miss Bardahl*, young Schumacher, and the Teeny Bopper crew now had won three out of four races in their maiden season together, thanks to Zuvich and team employing a winning formula that had been battle-tested in Vanden Berg's tenure.

"The engines were built the same way, the fuel was done the same way, the nitrous was done the same way, everything was done the same way," said David. "In '67, we basically ran the engines from the cabover. We didn't even dust them off, we had 'em sitting there. We put some oil in them and we ran them. All we had to do was build a boat."

Zuvich noted one significant engine development that he implemented later, in 1968. *Miss Bardahl* ran with Mickey Thompson's forged, flat-top pistons, which the team had explored since early 1965, and which were believed to be better than *Bardahl*'s home-made welded pistons. Dixon recalled the Thompson pistons didn't knock spark plugs out of the Karelsen boat, as the welded pistons had done with the Green

Dragon, because Thompson's were full-cast pistons that transferred heat.

Although blown spark plugs may not have been a concern with the Karelsen boat, Zuvich and David recall other problems.

"We had breakdowns the year we used those Mickey Thompsons," Zuvich said. "But when the motors did hold together, they definitely made more power."

"Those Mickey Thompson pistons were a disaster," David said. "They'd get hot and stick in the combustion, break the rods off and cut the motor in half."

But in July 1967, it wasn't yet an issue.

Seventeen hydros gathered in Seattle Aug. 6 for the $55,000 Gold Cup, which was marred by an early accident. Charging at 150 mph toward the first turn in heat 1A, *Notre Dame* bounced and dug its nose, which disintegrated, and slammed to a halt in a blast of water, pitching Regas into the lake. *Harrah's Club* trailed and driver Hickling had a split-second choice: Run over Regas, or plow into *Notre Dame*. He chose the latter. *Harrah's Club* crashed over the stricken U-7, launched upward, tossed Hickling overboard and sliced sideways under the surface. Regas and Hickling survived with broken ribs.

Miss Bardahl showed her superiority that day, consistently beating her foes through the turns and casting a stubby, short roostertail on the chutes that belied her speed. "Billy the Kid" Schumacher, 24, won three of four heats and earned 1,500 points to easily capture the Gold Cup at a 60-mile race average of 101.484, later telling bystanders, "I drive just fast enough to win."

* * * *

My friend Tom persuaded his dad to drop him, Mike, and me off near the pits for Gold Cup qualifying in 1967. All three of us were 13. Access into the innermost "hot pits" was restricted, and that's precisely where every kid wanted to be, because that's where the boats and drivers were. The only way into the hot pits was with a scarce and coveted pit pass.

However, for $1 you could buy a Seafair skipper pin that allowed access into the outer pits. The only thing separating the outer pits from the hot pits was a four-foot-high chain-link fence, plus a horde of overzealous pit-security guards who patrolled in orange Union 76 vests.

We learned a scheme watching older pit-crashers: Pool your money to buy one skipper pin, which one boy uses to enter the outer pits. Rendezvous away from the gate and covertly pass the pin through the chain-link fence to your buddy, who then enters through the gate and repeats the process. After three cycles, Tom, Mike and I were in.

The four-foot barrier to the hot pits was fairly close to the action. A 30-foot fire lane separated us from the hydros and their rolling stock – so near, yet so unreachable. We yearned to touch the boats and ask their drivers to autograph our Gold Cup programs.

Tom led the way.

Tom was more gutsy than most kids, a likeable guy but not shy of a scrap. He studied the security guards, watching their patrol patterns, spotted a gap and said "Follow me!" Tom hopped over the short fence and scurried behind one of the big equipment trucks. Mike and I took a few moments to get up our nerve, then followed suit.

We enjoyed several minutes in that forbidden zone before a guy in an orange vest approached and asked sternly, "Where are your passes?" Learning we had none, he escorted us back to the outer pits, where we looked for another chance. Soon we hopped the fence again.

That happened seven times, once eliciting the warning, "Kids, if I catch you in here one more time, you're going downtown in a paddy wagon!" In between capture we collected autographs from our heroes: Warner Gardner, Jerry Schoenith, Chuck Hickling, even *Bardahl* driver Billy Schumacher, who disheartened me by showing surly annoyance at my polite request.

But we made a great friend that day: Jack Regas, former *Hawaii Kai* champion and the recently unretired *Notre Dame* driver. Jack must have liked us because he took us under his wing for an hour or so, fending off security guards. "These boys? They're okay, they're with me," he said. Other times he'd warn us, "Uh-oh, here comes security," and steer us to safety. Jack Regas, our co-conspirator. What a thrill.

My friends and I sometimes made fun of Walt Kade, a grizzled 63-year-old veteran who drove the underpowered also-ran *Savair's Mist*. Regas was pleased to watch Kade qualify that day at a brisk 107 mph. Regas stood with us at water's edge with a stopwatch in hand and said, "Wow, boys, look at him go. Come on, Walt! Keep it going!"

We got Regas' autograph and treasured our time with him. Later, on race day, I felt distraught watching him crash right in front of me. Screaming down the front stretch at the start of heat 1A, *Notre Dame* bounced badly and nosed in, disintegrating at 150 mph. Moments later the *Harrah's Club*, which had been trailing, ripped over *Notre Dame*'s carcass and launched sideways into the air, then sliced into the water. We clearly heard wood shredding as the boats collided. Regas was hurt but survived to eventually race again.

Ole Bardahl offered insight into Schumacher's character years later, when I read Ole's 1980 interview in the March 1982 *Unlimited NewsJournal* and recalled the surly reception I'd received as a 13-year-old autograph-seeker in the Gold Cup pits.

"Billy is a darn good driver," Ole said. "He's kind of hot-tempered and a lot of people don't like him because they think that he has snubbed them. But that's just his way. He's thinking about driving the boat. He's not very communicative then and doesn't like to answer a lot of questions."

* * * *

Longtime fans lament the loss of Lake Washington's 3-mile racecourse (the current course is a mere 2-miler) and the benefits that came with it. Some good, some bad.

The larger course allowed lengthy high-speed straightaway battles on its long chutes, and the viewing area extended much farther down the beach. Overnight shoreline camping was tolerated, if not permitted, making it a two-day event for hardcore fans. And Seafair was free of charge right up through the 3-mile course's final year – 1973, the revered "race in the rain" with its blazing battles between Dean Chenoweth in *Budweiser* and Mickey Remund in *Pay 'n Pak*.

The bad included rude intoxicated spectators, fistfights among drunks and hooligans, and other unruly behavior because many who attended the then-free races didn't necessarily come to watch the hydros.

Ed Karelsen built the 1967 *Miss Bardahl* in Ole's Ballard shop, with the retired Green Dragon parked in the background.
© Eileen Crimmin photo 1967, used with permission of The Crimmin Collection

The *Bardahl*s often tested at Sand Point Naval Air Station over the years, thanks to a relationship with Commanding Officer William "Bull" Dawson.
© Eileen Crimmin photo 1967, used with permission of The Crimmin Collection

Miss Bardahl, shown racing on Folsom Lake near Sacramento, became the first hydro to win six races in a season, in 1967.
– Rich Ormbrek photo, used with permission of The Crimmin Collection

Huge crowds still were the norm when Seattle hosted the 1967 Gold Cup, won by Billy Schumacher and the fifth *Miss Bardahl*.
© Eileen Crimmin photo 1967, used with permission of The Crimmin Collection

In 1968 the fifth *Bardahl* became the Checkerboard Comet, winning its second straight Gold Cup and National Championship.
© Eileen Crimmin photo 1968, used with permission of The Crimmin Collection

During the 1967 Gold Cup, when I was 13, I heard a commotion on the beach below South Dakota Street and saw a circular pack of people on the grass, cheering and exhorting. Believing a fistfight was underway I squeezed through the crowd for a look until I saw not upright pugilists, but a prone unclothed couple with a whole lot of white flesh moving vigorously. I was astounded to see bare buttocks (and more) in public and retreated across the boulevard to our family's picnic blanket, knowing full well what I'd just seen, yet not quite believing it.

* * * *

Rookie driver Mike Thomas won the British Columbia Cup in Kelowna on Aug. 19, 1967, aboard the replacement *Miss Budweiser*. Bernie Little's new standard-bearer had been the 1962-63 *Notre Dame*, later rebuilt as U-5 *Shu-Shu*, a two-seat pleasure craft. The *Bud* crew converted the Allison-powered boat to Rolls power, and after five thrilling deck-to-deck laps in the final heat at Kelowna, *Bud* outlasted *Bardahl*, which threw two rods but limped home to take second.

Schumacher got revenge Sept. 17 when he drove *Bardahl* to victory in the Sacramento Cup over Thomas and *Budweiser*, which tied *Bardahl* on points but ran a slower race overall. That sewed up the national title for the U-40, which won the San Diego Cup a week later for good measure. Despite jumping the gun in the final heat, Schumacher tallied 1,100 points for the day and finished 27 seconds ahead of Muncey in *Miss U.S.* to win his sixth out of eight 1967 races.

"I adapted to it pretty well," Schumacher said with a smile of his new boat that summer. "I had a big advantage in the corners. I felt comfortable in it. Mira Slovak would come up to me every week saying, 'That was your turn, it's my turn now.' I'd think to myself, 'Nope, sorry, my turn again!' I knew the boat would beat him."

Miss Bardahl had become the first unlimited ever to win six high-points regattas in a single season.

That fall, Schumacher announced he was done racing, saying, "I've gotten about all the mileage I can out of boat racing. It's time to get a full-time job. A person just has to be able to work more than five, six months out of the year. And let's face it, this is a very dangerous sport."

Billy the Kid had a change of heart, however, and the *Bardahl* team pressed forward with offseason work. Maris Scuya joined the crew, and the most-visible change, one that fans applauded, was a new paint scheme and streamlined tailfin for the 1967 high-point champion, which also changed its number from U-40 to U-1 to signify its national title. *Miss Bardahl* emerged in the spring of 1968 decked out in yellow and black checkerboard, earning a new nickname: the Checkerboard Comet.

"Bill Voorhees was a good friend of mine because he was a designer, and I would always talk design with him," David said, referring to Bardahl's corporate artist. "He and I did the checkerboard together. I drew cowling designs, and he would input those. I said, one thing that always stood out in boat racing was the tail on *Miss Seattle*, the checkerboard. And he said checkerboard, that's kind of cool. Bill laid one out and said, 'Why don't we checkerboard the whole boat?' Yellow and black works visually, and Bardahl really liked it because we got to romancing Autolite, so we had Autolite on the yellow valve covers."

Sadly, promising *Budweiser* driver Mike Thomas, 32, had died the previous fall, but not on the racecourse. Thomas perished Oct. 10 when a bulldozer he was loading onto a flatbed truck overturned on him in New Jersey. Undaunted, Bernie Little proceeded with plans for Ed Karelsen to build him a copy of *Miss Bardahl*, and Bill Sterett was recruited to drive the new *Miss Budweiser* for 1968.

Bardahl debuted her new colors at the June 2 Dixie Cup in Guntersville, Ala., where a tough new challenger emerged. Dave Heerensperger, sponsor of *Miss Eagle Electric* in 1963-64, had bought the *$ Bill* from Bill Schuyler in August 1967. The "new" *Eagle Electric*, repowered with Rolls-Merlin engines and driven by Col. Warner Gardner, was painted in a gorgeous scheme of Indian red, gold flake, and black. The boat was an instant contender and won the Dixie Cup with three heat victories and 1,200 perfect points, while *Bardahl* failed to finish the final heat. Ironically, the Screaming Eagle was the same hull Schumacher had driven in 1963-64 as the underpowered *$ Bill*.

Wisconsin hosted its first unlimited race June 16 on Lake Monona in Madison, where *Bardahl* enjoyed a perfect day, winning all three heats and averaging more than 100 mph for the regatta. At the other Madison, *Bardahl* won its second-straight Indiana Governor's Cup on July 7, taking two firsts and a second on the Ohio River. In a bizarre twist, Bill Muncey's *Miss U.S.* withdrew from the race after being rammed by a houseboat.

While in Madison, Ole Bardahl told sportswriters that he and Lee Schoenith were in a joint venture to develop new turbine-powered hydroplanes, according to a July 8 *Seattle Times* AP story. Bernie Little said he was doing likewise and had plans to ship his 1967 *Budweiser* hull to San Diego where "we'll drop in an Electra turbojet." However, nothing materialized.

Bardahl ran into trouble on the Columbia River in the Atomic Cup. Schumacher and Gardner won their preliminary heats and entered the final tied with 800 points, but *Bardahl* blew its engine in lap two while chasing *Eagle* and *Bud*. Gardner and the Spokane-based *Miss Eagle Electric* went on to win.

More mechanical failures vexed *Bardahl* at Seattle in the UIM World Championship, which opened with *Eagle*'s near-record qualifying run of 120.267 mph. *Eagle* and *Bardahl* met in heat 1A, where *Eagle* quickly folded. But *Harrah's Club*, driven in 1968 by Jim McCormick and repowered with huge Rolls-Royce Griffon engines, showed surprising speed and durability to beat *Bardahl*.

Harrah's Club and *Bardahl* met again in heat 2B and scorched around Lake Washington at a blistering pace before McCormick used a final burst of nitrous at the finish to barely hold off Schumacher, 109.666 mph to 109.622. *Harrah's Club* blew its Griffon in a bright flash of light as the boats crossed the line and was done for the day. *Bardahl* threw a rod at the start of the final heat that was won by *Eagle Electric*, but it was Bill Muncey in *Miss U.S.* who earned enough points to win the regatta.

Bardahl returned to form Aug. 10 at the wind-delayed Diamond Cup in Coeur d'Alene, where at dusk the Checkerboard Comet raced *Eagle Electric* through the first turn of the final heat, then cruised to victory when *Eagle* blew its supercharger. *Bardahl* tallied 1,100 points in what proved to be the final Diamond Cup. Earlier, in heat 2C, Schumacher had been surprised by rookie Tommy Fults driving *My Gypsy*, which beat *Bardahl* in a close race on the new, shorter 2½-mile course.

* * * *

I finally attended a Diamond Cup in 1968, when I was 14. *Bardahl* and *Eagle Electric* headlined a competitive field that year, and we settled on the rocky slopes of Coeur d'Alene's Tubbs Hill for the day. It was a long one.

Rising winds chopped the water into a froth, delaying heats and even nudging the official barge free of its moorings. During the long afternoon delay a group of older teens drank beer steadily in the hot sun, occasionally jumping off a rock outcropping into the lake. Suddenly a girl's shrieks pierced the air, and we rushed to see what was wrong. She stood on top of a short bluff covering her face with her hands. Below, confused teens pulled her unconscious boyfriend to shore from blood-stained water. He had jumped head first into a shallow cove and struck rock.

My friend Mike and I watched the ugly scene unfold. The semi-conscious victim's left ear was torn off, and raw flesh dangled from the side of his bloody scalp and face. The girl continued screaming and sobbing as the youth was carried off for aid. We never learned the outcome.

The final heat eventually began at 8:15, quite literally at dusk. *Bardahl* and *Eagle* locked up in a battle until *Eagle* blew its Merlin in an explosive bright flash exiting the first turn. Schumacher steered *Miss Bardahl* to victory in the fading light, nearly in silhouette, the first and last Diamond Cup win for owner Ole Bardahl.

* * * *

Eagle Electric beat *Bardahl* in a preliminary President's Cup heat in Washington, D.C., and *Bardahl* later blew while racing alongside eventual race winner *Eagle* on lap three of the final. Gone were *Bardahl*'s days of unfailing reliability. So far in 1968, the Screaming Eagle and Checkerboard Comet had fought to a draw, three race wins apiece.

Next up was the Sept. 8 Gold Cup in Detroit. *Bardahl* won its first two heats, then faced *Eagle Electric* and the now-seasoned *Budweiser* in the final. (In 1968, the Gold Cup had just three heat sections, not four.) *Bud* jumped to the front ahead of *Eagle* and *Bardahl*, which trailed in third, when *Eagle* leaped on the backstretch of lap three, slammed to the river on its side, pitched Gardner overboard and disintegrated near the Detroit Yacht Club. Gardner was rushed to Detroit General Hospital in "extremely critical condition" where he underwent surgery for severe head injuries.

In the rerun, *Bardahl* and *Budweiser* dueled side by side for three electrifying laps, sometimes less than five feet apart, until *Bud* faded. Schumacher kept his foot hard on the throttle and *Miss Bardahl* won another Gold Cup at a fast 111.248 mph final-heat average, including a record lap of 120.8 mph.

The next afternoon, Sept. 9, 1968, Warner Gardner died from his race injuries. The popular driver, winner of three races on the 1968 circuit plus the 1966 Sacramento Cup, was 52.

"Few had the infectious enthusiasm of the Colonel," wrote the *Spokesman-Review*'s Bob Larrigan. "He was the kind of man who would be immensely popular if you'd never heard of him. Quick-witted, happy, a nondrinker. His courtesy was unwavering to everyone."

Indeed, the smiling Gardner often clutched a bottle of Coke and made time for his fans and reporters. He was survived by wife Gloria, two daughters, and 17-year-old son Warner Jr., a fixture on his dad's boat crews.

Bardahl led its first heat at San Diego on Sept. 22 but conked on lap three with a busted gearbox. Schumacher won his next heat as well as the final on the new 2½-mile Mission Bay course to finish second overall, behind *My Gypsy*. At the final race of the season on Lake Carl Pleasant north of Phoenix, *Miss Budweiser* came alive and won all three of its heats to snatch the Arizona Governor's Cup. *Bardahl* finished second overall and earned a second straight boat and driver National Championship with 9,300 points.

On May 14, 1969, Evelyn Manchester announced that *Miss Bardahl* would not compete any longer. The Rolls equipment was for sale, but Evelyn expressed hope that a new automotive-powered *Bardahl* would be ready the following year. Ultimately, that never happened.

Ole Bardahl had won more races – 27 – than anyone in unlimited hydroplane history. His Checkerboard Comet had racked up 10 wins in two years, including two Gold Cups and two National Championships. Altogether, Ole's *Miss Bardahl*s won six national titles: 1958, 1963-64-65, 1967-68; and five Gold Cups: 1963-64-65, 1967-68.

"The reason I quit boat racing is that over the years it began to cost more and more to participate. It got too expensive," Ole said years later. He also acknowledged, "We were having internal changes in our marketing organization at that time and our new group was not interested in racing."

1968 also was the final year of racing for Bill Harrah, who had campaigned his *Tahoe Miss* and *Harrah's Club* boats since 1962, and for Jim Ranger, whose *My Gypsy* had raced just three seasons.

With *Miss Bardahl* retired, Schumacher sat out the 1969 season to focus on business. Shirley Mendelson McDonald ordered a new *Notre Dame* from Ed Karelsen, and David Smith was recruited to the *Notre Dame* camp because of his familiarity with a Karelsen hull. At Seafair that year, David competed against his old *Bardahl* teammates when Ole allowed Zuvich and crew to bring the Checkerboard Comet out of mothballs on short notice for a final fling.

"We decided to race the final two races more for sentimental reasons than anything else," Ole said. "Billy was unavailable, so Fred Alter took over."

Schumacher gave a different reason. "The Bardahls refused to pay me for my services. Fred drove the boat for nothing," he said in January 2012.

* * * *

When Bill Harrah quit racing, hydroplaning lost a professional, competitive, hospitable team – and also one that occasionally joined in mischievous antics.

"We had some *neat* truck races towing these boats down the road!" recalled Zuvich, laughing. "Harrah's had a great big V-16 gas truck, and we had the biggest Ford block you could get, and everybody had the biggest truck – you know, 75 mph. I had a truck that shifted at 72 mph. So try that sometime!

"The crews were a lot closer in those days, I thought, and they weren't all challenging to make dollars off each other."

"We traveled with some of the boats," said Breakfield of his 1964 experience. "Two or three times we traveled together with *Tahoe Miss*, following each other on the road. We had a contest racing from race site to race site to see who's going to be there first to get the best pit area, little contests like that. The crews all kind of hung together. We'd stay at the same hotels, partying at different places."

* * * *

In 1969, the Sylte Ranch near Rathdrum, Idaho, again was my July home. Unlike previous visits where I'd largely goofed off, '69 was the first in a series of summers where I hauled hay for wages. Entering Sammamish High School and soon to be driving, I paid for that privilege by shelling out for my portion of Mom's car-insurance fee.

The ranch paid me $3 for each ton of hay delivered, and the Ford flatbed truck held three tons, a $9 load.

We hauled three loads per day, all done by hand: the baler left rows of 50- to 70-pound bales in the field, between which someone steered the truck. One guy bucked bales onto the bed where someone else stacked them in a precise interlocking pattern. Once fully loaded, we drove inside the ranch barn and tossed the bales off the truck to someone who stacked them roof-high. By hauling one load each morning and two in the afternoon, I earned $27 per day for hauling nine tons of hay.

Bucking bales in 90-degree heat etched some vivid, lasting images: sweaty blue jeans with fabric worn through just above the knees. Relentless itch from needle-like "fuzz grass" chaff that penetrated everything. Guzzling sunbaked warm water from rinsed-out Clorox bleach bottles. Hay dust suspended mid-air in the old barn, illuminated by narrow beams of sunlight shining through holes in the shingle roof.

I returned home to Lake Hills the week before Seafair to learn that on July 23, it was announced the checkerboard *Miss Bardahl* would come out of retirement for a last-minute shot at glory. Mom gave me some Bardahl stickers that had been handed out to rally interest.

* * * *

Zuvich and crew scrambled to prepare *Miss Bardahl* for Seafair, and for most of the Aug. 3, 1969, race it looked like she might replicate *Hawaii Kai*'s 1958 feat, when the Pink Lady came out of retirement for one race – the Gold Cup – and won it. Alter had blown two motors in Seafair qualifying, perhaps not surprising since they had been borrowed by Bob Gilliam for his *Mister P's* hydro in the Atomic Cup. But on race day Alter lead-footed *Bardahl* to victory in his first two heats at 108.564 and 106.973 mph, and he posted the day's fastest lap, 113.924.

"Fearless Freddy" started the final heat on the outside, shadowed Sterett and *Budweiser* through the south turn, and then shot *Bardahl* past *Bud* into the lead entering the backstretch.

And just as quickly, *Bardahl*'s Rolls-Merlin blew. *Bud* raced on to victory, while *Bardahl*'s 800 points earned third place overall.

"I went by him like he was tied to a post," Alter lamented afterward. The *Bardahl* crew told *The Seattle Times* that their engine was "just a junker, a stock block. We blew the two good ones we had in practice."

Rather than quit while they were ahead, the *Bardahl* folks decided to make one final curtain call, at the Gold Cup in San Diego. On a foggy, breezy Sept. 28 on Mission Bay, Fred Alter and *Miss Bardahl* brought to mind musician Neil Young, who once introduced a new song by telling his audience, "It starts out kind of slow and then fizzles out altogether." The defending Gold Cup champ finished fifth – dead last – in heat 1A at 88.307 mph, took a close second to *Bud* in 2B at 102.137, but again wallowed home last in 3A at 65.288, failing to score enough points to earn its way into the final heat. It marked the final race ever for a Bardahl-sponsored hydroplane.

Miss Budweiser went on to win the Gold Cup that day, the first of 14 for owner Bernie Little, and driver Bill Sterett nipped season-points leader Dean Chenoweth for the national title by just 100 points.

Later that year, Ole Bardahl ensured there would be no more comebacks for his Ballard boat. On Dec. 11, 1969, he sold *Miss Bardahl* to Bernie Little, who sought a backup hull and said he "bought everything" – boat, engines, truck and trailer. Conflicting reports said Ole sold his stockpile of Rolls-Merlin engines to Laird Pierce, for whom Ed Karelsen was building a new *Parco's O-Ring Miss* for the 1970 season. Ex-*Bardahl* crew chief Zuvich headed up the *Parco* team that included Gary Crawford and ex-*Eagle Electric* crew chief Jack Cochrane.

During the summer of 1970, the ex-*Bardahl* hull competed early on the circuit as *Miss Budweiser II*, taking an overall third at Owensboro with young Bill Sterett Jr. driving, and ran as *Miss U.S.* thereafter. Meanwhile the boat's former driver, Billy Schumacher, suffered throughout the season with the poor-riding *Parco*, which defied the crew's endless efforts to tame it. Schumacher did enjoy one shining moment on the Potomac River when he outran Bill Muncey aboard *Myr Sheet Metal*.

* * * *

In August 1970, I attended the Seafair race without my family for the first time. My friends and I were 16 and had our licenses, soon to be juniors in high school. We were independent and on our own that day. Woo-hoo! Party time!

Because of the sheer size of the crowd, Seafair was a somewhat lax free-for-all back then, with police semi-tolerating drinking as long as people were discreet and behaved themselves. Officers already had plenty to handle with fights and obnoxious, belligerent revelers. Even underage drinking largely flew under the radar.

Several guys in our group brought beer to the shoreline below Lake Washington Blvd. and South Dakota St., near the end of the front chute of the racecourse. Top hits getting KJR and KOL airplay that day included Eric Burdon's "Spill the Wine," Three Dog Night's "Mama Told Me Not To Come," Bread's "Make It With You," and "O-o-h, Child" by the Five Stairsteps. Now, I was no angel, but hydro racing has always been far too important to me to fog the race-day experience with alcohol, so I was a teetotaler.

On the other hand, a friend of mine drank for the first time that Sunday and managed to suck down eight Rainier beers, which he then threw up along with a whole lot of pretzels. He spent part of the race lying on his back with his eyes closed, hoping his head would stop spinning.

Of course I was too immature and selfish and to think about it at the time, but I wonder what kind of impression we made on the families with kids picnicking on their blankets nearby?

* * * *

For 1971, Tony Mulherin of Augusta, Ga., bought the former *Bardahl* and raced it as *Hallmark Homes*, with Leif Borgersen driving. The prolific hull came to an end when *Hallmark Homes* crashed, ripped apart, and sank in the Ohio River during heat 1A of the 1971 Gold Cup, best remembered as the race won by the hometown *Miss Madison*.

"Muncey came over from about the number-six lane and left me 'plenty' of room," Borgersen later told the *Unlimited NewsJournal*, "but for some reason my boat went in the air over the roostertail and crashed."

Mulherin was determined to resume racing, so designer-builder Ed Karelsen brought his original *Miss Bardahl* plans to fellow boatbuilder Don Kelson, who immediately began construction of a duplicate hull.

"They actually – and I still can't believe it – built a complete unlimited in 32 days, from cutting the frames to actually having it on the water," Borgersen said, noting that a crew worked "24 hours around the clock, taking shifts."

The new U-32 *Hallmark Homes* was rushed down to Lake Washington and raced in the 1971 Seafair Trophy Race, where its rudder failed, giving spectators like me a scare when the boat veered right at 155 mph, clipped *Atlas Van Lines'* stern, and headed straight for us on shore before coasting to a stop.

Though it was a copycat hull and not the true ex-*Bardahl*, fans of the Checkerboard Comet cheered for the "32-day wonder" when it raced at Seafair the following year as *Miss Van's P-X*. Jerry Zuvich, Leif Borgersen and friends joined forces under the name "Allison Wonderland" (even though the boat was Rolls-Merlin powered) to lease the hull from Mulherin, and Borgersen finished third overall at Seafair, averaging 104.040 mph for the 45-mile regatta. The boat finished its brief career in 1973 when Jim McCormick raced it as *Red Man*.

* * * *

I got a Seafair inner-pit pass for the first time in my life in 1972, thanks to my brother Dave. I don't recall his connection, but not only did Dave's pass allow me into the pits, it gave me access to the official barge, where I watched several boats qualify.

My companion and ticket into the pits one August day in 1973 was a girl named Jane who knew Bill Muncey as a family friend. We entered the hot pits and found Muncey near his *Atlas Van Lines* hydro, where Jane greeted him with a hug. "How's your ma?" the smiling Muncey asked, and then Jane introduced us. "Bill, this is my friend Jon. Jon, this is Bill." I shook his hand and said, "It's a pleasure to meet you."

I would expect most people to answer, "It's a pleasure to meet you, too." But instead Muncey responded, "Thanks."

Thanks? Apparently Muncey took my greeting as adulation, rather than good manners. I thought he was egotistical to perceive it that way. Muncey's response further cemented my tepid feelings about him and kindled my fondness of *Budweiser* driver Dean Chenoweth, who was humble as well as a great driver. Dean had pretty decent success that year on race day, the celebrated "race in the rain."

Chapter 31

Lost: Miss Bardahl *hydroplane*

In the post-*Bardahl* years, my hydro allegiance stuck with boats and personnel connected to the U-40.

In 1970, I pulled for Schumacher and *Parco*. In 1971 Schumacher moved to the *Pride of Pay 'n Pak*, which had been converted from a twin-Chrysler cabover to a conventional Rolls-powered, rear-seat picklefork. It became my favorite boat, and it was fast. The following summer Schumacher left the team, but Billy Sterett took over and drove the *Pak* hard, especially at the 1972 Atomic Cup, which I drove to with friends in the first car I ever owned, a tan 1961 Chevy Impala four-door.

Bernie Little bought the *Pak*, which he would race as *Miss Budweiser* in 1973. I remained a *Pak* fan until the day the new boat was launched at Stan Sayres Pits in spring 1973. What a disappointment. *Pay 'n Pak*'s gorgeous gold metalflake and orange paint had been supplanted by boring white, with orange and black stripes. I've always disdained white hydros. In my mind, white is not a color. For that fickle reason, on that day I became a *Miss Budweiser* fan since it was the former *Pak*, now painted gold with red and white trim, and Dean Chenoweth was its skilled and personable driver.

What I didn't know at the time was that *Pay 'n Pak* retained a *Bardahl* connection: Dax and David Smith were on the *Pak* crew. It was to be David's last hydro job, but for Dax – who worked at the time as Dave Heerensperger's corporate Lear Jet pilot – it preceded his years with *Miss Budweiser*. When you examine Dax's work history, it speaks of sustained excellence: *Miss Bardahl*, *Tahoe Miss*, *Pay 'n Pak*, *Miss Budweiser*. All national champions, all Gold Cup winners.

In December 1973, my life took a happy new direction. While still living at home with Mom in Lake Hills and attending Bellevue Community College, I met Luanne Wiuff. We dated shortly before Christmas and began a romance that became a lifelong bond. Luanne got indoctrinated into hydros in March 1974 when we went to a chilly Lake Washington *Budweiser* test session, not far from the Columbia City dentist office where she worked. For some reason she later chose the turbine *U-95* as her favorite boat. Maybe she thought driver Leif Borgersen was cute.

In June 1974 I finished spring quarter and dropped out of college, not knowing which major to pursue. Soon I found work at Sundstrand Data Control in Redmond, the world's leading manufacturer of ground-proximity-warning computers and flight-data recorders ("black boxes," which actually are orange) for the airline industry. I earned modest but steady money, moved out on my own, and later saved enough to buy my dream car, a 1970 Chevelle SS 396. The color? Metallic green, of course. (Actually, Chevy called it Forest Green.)

That July, Luanne experienced her first "Fiasco in Pasco," the silly name we dubbed the annual Tri-Cities hydro extravaganza. In those days Kennewick police would barricade Columbia Boulevard the Saturday evening before the race, and attendees would park on the roadway itself inside Columbia Park wherever they found themselves. All-night partying ensued, and at 6 a.m. the barricade was removed, an entry fee collected, and cars dashed eastward to park on the Columbia River shoreline, where fans staked out their spots for the day.

In March 1975 I met Bob Senior, longtime hydro enthusiast and Unlimiteds Unanimous club co-founder, at a hydroplane exhibit at the Custom Auto, Hot Boat and Speed Show, held at Seattle Center Exhibition Hall. We talked boat racing, and Senior apparently reckoned I knew enough about hydros and their history to join his pool of Seafair pit-tour guides. He invited me and I eagerly accepted, knowing that tour guides received pit passes. Yes! Here was my ticket for legitimate access to the inner pits.

In August 1975 I began giving pit tours for Unlimiteds Unanimous. My dialog generally went, "Here is the Miss Such-and-Such, which is the former This-and-That...." Many Seafair visitors asked what became of the third *Miss Bardahl*, so I'd recite the East Coast display story. However, my talks with hydro buffs revealed no one who had seen or heard of the boat since the early 1970s.

That summer and again in 1976 I cheered for *Bud*, now driven by Mickey Remund, even though Billy Schumacher had returned to racing aboard *Weisfield's/Olympia Beer*. My *Bardahl* loyalty simply could not pervert me to cheer for what I perceived as a weak, distasteful brand of beer.

Luanne and I were married in August 1977 in her hometown of Yakima, honeymooned in Vancouver, B.C., and moved into a Bellevue apartment across the street from where Pat O'Day staged his 1960s rock dances at Lake Hills Roller Rink. We later bought our first home, a fixer-upper near downtown Kirkland. I continued giving pit tours at Seafair, and the "Where's *Bardahl*?" questions persisted.

* * * *

To some, my passion for hydros is a bit extreme. One of my first projects after buying our Kirkland home – and two homes since then – was to landscape the yard with rhododendrons strategically chosen for a hydro theme.

Solid-color rhodies are okay, but I prefer the two-tone variety with dark throats and lighter petals. The rhodies I chose for our home evoke hydroplane colors: "Mrs. G.W. Leak," which blooms in April, is coral and dark pink, like *Hawaii Kai III*. "Vulcan" brings to mind *Miss U.S.*, "Mrs. Tom Lowinsky" approximates *Miss Century 21*, and *Miss Spokane* is represented in both of its paint schemes: "Blue Peter" is the lilac and purple boat, and "Sappho" mirrors the U-25's final white and purple *Eagle Electric* incarnation.

We also have two *Miss Spokane* lilac bushes and one *Miss Burien* white lilac in our current yard.

* * * *

In 1979 I added another hydro gig, freelance reporter for the *Chelan Valley Mirror* weekly newspaper. Veteran 1950s-'60s driver Norm Evans of Chelan had returned to hydro racing, and he brought his sons Mark and Mitch into the sport. Figuring Chelan might like some coverage of the hometown boys, I offered to write race reports and shoot photos in return for *Mirror* press passes. Publisher Rick Gavin agreed.

It was early in 1979, during the winter, that I became so perplexed and discouraged by *Miss Bardahl*'s disappearance that I determined, "I'm gonna find that boat."

I organized all the information and rumors I'd heard, trying to chart a pattern of clues. Much of the info was contradictory. That summer in the pits I asked friends, acquaintances, and people I didn't know – boat owners, crew members, hydro "insiders," hardcore fans from Unlimiteds Unanimous – what had happened to *Miss Bardahl*. I heard lots of conjecture but nothing concrete.

Hydro racing became extra exciting in 1979. Dean Chenoweth had unretired to drive a new cabover Rolls-Griffon powered *Miss Budweiser*, which though flighty showed flashes of greatness. On Oct. 23 at Sand Point, I stood on top of *Bud*'s trailer next to owner Bernie Little as we watched Chenoweth try to break the world straightaway speed record of 200.419 mph.

After hitting 193 mph, Chenoweth went out a final time and disappeared from view to the south. "Come on, Dean, let's get this and go home," Little said aloud. Chenoweth and *Bud* reappeared roaring north past Denny Park at an estimated 215 mph when suddenly, we saw a flash of brilliant gold – the sun reflecting off *Budweiser*'s deck as it flipped. "Oh, my God, no! No!" Bernie yelled. Exploding water engulfed the boat. Dean was thrown clear and survived the crash with broken ribs, but *Bud* was destroyed.

In March 1980 I phoned Evelyn Manchester, Ole Bardahl's daughter, at the Bardahl plant in Ballard. I explained my search for the Green Dragon, and she graciously invited me over for a chat. After a grand tour of the facility on March 12 we sat in her office to talk about the boat. As I understood it, this was Evelyn's account:

Miss Bardahl was given to Bardahl's sales division after the 1965 season for display duty. The boat was shipped to Boston in 1967. Sometime later the Boston and Los Angeles sales divisions merged, which fostered some intra-company problems. A corporate lawsuit followed, during which all company communication went through lawyers. Somehow, Bardahl "lost track of the boat" until a man from the East Coast who had possession of it called Ole Bardahl. The man was restoring the hull and wanted to race it. Ole said no, it's too old and worn to race again. The company went to court to recover it, but the attempt failed.

Driving home to Kirkland from Ballard, questions lingered. Who was the man who had spoken with Ole? How did the boat look when last seen? What color was it? And where is the boat now? Evelyn had said I should ask her father because "he has a photographic memory" and was best suited to add more details. I wrote Ole a letter that evening but never heard back, and I was unable to talk with him directly in follow-up phone calls.

I wrote a story for the April 1980 *Unlimited NewsJournal* that tracked the whereabouts of 43 inactive unlimiteds. Titled "Whistling Through the Boneyards," the story ended with the Green Dragon saga and a plea for anyone with information about its location to step forward. No one did.

That summer, the San Diego race committee ran my "Boneyards" story in its souvenir race program. Again I hoped my plea in the narrative would yield *Bardahl* answers, but again I heard nothing.

Over the winter I nearly gave up. While researching the "Boneyards" article I'd learned that, without proper storage, wooden hydros (like *Bardahl*) can – and do   rot away. Many had been burned. I learned that many owners, crew chiefs, and mechanics don't share my sentimental streak, and they discard their worn boats as easily as they discard a broken piece of hardware or a worn spark plug. The odds of finding the Green Dragon intact seemed slim. Still, I questioned more people throughout the hydro fraternity. My search became an obsession.

In 1980 Luanne and I moved into a new home on Education Hill in Redmond. My early memories of the house include a bleak Christmas season mourning the Dec. 8 murder of John Lennon, and documenting *Bardahl* clues.

In the spring of 1981, a man phoned from the Detroit suburb of Taylor, Mich. Randy Roe was starting a newsletter for hydro fans. Roe shared my concern for finding *Miss Bardahl* and ran my "Boneyards" article in his first issue. Although no *Bardahl* clues surfaced, we struck up a cross-country friendship that later played a crucial role in finding the boat.

More questions, more false leads, more dead ends. Even if the boat had been destroyed, I figured there must be a witness somewhere who could verify its demise.

* * * *

In August 1981, Seattle hosted the Gold Cup on a blue-sky day that reached a record 99 degrees. After Dean Chenoweth whipped the field in his Rolls-Griffon-powered *Miss Budweiser*, my buddy Kerry and I cooled off in Lake Washington while the crowds thinned out. I used a small bar of soap from my camera bag to wash off the sweat, then drove home and showered before going to bed.

While showering I discovered my wedding ring was missing – flat-out gone from my finger.

I fretted and pondered what might have happened, reconstructing the day's events in my mind, and then realized: wading out into the lake chest-high … washing with soap … slippery suds … did my ring slip off into Lake Washington?

The next morning I phoned around and found where I could rent a metal detector. Costly, but worth it. Next I called my friend Tom VanSteenvoort, who scuba-dived as a hobby. Tom happened to be former Bardahl chemist Don VanSteenvoort's son. Would Tom meet me at Lake Washington after work and use the metal detector to search for my wedding ring? Yes, he'd be there.

Tom and his wife Laura, Luanne's friend and Kenworth Truck Co. co-worker, met us at Lake Washington that evening just before dusk. Tom scrambled to put on his gear in the fading light and walked out into the lake, slipping underwater where I had bathed. He came up once or twice, submerged, surfaced, and then walked out of the lake toward shore with his index finger pointing skyward. On its tip was my wedding ring!

Tom said when he first swam down he inadvertently kicked up silt and clouded the water, obscuring the lake bottom. So he scooted off to the side, and the instant he emerged from the muddy cloud, a slim glint caught his eye. My ring was already buried more than halfway in silt, but the fading daylight fortuitously glistened off the gold.

"The metal detector never even went off," Tom said. "If I hadn't seen your ring with my eyes, I'd never have found it."

I was elated. Later I learned it pleased Luanne too, mainly because I made such an effort to retrieve the ring. Tom was tickled simply to have helped, but Laura advocated for payback: dinner at Victoria Station, one of their favorite Seattle restaurants. So we set a double date and the four of us dined there, where I cheerfully bought the best steaks on the menu.

* * * *

My brother, Dave, was my biggest advocate when as a young adult I tried to get a toe-hold covering hydro races for the media. He encouraged my early submissions to the *Chelan Valley Mirror* and *Coeur d'Alene Press*, he arranged to have me broadcast the 1979 Seafair heat reports on Coeur d'Alene's KIOB-FM Radio, and he even met with KING-TV Sports Director Don Poier after the 1980 Seattle race to suggest a Seafair feature based on my "Whistling Through the Boneyards" article. Dave urged Poier to collaborate with me, which would bolster my writing portfolio. Poier agreed, and I mailed him a three-page outline of my story ideas on Aug. 24, 1980.

We never heard back from Poier. But the following August, KING aired a feature during its 1981 Gold Cup telecast that closely mimicked my April 1980 *Unlimited NewsJournal* "Boneyards" story, uncredited. For me it was a harsh lesson in naiveté.

* * * *

During Gold Cup race week in Seattle I was thrilled to be introduced to Leo Vanden Berg, who had generally steered clear of the hydro scene for many years. Finding Leo proved to be my best reward in the search for *Miss Bardahl*. He was friendly, gracious, receptive to my endless questions, and we hit it off right away. He later became a good friend, a man I respected for his honesty, humility, and authenticity.

Randy Roe called one night in September 1981. He'd just returned from the San Diego race, where he'd struck up a conversation with *Captran Resorts* crew chief Ron Giese. When Roe offhandedly mentioned our *Bardahl* search, Giese perked up, saying he'd met a man a few years earlier in Miami who claimed to own the boat. I thanked Roe and dialed Giese in Fort Meyers, Fla.

Giese said that years earlier, while attending the Miami race, he had met an older man who claimed to own the third *Miss Bardahl*. The boat was for sale, but Giese wasn't interested. The man also claimed to own "the largest motorcycle dealership in Daytona Beach" and said the *Bardahl* was parked on its trailer outside the cycle shop. Giese couldn't remember the man's name but thought he had his business card and promised to look for it.

On Oct. 18, 1981, hydroplane racing lost its biggest all-time celebrity. Bill Muncey flipped *Atlas Van Lines* on a lagoon in Acapulco, Mexico, while leading the field up the backstretch on the first lap of the World Championship final heat. Muncey was steering into the sun without his prescription goggles, which had broken earlier, likely hindering his ability to "read" the water. *Atlas* blew over and landed upside down on top of Muncey, who later died from the impact. He was 52 and had amassed 62 victories in his long career.

In the following months I postponed my *Bardahl* search. Giese hadn't called back, and I'd returned to college. After years of uncertainty over choosing a major, I realized I could cultivate my inclination for writing into a paying job by earning a journalism degree from the University of Washington. But first, I had to meet the mandatory foreign-language prerequisite. For two quarters I labored to learn French and balance a full credit load with my full-time job at Compugraphic Corporation, a leading manufacturer of phototypesetting equipment. It wasn't until spring break that I found time to go hydro hunting again.

I phoned Giese in Florida. No, he hadn't found the man's business card, but he thought the dealership was for Honda, Yamaha, or Harley-Davidson. He wasn't sure. I phoned the Daytona Chamber of Commerce, explained my search, and asked if someone could mail me photocopies of the Daytona Yellow Pages listing all the motorcycle dealers. (How did mankind survive before the Internet and email?) Four pages arrived via U.S. Mail on April 10, 1982.

I called every motorcycle dealer in the Daytona area, but no one had seen the *Bardahl*. I now owed the phone company a huge long-distance bill and had nothing to show for it.

On April 15, I phoned the *Daytona Beach News-Journal* to run a lost-boat ad under "Motorcycles For Sale." However, the ad manager refused to place my ad in the Motorcycles section. Frustration!

The Florida calls had been fruitless. What I needed was less-costly, long-term exposure – something like a "wanted" poster. So I created one by gluing a *Bardahl* photo on a sheet of paper with the word "LOST" in bold letters. Below that read:

Miss Bardahl hydroplane. Last seen at a Daytona Beach-area cycle dealership in mid-1970s. 30' long, possibly still painted green and yellow, may be in disrepair. Anyone with information on its whereabouts, please call Jon toll free at (number), 8 to 5 weekdays, Pacific Daylight time. Thanks!

I mailed copies of the poster with a cover letter to the Daytona Chamber of Commerce and every motorcycle dealer in the Daytona phone book – nearly 50 mailings altogether. Then I waited, hoping for a call but prepared for failure.

By May 18, 1982, I'd decided my silly posters had flopped. Driving to work, my thoughts centered on business and term papers rather than dragons and roostertails. Then came a mid-morning phone call. An unfamiliar voice said, "I understand you're looking for *Miss Bardahl*."

Stunned, I leaned forward and asked the man what he knew.

"*Miss Bardahl* is up at Lake Winnipesaukee, New Hampshire," he said. "The phone number of the guy who owns it is…."

Out of the blue, here was a man – Sammy Packard – who not only knew what *Miss Bardahl* was, he had the boat's phone number!

Packard lived in Daytona Beach. I learned years later that on Dec. 14, 1947, Sammy Packard had been one of 32 men who met at the Streamliner Hotel in Daytona Beach to create NASCAR. On the day he phoned me, Packard had walked into Robison Harley-Davidson in Daytona at the moment the manager was opening my letter. Noticing the boat photo on the poster, Packard asked to read it, then phoned me from the motorcycle shop.

Incredibly, Packard knew nothing of *Bardahl*'s owner being a Daytona resident, and he'd never seen the boat in town. (I later learned *Miss Bardahl* never had been in Florida at all.) By sheer coincidence, Packard knew the man he believed owned it – Robert Valpey, who lived 1,350 miles away in Center Harbor, N.H.

Over and over I thanked Packard, who didn't grasp the importance of his call. (It later proved to be crucial: No one else answered my posters.) I was sure I'd found *Miss Bardahl*. Its condition, though, was unknown.

* * * *

For two days I tried to reach Robert Valpey. He finally returned my call on May 20. I told him about Sammy Packard and asked Valpey if he still owned the *Bardahl*.

My heart sank at his answer: Valpey never had owned the boat. However, he knew the man who did, and Valpey had seen it five years earlier. Valpey gave me the number for Sam Rogers of Hollis, N.H., and I phoned Sam at 10 p.m. Eastern time.

Rogers was cordial despite the late hour. He talked a blue streak and offered a wealth of information. This is the *Miss Bardahl* story according to Sam Rogers, subsequently updated following a May 2012 interview:

Sometime around 1973 or 1974, word came that Bardahl was closing its packaging plant in Norwood, a Boston suburb. Everything in the warehouse eventually was liquidated except one item – *Miss Bardahl*. Ole instructed the Norwood staff either to put the boat in a museum or destroy it. They tried to give it to the Larz Anderson Auto Museum in Brookline, Mass., but the museum had no room for it.

Ted Larter, a friend of Rogers, heard from the museum about *Miss Bardahl*, and he and Rogers drove down to Norwood together "just to have a look." Rogers already owned some boats, including *Juno*, "the first hydroplane with sponsons to compete against the step hulls," which Larter had given to him. When they arrived in Norwood the Bardahl warehouse – which literally was in the process of being demolished – was empty except for the Dragon, which sat on its hydraulic trailer. The boat was beautiful, still shiny and wearing its original green and yellow colors.

Inside the office next door, Rogers and the plant manager began talking but were interrupted by an emergency phone call: The manager's son had been in a bike accident. Hurriedly, he introduced Rogers to a man named Laterno (or Letourneau), who had been hired as the comptroller to liquidate Bardahl property. Then the manager rushed off.

Rogers asked Laterno how much he wanted for the boat and was told "around $10,000." Rogers said that was way too high, thanked him for his time, and walked out. Just as Rogers and Larter reached their car, Laterno ran up from behind and said, "OK, I'll give it to you for $3,500." Rogers and Larter calculated their spare funds and Rogers offered Laterno $1,500, which he agreed to. Rogers bought *Miss Bardahl* for $1,500, paid with a personal check.

Back inside the plant, Laterno typed a crude bill of sale that read, "Sold, to Sam Rogers for $1,500. *Miss Bardahl* U-40 hydroplane and trailer. This boat may not ever be raced." Rogers signed the paper, handed over the check, and drove home with Larter. Rogers contacted his friend Bruce Barnard, who owned a former U-Haul International box truck, and a day or two later they drove down to Norwood to retrieve the boat. They hauled *Miss Bardahl* to Roger's home in Wolfeboro, New Hampshire, next to Lake Winnipesaukee, where Roger's built a temporary 18-foot by 40-foot wood shed to house it. The boat remained under cover the entire time he owned it, and he would "admire it from the bathroom window."

Rogers and his son, Joe, attended the 1975 President's Cup in Washington, D.C., where they introduced themselves to Bernie Little and Mickey Remund. They also met Jerry Zuvich, who was there racing the Billy Schumacher-driven *Weisfield's* hydro, and Sam told Zuvich he owned the old *Bardahl*. Sam said Zuvich advised that he forget any notion of racing the Green Dragon because when they retired it in 1965, it was worn out and needed major repairs.

Though within a few years *Miss Bardahl* seemed "lost" to most people in the hydro community, in early August 1975 she was conspicuous to anyone attending the Weirs Beach Boat Show near Laconia, N.H., where the U-40 was tilted on display.

In 1976, Rogers planned to move and decided he had to sell *Miss Bardahl*. One person showed interest, John Sweet. He was a man about 30 years old who would show up at Rogers' house, sit in *Bardahl's* cockpit, and dream of owning the boat. Sweet was unable to meet Rogers' full price, but Rogers finally sold it to Sweet for $1,500, plus one of Sweet's motorcycles and a sidecar.

In our May 1982 conversation, Rogers said Sweet still had it "as of two months ago," near Derry, N.H., the birthplace of astronaut Alan Shepard. "The boat is in good shape with the display engine, but no shaft. If you buy it, I'd love to tow it back to Seattle," said Rogers, adding that *Bardahl's* tail cowling and fin had been "used as a dog house for Sweet's black lab." He told me where Sweet lived and gave me some phone numbers.

I thanked Sam Rogers profusely. The next day I phoned Sweet, but all the numbers were disconnected except for one, a beauty salon. The woman who answered was aloof but, after some prodding, admitted she was Sweet's sister-in-law. She gave me the phone number for Sweet's mother in Salem, N.H. Sweet, she explained, had no phone of his own.

The next day I reached Mrs. Sweet. I explained I was a writer from Seattle doing a story on *Miss Bardahl* and needed to speak with her son. All she promised was she'd give him my message and number.

For two days I heard nothing. Crazy thoughts surfaced: What if Sweet thought I was a lawyer trying to repossess the boat for Ole? What if he didn't want anyone to know he had the boat? Might he never return my call?

Finally, he did. On May 25, 1982, I spoke with the man who owned the third *Miss Bardahl* unlimited hydroplane. This was John Sweet's story, updated with details he provided in May 2012:

Sweet lived in Salem, N.H. He'd been involved with hydros a long time, most recently as a Grand Prix-class driver. In 1976, Sweet and his father – the man Ron Giese met in Miami – bought the *Bardahl* from Sam Rogers. The boat was complete, having everything except the rudder, and rested on an old *Notre Dame* trailer. Sweet paid $1,500 cash, plus he gave Rogers a Honda 750 motorcycle and a blue My Sweet SL-110 sidecar, which Sweet manufactured. The sidecars at the time sold for $635 and the bike's value was around $1,000.

Sweet found dry rot in *Bardahl's* left sponson and intended to rebuild and race her, so he asked the Unlimited Racing Commission for a "certificate of intent to rebuild and race." But he got what he called "overwhelming resistance" from Lee Schoenith, including a steep fee for Schoenith to come to New Hampshire to inspect the boat. Sweet dropped his plans to race *Miss Bardahl*.

Earlier published accounts of this saga include a paragraph based on my May 1982 interview notes: Sometime in 1975 Rogers got a call from Ole Bardahl, who until then had been unable to trace his old hydroplane. Ole never had intended for the boat to be sold. He told Rogers, "It's mine, you don't own it, and I want it back." Rogers said, "Fine, I'll sell it back for what I paid for it – $1,500." Ole refused to "pay for something I already own." Rogers pointed out he had a legal bill of sale for it. Ole cut the conversation short, telling Rogers, "Don't you dare try to race that boat!" That was the last time Rogers heard from Ole.

In May 2012, Sam Rogers said he never heard from Ole and thinks the conversation might have been between Ole and Sweet. Yet Sweet recalls Rogers telling him the Ole story, too, when they met in 1975.

Perhaps the conversation has been lost to Rogers' memory, or perhaps after years of reflection there's a desire to sidestep a less-than-flattering exchange with a revered man who meant so much to boat racing.

Without question, if the story is accurate, it should not present Ole in a bad light. If anything it invites sympathy, considering the understandable frustration Ole must have felt after learning his most-celebrated hydroplane had been mistakenly sold, and worse, might be raced again in unsafe condition.

Sweet decided to strip the boat, replace the rotten wood, and restore it in "show" condition. But something on the boat had to change. Ever since Sweet was in the U.S. Army he'd hated the color green. After digging up photos of the 1968 *Bardahl* in old issues of *Powerboat* magazine, he painted his boat – except for the tail and cowlings – in a yellow and black checkerboard design that somewhat resembled the '68 scheme.

Sweet stored the boat indoors. While his custom-auto and sidecar shop was in business, *Miss Bardahl* hung from the rafters in the warehouse, and more than once Sweet and his co-workers bumped their heads on it. Shortly before May 1982, Sweet sold his business and vacated the warehouse. For the first time in its life, *Miss Bardahl* had no permanent shelter and was parked outdoors. Sweet had a friend named Bob Mackey (by crazy coincidence, the same name as the man who helped build *Bardahl* in 1962) who ran a truck/auto body shop in North Salem. Mackey let Sweet park the *Bardahl* alongside the shop.

I told Sweet why I was looking for the boat, at which point he said it was for sale – for $20,000. I was shocked at the high price, but Sweet explained the boat had cost him much time, labor, and inconvenience. He said he'd torn off the decking and replaced it, battens and all, before painting it checkerboard.

That blew my fantasy to pieces. Until then I'd had visions of finding the boat, buying it for around $1,000, towing it home to Redmond, and repainting it myself. Sweet asked if I wanted to buy it, but I said I had nowhere near that kind of money.

Sweet asked what I'd like to see done with the boat. "I'd like to see it come home to Seattle where people could pay tribute to it, like *Slo-mo IV* and *Miss Thriftway*," I said.

Sweet said he, too, would like to see the *Bardahl* go home to Seattle and told me to "try and find a buyer." He also said he was willing to trade *Bardahl* for a 7-litre hydro without an engine. We exchanged phone numbers and hung up. At last, I'd found the Green Dragon! Yet my hopes sagged. Who was going to pay $20,000 for an antique hydro with rotting sponsons?

* * * *

My employer from 1977-83, Compugraphic, was based in North Reading, Mass. In May 1982 a co-worker from my Redmond, Wash., district office, George Brennan, visited corporate headquarters. I called him and asked if he'd drive north and take pictures of the *Bardahl*; he did so May 26.

Five days later I received Brennan's developed 35mm slides and, for the first time since August 1965, saw *Miss Bardahl*. It was checkerboard, all right, but not an accurate replication of the 1968 paint scheme. Still, the boat seemed to be in fine shape.

Also in May 1982, a writer learned through my brother, Dave, of my *Bardahl* search. C.R. Roberts was the associate editor of *State* magazine, based in Spokane. With the Tri-Cities and Seattle races approaching, he thought a hydro story about my search would be timely.

C.R. Roberts' two-page story with photos later appeared in the August 1982 issue of *State* magazine, titled "Hydros on my mind: The Quest for *Miss Bardahl.*" Roberts reported the boat was for sale or trade, but no one stepped forward with an offer.

In early June, after finishing spring quarter at the University of Washington, I had talked with many people as I tried futilely to round up interest in bringing *Miss Bardahl* home. On June 16, 1982, I phoned Evelyn Manchester, told her I'd found the boat, described its condition, and suggested she reacquire it for display. She sounded somewhat enthused until I told her Sweet's asking price – $20,000 or trade. "That's ridiculous," she said. Which it was. I suggested she make a counteroffer or convince Sweet he'd enjoy a nice tax break if he unloaded it for next to nothing.

Evelyn explained it would be hard to store a boat that size but thanked me for the information and said she'd let me know if there was any way Bardahl could reacquire the boat. Apparently there wasn't, because I never heard back.

John Sweet phoned every few weeks during the summer to see if I'd made any progress. I told him politely he'd priced himself out of the market. He made some counteroffers concerning down payments and trades, and finally he said he'd trade the boat straight across for a jet engine. I asked around but found none, and soon Sweet quit calling.

* * * *

1982 was a difficult summer for hydro fans. Bill Muncey had died the previous fall when he flipped *Atlas Van Lines* in Acapulco, Mexico. At the Tri-Cities in July, now covering hydro races for the daily *Coeur d'Alene Press* as well as the Chelan newspaper, I watched from inside the pits as my favorite driver and acquaintance, Dean Chenoweth, took *Miss Budweiser* out for an early morning record-qualifying attempt.

Dean roared down the Columbia River frontstretch until *Bud*'s nose lifted, wavered, leaned to its left, and the big gold hydro blew over backward and landed on its back with a huge splash. I climbed atop a small building and watched the rescue unfold. I recalled witnessing Dean's Sand Point flip in October 1979 and watching as he was rolled past me on a stretcher to the aid car. That time Dean was very pale but – to my profound relief – wide awake, his eyes as big as saucers.

Now, as I looked out on the river, a rescue sled was rushing toward shore with Dean aboard, and my heart sank at the image: Kneeling over Dean was a medic, vigorously pumping Dean's chest with both palms. Instantly I sensed that Dean was gone. And he was.

* * * *

That same summer I became better acquainted with Leo Vanden Berg and his wife, Elsie. We socialized in the hydro pits and later took turns hosting each other for dinner in our homes. I remember Leo's lawn and trees in his Ballard yard, on N.W. 65th near 34th N.W., being neat and crisply trimmed.

While eating at the Vanden Berg's dinner table I mentioned in passing that our '79 Chevy Monza had developed a surge problem. Leo said it should be easy to fix and had me pull our car into his garage. Although he admitted to being a Ford guy who hadn't touched a Monza before, he pulled out his tools and quickly disassembled the carburetor. Being a "follow the directions" guy, I got nervous because Leo consulted no diagrams, no manuals. He just dove in and started pulling pieces apart.

But soon, he had the carb reassembled and told me to start the motor. It purred smoothly. Leo just smiled and tried to explain how simple the repair was, but to me, he had worked his *Bardahl* magic.

* * * *

In September 1982, Luanne and I drove our Monza south to the San Diego race. We spent time with Randy Roe and another Detroit friend, Bill Hardy, who knew about my *Bardahl* search. Hardy thought the boat belonged in Seattle and made a generous offer: He would give his 1967 national champion 145-class hydroplane to John Sweet, either in trade or as a down payment, for the *Bardahl*. Hardy's boat was in running condition, complete with motor, trailer, and a solid coat of paint.

Sweet declined the offer Sept. 29, saying that even a top-flight 145 was worth no more than a few thousand dollars. He told me to keep looking for a jet engine.

At that time life grew hectic again. Fall quarter started at the University of Washington and I spent all my time either at work, night school, or doing homework. Nothing developed with *Bardahl* over the winter, and I anguished over the thought of it sitting outside that New Hampshire garage, unprotected from the harsh New England weather. Although this was the first time the boat had ever been unsheltered, I feared that wind, rain, and snow could deteriorate the old wood hull quickly.

* * * *

An unexpected break in my quest came in May 1983. A friend at Compugraphic's Massachusetts office, Neil Stewart, subscribed to the Lawrence, Mass., *Eagle-Tribune*. In that newspaper a former Detroit resident, Kathie Neff, wrote a local-interest column. One day Stewart phoned her and suggested she do a story on the *Bardahl*. Neff remembered the boat, having attended Detroit hydro races.

The next morning Neff called, and we spoke for an hour. Knowing of Bob Williams' October 1982 announcement that he was forming the Unlimited Hydroplane Hall of Fame and Museum in Seattle, I asked Neff to write that the boat would have a home if it returned to the Northwest. On Sunday, June 5, 1983, the *Eagle-Tribune* ran Neff's article, "Long Search for *Miss Bardahl* Ended in Salem."

Not surprisingly, I got a long-distance call June 13. It was John Sweet, whom I hadn't heard from in nearly nine months. "I saw the article in the paper," he said, "and I've been giving this a lot of thought. I'd like to work a deal."

Again, my hopes soared. But was this another false alarm?

"I'm willing to drop my price," said Sweet. "I'm going through a divorce, the boat is starting to deteriorate, and I've got no place to store it. The last thing I want is for that boat to fall apart. I'd like to get about $5,000 out of it. I've got at least that much invested in time and materials."

Sweet said that after sitting outside all winter, *Bardahl*'s deck had delaminated. (Inexplicably, Sweet had not fiberglassed it before painting it checkerboard.) He took the deck off and deemed the remaining wood unblemished. "I'm willing to work in any direction to make a deal for the boat," he said.

However, his lowered price was conditional, and problematic: Sweet wanted *Bardahl* to return to Seattle along with *Joy Boy*, his 7-litre hydro built and formerly owned by Joe Gimbrone, Sweet's friend who died driving *Nordic* in a Grand Prix race at St. Timothee, Quebec, in 1978. "Gimbrone was better than Howie Benns and deserved to drive the *Budweiser*," Sweet said. "I want *Joy Boy* to be restored and go on display in your hydro museum, so people out there will know who he was and remember him." Sweet said he could weld frames onto *Bardahl*'s trailer to carry *Joy Boy* above the Green Dragon.

I shared that with Bob Williams, who groaned and said the Museum's focus was unlimited hydros, not the smaller classes. *Joy Boy* clearly was an obstacle to acquiring *Miss Bardahl*. I relayed the message to Sweet.

The next day Sweet phoned again. "I thought about this all night long," he said. "I'm willing to go a step further." Sweet generously offered to donate *Miss Bardahl* to the Museum for one dollar, but only if he – not the Bardahl company – was credited with donating the boat, and only if the agreement was legally documented. By donating the boat, Sweet would enjoy a substantial tax write-off for the next three years.

Sweet asked me to make the offer, and I phoned Williams with the news. He was thrilled.

Two weeks earlier, I had asked another Redmond co-worker to take current *Bardahl* photos. Bob Allen was at Compugraphic's North Reading plant for training, and on June 5 he drove up to North Salem and shot a roll of 35mm slides.

I met Bob Williams on June 20 at his Burien home, where I showed my *Bardahl* slides to him, his wife Shirley, and Stan Hanauer. Stan was encouraged by the boat's condition and said it would be "no problem" to restore it. Bob said Sea Galley restaurants, at that time a Seafair sponsor, had offered a generous sum to finance the recovery of the *Bardahl*.

The next day I called John Sweet and asked him to phone Bob Williams directly. They talked for the first time, and Sweet agreed to donate the third *Miss Bardahl* unlimited hydroplane to the Unlimited Hydroplane Hall of Fame and Museum for $1.

Williams called me two weeks later to say the departure date for his cross-country journey was set. Finally, someone was going to New Hampshire to tow home an icon of boating history and a slice of my past.

* * * *

On July 16, 1983, Bob Williams sat in his Burien home with Bob Burd, the Museum's historian, making last-minute plans to recover *Miss Bardahl*. Early the next morning they would leave for Salem, N.H., in a ¾-ton Ford Super Cab pickup truck generously loaned by Williams' neighbor, Gene Bolanga.

As Williams and Burd talked, they became antsy. Around 9 p.m. one of them said, "We'll never get any sleep, we're too excited. Let's go now!" And so they did.

To avoid bad weather in the northern states, they traveled south to Portland, east to Pendleton, and southeast to Boise and Ogden – past the site of *Miss Bardahl*'s 1965 Utah Cup victory – and east onto Interstate 80. When one of them grew tired he'd crawl in the back and sleep for two or three hours while the other drove. They pressed on at 65 mph through sweltering heat that topped 100 degrees. The truck had no air conditioning.

"After about 48 hours, boy, did we smell!" said Williams.

Towns and cities whizzed by: Cheyenne, Lincoln, Des Moines, Chicago. They stopped for gas only at places that sold burgers and fast food. From Toledo they followed Interstate 90 through Erie, Buffalo, Syracuse, and Worcester, then turned north to Salem, N.H., home of John Sweet and *Miss Bardahl*.

It was Monday morning, July 17, when they turned onto a rural, dirt road near Interstate 93. They had driven straight through from Burien in 60 hours, 5 minutes. Suddenly, the bleary-eyed travelers caught a glimpse of a boat through tall firs. Williams let out a yell and said, "My gawd, there it is!"

Miss Bardahl was parked outside Sweet's fiberglass shop. No one was there. After looking around, the fragrant wayfarers found the nearby Brookside Motel on old Highway 28 and checked into cabin 9. "We each took a two-hour shower, changed clothes, relaxed, and ate a good meal at a nice restaurant," Williams said. As planned, he then phoned Museum adviser George McKernan and asked him to catch the next flight from Seattle to Boston.

The next morning, Williams met McKernan at Logan International Airport while Burd began rewiring *Bardahl*'s trailer. All its tires, mounted on old-style split rims, were flat. Surprisingly, the hydraulic lift worked perfectly.

Williams had heard New Englanders are unfriendly. "Not true," he said. "I've never been treated any nicer. Once people found out we were that far from home and needed help, they were wonderful. Nobody will ever convince me New Englanders are aloof."

Chandler Serv Inc., a Salem tire dealer, sold the men four wheels, inner tubes, and tires at cost. A man at Northeast Welding in Salem opened his shop one night, worked three hours, and charged just $30 for materials and labor.

McKernan, Burd, and Sweet had a rough time rewiring the lights, delaying the trip home by a day. While the others struggled with the trailer, Williams scoured the property for boat parts. He found them buried in the weeds and scattered throughout Sweet's shop – *Bardahl*'s seat, windshield, steering wheel, magneto, carburetor, fuel pump, engine stacks, and more.

The tail section also lay outside. Bob nailed it to the hull with roofing nails, then roped it down. *Bardahl*'s Rolls-Merlin engine was loaded into the truck bed.

Sweet wrote a bill of sale, then gathered his receipts and drove everyone into town, where *Miss Bardahl*'s sale to the Museum was notarized. Williams handed Sweet $1. "John autographed the dollar and gave it back to us," Williams said. "He was great, a real nice guy."

At last Williams, McKernan, and Burd hooked up the trailer and headed home with *Miss Bardahl*.

Seven miles down the road, one of the new trailer tires went flat. They mounted the spare, an old split-rim, then stopped and had the new tire repaired. They never remounted it, though, and it was the spare that eventually took them all the way to Seattle.

Just into Massachusetts, a strong side wind hit. Burd hollered and the others craned their necks to see *Bardahl* lifting off the trailer more than a foot. They stopped, tied a huge rope around the hull and trailer, and continued on.

The men stayed in motels every night, traveling 12 hours per day. One evening they stopped at a toll booth on the Ohio Turnpike. The toll-taker eyed them dubiously and said, "You owe $7.20, but you ain't going nowhere until you tell me what that is." "It's a race boat," they said, laughing.

Nearing Chicago at rush hour, they almost got stuck on an exit ramp that funneled traffic downtown. Williams cut off a few cars as he veered over to the through-lanes. "If we'd have taken that exit, we never would have gotten out of town until 10 p.m.," McKernan said.

When the men reached Ogden and realized it was Tuesday of Columbia Cup week, they decided to

Sam Rogers bought the third *Miss Bardahl* at a liquidation sale and towed her to his home in Wolfeboro, N.H., to accompany Sam's historic *Juno* hull.
– Sam Rogers photo, used with his permission

The third *Miss Bardahl* as she appeared in May 1982, when Jon Osterberg tracked her down to then-owner John Sweet of Salem, N.H.
– George Brennan photo, Jon Osterberg collection

After *Bardahl* endured a harsh New England winter outdoors, Sweet stripped her decaying deck. Shown in Salem, N.H., May 1983.
– Bob Allen photo, Jon Osterberg collection

Sweet had intended to recondition *Miss Bardahl* and race her, but said he encountered "overwhelming resistance" from URC official Lee Schoenith.
– Bob Allen photo, Jon Osterberg collection

Leo Vanden Berg views his once-proud Green Dragon at the 1983 Tri-Cities Columbia Cup, where she was transported by Museum founder Bob Williams, left.
© Jon Osterberg photo 1983

detour through Tri-Cities. Pushing on to Seattle would leave them too tired to return for the race. On Wednesday, July 27, 1983, they arrived at Columbia Park and got permission to park behind the pits near the motorhomes.

Chuck Hickling approached Bob Williams as soon as Williams pulled in with the boat. After inspecting *Bardahl*'s display engine, Hickling offered to assemble another motor in exchange for it. Although the Dragon's dash 9 Rolls-Merlin was considered junk after throwing a rod in 1965, Hickling said it was in mint condition "compared with what we weld together nowadays."

Race officials came by two hours later. "The old-timers remembered *Miss Bardahl* and went nuts," Williams said. "They told us, 'We want her inside the pits, out on the line.' So that's what we did."

One of my biggest thrills was watching former *Bardahl* crew chief Leo Vanden Berg's face light up when he saw his old boat for the first time in nearly 18 years. The once-proud hull, skeleton-like without its deck, sat at the west end of the pits next to the current hydro fleet. Seeing the boat kindled many of Vanden Berg's memories, and he shared fascinating stories that weekend.

Following the Columbia Cup, Williams towed *Miss Bardahl* westward over the boat's old U.S. Highway 10 stomping grounds – past Ellensburg, through Cle Elum, over Snoqualmie Pass, through Eastgate, and across the Lake Washington Floating Bridge near the site of her third Gold Cup triumph in 1965. The Green Dragon was back home in Seattle at last.

Gene Bologna's truck had run perfectly. It never overheated or used any oil the entire 7,014-mile journey. Altogether the trip cost the Museum $3,500 including repairs, gas, food, and motels.

Williams pulled up to his Burien house, got out of the truck, and gazed at the rickety old boat. It had no deck. The battens were decaying and cracked. Dry rot gnawed at the entire left sponson. Corrosion covered the aluminum sheathing.

There was much work to do.

* * * *

1983 was my fifth year of covering the Evans brothers, who were doggedly determined to succeed in unlimited hydro racing. It had been a struggle, particularly after their father Norm was murdered at his Chelan home on April 11, 1981. The boys made their own way, teaming with friends to scrape together teams that ran aging hulls practically held together with baling wire and duct tape.

Mark got the first shot, driving *Evergreen Roofing* – originally the 1962 *Notre Dame* – at Tri-Cities and Seattle in 1979 and 1980. Its tired old Allison couldn't muster enough speed or stamina to qualify, despite the efforts of aging veteran mechanic Hap Dexter. Mitch joined the fray in 1980, driving the anemic Chevy-powered *KW3 Radio*, and after three seasons of trying the best he had mustered was a lap of 97.954 mph, too slow to qualify for the 1982 Emerald Cup.

But at the 1983 Emerald Cup, Mitch found success. Driving Rick Bowles' same hull, now repowered with an Allison engine and sponsored by a nearby home-security firm, Mitch drove *Island Security Systems* to a 100.727-mph lap on Lake Washington, qualifying for the race. On Sunday he made a perfect start in heat 1A and dueled for four laps with *Princess Yachts*, the Pat O'Day-owned boat driven by Brenda Jones. Mitch came from behind on the inside to pass Jones before punching a hole in his right sponson, and his bright yellow hydro sank at the dock.

No matter. It was a conquest over adversity, one that warranted *two* articles of mine that ran in the Aug. 17 *Chelan Valley Mirror*. Mitch, Bowles, and friends had turned the corner, and it was fun being friends with the rags-to-riches team.

Chapter 32

First a facelift, then a rebirth

Miss Bardahl had been gone 16 years, was found after a three-year search, and returned to Seattle. That alone was reason to celebrate. But after the excitement of the "rescue mission" had worn off, a cold fact remained: *Bardahl* was more of an emaciated albatross than a revered Green Dragon.

Bob Williams' vision was to restore *Bardahl* cosmetically to "show" condition, not to running condition. "Nothing would be worse than to restore one of those treasures and risk having it sink," he said, thinking ahead to a fleet of additional Museum hydros.

After months of searching for a workshop to cosmetically restore the boat, Williams and the Museum staff settled on a warehouse in Maltby, Wash. The rural location – 24 miles northeast of downtown Seattle, not far from the home of former *Bardahl* crewman Skip Schott – required long commutes for the work crew, but the facility was good and the rent reasonable at $500 per month. On Feb. 1, 1984, *Miss Bardahl* moved in.

Mike Allen borrowed a crane from Woodinville Lumber to lift the boat off its trailer, which Burd made his special project. For the next several weeks, Burd lived on-site in his motorhome, repairing the trailer and working on the Green Dragon.

McKernan, once a crew chief for *Bardahl* and many top-notch hydro teams in the 1950s, '60s, and '70s, set up a work plan and supervised the project in its early months. The first task was to remove the few remaining deck pieces and all rotten wood, sand and clean what remained, and repair most of the boat's battens. Key players were Burd, Norm Arndt, Dale Dutton, Harvey McLemore, and Dick Schlemmer.

Meanwhile, Hickling and Mike Baxter set to work rebuilding and painting a Rolls-Merlin display engine at Chuck's Bellevue home.

Williams, Bob Banker, and June Banker toiled inside the hull weekdays, painting the wood with brown epoxy. Roger Newton joined the team at that point and proved to be vital. Everyone who volunteered helped ensure success, but Newton and Schlemmer in particular logged monstrous hours and effort. Schlemmer teamed with Stan Hanauer every weeknight they could, plus weekends, which Schlemmer called "a great learning experience."

Once the framework was sound, workers flipped the boat and started on its bottom. Dutton, McLemore, Newton, Schlemmer, Williams, and Rocky Fridell stripped corrosion off the aluminum with buffing wheels and high-grit compound. Schlemmer and Williams stripped and buffed the nontrips on the afterplane to a mirror finish – a tedious job that took four days per side.

Newton, Schlemmer, and Burd rebuilt the sponsons. The left one was especially decayed, being the lowest and wettest point when the boat sat tilted on its trailer. Then Schlemmer and Stan Hanauer installed a new deck of 3/16-inch mahogany plywood.

Tim Ramsey, an *Atlas Van Lines* crewmember at the time, gave Schlemmer a two-night crash course on laying fiberglass. With help from Tim and Jim Olson, Schlemmer sealed the deck. Next came Newton's and Schlemmer's never-ending task of filling imperfections with Bondo and sanding by hand with wet/dry sandpaper.

Until then, I hadn't joined the *Bardahl* restoration project. From September 1983 to June 7, 1984, I was strictly a college student, taking as many as 21 credits per quarter at the UW. I'd quit my Compugraphic job so I could cram four quarters' worth of classes into three quarters and get my bachelor's degree in editorial journalism. The day after graduation, I drove out to Maltby to check on the boat.

By now Newton and Schlemmer had become the primary crewmembers. Newton worked on *Miss Bardahl* every day he wasn't on call as a Renton firefighter, and Schlemmer toiled every night after working at his daytime job at Firestone in Renton. Both used vacation time for the project.

Newton and Schlemmer asked me to help them get the *Bardahl* finished before the July 29 Tri-Cities race. I was thrilled! Not only had I found my favorite boat after a three-year search, I now was going to help with its cosmetic restoration.

For the next five weeks I worked 10 hours a day, six days a week on *Miss Bardahl*. We primed it, filled imperfections, and sanded, sanded, sanded. Then we repeated the process. Over the July 4 holiday, Newton and Schlemmer sprayed the boat with its familiar green and yellow paint. Outside the warehouse, Bob Banker painted the rebuilt trailer.

Leo Vanden Berg provided photos showing *Miss Bardahl*'s original paint scheme. John Mason, the Museum's talented illustrator, spent two days outlining, masking, and painting the boat's monikers and U-numbers.

Kirk Pagel helped around the shop and brought a sign painter, John Masterson, who hand-painted small lettering and the Bardahl detective on the boat's cowling and tail. And I had the honor of penciling and masking the "scallops" on the bow. (*Bardahl*'s original scallops had irregular curves, an imperfection that always bothered me. Mine, I thought, were better.)

One day Mason, Pagel, and I took turns sitting behind the boat's steering wheel, posing for photos like we were 10-year-old kids. Then Newton sprayed the boat with several coats of clear paint. Dutton and Olson installed the cowlings, tail, and cockpit.

Five days before the Gold Cup, Mike Allen lifted the hydro out of the warehouse with a crane and set it on its trailer. Then he lowered the Rolls-Merlin into its engine bay. Magically, that familiar old profile returned. *Miss Bardahl* looked exactly like she had in her racing days – sleek, sturdy, sparkling in the sunlight.

Several people joined us that evening to buff and polish the hull with rubbing compound and give it a thorough wash. Among the helpers was Rocky Fridell, who as a sixth-grader had toured the *Bardahl* shop in 1965 with Ron Musson. At dusk a motorcyclist drove past on nearby State Route 522, raised his fist and shouted, "*Miss Bardahl*… all RIGHT!"

On Wednesday, July 25, 1984, Ole Bardahl and Evelyn Manchester rechristened *Miss Bardahl* at a ceremony in front of the Seafirst Tower in downtown Seattle. The volunteer Museum crew stood proudly as newspaper reporters and TV cameramen recorded the long-awaited event. Among the honored attendees were Leo and Elsie Vanden Berg.

The next morning *Miss Bardahl* hit the road for Tri-Cities. She occupied the same spot in the Gold Cup pits as the year before, when she was little more than a ragged hulk. The *Tri-City Herald* ran an article July 29 recapping *Bardahl's* disappearance and recovery, along with before-and-after photos. After the Gold Cup, the boat returned to Seattle where she appeared in the Seafair Torchlight Parade and at Stan Sayres Pits during Seafair race week.

The following months found *Miss Bardahl* taking part in fairs, parades, exhibits, supermarket and auto dealer displays, and fund-raisers. After years in limbo, she had embarked on what was envisioned as a long display career.

The Green Dragon had been lost, found, and revived.

* * * *

The Unlimited Hydroplane Hall of Fame and Museum had no permanent facility to call home. President Bob Williams searched for willing partners over the next several years and became increasingly frustrated that no Seattle venue could be consummated. The Museum acquired other revered hydros, including *Hurricane IV* from the Stead family in Nevada, in 1986; the Gray Ghost *Tahoe Miss* from Harrah's auto museum, also in 1986; Muncey's Blue Blaster *Atlas Van Lines*, from the Smithsonian in April 1987; and the third *Miss Thriftway*, which had been acquired first.

By spring 1987 the Unlimited Hydroplane Hall of Fame and Museum possessed 12 hulls, and with no facility or funds to pay for indoor storage, the boats were kept wherever the Museum could safely tuck them. *Atlas* was parked in Williams' Burien carport, *Bardahl* spent a winter at Jim's Detail Shop near Sea-Tac Airport, and in September 1988 Williams reported that eight Museum boats had to be moved from the Garbush residence near South Park to temporary storage because of "a very serious torching threat." *Thriftway* ended up parked at an RV dealer on the west side of Interstate 5 near Fife.

Former *State* magazine writer C.R. Roberts, who had joined the Tacoma *News Tribune* as a columnist in April 1987, saw the Nifty Thrifty decaying in the elements and described her vividly in a story that ran March 7, 1989. "Rust curdles on the edges of her speedometer and rot bubbles under her deck … warped wood swells her hull. Her paint flakes, it chips, it breaks," he wrote.

Soon after Roberts' column appeared, the City of Tacoma offered Williams the Tacoma Municipal Dock, a waterfront facility and former Mosquito Fleet port that needed extensive renovation. Elated to finally have a suitor – he had even considered a Museum site in distant Monroe – Williams announced in 1989 the Museum was "racing to Tacoma" to accept a 30-year lease, which he signed March 21, 1990. Williams and his colleagues aimed to raise $5.3 million to transform and reopen the building.

But the Tacoma deal never materialized.

Instead, Bob and Shirley Williams retired, and their Museum merged in June 1991 with the Antique Raceboat Foundation, located in a 5,000 square-foot warehouse at 1605 South 93rd Street in Seattle's South Park industrial area. The Foundation had restored *Slo-mo-shun IV* to running condition in 1990, and in 1991 it did likewise with *Breathless II*, configuring it to replicate the *Hawaii Kai III* that had been burned near Edgar Kaiser's Orcas Island estate in a 1974 "Viking funeral."

Philosophically, the Museum and the Foundation differed. The Museum believed its hydros should be cosmetically restored and then preserved against any risk of damage, while the Foundation believed its boats, being *boats*, should be fully restored to run on the water. The merged entity carried on the Foundation philosophy.

Dr. Ken Muscatel took the helm of what soon was renamed the Hydroplane and Raceboat Museum. Its cramped South Park site became home to a select few of the vintage hulls, including the Blue Blaster *Atlas*, the "quasi *Kai*," and while it remained on loan, *Slo-mo IV*. With insufficient space and no options for donated indoor storage, Muscatel chose to put much of the fleet up for "adoption" by friends of the Museum who owned indoor or covered storage. Some hulls were sold to private collectors to settle existing Museum debt.

"Those boats are not under our direct control, though by sale agreement they may be loaned to the Museum for display from time to time," Muscatel told the *Unlimited NewsJournal* in 1992. "Foster parents will restore those boats to running form as their time, efforts, and funds allow."

Miss Bardahl – like the rest of the original Museum's fleet – had been relegated outdoors for several years and was losing her luster. Curt Erickson of Eatonville, Wash., an associate of the Museum, had become *Bardahl*'s "foster parent" in 1989 when he took possession of the Green Dragon and parked it in a metal storage building near his home on Tanwax Lake, intending to refurbish it to running condition.

* * * *

On Aug. 11, 1989, Ole Bardahl died of emphysema at age 87 at Ballard Community Hospital, which he had helped establish. He left behind wife Inga, with whom he had celebrated their 65th wedding anniversary a month earlier, and who lived until May 20, 2001, when she died at 98 in the family home above Golden Gardens Park in Ballard.

The Seattle Times quoted daughter Evelyn McNeil saying her mother's cooking was legendary, producing lamb and cabbage, fish cakes, meatballs, and an estimated 1 million Norwegian pancakes. McNeil said her father could be in a business meeting, answer a phone call, and suddenly bolt from the room. "Mother said the soup's on," he'd say.

The progeny of another longtime hydro family got his big break in 1991. Mark Evans was tabbed to drive the *American Spirit*, a veteran turbine-powered craft managed by acclaimed boatbuilder Ron Jones Jr., son of Ron and grandchild of Ted. Mark joined younger brother Mitch as a full-time competitor on the hydro circuit and won the Indiana Governor's Cup that season, his first of 10 career wins. With Mark and Mitch's hometown of Chelan just a 45-minute drive from Wenatchee, *The Wenatchee World* daily newspaper sought coverage, and sports editor Nick Babcock added me as a contributing hydro beat writer in June 1991, an enjoyable association that continues today.

* * * *

Fresh off its success with *Miss America VIII*, *Slo-mo IV*, and the quasi *Kai*, the Hydroplane and Raceboat Museum took on a colossal task and fully restored Stan Sayres' second unlimited, *Slo-mo-shun V*, which Muscatel drove at Seafair in 1993. Next, the Museum restored the 1959 *Miss Thriftway*, which was relaunched by then-owner Joe Frauenheim at Tri-Cities on July 30, 1994, and ran an exhibition at Seafair with *Slo-mo V* and the quasi-*Kai*. Barb Carper bought the ivory and persimmon *Thriftway* in early 1995. Subsequent Museum restorations included the 1960 *Miss Burien* and 1967 *Miss Budweiser*.

In early 1999 I reveled in a dream come true. My employer, PEMCO Insurance, where I oversaw communications and advertising, agreed to sponsor two Seafair events to help mark PEMCO's and Seafair's 50th anniversaries. The first event was a June 26 re-enactment of *Slo-mo IV*'s mile record run at Sand Point, and the second was an Aug. 8 exhibition race between six vintage hydros during the General Motors Cup at Seafair.

I was on point for our Seafair partnerships, a role I enjoyed for four summers after our marketing director, Rod Brooks, renewed the PEMCO Classic each year through 2002. I had the ideal job, getting paid to help manage a hydroplane project, working with Seafair and David Williams, the executive director of the Hydroplane and Raceboat Museum.

One weekday in May 1999 I drove down to Stan Sayres pits to watch a PEMCO Classic test session for the Museum's vintage hydros.

* * * *

Even with earplugs, the roar was deafening. Hot fumes from a World War II fighter engine scoured the cockpit. Lake water sprayed my face. I felt vulnerable and exposed sitting atop this big, snarling boat, an unlimited hydroplane.

An hour earlier I'd been watching *Miss Burien* and *Miss Thriftway* test on Lake Washington. After *Burien* returned to the dock, driver David Williams waved me over.

"You want to go out in the boat?" he asked. I got excited, thinking he meant one of the patrol boats that would offer a great vantage point for taking photos.

"No, I mean *Miss Burien*," he said.

I thought for a moment and said, "Sure!" Before I could reconsider and ponder the possible danger, a nice woman named Linda from the Hydroplane and Raceboat Museum began fitting me for a lifejacket, helmet, and goggles. I looked like a dork: Under some too-short *Hawaii Kai* coveralls I wore slacks, a dress shirt, dress shoes, and tie – the usual PEMCO business garb at the time.

I approached a clergyman who earlier had blessed *Miss Burien* during its rechristening. "Hi. What denomination are you?" I asked.

"I'm a Roman Catholic priest," he said.

"Well, does your blessing work on Presbyterian passengers?" I teased.

"Oh yes," he answered with a smile, "a Roman Catholic blessing is more than adequate for you."

A crane lowered *Miss Burien* into the water. To fit two people inside, a padded wooden board replaced the driver's seat. Time to go.

I stepped in the cockpit and wedged onto the board. Williams, on my right, instructed me to grip a yellow tether and brace my left foot against a steel coupling. Clutching my Canon AE-1 camera with my other hand, I realized that once underway my lens cap would be a hassle. I handed it to someone on the dock.

Williams flipped a switch and a red light glowed atop the dash. He pushed the starter. The engine snarled, and for a moment the entire hull vibrated. Wow. I felt its raw power in the seat of my pants before the engine died. Williams restarted, and the Allison V-12 roared to life. We heaved forward, the bow rising.

Several sensations exhilarated me: the Allison's loud growl. The sight and sound of water spraying up behind the sponson. Hot exhaust sweeping my face. The smell of aviation fuel, different from auto gas. The lake surface rushing by.

Williams curled to the right out of the Sayres lagoon, and the bow dropped as we came on plane and accelerated down-lake. I saw the familiar grassy point where as a kid I had watched the hydros race on the old 3-mile course, and it struck me: Here I am riding in a hydroplane, a cool old-style hydro with a full bow, on Lake Washington!

We began a wide left turn. Suddenly, the stern fishtailed, caught itself with a jerk, fishtailed, jerked again. The boat seemed to lean outward with every jolt. Not a frightful sensation, but unsettling. The speedometer said 75 mph.

A name came to mind: Tommy Fults. At San Diego in 1970, Fults turned Pay 'n Pak's *Li'l Buzzard* past photographers at low speed when the boat abruptly hooked. Fults broke his neck and died.

Burien straightened and accelerated northward. I gripped the strap tightly, but the ride smoothed out the faster we went. This was fun! The sound surprised me. Conditioned to expect the Doppler effect – the high pitch of an approaching engine, dropping pitch as it passes – I instead heard a steady blare, similar to the drone when pushing a lawn mower around the yard.

Williams slowed and veered left. Once again *Miss Burien* turned fitfully in a series of lurches; she did not carve a steady arc like modern hulls. Amid our bouncing I saw a plastic milk carton shoot past, a small buoy marker. Then we nosed southward again. I jabbed my thumb up, the sign to go faster. Williams obliged. *Miss Burien* surged forward and a brutal sensation of power engulfed me, yet the boat rose softly on its air cushion and glided smoothly. It startled me to look at the speedometer and see 135 mph, because it didn't feel that fast. I shot photos with little trouble. Forty mph on choppy water in my 19-foot Bayliner felt faster and more precarious.

Another jerky turn, a wave at a patrol boat, and up the backstretch again. Bilgewater soaked my right foot. Williams tapped my arm and motioned for me to take the steering wheel. I gripped it, expecting some sort of shimmy, but felt none. Williams took the wheel and set the rudder for the turn, cranked *Burien* through an arc, and gave me the wheel again. What a rush! Just don't hook the boat, I thought. Rudders fail all the time – *Thriftway* in 1958, *Hallmark Homes* in 1971, *Budweiser* in 1980....

We dashed down the chute again, and I saw 3,500 rpm before we looped around the course, slowed, and angled toward the pits. I took more photos, then stood up partway in the cockpit to shoot over the windshield and bow. I also extended my camera at arm's length and snapped a self-portrait of me wearing Billy Schumacher's old goggles, my PEMCO tie, and a goofy smile. Entering the lagoon Williams shut down the engine and we coasted to the finger pier. My thrill ride was over.

Back on shore I thanked Williams for the ride, and we chatted with Dixon Smith about his drive that day in *Miss Thriftway*. "Geez, going up the backstretch I passed a big log," he said. "Yeah, I saw it too," said Williams.

A log, while I was out there going 135 mph? I'm glad I didn't see it.

* * * *

The 1999 PEMCO Classic featured *Miss Burien*; a *Miss Madison* facsimile that actually was the former *Savair's Mist*; the *Hawaii Kai III* replica; an old *Atlas Van Lines* facsimile, which truly did race in 1970 as *Li'l Buzzard*; the 1967 *Miss Budweiser*; and *Miss Thriftway*.

When Barb Carper recruited Dixon to drive *Thriftway*, Dixon reunited a crew of former *Bardahl* and *Pay 'n Pak* associates – Skip Schott, David Smith, and Dwight Thorn, plus Dixon's 16-year-old son Ryan. The Aug. 8 vintage "race" generated much fan excitement, and Dixon beat the field to the checkered flag despite a pre-race script that called for a different ending.

"There was some kind of arrangement as to the finishing order, but during the last lap Dixon had a 'memory problem' and he crossed the finish line first," Schott said. "Then we cleaned everything up and went to dinner at the Outback Steak House. After prime rib and several glasses of wine, the conversation turned to, 'We should restore an old boat.' Dixon said he knew the fellow who owned the *Bardahl* and that we should talk to him."

Curt Erickson still owned the Green Dragon, and Dixon had told Curt that if he ever restored the boat, he would make an engine and gearbox available.

"At this point in the conversation, after more wine, I said, 'Well, if we're going to do it, we'd better do it now, before we're too old and wished we had," said Schott.

Dixon approached Erickson about working together to restore *Miss Bardahl*, but Erickson decided instead to sell it to Dixon. On June 24, 2000, the former kid from Beacon Hill and teenage crew member purchased a piece of his past. Dixon Smith now owned *Miss Bardahl*. Always a perfectionist and a stickler for doing things right, he knew exactly who had the knowledge and skill to lead a top-notch restoration: boatbuilder and hydro driver Mike Hanson.

Hanson drove the *Miss Madison* for 10 years before joining Mike and Lori Jones' U-9 racing team in 1999. A two-time winner – San Diego in 1993 and Lewisville, Texas, in 1994 – Hanson was known as a meticulous wood butcher. Arrangements were made for him to rebuild *Miss Bardahl* in the Jones' rural shop just west of Enumclaw, Wash., about 12 miles from Hanson's Bonney Lake home.

On June 24, 2000, three Smiths and a Schott drove past Graham, Wash., to Tanwax Lake to retrieve the U-40 from Erickson. They towed it to the *Miss Budweiser* shop in Tukwila, where Dixon worked as a *Budweiser* team member. *Bardahl's* display engine had not been removed in years and the mounting bolts were corroded so badly that Dixon needed to cut them with a torch. The tail and cowlings also were removed. After taking careful, copious measurements of the hull and its hardware in July, "deconstruction" began Aug. 11 at Dixon's storage shed in Redmond, where the dry-rotted deck and battens were removed, along with the corroded rudder, rudder bracket, and struts.

Meanwhile, notable hydro happenings had taken place. On June 15, 2000, someone finally broke the world straightaway speed record for propeller-driven craft: Russ Wicks, driving the turbine-powered *Miss Freei* near Sand Point, averaged 205.494 mph through the 1-mile trap, breaking *Miss U.S. I*'s 1962 mark of 200.419 mph. *Miss Freei*'s crew chief was Roger Newton, who had led the final stages of *Miss Bardahl*'s 1984 cosmetic restoration.

It was also at the *Miss Freei* record run that I stumbled upon and met Skip Schott, to whom I babbled something about being excited to finally find the former *Bardahl* wrench.

By summer 2000, the Hydroplane and Raceboat Museum had acquired another *Miss Bardahl*: the original Green Dragon, the 1958 hull that Ole Bardahl had donated to Seattle Goodwill in 1969. The boat had been displayed on tilt for years at the Goodwill store on South Dearborn Street until the Museum got it and, setting its sights on that summer's PEMCO Classic, performed a minor renovation. The boat was relaunched July 20, 2000, at Stan Sayres Pits.

Bill Schumacher later steered the '58 *Bardahl* to "victory" in the 2000 PEMCO Classic at Seafair, which was promoted as a much-delayed finish of the 1960 Gold Cup on Lake Mead that had been canceled by high winds. Other PEMCO Classic participants were *Nitrogen Too* (ex-*Savair's Mist*, painted in *Nitrogen* colors), *Miss Burien*, *Miss Century 21*, and the 1967 *Miss Budweiser*, which the Museum had planned to paint as *Miss Seattle Too*.

* * * *

In March 2001, the 1962 *Miss Bardahl* was towed to the Jones Racing shop near Enumclaw and parked alongside the U-9 turbine hydro. Deconstruction continued at the direction of Mike Hanson, who with his brother Larry logged many hours on *Bardahl* for more than three years. The Smiths and Schott also came frequently. The harder they looked, the worse the hull appeared. Corrosion ate at aluminum plates and brackets. The wood bow, transom, and left side of the hull were rotting and had to go. Ditto for all of the sponson frames, which later served as templates for replacements. *Bardahl*'s sponson remnants were unbolted and removed, leaving just the center section of the hull. Though some of the main frames could be saved, several also had decayed and needed replacing.

Around that time Ryan Smith created the missbardahl.com website, on which he carefully documented the step-by-step restoration and rebuild of the Green Dragon.

Once the boat was stripped as far as it needed to go in April, reconstruction began. New spruce was spliced onto the engine stringers, which then were sheathed in a continuous sheet of 6061 aluminum. *Bardahl* received a new transom, new engine rails, repaired port frames, and a new left side to replace the rotted original that suffered from being the waterlogged low point when *Bardahl* sat on tilt.

Mike and Larry Hanson took a break for the summer to race the Jones' speedy U-9, and Mike won hydroplane racing's most-coveted prize July 15 in Detroit, the Gold Cup. The name "Mike Hanson" now adorned the revered trophy along with superstars like Gar Wood, Muncey, Musson, Chenoweth, and Hanauer.

That August PEMCO's sponsorship of the vintage hydros at Seafair included a lakeside hospitality pavilion, where we hosted a very special guest: J.P. Patches, the beloved Seattle clown and rascally "mayor of the City Dump" whose popular KIRO-TV show ran from 1958-81. Julius Pierpont Patches (a.k.a. Chris Wedes) entertained our PEMCO guests on race day and caused quite a stir among the adoring crowd, particularly baby boomers. I was delighted to introduce my teenage daughter, Kristin, to J.P., who still had great rapport with kids. What a guy, a real Northwest treasure.

* * * *

Christmas Eve 1959 must have been a weekday, because I vividly recall watching J.P. Patches' afternoon

TV show. I was 5 years old, and J.P. was supposedly broadcasting from the North Pole, where he had somehow magically transported himself.

Onscreen J.P. was talking with Santa – and just then Mom bolted into the room and clicked off the TV. I squawked, but she quickly asked, "Hey, what's that sound?" I heard sleighbells and a "Ho-ho-ho!" coming from the patio, and Mom said, "Santa is here!"

I darted to the sliding glass door, and there on the patio was a big cardboard box from Frederick & Nelson that contained my American Flyer electric train. My big brother Dave had pretended to be Santa dropping it off. Years later Mom said she turned off my TV show because "we were worried that if you saw Santa on TV at the same time you heard him on the patio, you would be suspicious since he couldn't be in two places at once."

* * * *

With all of the main frames now repaired or replaced, *Miss Bardahl* was turned over in November 2001 to begin work on the bottom, which was badly deteriorated. Hanson and crew removed it. All of the brown epoxy paint applied inside the hull in 1984 by Bob and June Banker was stripped, a tedious job. Instead of attaching the frames to the stringers with wooden blocks, Hanson and team used aluminum angles to increase the hull's strength and durability. They later did likewise with the sponson frames.

Bardahl received a new bow and airtraps around Christmas, and spruce shims filled voids where dry rot had been cut away. Then the oak keel was laid Jan.2, 2002. Like all of the wood in the boat, the keel was sealed with West Systems Epoxy for water-proofing and protection. New battens were screwed and glued to the bottom, followed by plywood panels that were skinned with aluminum in June. Mike Hanson built new sponson frames before taking another summer hiatus to race the U-9. Likewise, Dixon went racing with the *Miss Budweiser* team in his capacity as "Chief Science Officer," as the team had dubbed him years earlier.

Leo Vanden Berg also had worked with the *Bud* team for many years. After returning to hydro racing with the *Squire Shop* team from 1984 through '86, Vanden Berg was lured to the *Bud* camp in 1987. Bernie Little recalled getting his fanny kicked by *Miss Bardahl* early in his hydro career and, recognizing Leo's talent, put him to work on the beer boat. Leo often drove around Seattle chasing parts and sometimes took a young friend with him, grade-schooler Ryan Smith.

As the 1990s wore on, Leo slowed down, limited by bad knees. By 2002 he was largely housebound, but pleased to know that his former protégé Dax – Ryan's dad – was restoring the Green Dragon to glory.

The fourth PEMCO Classic vintage hydro race took place at Seafair Aug. 4, 2002. David Williams and the "Mist" *Madison* averaged 81.902 mph to edge Mark Evans in the quasi-*Kai* across the line, along with the '67 *Budweiser* and '60 *Miss Burien*. *Miss Century 21* broke down and did not finish, but technically, neither did any of the vintage hydros – race officials inexplicably cut the exhibition short after just two laps and never gave PEMCO or the Museum a satisfactory reason why. It proved to be the final PEMCO Classic.

Miss Bardahl's rebuilders attached sponson frames in October, and Dixon fitted the distinctive angled aluminum plates that had capped the rear of each sponson as part of Ron Jones' 1963 modification. *Bardahl*'s new sponsons now were configured identically to those used from 1963 through 1965. A hole was cut in the hull's bottom for the propeller shaft, and laminated oak sponson battens were attached around Thanksgiving. The sponson runners were screwed on beginning Dec. 30, and starting Jan. 10, 2003, the team fit aluminum over the runners and nontrips. In late February, with the bottom now finished, the crew rolled the hull rightside up. Significant progress halted for the summer as Dixon and the Hansens again went racing.

The summer of 2003 would be different for Dixon, the *Bud* team, and the entire hydro community. Bernie Little, who had raced unlimiteds since 1963 and campaigned a long line of boats named *Miss Budweiser* continuously since 1964, died at age 77 on April 25, 2003. Son Joe Little took over the *Bud* team, which added two more regatta wins that year to its gaudy total, 136 victories through 2003.

2003 might best be remembered as the year that Ed Cooper's turbo-Allison-powered U-3 won three out of six races. Driver Mitch Evans drove smart and fast, winning Thunder on the Ohio in Evansville, Ind., the APBA Gold Cup in Detroit, and the Bill Muncey Cup in San Diego, where one year later Evans would qualify at an all-time piston-record lap of 162.602 mph.

For Captain Dixon J. Smith, the summer of 2003 also was the year he turned 60 and retired as a United Airlines pilot.

Work continued in October 2003 on *Bardahl*'s deck frames. Dixon fitted the rear and intermediate struts, and an aluminum and fiberglass box was constructed near the cockpit, at the hull's center of gravity, to hold the fuel cell. Through the rest of the fall deck battens were cut, fitted, planed, and attached. Dixon built an oil tank directly in front of the engine compartment, and he refurbished and installed *Bardahl*'s original ADI tank that had been fabricated and first installed in September 1965. While digging through old hydro equipment in the spring of 2001 at Bob Gilliam's Kitsap Peninsula shop, Dixon had amazingly come across it.

On Dec. 11 the hull was flipped upside down again, thoroughly blown out with compressed air, and sprayed with three coats of clear epoxy by *Miss Budweiser* crewman Mike Campbell, sealing the entire interior. The boat dried for several days before being flipped rightside up. Dixon and David fit the original transom over the new one after Christmas to trace rudder-bracket holes, ensuring identical placement.

After Schott built butt-blocks for the deck and Mike Hanson finished fairing the battens, the two began fitting 4' x 8' plywood deck panels on Jan. 17, 2004. Meanwhile, Dixon installed plumbing and hardware such as the water pickup line, oil cooler, and oil thermostats. The deck was completed Feb. 13, and work progressed on a slightly altered cowl: Knowing he would give rides in *Miss Bardahl*, Dixon widened the cockpit six inches to better accommodate two people squeezed side by side. To accomplish this, *Bardahl*'s original cowls were cut down the middle and wood spacers were inserted, making the cowls commensurate with the widened cockpit.

The core crew plus additional volunteers fiberglassed the entire deck in 10½ hours on Feb. 21. Next, new cowls were made using the originals as molds. *Bardahl*'s heavy originals had been made of roving that added unnecessary weight; the replacements comprised strong but lightweight carbon fiber and fiberglass. Mike Hanson and Schott also constructed a new, lighter tail of fiberglass honeycomb with fiberglass skin, using the original tail – made of marine plywood, now bent and rotting – as a template. About this time the rear and intermediate struts, now plated, were permanently fastened.

Schott, David, and Mike Hanson glued and glassed the tailfin to the rear cowl on March 22. In mid-April the boat was primed and sanded several times. Finally, after more than 4,000 hours of labor, *Miss Bardahl* left the Jones Racing shop for good on April 26, 2004. The bulk of the rebuild was finished, and Mike and

Roger Newton, left, led the Museum's later stages of *Bardahl*'s 1984 cosmetic restoration in Maltby, Wash.
© Jon Osterberg photo 1984

The author wet-sands the boat at Maltby in mid-July 1984.
– Jon Osterberg collection

Newton and Dick Schlemmer unmask *Bardahl*'s bow scallops as the restoration nears the end.
© Jon Osterberg photo 1984

Buffing party outside the Maltby warehouse the evening before *Bardahl*'s rededication ceremony.
© Jon Osterberg photo 1984

Cosmetic transformation complete: *Miss Bardahl* was the hydro museum's first restoration.
© Jon Osterberg photo 1984

Ole Bardahl cuts the ribbon outside the Seafirst Tower while daughter Evelyn Manchester and Bob Williams look on, July 25, 1984.
© Jon Osterberg photo 1984

E.K. Muller, right, was a bright, ever-inquisitive student of the sport until his 2004 passing. Shown here in 2002 with Bob Burd, who helped retrieve *Bardahl* from New Hampshire in 1983.
© Jon Osterberg photo 2002

Leo is prompted to identify the original Keeper of the Dragon.
© Jon Osterberg photo 1984

After Dixon Smith acquired the Dragon in June 2000, Mike Hanson oversaw a major rebuild, shown here in March 2002.
© Jon Osterberg photo 2002

Mike Hanson performed his magic in a shop near Enumclaw, Wash. Hanson estimates only 30 percent of *Bardahl*'s original hull was salvaged, because of dry rot.
– Dixon Smith photo, used with his permission

Miss Bardahl as she appeared after reconstruction, May 2004.
© Jon Osterberg photo 2004

The final phase of *Bardahl*'s reconstruction took place in Redmond, Wash., where Dixon and Skip Schott, in particular, logged many hours in 2004-05.
© Jon Osterberg photo 2005

Larry Hanson waved goodbye to the product of their superb craftsmanship.

"The boat is, at most, about 30 percent original because of dry rot and questionable structure," Mike Hanson said. "It's probably stronger now than when it was new."

Dixon towed the boat to the *Miss Budweiser* shop in Tukwila on May 29 for painting, the majority of which was done by *Bud* crew members John Rheinberger, Jeff Campbell, Mike Campbell, and John Rice. The hull was suspended from cables and sprayed yellow on its sides and transom. Once it cured, Rheinberger and Loren Sawyer painted the black and white "Miss Bardahl" to the sides in 1965-style block lettering. Next, after flipping the boat upside down, metallic green and clear-coat paint were sprayed on the deck, followed by black bow scallops and "U-40." On June 10 the entire hull was clear-coated while upside down, after which *Miss Bardahl* hung for a week to cure.

Hydro purists later claimed the metallic green on the restored *Bardahl* was not the authentic 1965 color, and said it appeared a shade lighter than the 1962-64 paint. David Smith acknowledged that metallic green was chosen for the restoration over 1965's tractor green, mainly for aesthetics, and also because the 1965 color had been a limited-options choice necessitated by the time crunch. During the restoration, he and Dixon gradually stripped a piece of original deck to reveal the 1962-64 color.

"It was all there. It's like a tree, you just go down and look at the different layers," David said. "Dixon and I looked at the paint and decided to go back to the metallic because it looks much better, so we found a PPG paint on the color chart. And the yellow was really easy, because it's just a fleet yellow. The paint we used for black was already at the *Bud* shop, and the clear Sickens was compatible.

"We went over to Bellevue Paint and had them mix the stuff," he said. "For the green, we picked something that was really close. We couldn't get it dead-on, but we got it close and said this looks good. The *Bud* guys taped it, painted it, everything. Very nice."

The *Budweiser* team then embarked on its farewell tour, racing in 2004 for the last time. Joe Little had decided two years of running the boat in tribute to his dad was enough, and soon unlimited racing's longest-running commercial sponsorship would come to an end.

My daughter graduated from Redmond High School in June 2004, and soon the family drove east on a two-week road trip that included a weekend in Madison, Ind., where we saw *Miss Budweiser* win the Governor's Cup. After returning home in July we finalized the purchase of a cabin near Cle Elum, Wash., where much of this book later was written while gazing at craggy 9,415-foot Mount Stuart.

That summer of 2004, *Miss Bardahl* resided in a spacious Redmond shop owned by Greg Draper. The tail and cowlings were painted, including the Bardahl detective. Decals were made for detailed graphics like the cans of B1 and B2 Bardahl oil, Musson's and Vanden Berg's names, the national championship crest, Seattle Yacht Club burgee, and Champion Spark Plug logo – the only vinyl on the boat. Dixon and Schott worked almost daily on the boat fabricating hardware and installing plumbing, systems, and steering.

* * * *

Sad news swept the hydro community Oct. 24, 2004. Leo Vanden Berg, the "Keeper of the Dragon," died at age 87 after an extended illness, leaving behind his wife Elsie, son Mel, stepdaughter Teresa, sisters Mary and Ann, eight grandkids, and 14 great-grandchildren. Leo would not see his old charger roar to life and kick up roostertails again.

I quickly tipped off *Seattle Times* reporter Dwight Perry, who I first became friends with in 1983 when we covered the hydros, he for the *Seattle P-I* and me for the *Coeur d'Alene Press*. I knew that Perry, like me, had grown fond of Leo and understood his prominence in hydro racing. I offered Perry a few details about Leo's career and lent the *Times* a color photo I'd shot, and Perry crafted a poignant news story that ran in the Oct. 30 *Times*. In it, he quoted Dixon talking about Leo.

"He was quiet, unassuming, modest, and he had to have patience like you wouldn't believe. He had guys like me, 19 to 23, for a crew, and he rode herd on us. He was very even-tempered, patient and very fair, one of the most honest people I've ever met in my life."

"Leo was a lot like Edgar in that he probably never had an enemy in the world, which in hydroplane racing especially is really saying something," Perry told me, comparing Vanden Berg to Seattle Mariner Edgar Martinez.

I had the somber privilege of writing Leo's obituary for the November 2004 *Unlimited NewsJournal*.

Leo Vanden Berg, the hall of fame "keeper of the Green Dragon" crew chief, passed away Oct. 24 in Seattle. He was 87.

Under Leo's watch, Ron Musson and Miss Bardahl won three consecutive Gold Cups and National Championships in 1963-65. The U-40 won 12 races altogether and, in its final appearance at San Diego in 1965, set records for fastest lap (117 mph), heat (116), and 45-mile race (115) that stood for years.

A disheartened Leo walked away from hydro racing the following year after Musson died racing a new Bardahl on the Potomac River. The cabover boat nosed in and disintegrated. Leo didn't return until 1984, when he worked on the Squire Shop crew. Bernie Little, well aware of Leo's sparkling past and talent, later lured him to the Budweiser team for several years.

Sometimes a friend's death hurts all the more because of things left unsaid. Such was the case with Leo, who became my friend in 1981. He never heard the reasons why I admired him so much. Assuming that Leo, a man of faith, is somehow still aware of worldly things, I offer those reasons now.

Leo, although you were one heck of a crew chief, I respected you far more for your character. You were decent, humble, kind to others, and honest as the day is long. I spent three years searching for your old hydro, and although I was elated at finding it in a New Hampshire field in 1982, that search led to an even more-valuable find: meeting you.

I'll remember your laugh, your perpetual crew cut, that odd squint, your patience, and your great stories – like how you and Chuck Thompson would go get milkshakes when other racers headed off to the bar. And forever, I'll remember how you made that beloved Dragon of my childhood roar.

Thanks for the memories, Leo. God bless you.

A few days earlier, another good pal and friend of hydroplaning had passed away, on Oct. 15, 2004. E.K. Muller, a fellow pit-prowler, photographer, and hydro historian I'd met in the 1970s, died at age 75 at Park Shore in Seattle's Madison neighborhood after a brief battle with cancer. E.K. had a keen intellect and appreciation for not just the spectacle of racing, but for what makes boats and motors go, befitting his engineering degree from Cal-Berkeley and his long tenure as a Boeing civil engineer.

Ekay (as he sometimes wrote his name) also possessed a sharp wit, solid writing and editing skills, an innate curiosity about all things, and several goofy, unfashionable porkpie hats that adorned his head at all hydro events.

E.K. was the driver behind "the Colonels," his name for our group of hydro enthusiasts who planned a series of in-depth booklets about noteworthy thunderboats, to be published by Unlimiteds Unanimous. Only one made it to print, Weldon Johnson's superb *Profile: Slo-mo-shun IV* in 1986, but others were outlined or drafted by Unlimiteds Unanimous members such as David Speer, Jim Dunn, Bill Osborne, and Craig Fjarlie. This *Bardahl* book began as my own installment in that series, and E.K. was the impetus who set it in motion.

* * * *

Around Thanksgiving 2004, Schott began renovating Ron Musson's original seat, which was salvageable. David and Dixon finished the dashboard, installing its gauges and windshield during the holidays.

By February Corky Peterson had built much of *Bardahl*'s new low-profile hydraulic trailer, which cradled the hull close to the ground for easy access. The rudder bracket, flash pans, foot pedals, linkages, fire extinguishers, guy wires, deck cleats, and cockpit upholstery were added before May arrived.

On May 13, I met with Dixon in Redmond to see *Bardahl*'s progress and discuss a brochure he asked me to write recapping the boat's racing history and renovation. Dixon had named me "team historian," which was flattering, and I happily wrote the three-fold brochure that's still shared when *Miss Bardahl* runs or is displayed.

On July 10, 2005, *Bardahl* was lowered onto its trailer, and Dixon used his new Chevy Silverado 1-ton pickup to tow the completed hull outside into daylight for the first time. He installed a Rolls-Merlin display engine at the former *Bud* shop in Tukwila along with the rudder and propeller, and after washing the boat July 17, *Miss Bardahl*'s rebirth was virtually complete.

Dixon towed the Green Dragon on a sunny July 18 to the Museum of Flight at Boeing Field, where he had been invited to display *Miss Bardahl* for the "Boats That Fly" exhibit. There, the U-40 remained on display next to the venerable *Slo-mo-shun V* and *Tempo VI* from July 30 through Jan. 15, 2006.

On Oct. 2, 2005, almost 40 years to the day since *Miss Bardahl* was hoisted out of the water for the last time on Oct. 3, 1965, in San Diego, the restoration team gathered with friends and family at the Museum of Flight for a commemorative celebration. Schott related "how we got here" to the crowd, which aside from the core team and their families included Jerry Zuvich; Evelyn Bardahl McNeil; John Rheinberger; Mike Campbell; the restored *Miss Thriftway*'s owner and driver, Barb Carper and Ike Kielgass; former *Bud* crew chief Mark Smith; and me. I was delighted to be invited.

Organizers of the Syttende Mai (Norwegian Constitution Day) Parade in Ballard wanted *Miss Bardahl* to appear, and on May 17, 2006, she returned to her home turf near Bardahl Manufacturing Corporation and drew an enthusiastic welcome from the crowd lining Market Street.

Meanwhile, work progressed on *Miss Bardahl*'s Rolls-Merlin engine, a hybrid dash 7/dash 9 model that Dixon and Ryan had disassembled in 2002-03 and began rebuilding in 2004. With the hull now finished, engine work ramped up in the shop at Dixon's Issaquah home, and by early May 2007 the Merlin's lower end, wheelcase, banks, and supercharger were finished. Final assembly was completed June 1, the engine was hoisted into Dixon's Chevy truck and driven to the *Bud* shop and installed, and on Sunday, June 3,

Dixon trailer-fired *Miss Bardahl*'s Merlin as the U-40 sat on its sparkling new trailer.

The next day, Ryan Smith became the third-generation Smith to start a Rolls-Merlin. The Green Dragon roared to life effortlessly and once again breathed fire.

Aficionados noted that *Bardahl*'s Merlin looked different from its racing days – whereas Vanden Berg's engines were painted entirely black with "Bardahl" lettered in white on the valve covers, Dixon preferred polished-metal valve covers and carburetor scoops, as sported by the *Pay 'n Pak* Merlin-powered hydros.

Dixon acknowledged his rebuilt Dragon is not a concours (fully identical) restoration, noting changes like the widened cockpit, honeycomb tail, modern fuel cell, and plentiful aluminum brackets that strengthen the frame. But those subtle improvements go unnoticed by the untrained eye.

That week, the *Bardahl* guys weren't the only vintage-hydro enthusiasts who wrestled at bedtime with insomnia caused by eager anticipation. A roostertail reunion was slated for Thursday.

Chapter 33

The Dragon roars again

June 7, 2007, dawned overcast and brisk with showers, though later in the afternoon the sun emerged and warmed Seattle to 63 degrees. For the throng of hydro fans at Stan Sayres Pits, the weather didn't matter – it was a brilliant and glorious day. Perched on their trailers near the west finger piers were two resurrected and hallowed hydros: a marvelous replica of the 1955 *Miss Thriftway*, owned and built by Vashon Unlimiteds LLC, and the 1962 *Miss Bardahl*.

For the Green Dragon and team members Dixon Smith, David Smith, and Skip Schott, it marked a return to the site of *Miss Bardahl*'s third-straight Gold Cup victory, and it marked her first visit back to her former August lakeside home.

Hundreds of well-wishers jammed the pits – current and former drivers, crew, reporters, photographers, fans, and curious joggers. Among the crowd were Jerry Zuvich, Chip Hanauer, current *Miss Spokane* owner Pancho Simonson, Ron Jones Sr., Evelyn Bardahl McNeil, Mark Manchester, Roger Newton, shutterbugs Bill Osborne and Owen Blauman, and former *Bud* crew chief Mark Smith, who lent a hand that day with the Green Dragon. Hydroplane and Raceboat Museum personnel tended their own boats, the 1960 *Miss Burien* and 1961 *Miss Lumberville/Savair's Mist*, now painted as *Oh Boy! Oberto*.

"Evelyn told us the boat looked great, that it 'never looked this good when it was new,' and she thanked everybody," said Schott.

Other noteworthy attendees were the team members' wives, each of whom had supported their spouse's hydro passion and spent many days and evenings alone as hulls took shape in distant workshops. Judy Smith, Jody Smith, Karin Schott, and the *Thriftway*-team wives and girlfriends watched the culmination of their husbands' long efforts.

After the crew trailer-fired *Bardahl*'s Rolls-Merlin, a crane hoisted the boat aloft and settled it on Lake Washington. Tending *Miss Bardahl* were the same people, manning their same positions, as when the hull had last been pulled from the water Oct. 3, 1965, at Mission Bay: David with the stern rope, Schott with the bow rope, and Dixon directing the crane. Ryan assumed Vanden Berg's role as keeper of the checklist.

Dixon and David donned their driving suits – Dixon in yellow, with a white Navy flight helmet adorned with yellow lightning bolts and tomahawks; David in bright red, with a white full-face Ferrari helmet. They stepped off the wood-plank dock onto *Bardahl*'s metallic green deck, buckled on old-style orange life jackets, and cinched their chin straps as the Vashon Unlimiteds crew lowered its *Miss Thriftway* replica into the adjacent slip. Chip Hanauer stepped forward, grinning broadly, and shook Dixon's hand in congratulations. The moment had come: *Miss Bardahl* was poised to roar to life.

David stepped into the cockpit and sat on the bench seat, then Dixon. They pulled their gloves on, lowered their visors, and Dixon manipulated the controls. Without hesitation the black Rolls-Merlin barked, puffed smoke through its white stacks, and thrust the hull forward. *Bardahl* carved a trough across the lagoon, lifted her nose, and gained speed as she curled to the right and onto the Lake Washington racecourse.

* * * *

"When we were growing up, my father prided himself in building things," said David Smith. "He built nearly all our toys that we played with. One year they didn't have much money, and all the toys under the Christmas tree were ones my father built. I got an aircraft carrier, my brother got the *U.S.S. Missouri*, my sister got something. The trike, the bike, all the stuff we rode on, my father built from scratch in the basement. Dad built two runabouts in the garage in the basement, and the third boat – the one that Dixon owns today – was built in grandma's garage, because it's bigger.

"So this is in 1953, 1954, 1955? I don't know; we were all very young. Dad had put the boat in, and we're chugging along in Lake Washington. And the *Gale V* comes by! And it stops. So my dad powers over there, we get real close, and it's Bill Cantrell in the cockpit, and I don't remember who else, but they're testing some kind of carburetor.

"They were about to start up and take off again. Dad says, 'Boys, this is the closest you'll ever get to an unlimited hydroplane. Take a really good look right now.' And we sat there making ga-ga eyes at the *Gale V*. Or maybe it was the *Gale IV*. It had to have happened during Seafair week. The boat was launched at Jett's Marina and they ran up by Seward Park, and we were by Seward Park," David said.

* * * *

Dixon rounded the south turn and steered *Miss Bardahl* up the backstretch. The Smith brothers were seated inside an unlimited hydroplane, much closer than they'd been that summer day of their youth when they gawked at *Gale*.

Bardahl churned an arc and straightened for the southward leg down the frontstretch. Dixon pressed the throttle harder this time, casting a glorious roostertail behind the green and yellow craft in concert with the Merlin's urgent roar, and the brothers briefly saw 150 mph on the speedometer. The hull rode level and true.

Success!

Boisterous applause greeted boat, driver, and rider at the dock. Then attention quickly shifted a few yards to the east as Larry Fuller guided *Miss Thriftway* onto the lake for its maiden voyage.

Skip Schott suited up on shore as *Bardahl* received careful inspection on its trailer before returning to the water. When Dixon and Schott streaked past the pits at 140 mph on their first full lap, Schott raised his left fist high in exhilaration. In all his years working on *Miss Spokane* and *Miss Bardahl*, it was just his third hydroplane ride – once in the Lilac Lady at Coeur d'Alene, plus the slow ride on *Bardahl*'s deck with Musson and crew before the '65 Gold Cup. Schott soaked in everything his senses could seize: the roar, the spray, the wind in his beard; he leaned far to his left and pressed his palm on the deck, feeling it pulsate; he welcomed the heat from the engine, sniffed its exhaust.

Thriftway went out again with Fuller and Steve Compton taking turns at the wheel. *Bardahl* again was inspected onshore, and when the time came to hoist her onto the lake for Ryan Smith's ride, Dixon invited

Jerry Zuvich to relive his past. Zuvich snapped on *Bardahl*'s sling and invoked Vanden Berg, shouting, "Put 'er in, boys!"

With Dixon working the throttle, Ryan took the wheel for a time as *Miss Bardahl* circled the lake a final time, again hitting 140 mph under brightening skies. At the dock I shot candid photos of a 1965 crew reunion: Jerry, Dixon, David, and Skip, alone on a finger pier alongside the iconic Green Dragon, reminiscing, laughing.

Sunshine bathed the pits as *Bardahl* and *Thriftway* personnel buttoned up their boats, raised them on tilt, and posed alongside for team photos. Then it was over.

Driving home I realized June 7 had become a significant date for me: It was the day Luanne and I embarked on our first memorable road trip, in 1974; it was the day I graduated from the University of Washington, in 1984; and now it marked the launch of the reborn *Miss Bardahl*. A long 28 years had passed since I began my serious search for the boat.

One week later, on June 14, Dixon phoned with an exciting invitation: Would I like to join the *Bardahl* team as the fifth crew member? "David, Skip, Ryan and I met last night and unanimously agreed to invite you on board," he said. I answered "Yes!" before we even clarified my role.

Dixon asked that I handle publicity and media relations, mirroring my PEMCO job responsibilities. I would be the team photographer and continue as historian, and having recently agreed to run *Miss Bardahl* in exhibitions sponsored by HAPO Credit Union at the Columbia Cup in Tri-Cities, Dixon also asked me to help with random crew tasks. David would be busy that weekend preparing a car for the 2007 Pebble Beach Concours d'Elegance, and Ryan would miss the first day while flying in from Cincinnati, where he worked for General Electric Aviation while pursuing an engineering master's degree from Purdue. Dixon also later recruited former *Miss Budweiser* colleague Ron "Bub" Hornung to ensure experienced help.

Schott soon welcomed me to the team. "We all want you to be part of 'this,' whatever 'this' turns out to be," he said. "We could not have done this if you hadn't found the boat."

I helped arrange for Dixon to be interviewed live on Seattle's KIRO Newsradio by Vinnie "New York Vinnie" Richichi on July 20, 2007. We hoped to publicize the Tri-Cities vintage-hydro exhibition the following weekend, and what I didn't know is that Vinnie had a *Bardahl* connection of his own with fond boyhood memories. His father owned gas stations in New York and sold lots of Bardahl products, and in exchange, local Bardahl rep Tony Milano had arranged for the elder Richichi to display *Miss Bardahl* for a day at one of his gas stations in the 1960s.

"All my friends came down to see it, and it was great," Vinnie said during the 20-minute KIRO interview. "*Miss Bardahl* was a piece of my childhood, 3,000 miles away from here."

When we parked *Miss Bardahl* inside Kennewick's sweltering Lampson Pits on Thursday, July 26, I was living the dream. Dixon gave each of us green crew shirts tailored by Don's Group Attire, the original supplier of *Bardahl*'s 1960s team apparel. The U-40 sat at the far west end of the pits in a designated vintage-hydro area. Parked immediately to the east were the 1955 *Miss Thriftway* and the Hydroplane and Raceboat Museum's *Miss Burien*, *Oh Boy! Oberto*, and *Hawaii Kai III*. We had our own dock for the vintage boats, separate from the hectic commotion of the turbine-powered hydros competing for the Lamb Weston Columbia Cup.

The warm reception I had enjoyed weeks earlier from Dixon and team perhaps faded a bit once I added my "skills" to the mix in Tri-Cities. I had warned the guys I wasn't too mechanically inclined, and I think the scope of my mechanical talent became clearer to them that weekend. Asked at one point by Dixon to fetch a speed handle from the tool box, I had to ask what it was, and then brought him the wrong gizmo.

I also gained insight into the precision and rigor that served Dixon so well during his successful hydro career. An acknowledged perfectionist, he performs all tasks, both large and small, just one way – the right way – with little tolerance for anything less. My meager mechanical aptitude and unfamiliarity with routine crewmember chores kindled his impatience at times, and I grew hesitant.

Still, I found a niche of sorts that weekend and at subsequent events, doing simple but helpful odd jobs in addition to shooting photos: laying and sweeping the ground tarp, holding a rope or fending pole at the dock, wiping the boat down when it came in from a run, manning the fire bottle, and helping Schott fuel the boat. An astute man, Schott recognized the work of a liberal-arts major when he saw it, and he patiently coached and directed me.

* * * *

It was Friday, July 27, 2007, my second day as a working member of the *Miss Bardahl* hydroplane crew. I had just finished helping Skip Schott fuel the boat when owner Dixon Smith waved me over.

"Go find yourself a driver's suit."

Dixon's order was unexpected. And baffling. But clearly, he had said "find *yourself*," not "find *me*" a driver's suit.

"Go find Steve Compton of the *Thriftway* crew," he added. "He's about your size."

Schott smiled. He apparently knew what was up: I was going for a ride in *Miss Bardahl*, my magnificent obsession.

Compton graciously lent me his red suit and showed me how to strap on his lifejacket. I dressed quickly and retrieved Ryan Smith's helmet. It was hot, in the 90s in the shade. Soon I stood on the Lampson Pits dock alongside the U-40 Green Dragon. My wife, Luanne, beamed and shot grainy photos with her cell phone. A few friends – fellow *Bardahl* fans – looked on, smirked, and shook their heads. Their thoughts were clear: "That lucky dog…."

One of those friends was Joe Kettner, who oversaw the props and stern on Ed Cooper's speedy turbo-Allison-powered U-3. Joe and I first got to know one another during the six years I handled publicity for the Cooper team, and seeing our team shorthanded he offered to hold *Bardahl*'s stern rope at the dock. That in itself was a thrill for Joe, a student of the sport who appreciates its history.

I climbed inside *Bardahl*'s cockpit and onto the padded bench seat temporarily installed to accommodate Dixon and me. The Columbia River lapped at the rim of the green deck as the midday sun baked me and my thick garb. Dixon lowered my helmet visor. "Brace your left foot here," he said, pointing at a foot mold. We packed the cockpit tightly, so I rested my right arm on the tail cowling.

Dixon pushed levers and flipped switches. The starter whined, the 3,150-horsepower Rolls-Merlin aircraft engine snarled to life, and we surged onto the big 2½-mile Columbia River course. Instantly I felt hot exhaust blowing back from the stacks.

An ecstatic Skip Schott pumps his fist on the day *Miss Bardahl* was relaunched, June 7, 2007.
© Jon Osterberg photo 2007

The author leaves the dock for his 140-mph Columbia River ride in the Tri-Cities, July 27, 2007.
– Owen Blauman photo, used with his permission

The 1965 *Bardahl* team, minus Vanden Berg and Kruse, reunited June 7, 2007: David Smith and Jerry Zuvich (standing), Dixon Smith and Skip Schott.
© Jon Osterberg photo 2007

We curled around the east turn. Strange, I thought – surely we must be going more than 60 mph. Yet the needle on the speedometer, which starts at 60, had not moved.

Dixon straightened upriver and tapped my forearm, gesturing for me to take the steering wheel. Cool! I gripped it and steered *Miss Bardahl* up the backstretch in about lane four or five, feeling her power buzz through my palms and fingers. What a thrill. Nearing the west turn I expected Dixon to take back the wheel. Sure enough, he reached over … only to point at the yellow entrance buoy marking the turn. "Aim for that" was the message.

What? He's actually going to let me *turn* this hydro? Ohmygosh. This, I knew, was a rare chance. In May 1999 when I rode in *Miss Burien* on Lake Washington, driver David Williams had let me steer down the chutes. But turning required more skill, more responsibility.

I thought to myself, "If Dixon's going to let me turn, I'm going to do it like Ron Musson did." Which was a rather silly thought since Musson turned the *Bardahl* at more than 90 mph. My speedometer registered just below 70.

I veered left and brought the boat close to the entrance buoy, then held a tight arc in lane 2. Dixon probably didn't want me any closer. And besides, Leo Vanden Berg and crew had told me that Musson's preferred lane was 2, not 1 as many believed.

Bardahl turned with surprising ease. It felt almost like power steering. She didn't lean outward or fishtail as I rounded the exit pin and headed east downriver. Dixon took the wheel, then tapped the speedometer as if to say, "Watch this."

He mashed the gas. We surged forward, pinning me against the seat rest. The Rolls engine blared loudly. *Bardahl*'s hull vibrated, the scorching exhaust got hotter, and I watched the speedometer quickly climb past 90, 100, 110, 120. Then my vision blurred. Despite wearing a visor and sunglasses, wind curled over the windshield and shot its way inside my helmet. *Bardahl* continued to surge, but all I saw were fuzzy glimpses of dashboard, shoreline, patrol boats, and our big black motor.

Dixon later said we ran 140 mph, but I never saw those numbers with my own eyes.

As we slowed for the east turn my vision cleared. We turned left. That's when I *really* felt the heat from the stacks. I'd forgotten to wear gloves, and exhaust baked my hand that rested outside the cockpit.

Like with my first ride in 1999, the thought struck me that the sound onboard a hydro was like a lawnmower. Seated in the cockpit a constant distance from the motor, you have no Doppler effect and instead hear a constant drone. Just like circling the lawn with my Toro.

Meanwhile, *Hawaii Kai III* had entered the course and rounded the west turn ahead of us. Dixon cut across the infield and straightened out in lane 1. *Kai* quickly closed on us from behind, its tall roostertail indicating acceleration. Dixon pushed the throttle, and a brief race ensued! *Bardahl* shot forward, but all too soon he was off the gas as we circled near the Blue Bridge and glided back to the dock.

Once onshore, photographer Owen Blauman asked me to describe my ride. When I griped that my vision blurred at top speed, he accessed his pictures on the screen of his digital SLR. "Anything look funny to you?" he said. Yes, it looked like I was standing up in the cockpit. "That's because Musson was a little short guy. You sit way up high, with your head catching the air over the windshield."

Next time – if there is a next time – I'll wear goggles so I can witness 140. Or faster.

Chapter 34

Completing the puzzle, extending the legacy

Eric Schwartz of the *Tri-City Herald* watched what he called my "finder's fee" ride aboard *Bardahl* and wrote a story that ran July 28, 2007. Over that weekend the vintage boats put on a good show and excited the fans, judging from the cheers on the beach. *Bardahl* "won" the exhibition races and circled the buoys at respectable speeds, including average laps of 86.339 and 85.886 mph. Not bad, considering the script directed the boats to queue up in each turn and wait for one another to ensure side-by-side "racing."

Official inspector Peter Thomson brought his digital scale to vintage alley and attached it to *Bardahl*'s sling, and when the crane lifted the boat off its trailer the display read 6,770. Dixon had to be pleased, knowing the Green Dragon weighed more than 7,100 pounds in 1965 with fuel and oil. Rebuilt, strengthened, and loaded with fuel and oil, the new incarnation weighed at least 330 pounds less.

The vintage fleet reconvened at Lake Chelan on Sept. 29 for the Hydroplane and Raceboat Museum's annual volunteer-appreciation event. By working a sizable number of hours throughout the year, volunteers earn a ride in one of the Museum's vintage hydros. It was during such an event on Oct. 1, 1994, that young Ryan Smith went for a ride aboard the restored 1959 *Miss Thriftway*, which had benefited from Dixon's handiwork.

Miss Bardahl and the 1955 *Thriftway* replica tagged along for the 2007 Chelan event. Judy Smith, Jody Smith, and Karin Schott were rewarded for their years of support by riding with Dixon, thus joining *Miss Bardahl*'s 100-mph Club as members No. 6, 7, and 8. Also rewarded that day were restoration workers Mike and Jeff Campbell and Mark Smith. David Smith went for another ride with Dixon but steered and controlled the throttle this time, and Dixon later took *Bardahl* out solo and ran her fairly hard, testing a three-blade prop that soon became the propeller of choice.

"Spring Training" marks the start of each hydro season at Stan Sayres Pits on Lake Washington, and *Miss Bardahl* began attending April 17, 2008. Four riders of note joined Bardahl's 100-mph Club that day: Jim Bevart, who went 150 mph; Joe McDonald, who briefly hit 155; and *Bardahl*'s resurrector Mike Hanson, who steered her at 150.

But the most noteworthy ride went to 100-mph Club member No. 13, Maxine Morrow, Judy Smith's mother from Elma, Wash., who set what was believed to be a world "senior class" speed record by going 140 mph at age 84. (In August 2011, Mira Slovak drove *Miss Wahoo* at about that speed, but he was "only" age 82.) With exuberance belying her years, Maxine thrust her arms skyward and repeatedly flashed thumbs up while returning to the dock.

Bardahl participated in the oddly named Tastin' and Racin' at Lake Sammamish June 7-8, 2008, where Dixon circled a tiny 1-mile course literally a stone's throw away from the dock of his Issaquah lakeside home. On that day *Miss Bardahl* matched roostertails with *Miss Beacon Plumbing*, a modern turbine-powered hydro owned by 1967-68 *Bardahl* driver Bill Schumacher. Photographers drooled at the juxtaposition of vintage versus contemporary.

By this time I had become somewhat fixated on finding yet another missing piece of the *Bardahl* puzzle: Roger Kruse. No one on the team knew of the 1964-68 crewmember's whereabouts, or whether he was even alive. Schott had probed the Internet, armed with what he recalled of Kruse, searching for clues. I had joined the search in spring 2007 at Schott's urging. "You found the boat, so you should be able to find Roger!" he said in mock indignation.

Roger H. Kruse had worked in the 1960s as a mechanic for Los Angeles – Seattle Motor Express (LASME), which was melded into T.I.M.E.-DC Inc. trucking of Lubbock, Tex., before it went bankrupt in 1988. Schott recalled Kruse was married to a woman named Joann from Gorst, Wash., until around 1966-68, when they divorced. Joann then married a "tall, skinny shipping clerk at Bardahl" whose name Schott had forgotten. Roger and Joann had lived in north Seattle, east of Interstate 5, and Kruse was believed to have started a laundromat business in the late 1960s. Based on the 1965 *Bardahl* press kit that said Kruse was 26, we believed he was born in 1939.

Despite all those clues, despite corresponding with the men who maintain the online LASME photo archives, despite quizzing the Manchester family about the shipping clerk, and despite tips from my sister, who taught genealogy at North Idaho College, Kruse remained a phantom.

I thought of a last-chance resource, an old friend in law enforcement who I presumed had access to databases unavailable to the general public. His phone was unlisted, but I found his Facebook page on a Google search and decided to join Facebook so I could reach him. (Joining Facebook soon prompted this post from my son Sean, then 23: "The end of the world is nigh. My dad has added me as a friend on Facebook.")

I connected with my friend. Could he – *would* he – find Kruse, without violating ethical principles?

Yes. He later told me that I could have tapped the same resources myself, had I simply paid a private investigator for less than an hour's work.

On Aug. 4, 2008, I got an email from him: "Good news – we've located Roger. He lives in Portland, Oregon. He confirms he was on the *Bardahl* team, and he's very happy to be found." Included was Kruse's phone number.

I emailed my *Bardahl* teammates with the news and deferred to Dixon to phone Kruse. The next day he called me with an unexpected reaction: Because he'd had an ugly experience with identity theft, Dixon was uncomfortable with the method I used to find Kruse. I respected his perspective and apologized for possibly embarrassing him by association.

In the end, Dixon did call Kruse, who with his wife Anna attended the Chelan hydro event Oct. 4, 2008, the day John Rheinberger got his 150-mph ride. The following spring Kruse joined our team for Spring Training and added veteran help in Seattle, Tri-Cities, and Chelan, where he enjoyed his own ride with Dixon at 150 mph.

Dixon used *Miss Bardahl* as a vehicle to do good, selling rides at auctions that benefited charities. The U-40 ran at Seattle, Tri-Cities, and Chelan in 2010 and 2011, including a speedy run on the Columbia

David Smith steers the Green Dragon on a high-speed run across Lake Chelan, September 2007.
© Jon Osterberg photo 2007

Before long, driver Dixon Smith was hitting 150 mph on the chutes.
© Jon Osterberg photo 2008

August 2010, Coeur d'Alene: Mira Slovak wears a "Who, me?" expression while showing the aftermath of his 1963 *Miss Exide* crash.
© Jon Osterberg photo 2010

Dixon shared Lake Sammamish in 2008 with Jean Theoret, driver of Billy Schumacher's *Beacon Plumbing* turbine-powered hydro.
© Jon Osterberg photo 2008

A mischievous Dixon enjoyed buzzing the photographer's boat on Lake Chelan in October 2008.
© Jon Osterberg photo 2008

Columbia Cup vintage exhibition race, July 2011: *Miss Wahoo, Oh Boy! Oberto, Miss Thriftway, Miss Bardahl, Miss Burien.*
© Jon Osterberg photo 2011

Hydro pals Steve Compton, driving *Miss Thriftway*, and Dixon Smith eye each other as they roar past Kennewick spectators.
© Jon Osterberg photo 2011

Luanne Osterberg was just a wee bit emotive about her 145-mph ride aboard *Miss Bardahl* at Chelan, October 2011.
© Kristin Boyett Photography 2011

Tri-Cities fans stood and cheered at the sight and sound of piston thunderboats, July 2011.
– Anna Kruse photo, used with her permission

River July 23, 2010, where Dixon and Water Follies volunteer Jason Wolcott hit racing speed on the Pasco backstretch – 160 mph.

Wolcott's fast speed might have been aided by a new wrinkle in *Bardahl's* equipment. Earlier that year, Dixon had installed a fully functional nitrous oxide system. Squirts of liquid laughing gas certainly gave *Bardahl* some extra kick, even though Dixon used it cautiously and sparingly.

An exhibition event oozing nostalgia and promise took place Aug. 20-22, 2010, in Coeur d'Alene: the Diamond Cup Regatta, as organizers called it. Conceived as a fundraiser for North Idaho Museum by the Hydromaniacs – some being the offspring of the organization's founders who staged the Diamond Cups of the 1950s and '60s – the first day was Nirvana for local baby boomers who flocked to The Coeur d'Alene Resort. They saw three hydros of their youth on display: a new 1956 *Miss Wahoo* replica, the 1955 *Thriftway* replica, and *Miss Bardahl*.

Exuberant crowds gave us loud ovations Saturday merely for trailer-firing! Men and women engaged us with lively stories of past Diamond Cups, their encounters with drivers and owners, and questions about our boats and the whereabouts of past hydro luminaries. It was a warm, glorious, blue-sky day in the Lake City. I fed off the energy of the earnest visitors, met kindred spirits like local hydro historians Stephen Shepperd and Barry Sartz, met 1963 "Miss Diamond Cup" Sheri Mar Carlberg, toured the wooden boat show on the resort's floating boardwalk, and handed out many of my *Bardahl* brochures. It was a publicist's dream.

The center of attention was Mira Slovak, who returned to the scene of his 1966 *Tahoe Miss* Diamond Cup victory and 1963 *Exide* crash. The *Coeur d'Alene Press* ran a charming story and photo of Slovak finally cashing in on a free cheeseburger promised to him decades earlier by iconic eatery Hudson's Hamburgers. Slovak proved to be an engaging, cordial man, a rapt storyteller, and talking with him was the highlight of my weekend.

The Hydromaniacs' commendable excitement and deep commitment was somewhat tempered by a lack of logistical experience at staging a hydroplane exhibition – a complex undertaking – and by civic restrictions slapped on hydroplanes years earlier. Fearing the return of hydro races and the boorish antics that sometimes accompanied them, Coeur d'Alene voters passed a 1985 advisory measure and a 1996 initiative banning the boats after local tycoon Duane Hagadone explored reviving the Diamond Cup. Because of that, our Sunday exhibition race was exiled to the middle of Lake Coeur d'Alene, far from public beaches, and our pits were relegated to distant Murphy's Landing, requiring a tedious tow through a maze of boat slips and log booms to open water.

Worse, Mother Nature pitched us a nasty curveball. Sunday brought clouds, showers, cool air, and stiff winds that churned whitecaps on Lake Coeur d'Alene. In the end only the Hydro Museum's David Williams ventured out, nursing *Miss Wahoo* through stout waves at speeds barely sufficient to raise a meek roostertail. TV and newspaper reporters chronicled the run, though, generating helpful publicity.

Another Diamond Cup exhibition and auction dinner took place Aug. 19-21, 2011. Dixon had a prior commitment so *Miss Bardahl* didn't participate, but he and wife Judy flew from Seattle to Coeur d'Alene in their Moonie 231 airplane on Saturday to observe several hours of the event, which was much improved over the previous year. I took vacation time and drove my 1962 Impala to visit family at Sylte Ranch in Rathdrum and also attended Saturday's events at the lake. Sunshine prevailed, the pits were conveniently located downtown at Independence Point, vintage limited-class hydros augmented the fleet, and larger crowds attended. The lake surface was much smoother than in 2010, though still choppy.

The major concern was pleasure-boat traffic. Despite efforts of the Kootenai County Sheriff Marine Patrol, event organizers were unable to enforce a no-wake zone. Several photos I shot that day during the four-boat heats inadvertently caught recreational craft in the background plowing large bow waves and whitewater wakes close to the racecourse, a danger to speeding hydroplanes. When those challenges are resolved, Coeur d'Alene and the Hydromaniacs offer a venue so rich in history and passion that it could be the apex of a vintage-hydro circuit.

* * * *

Luanne's opportunity arrived Oct. 1, 2011. Having recovered from her neck surgery 10 months earlier, she was invited by Dixon to ride aboard *Miss Bardahl* at Chelan's annual Mahogany and Merlot event. I had several weeks to mobilize our family to attend and help document the occasion. My daughter, a professional photographer (Kristin Boyett Photography), would shoot close-up stills onshore; son Sean would shoot video; son-in-law Jason would take digital snapshots; and I would take telephoto action shots from inside the Lake Chelan course, thanks to rescue diver Nick Ehli, who kindly allowed me on his boat.

Luanne was giddy with excitement, as many people later attested. She and Dixon powered onto the course and turned a warmup lap, after which Dixon gave her the wheel and generously allowed her to steer a full lap and a half. My telephoto shots show Luanne smiling broadly. Her 100-mph Club card later said she went 140 mph, but she swears she saw 145 on the speedometer. (One-upsmanship? I had gone 140.)

Post-run photos taken at the dock show an animated Luanne hugging Dixon, family, and anyone else within reach, mugging for the cameras and gesticulating wildly as she recounted her ride. She felt no fear and was thrilled with every moment, she said, especially the straightaway sprints. Ever the mom, she then left the pits to enjoy time with her brood at Chelan Lanes, where they bowled a few games.

* * * *

As this book goes to press, 2012 presents several significant anniversaries. Feb. 20 marked 50 years since Mercury astronaut John Glenn blasted into space and circled the Earth three times aboard *Friendship 7*. America will commemorate May 24 and Oct. 3, when in 1962 Scott Carpenter and Wally Shirra rode their Mercury capsules into orbit.

April 21 marked 50 years since Seattle's World's Fair opened, the Century 21 Exposition that imparted civic treasure Seattle Center and its Space Needle, Pacific Science Center, KeyArena, and Belgian waffles.

May 25 denotes exactly 30 years since I hunted down *Miss Bardahl* in Salem, New Hampshire, upon finding John Sweet.

And on July 18, 2012, *Miss Bardahl*'s days of casting roostertails will span 50 years. Amazingly, her string of 57 consecutive heats without a mechanical failure has expanded to encompass every jaunt of her new exhibition career – a reliability record that might transcend even the turbine-hydro era.

May the Green Dragon of my youth continue to summon magic and stir the imagination of generations to come.

Acknowledgments

Many people supported the creation of this book, directly and indirectly.

I'm grateful to the late Ole Bardahl, Leo Vanden Berg, and Ron Musson for bringing *Miss Bardahl* to life. I'm grateful to all of the 1960s team members who prepared and repaired the Green Dragon so successfully, and in particular Leo's original "Keepers of the Dragon" who are my friends today, and who along with Leo allowed hours of my taped interviews: Dixon Smith, David Smith, Skip Schott, Roger Kruse, and their wives Judy, Jody, Karin, and Anna. Without the thoughtfulness and generosity of Dixon, in particular, I would not be reliving my past and now be an "insider" on the vintage *Miss Bardahl* team.

Thank you to original crew member Jerry Zuvich, and Ryan Smith, who not only is crucial to running the restored *Bardahl*, but who keeps our team energized with his youthful vigor, who helped refine my Hydrospeak primer, and who built and maintains missbardahl.com.

Other key *Bardahl* figures welcomed me into their homes or endured long phone and email interviews: Gary Breakfield, Ron Jones, Evelyn Bardahl McNeil, Mira Slovak, Mel Vanden Berg, Josette Musson Hess, and Anne Gustafson. Jim Osborne shared valuable insightful memories, as did Bill Schumacher, Jerry Schoenith, Wally Bostick, Jeanne Lamontia, Sam Cole, Bob Woolms, and Teresa Cain. I'm indebted to them all.

Thanks also to the kindred spirits whose vignettes appear in this book: my sister Judy, Stephen Shepperd, Dave Walker, Rocky Fridell, Bill Osborne, Craig Fjarlie, Dave Peterson, Randy Roe, Mark Evans, and Doug Brow.

Several people graciously contributed their own photos, or photos from their collections, to this book: Jan Kaulins, Troy Cain, David Newton (whose dad, Roger, I greatly miss), Sandy Ross, the family of Marg Smith, and in particular, Ned Crimmin. Ned allowed me to use color photos shot by his mother, Eileen, the superb 1960s hydro scribe. Ned is looking to sell Eileen's entire hydro archives, and interested parties can contact Ned at khabt114@att.net. Thank you to Bill Carver for permission to use his dad's great photos. I'm also grateful for the help of my former Compugraphic colleagues George Brennan, Bob Allen, and Neil "Rocky" Stewart, who in 1982-83 photographed the deteriorating *Miss Bardahl* in Salem, N.H.

We're all indebted to *Miss Bardahl's* former owners for extending her life – Sam Rogers; John Sweet, who ultimately donated the Green Dragon to Seattle's fledgling hydro museum for $1; the Hydroplane and Raceboat Museum; and Curt Erickson.

Thank you to the veteran Seattle sports journalists who brought 1960s hydroplanes to life with their gifted prose and colorful oratory, and who answered my questions about those days long ago: Keith Jackson, Rod Belcher, Bill Knight, and John Owen. Thanks also to Chip Lydum, Don Young (cover-design help), William Hoard, and to Dwight Perry for his thoughtful *Seattle Times* story on Leo Vanden Berg's passing in 2004.

There would be no fascination with *Miss Bardahl* for me were it not for my late father, Dean; my brother, Dave; and my sister, Judy. And yes, despite her preference for "The Edge of Night" over thunderboats, my mom Gretha also kindled my hydro fever. Thank you also to Gordon Sylte, who took me throughout junior high to Seafair and to the '68 Diamond Cup, and to my childhood friends Mikey, Peewee, Brad, and all the other Lake Hills kids who joined me in towing wooden hydros and drawing pictures (thanks, Roby) of our favorite boats.

Several people helped me research historical archives, particularly the staff at the University of Washington's Suzallo Library Microfilm Dept., Paula Dasher at Coeur d'Alene Public Library, Dorothy Dahlgren at Museum of North Idaho, and Carla Guinness at Redmond Public Library.

Thank you to E.K. Muller, my departed friend and fellow hydro geek who encouraged my hydro writings over the years, and who in 1984 planted the seed that ultimately reached fruition with this book.

Last, I'm profoundly grateful for the love and support of my immediate family: Luanne, who sacrificed my companionship for three years whenever I disappeared to the computer to write; Sean and Kristin, who with Luanne created cherished memories of our family gathered on shorelines in Seattle, Tri-Cities, San Diego, Kelowna, and Madison to cheer the hydros; and Jason, who with Sean and Kristin faithfully documented Luanne's 145-mph ride in *Miss Bardahl* on Lake Chelan.

Bibliography

Aircraft Engines of the World 1946, Paul H. Wilkinson, New York, 1946
Allied Aircraft Engines of World War II, Graham White, 1995, Society of Automotive Engineers.
"The Engine That Saved the Free World: The Story of the Rolls-Royce Merlin," Ryan D. Smith, Purdue University, 2006
"Musson v. Department of Labor and Industries," Supreme Court of Washington, June 4, 1970
"Nitrous Oxide Supercharging of an Aircraft-Engine Cylinder," Max. J. Tauschek, National Advisory Committee for Aeronautics, June 26, 1945
Bardahl Press Kit (1962-66)
Boat News
Boat Racing Yearbook, 1964 and 1965
Boating News magazine
Bremerton Sun
Cariboo Observer
Coeur d'Alene Press
Deseret News
Detroit Free Press
Ellensburg Daily Record
Evening Independent (St. Petersburg)
Hot Boat magazine
Hydro Legends
Las Vegas Sun
Lodi News-Sentinel
Los Angeles Times
Madison Courier
Master Motor Builders, Robert J. Neal
Milwaukee Journal
Motor Boating magazine
Motor Trend magazine
Nevada State Journal (Reno)
Northern Kittitas County Tribune
PPG Chemicals magazine
Pay 'n Pak Racing News
Popular Boating magazine
Popular Mechanics magazine
Powerboat magazine
Propeller magazine
Reno Evening Gazette
Rocky Mountain News
Sacramento Bee
Sea and Pacific Motorboat magazine
Seattle Post-Intelligencer

Spokane Daily Chronicle
Sports Illustrated magazine
St. Petersburg Times
The Detroit News
The Evening Independent (Massillon, Ohio)
The Evening Star (Washington, D.C.)
The Florida Times-Union (Jacksonville)
The Huntsville (Ala.) *Times*
The Independent Star-News (Pasadena)
The Kelowna Daily Courier
The Miami News
The New York Times
The News Tribune (Tacoma)
The San Diego Union
The Seattle Times
The Spokesman-Review
The Tampa Tribune
The Tuscaloosa News
The Washington (D.C.) *Daily News*
The Wenatchee World
The Windsor Star
Time magazine
Tri-City Herald
Unlimited NewsJournal
Vancouver Sun
Washington Daily News
Williston Herald
Wisconsin State Journal
World of Boat Racing magazine
Yachting magazine
Race programs – various
www.aafo.com
www.bardahl.com
www.historylink.org
www.missbardahl.com
www.sandiegohistory.org
www.thunderboats.org
www.vintagehydroplanes.com
www.wolfmanjack.org

Interviews
Evelyn Bardahl McNeil, March 1980, March 2011
Sam Rogers, May 1982, May 2012
John Sweet, May 1982, May 2012
Leo Vanden Berg, July 1983, May 1989
Dixon Smith, June 1987, July 2010, July 2011, April 2012

Jerry Zuvich, February 1988, February 2012
Mel Vanden Berg, multiple, November 2004 through April 2012
Ron Jones, May 2005, April 2007
Skip Schott, May 2007
David Smith, September 2008, February 2010
Mira Slovak, March 2011
Keith Jackson, March 2011
Jim Osborne, March 2011
Roger Kruse, June 2011
Jeanne Lamontia, September 2011
Ann Gustafson, February 2012
Gary Breakfield, February 2012
Wally Bostick, February 2012
Josette Musson Hess, February 2012
Bob Woolms, March 2012

About the author

Born in Seattle, Jon Osterberg grew up in the Lake Hills neighborhood of east Bellevue, where it seemed every kid under 13 pulled a wooden hydro behind his bike. By the time Jon earned his degree in editorial journalism from the University of Washington, he already had been a contributing reporter for five years, ultimately covering hydro racing for the *Chelan Valley Mirror*, *Coeur d'Alene Press*, and *Wenatchee World* newspapers. He currently manages marketing communications for PEMCO Insurance in Seattle, is active in his church, claims to enjoy playing guitar and piano (but seldom does), and loves to camp and hike with his family. Jon and his wife, Luanne, live in Redmond and enjoy weekends at their cabin near Cle Elum.

To order *Dragon Days*, go to dragondaysbook.com